T0345898

About Island Press

Island Press is the only nonprofit organization in the United States whose principal purpose is the publication of books on environmental issues and natural resource management. We provide solutions-oriented information to professionals, public officials, business and community leaders, and concerned citizens who are shaping responses to environmental problems.

In 2004, Island Press celebrates its twentieth anniversary as the leading provider of timely and practical books that take a multidisciplinary approach to critical environmental concerns. Our growing list of titles reflects our commitment to bringing the best of an expanding body of literature to the environmental community throughout North America and the world.

Support for Island Press is provided by the Agua Fund, Brainerd Foundation, Geraldine R. Dodge Foundation, Doris Duke Charitable Foundation, Educational Foundation of America, The Ford Foundation, The George Gund Foundation, The William and Flora Hewlett Foundation, Henry Luce Foundation, The John D. and Catherine T. MacArthur Foundation, The Andrew W. Mellon Foundation, The Curtis and Edith Munson Foundation, National Environmental Trust, National Fish and Wildlife Foundation, The New-Land Foundation, Oak Foundation, The Overbrook Foundation, The David and Lucile Packard Foundation, The Pew Charitable Trusts, The Rockefeller Foundation, The Winslow Foundation, and other generous donors.

The opinions expressed in this book are those of the author(s) and do not necessarily reflect the views of these foundations.

Mediated Modeling

Mediated Modeling

A System Dynamics
Approach
to Environmental
Consensus Building

Marjan van den Belt

Island Press
Washington • Covelo • London

Library of Congress Cataloging-in-Publication data.

Van den Belt, Marjan.
 Mediated modeling : a system dynamics approach to environmental consensus building / Marjan van den Belt.
  p. cm.
  ISBN 1-55963-960-1 (cloth : alk. paper) — ISBN 1-55963-961-X (pbk. : alk. paper)
  1. Environmental sciences—Simulation methods. 2. Environmental management—Decision making. I. Title.
  GE45.D37V36 2004
  363.7′00684—dc22

                                                              2003021165

British Cataloguing-in-Publication data available.

Printed on recycled, acid-free paper ♻

Design by Teresa Bonner

Manufactured in the United States of America
10 9 8 7 6 5 4 3 2 1

To Robert,
    Kaia, and Milo

Contents

Foreword

In this volume Marjan van den Belt articulates a promising method for meeting a fundamental challenge of the twenty-first century—integrating science and democracy. The problem is not a new one. Humans have engaged in discourse to make collective decisions throughout the history of our species. Indeed, group deliberation may be as much a defining characteristic of Homo sapiens as any of our morphological traits. Much of that deliberation was to make decisions about the environment, such as, where, when, and how to gather and hunt. We can imagine discussions around the campfire engaging indigenous ecological models—When will various kinds of fruits or nuts be ripe? Where will the animals be? What predators (both competitors and threats) might be encountered? Some part of these debates was undoubtedly about values—trading off different food types and habitat qualities based on preferences, expressing different degrees of aversion to the risks of predators, and so on. But I expect that much of the debate was about the quality of the models used to understand the environment—who had the right answers to questions about the environment?

So in one sense, democratic deliberation around models of environmental processes is basic to the human adaptive complex. But the Enlightenment, whatever its benefits, led to an estrangement of science and democracy even as it promoted both. The twentieth century has amply demonstrated that neither science nor democracy can enhance human welfare in the absence of the other. This was recognized and clearly articulated by John Dewey in his prescient analysis, *The Public and Its Problems* (1923). The eminent social theorist Jürgen Habermas also has examined the dysfunctional relationships between science and democracy. He notes that in some cases there is an illusion that science alone is sufficient to make public decisions, a pathology labeled "technocratic." In other cases, science is used primarily to legitimate decisions made on other grounds, a pathology labeled "decisionistic." Habermas calls for an approach grounded in Dewey's pragmatist arguments. He advocates an honest integration of scientific understanding with democratic discourse—decision making that is both fair and competent in the broadest sense of those terms.

In the 1970s and 1980s a number of scholars, including John Dryzek, John Forester, Ortwin Renn and I, drew on Habermas to argue that environmental decisions must be grounded in both sound science and fair and competent public discourse processes. We proposed that good science and good public discourse must be intertwined. In the 1990s, this idea gained much influence, reflected in both growing concern with public involvement on the part of environmental agencies and in important policy documents, such as the U.S.

National Research Council's *Understanding Risk: Informing Decisions in a Democratic Society* (1996). Now there is a broad consensus that scientific analysis and public deliberation must be integrated.

The challenge for the twenty-first century becomes how to integrate science and deliberation. At the heart of this challenge is the problem of getting ordinary citizens, the public in Dewey's sense, to engage with environmental science. Few of us, unless we are trained in the sciences of uncertainty and complexity, are very successful at unpacking probabilities and the dynamics of nonlinear systems. Yet bringing technical information to bear seems at first antithetical to having broad and meaningful public participation. The public is naïve of the science underpinning most environmental problems. I don't believe this should make us cynical about the capabilities of the average citizen. It's true that the public does poorly on the "pop quizzes" that are too often used to assess public understanding of science in surveys. But this seeming ignorance shows a canny rationality on the part of the public. Acquiring and retaining information has costs. Most items used to assess public understanding of science, while they seem important, even foundational, to scientists are not the kind of information used in making day-to-day decisions by most members of the public. As Sherlock Holmes once said to Dr. Watson (clearly pulling Watson's leg): ". . . you say that we go round the sun. If we went round the moon it would not make a pennyworth of difference to me or my work." (*A Study in Scarlet*, Chapter 2, p. 2). For most of the public, holding detailed scientific knowledge about environmental problems would be a waste of time unless such knowledge is part of an avocation, such as birding, or unless their community is faced with a decision regarding the problem. Since most citizens do not have a natural history hobby and have no direct input to public environmental decisions, knowing much about environmental science might be edifying, but it is not terribly useful. We can't expect people to study for a quiz for a course they are not taking. In contrast, hobbyists and those who can influence a consequential decision often display impressive scientific understanding. Unfortunately, the latter kind of expertise usually emerges only in times of intense conflict when options have been reduced to a "yes" or "no" on a specific proposal. By that time the chance for creative solutions has been lost, and whatever decision is taken the outcome will be costly and unsatisfactory to many.

Our greatest opportunities arise when the public actually has a chance to influence a decision early enough that creative and flexible solutions can be proposed. Indeed, we need to move from thinking about decisions as isolated events to a process of governance. To realize this opportunity we have to answer a number of difficult questions: How can the public be engaged in a way that leads to competent deliberation using the best available science? How can the science be engaged while taking proper account of the limits to our knowledge and the uncertainties inherent in even the best analysis? How can a process make use of quantitative information while giving proper weight to qualitative information? How can the public discourse help understand the limits of the models and the need for further research? How can the discourse proceed in ways that are respectful of all viewpoints while encouraging learning and change on the part of individuals and groups? How can a process move toward consensus and a decision while not forcing premature and fragile agreement? In order to integrate science and democracy in environmental governance, we must be able to implement answers to these questions. The admonitions to use deliberative processes have been heard for two decades, but we don't know how to practice what has been preached. *Mediated Modeling* offers a practice that respects both scientific analysis and public discourse.

In this volume, van den Belt deploys one of the most broadly integrative tools in the sciences—systems dynamics—in the service of public discourse. Her discussion of mediated modeling shows that it can be both robust and subtle. It acknowledges the tentative and partial character of all systems models. It is thoughtful about the process of interaction with a model and, more important, the process by which discourse leads to changes in the perspectives of participants. And in perhaps the most important contribution of the book she not only proposes a methodology but shows how it can be implemented in a variety of contexts. Every environmental problem is unique in its details, every public discourse has its own dynamics and context. There is no single approach that will yield good results everywhere. It is only by learning from experiments conducted in different situations that we can develop better methods. Van den Belt's contribution is rich with consideration of the contexts in which mediated modeling has facilitated analysis and deliberation and how we can learn from that variation.

As you read *Mediated Modeling* you will learn about a flexible and innovative tool for linking science and democratic process. But equally important, you will be challenged to think deeply about the fundamental issues of the twenty-first century—how to link our growing scientific understanding with our hopes for fair and competent governance processes. It is a book that is at the same time practical and thought-provoking—a rare and refreshing combination.

Thomas Dietz
Chair, U.S. National Research Council Committee on Human Dimensions
    of Global Change ·
Professor of Sociology and Crop and Soil Sciences
Director of the Environmental Science and Policy Program
Associate Dean, College of Agriculture and Natural Resources, College
    of Natural Science, College of Social Science
Michigan State University

Preface

Historically, the process of building simulation models with a variety of participants was often limited to private business settings for the purpose of strategic decision making. Royal Dutch Shell pioneered this approach in the late 1980s. This book concerns the expansion of group modeling into the area of environmental issues where multiple stakeholders are involved. It is written for three different audiences. First, it is aimed at environmental professionals who might be considering the use of a mediated modeling process. Hopefully these readers can gain enough information about the process to decide if it might work for them. Second, it is aimed at students to help them explore practical applications of modeling in the context of group dynamics and facilitation. Finally, it is aimed at both modeling and mediation practitioners (usually two distinct groups) as a report on recent experiences in using modeling to help build consensus.

Three of the models discussed in this book can be downloaded from www.mediated-modeling.com. In order to run the models, you will need to also download a free run-time-only version of STELLA from High Performance Systems Inc., at their website: www.hps-inc.com. The run-time only version of STELLA will allow you to explore the models on your computer and see the effects of making changes, but will not allow you to save any changes you make. To do this you will need to purchase the STELLA software.

It is not always easy to access models produced during a group modeling intervention. Many of the models are the product of consulting assignments and belong to the commissioning authority. For example, the Banff model presented in this book is not posted owing to privacy considerations. Other models have been produced for a single private client within companies where the stakeholders consist of different departments within a company. These models are also not usually made available to a wider audience. With this book and the accompanying models, the contributors of the case studies and myself hope to provide insight into an emerging and promising process that is evolving from private business into the public arena of environmental consensus building.

I would be happy to answer any further questions you might have about mediated modeling. You can contact me at: m.vandenbelt@verizon.com.

Marjan van den Belt
Burlington, Vermont
August 30, 2003

Acknowledgments

My interest in the environment started at an early age in The Netherlands. My father, Bart van den Belt, had a vegetable garden and the way he went about farming that piece of land, the energy and love he put into it, served as the seed for my lifelong interest in living systems. This, together with the documentaries of Jacques-Yves Cousteau (whom I eventually had the honor to meet in person) laid the foundation for my environmental interests and ultimately for this book.

Even though biology was my best subject in high school, I stubbornly went on to study economics. While studying business economics at Erasmus University in Rotterdam, I was often frustrated with the lack of coherence among the economics courses that were taught. For example, in microeconomics, economic systems miraculously return to equilibrium, but an hour later in macroeconomics, these systems would continue to grow indefinitely, on a finite planet with finite resources. Management and (European) integration issues caught my interest within business economics. But to the frustration of many of my professors, I questioned why the environment was missing from my economics courses. In December 1989, I attended a lecture by Dr. Donald Huisingh about Waste Minimization. Dr. Huisingh promoted the idea that pollution prevention pays, and this lecture had a profound impact on my thinking. Suddenly, the incoherent thoughts about linking environment and business economics became a concrete possibility. As a result of Don Huisingh's encouragement I became a student assistant at the Erasmus Center for Environmental Studies and took a Waste Minimization course/internship at Scandinavian Airline System in Copenhagen. After Donald Huisingh crossed my path, environment and business/economics became inseparable in my mind. This idea solidified during an internship at the Environment Unit of the United Nations Center for Transnational Corporations in New York.

After graduation I went to work for Vattenfall AB, in Stockholm—Sweden's largest energy producer and distributor. Gunnar Hovsenius, who at the time led the Environment Unit at the Research Department, convinced me to stay beyond the initial four-month traineeship. He was the type of mentor anyone would enjoy working with. He always provided opportunities for growth and exploration and always acknowledged my contributions. My assignments started in the field of environmental economics (applying economic theory to environmental issues) but gradually moved toward environmental systems management. The systems approach seemed to make the most sense to me.

Vattenfall had to downsize and I had to leave the company. However, the Swedish social system was such that even a foreigner received plenty of assistance for moving on. At Vattenfall I was introduced to Tommy Steinmetz who coached me into starting my own company. Waste Reduction International was created and initially focused on what the name suggested. But the systems considerations quickly gained ground and led to environmental management system design for industrial clients. I gratefully acknowledge Dr. Howard Ross for providing several projects and contacts during the years that followed in Stockholm.

I had already left the environmental economics approach for a more systems-oriented approach, but my exposure to Ecological Economics gave more substance to the idea of ecological systems as the starting point, leaving economic systems to be designed within the productive capacity of ecological systems. Dr. Robert Costanza introduced me to computer modeling during a course at Stockholm University, which I adopted as a key tool to assist in systems thinking.

Fran Irwin, then at World Wildlife Fund, gave me the opportunity to work on a feasibility study with respect to a Pollution Release and Transfer Register, in Trinidad and Tobago. This project proved a turning point for me. A view emerged that companies are participants along with other interest groups. In addition, I discovered the power of bringing stakeholder groups together and this led to an expansion of my interests in group dynamics, facilitation, and mediation.

Since then, several multistakeholder projects have brought all these threads together and contributed to the concept of mediated modeling from a combined practical and research perspective. Dr. Herman Daly, my Ph.D. advisor at the University of Maryland helped to give mediated modeling a place within ecological economics. I received a Ph.D. for solidifying consulting-based experience with mediated modeling and expanding on it from a research perspective; i.e., discovering some of the science behind the art. During my graduate studies at the University of Maryland, I delved more deeply into the System Dynamics literature and realized that an entire field had developed similar lines of thought to my own and that the origin of group model building could be traced back to Royal Dutch Shell in the late eighties. A host of people had evidently discovered the power of group model building, often from a practical point of view. I'm a great admirer of Donella Meadows, whom I consider one of the pioneers of bringing the human component into modeling. However, relatively few case studies dealt with environmental problems, where multi-stakeholder groups used quantitative group modeling in a process of conflict resolution or joint fact finding. When the opportunity arose to consolidate my experience and that of my colleagues and write this book about mediated modeling, I gratefully took it. I thank Island Press (especially Todd Baldwin) for taking this project on and providing encouragement and several editorial passes at the manuscript. In addition to discussions with the contributors of the case studies in this book, discussions with Tom Maxwell, Helena Voinov, Bud Harris, Robert Wenger, Rosimeiry Portela, Caroline Hermans, and Per Olsson, led to a better overview of how mediated modeling can serve a broader program, and support or be supported by other available tools.

This book would not have come about without the efforts of many people over many years. The authors of the contributed case studies were instrumental in the effort to synthesize our experiences. Equally important, the case studies would not exist without the dedication of the participants in the case studies themselves.

This book would also not have come about without the loving support of my husband, Robert Costanza, who also helped with editing the manuscript. Special thanks for reviewing and/or editing the manuscript also go to Cynthia Gonzalez, Nuno Videira, Ellen Pedersen, Guy Hager, Isabel de la Torre, Amanda Walker, and Jac Vennix. Their constructive critique has made this book a much better product. Bob Wenger not only reviewed and edited the manuscript, but his thoughtful explanation of English grammar and style helped me extend my writing skills well beyond this manuscript.

1

Introduction

Human economic activity now influences ecological systems not only at the local but also at the global level. Problems like climate change, induced by our carbon emissions, are encroaching on the natural environment to the extent that it is now impossible to find pristine systems. Ecosystem services can be lost owing to human activities, like agricultural expansion, that depend on these same services (Costanza et al. 1997; Daily 1997). Humans are a part of the ecological system. But we are currently capable of irreversibly damaging it.

Our current environmental problems are due in part to our inability to make many small, consistent decisions that lead to a broad, sustainable outcome. The world is becoming less forgiving of our mistakes as it becomes relatively "full" with human activity (Daly and Cobb 1989). In a full world, the interlinkages between human and natural systems are stronger, more pervasive, and more complex. In the past, when the world was relatively "empty," we could address these environmental problems in a linear, compartmentalized manner. In today's full world this approach is no longer adequate.

The problems of the environment are particularly difficult because their complexity, interrelatedness, and dynamic behavior are beyond the cognitive capacity of most humans to fully understand and manage. Humans respond to a strong signal that something is wrong but have more trouble stopping a negative trend that evolves with a slow pace and which involves many interlinked variables that are hard to track. The result is that we are gradually destroying the environment through our shortsighted, ill-coordinated management of it. Some refer to this phenomenon as "death by a thousand cuts."

Policymakers usually serve relatively short terms compared with the time scale on which structural environmental changes may occur. The short-term political orientation may continue to exist because of the lack of a coherent systems perspective in which actively involved stakeholders hold policymakers and politicians accountable. Trade-offs between short-term, usually economic, interests and long-term benefits—as well as the risk of long-term unintended and undesirable effects—of a policy are difficult to make and involve many stakeholders.

People occupied with environmental issues invariably face very challenging problems concerning the complex interactions between human systems and ecosystems (Costanza and Jorgensen 2002). For example, tourism, fisheries, and salt making are important economic activities in the Ria Formosa, a coastal wetland in the south of Portugal. These economic activities are affecting the ecosystem they are also depending on for their prosperity. In addition, these economic activities are interdependent. Tourists appreciate fish, and they enjoy the atmosphere a traditional fisheries fleet creates in the harbor of a town. However, the pollution caused by tourism to some degree affects the health of the fish stock. The cultivation of fish farms competes with traditional fisheries on the market and in addition competes for space with the local salt industry.

There is no single, simple answer available or a single discipline capable of adequately addressing such problems. Equilibrium-centered, command-and-control strategies are not necessarily well suited for the challenges posed by today's full world. Equilibrium-centered strategies are based on the assumption that a steady state for a system exists and that all we have to do is to guide a system there with appropriate policies, while command-and-control strategies assume that a system will actually respond on command as predicted.

Many environmental professionals, industry leaders, and academics have to deal with existing or anticipated conflicts over the alternative use of resources, their economic implications, and the distribution of social impacts over the medium and long term. Economic prosperity is just as much, if not more, a part of many people's preferred visions of the future as is the sustenance of natural systems.

All of these factors make the environmental manager's job more difficult, to say the least. In recent years, complexity has become more readily accepted as an intrinsic part of environmental management and policymaking. For example, dealing with complexity means that an increasing number of actors are recognized as being involved in the problem. It suddenly appears as if everyone is affected by a complex problem. Pursued to the extreme, this realization can paralyze efforts to improve a situation. In practice, environmental practitioners try to strike a balance between the philosophical ideal of encompassing complexity and what is currently feasible to improve a situation. Therefore, dealing with complexity in environmental management and policymaking manifests itself in a variety of ways reflecting different levels of comfort with complexity.

Finally, in our complex world, uncertainty is an unavoidable and often uncomfortable companion (van Asselt 2000). Uncertainty triggers the sense that something may go wrong because not all the aspects of a problem are under control or the outcome surpasses a limited time span. Uncertainty and associated risk also depend on the perspective of stakeholders (consider the perspective of a real estate developer versus that of an environmental activist in the Upper Fox case study in Chapter 5) and their personal attitudes (risk-adverse or risk-seeking).

The purpose of this book is to introduce professionals (and those who are training to become professionals) to a new tool that can help society to cope with this complexity and make sound decisions about the environment. It involves modeling, or simulation, which may seem daunting to some readers but which is in fact both easily understandable and necessary if we are to confront our environmental problems effectively. Models offer us the ability to expand our mental capacity in ways that enable us to better understand ecosystems and the implications of our many small management and policy decisions as they relate to ecosystem and human health.

Building a simulation model helps us to perceive interconnections and to connect past, present, and future. The simulation models come from a field known as system dynamics, which is concerned with the understanding of how systems change over time. The behavior of systems is studied through identifying a minimum of building blocks that can explain the bulk of the behavior. Feedback loops and time lags characterize the relationships among the building blocks of a system dynamics model. Building system dynamic computer models helps us to try to understand systematically these time delays, nonlinearities, and feedbacks.

Mediated modeling is based on system dynamics thinking but emphasizes the interactive involvement of affected stakeholders in the learning process about the complex system they are in. It allows a group of stakeholders to understand how seemingly small decisions may spiral a system onto an undesirable course. Such understanding provides opportunities to jointly design strategies to abate the negative spiral or to curb a trend into a more positive one.

Mediated modeling can also allow policymakers and other stakeholders to see the consequences of their actions over longer time scales. Not only are the time and space scales on which many environmental changes occur not in sync with institutional structures and political cycles but the incentives are lacking to close this gap (Costanza et al. 2001). The lack of appropriately structured institutions is not surprising considering the way the human mind works.

Bounded Rationality

Extensive research shows that human rationality is limited, or bounded, and this limitation can create persistent judgmental biases and systematic errors (Simon 1948). "Bounded rationality" means we are limited by a lack of full information and cannot process all that we have. We therefore end up with suboptimal solutions (Simon 1948, 1979, 1985; Kahnemann and Tversky 1974; Kahnemann et al. 1982; Hogarth 1987; Ehrlich 2000). The human mind works in a rather short-term manner and favors linear relationships over a dynamic systems perspective (Weiner 1985; Shoham 1990; Ehrlich 2000, 2001). Personal positions are often static and defended on the basis of convictions and perceptions, and people select information that reinforces their initial position (Bakken et al. 1994).

A linear relationship can be pictured as a situation in which A leads to B, which leads directly to C. A complex system–based relationship can be pictured as a situation in which A, B, and C are interrelated to the extent that C, in turn, may have an impact on A (see Figure 1.1). Such an interrelationship implies that there are dynamic or time-related issues at work. For example, A may influence B relatively quickly, but in return, B may influence A with a time lag. In addition, a feedback of a third element, C, may cause the pattern to change again. Humans have trouble taking time lags and feedback loops into account in a dynamic manner.

In practice, decision making and the resulting outcomes often lag in time

Linear relationship

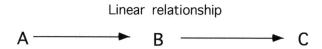

Dynamic relationship may include time lags and feedback loops

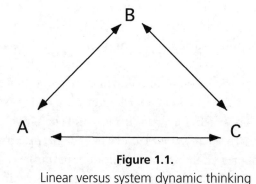

Figure 1.1.
Linear versus system dynamic thinking

and space. The consequences of decision making are only weakly connected to current reality. Impacts of decision making are seldom satisfactorily monitored. Negative impacts are rarely acknowledged. All these factors prevent effective learning and reinforce reliance on (politically motivated) beliefs rather than facts. The lack of understanding of the dynamics within and among systems and the participation of affected stakeholders cause many policy decisions to have unintended, potentially disastrous consequences.

Decision Making

As an artifact of our limitations in dealing with dynamic systems, decision making is often compartmentalized and fragmented into economic, environmental, and sociocultural spheres. The bigger, integrated picture gets lost, and trade-offs may not be obvious. Even though the following key elements to achieve sustainable development may not be sufficient, they are necessary to include in the decision-making process:

- Integration of insights from ecology, economics, and social sciences (Costanza 1993)
- Integration of impacts at different scales
- Effective stakeholder participation at the appropriate scale (Chambers 1997)
- A linked understanding of past, present, and future relationships (Senge 1990)

These key elements for sustainable development are often not deliberately addressed, and as a consequence, policymaking (and the underlying studies and decisions leading up to policymaking) is often accomplished through compartmentalization. The values assigned to environmental and economic activities may have different conceptual and empirical bases. The weighing of one against the other occurs at stages in the decision process at which a competitive win-lose situation results. It may be beneficial for some aspects of policymaking not to separate the questions of interest based on ecology and economics as different disciplines. By integrating ecology and economics (and any other relevant aspects) from the start of a decision-making process, the system can be thought of as a more multidimensional, dynamic, interactive one. Making the overall goals clear and understanding the trade-offs can harmonize the value basis up front.

If ecological and economic aspects of a system under study are included in a quantitative model structure, different units have to be converted for these aspects to relate to each other in a meaningful way. For example, while we are used to expressing economic values in monetary terms, the ecological values often lose out because it is more difficult to express them in monetary terms. Costanza, d'Arge, et al. (1997) argue that values of ecological services can be made more tangible and in some cases could help to get the ecological services on the monetary map.

Mediated modeling provides a structured process based on dynamic systems thinking to include the most important aspects of a problem in a coherent and simple but elegant simulation model.

Knowledge Accumulation by Experts

Policymaking is not the only field in which fragmentation and compartmentalization exist. Academia has traditionally embraced a logical positivist perspective based on the Greek ideal for understanding the world. These ideas still strongly influence the modern course of science. The logical positivist philosophy asserts that one "right" answer exists. In this view, the "right" answer will emerge if one keeps looking in increasing detail. Scientists are supposed to be the objective unbiased searchers for this answer. Two significant outcomes occur owing to this philosophy. First, it has led to the compartmentalization of science, which has produced many disciplines and well-guarded, hard-to-cross disciplinary boundaries. Second, in today's educational system people are trained predominantly in analysis—the art of taking problems apart to study the parts in ever-increasing detail. Very little attention is given to synthesis— the art of putting the pieces back together into a well-functioning apparatus.

As Connie Ozawa elegantly describes in *Recasting Science* (1991), scientists are often used by different parties to drum up support or discredit claims when conflicts have made it to the courthouse. Mediated modeling sees a role for scientists as one of the stakeholders. During a mediated modeling process scientists learn from other stakeholders what the practical questions are. Scientists can provide pieces of information as the stakeholder groups see the need for it. There is a value not only in one person knowing all about a small area but also in a group determining if there is a need for certain information and how it dynamically connects to other pieces of information. Furthermore, research needs to be adaptive if it is to benefit adaptive managers and support policymakers in becoming more responsive.

Stakeholder Participation

Policies directing or guiding the everyday decisions by many individuals are usually not developed by the people affected by these policies. Background studies for input to environmental decision making, including computerized models, often don't involve the relevant stakeholders. At best, experts consult individual stakeholders for their studies or models. At worst, the studies or models are *about* the stakeholders. These studies are most often performed by experts, after which decision makers weigh the outcomes against society's needs (or political agendas). Consequently, the broader stakeholder groups often do not accept the results of these studies or models because stakeholders don't understand or don't agree with the underlying assumptions, do not agree with the structure of the models, or refuse to accept the outcomes because they feel left out of the decision-making process. For these reasons, conflicts are likely to arise during the implementation phase (Mazmanian 1976; Cupps 1977; Rosener 1982; Thomas 1990).

Broader participation, however more expensive at the front end, should make the overall decision-making process more effective and less expensive at the implementation end. Early involvement of broad stakeholder groups (government or municipalities, industry, environmental nongovernmental organizations [NGOs], etc.) seeking common goals and consensus on an issue may increase the shared level of understanding in a community and reduce the conflicts and costs at the implementation phase. This book presents case studies at local and regional scales. However, a trend toward participatory processes is also visible at higher scales.

There are numerous examples of governing bodies embracing the participatory principle. For example, the European Commission (EC) is working to open up the policymaking processes to get more people and organizations involved in shaping and delivering European Union (EU) policy. The principles in this effort are, according to the European Commission (2001):

- Openness—e.g., between institutions, active communication, common languages, increasing confidence in complex institutions
- Participation—i.e., the quality, relevance and effectiveness of policies depend on wider participation throughout the policy chain, following inclusive approaches
- Accountability—i.e., more involvement will mean clearer goals and greater responsibility

At the global level, a move toward a participatory attitude in addressing global environmental problems can be traced back to Principle 10 of the 1992 Rio Declaration. This principle suggests that environmental issues are best handled with the participation of all concerned citizens at the relevant level. Ten years later at the World Summit for Sustainable Development in Johannesburg, the Partnership for Principle 10 was developed. This partnership provides a way for governments, civil society organizations, donors, and other stakeholders to work together to implement practical solutions to provide the public with access to information, participation, and justice for environmentally sustainable decisions.

Adaptive Management

In many places in the world, managers have begun to shift environmental management away from individual planning tools for separate economic sectors or single species and toward an ecosystem management approach in which a range of different stakeholders are included. To improve decision making for sustainable development, new tools to facilitate common goal development and to test alternative scenarios are needed. These tools must be able to communicate the complexity and associated uncertainties of the decisions and to allow for broad stakeholder participation while integrating different aspects (economic and ecological) of the situation involved.

Integrated assessments use tools and inputs from multidisciplinary, multiscale, and a variety of demographic and ethnic backgrounds to support decision-making processes (van Asselt 2000). Rather than the equilibrium-based view of decision and policymaking, adaptive environmental management (Holling 1978) assumes an ever-evolving cyclic goal for societal organization structures centered on the behavior of ecological systems.

Practically, in adaptive environmental management, policymaking is designed more as an experiment. A policy is closely monitored for its intended and unintended effects. Consequently, policies are appropriately abandoned, adjusted, or fine-tuned in an ongoing effort to develop an effective and efficient government system in an ever-changing world.

In adaptive environmental management, as in ecosystem management, ecological boundaries such as watersheds define the geographic scope (Yaffee et al. 1996). Adaptive environmental management may gain strength when a process-oriented approach from a team learning perspective is adopted, emphasizing collaborative learning (Daniels and Walker 1996).

Addressing today's complex environmental challenges deals with finding balance between different sides of an issue. There is constant tension between the opposite sides of the same coin, and the game is played with a variety of coins of varying values and even varying currencies. For example, should one person make decisions or should all stakeholders be involved? Should we strive for a single answer to a problem or instead should we not commit to any answers in the face of overwhelming uncertainty? Should we rely on answers generated within the borders of individual disciplines or do we need to move beyond disciplinary analysis? Many different forces are at work at the same time.

Most likely there is no black or white choice involved, but rather the need to choose an appropriate position along many different continua. For example, rather than having decisions made by one or by all, we can examine the trade-offs and choose a position in the middle where relevant stakeholders can participate in designing an answer. Rather than assuming one compartmentalized answer that fits the static legislative structure or becoming overwhelmed by the uncertainty pointed out by scientists, we can acknowledge a complex, dynamic situation and manage it in an adaptive manner.

Building Environmental Consensus

Environmental conflicts are often based on the values of individuals and groups and contrasting beliefs about the distribution of costs and benefits. Environmental disagreements when left to themselves often become entrenched conflicts. Mediation and negotiation are alternative ways to address conflicts before they require litigation.

Courts are unable to address these interpersonal values when there is a lack of scientific consensus. In fact, science is often used to justify opposing points of view (Ozawa 1991). The judicial process is concerned with the legal arguments rather than establishing a consensus. Mediation, as an alternative to the litigation, can maintain fairness and offers improvements in the overall competence of the process. It is increasingly preferred over confrontation in the legal arena (Bingham 1986).

With current technological advances, the mediating discussion among multiple parties can be facilitated effectively with the aid of computer modeling. An increased level of shared understanding of a problem improves the chances that a mutually acceptable solution can be found.

But more broadly, addressing today's complex environmental problems requires consensus building (Susskind et al. 1999). Consensus building is important in several domains, from local to regional to global, and ultimately to developing a clear vision of what a sustainable future encompasses for all of us. Consensus building is a central part of the mediated or negotiated decision-making process. The *Consensus Building Handbook* describes consensus building as "an agreement seeking process" and provides the following insight:

Consensus building is a process of seeking unanimous agreement. It involves a good-faith effort to meet the interests of all stakeholders. Consensus has been reached when everyone agrees they can live with whatever is proposed after every effort has been made to meet the interests of all stake holding parties. Thus, consensus building requires someone to frame a proposal after listening carefully to everyone's concerns. Participants in a consensus building process have both the right to expect that no one will ask them to undermine their interests and the responsibility to propose solutions that will meet everyone else's interests as well as their own. (p. 6)

The above definition states that "seeking unanimous agreement" is the ultimate goal, but there is a continuum from strong to weak consensus.

Specifically for multistakeholder groups, there are two important aspects in the evaluation of the strength or weakness of consensus (see Table 1.1). First, strong consensus reflects a situation in which no participants have dropped out during the process for other than personal reasons. A weak consensus involves the loss of participants for one strategic reason or another. Susskind et al. (1990) terms these participants "holdouts." Second, a strong consensus is reflected in an endorsement of the resulting recommendations, action plan, or proposal to resolve a conflict. A strong consensus is embraced without reservation and is considered empowering to each participant. Alternatively, a weak consensus is one that participants "can live with" and will comply to but which is not necessarily empowering.

A strong consensus should make implementation of proposals easy, provided the appropriate stakeholders were part of the process. A weak consensus remains a relatively fragile basis for implementation.

With consensus among a critical empowered group, the focus can shift back to inclusion of the parties left behind, which can take many forms. There may be room for broadening the stakeholder involvement, because some parties are lagging in the process. Deepening the stakeholder involvement occurs when a broad enough stakeholder group draws their specific-interest network into the process. A consensus at the "can-live-with" level among all participants may need strict rules for implementation, accountability, and monitoring to ensure that the process moves forward. Deepening the stakeholder involvement can be an appropriate step.

The Role of Mediated Modeling

The definition in the *Consensus Building Handbook* (Susskind et al. 1999) mentions the framing of "proposals." Mediated modeling helps to build consensus in small increments by finding common ground regarding the goal of the model, constructing a simulation model, and running scenarios to evaluate the desirability of the potential outcomes of various actions. Confidence in the

Table 1.1.
Degree of consensus

	All participants stay involved	A critical mass of participants stay involved
Empowering conclusions	Strong consensus: a strong basis for implementation	Consensus with clues for follow-up
"Can live with" conclusions	Consensus with clues for follow-up	Weak consensus: a fragile basis for implementation

model structure and the level of consensus that was reached during the process of model construction builds confidence in the crafted statements or "proposals." In the case of mediated modeling, proposal drafting is a collaborative process based on a higher level of shared information about the system and its dynamics.

In the consensus- and model-building process three domains are implicitly addressed:

- How the world works in a certain domain or worldview.
- What would constitute a more desirable state of the world or vision of the future?
- What policies will lead to that better state, given how the world works?

The focus during the modeling process oscillates among these domains at different times during the process. Trying to understand consensus does not mean that consensus is the only desired measurement of success. Conforming to system dynamics thinking, a mediated modeling process appreciates any improvement or insight in a complex situation. For example, an improvement in interactive communication is regarded as an improvement over the old situation. But then again, an improved interactive communication among relevant parties is a prerequisite for consensus as well as for collaborative action.

Rather than relying on a single discipline or doing away with deep analysis, mediated modeling provides a format wherein relevant disciplines can constructively contribute toward synthesis and practical problem solving. It allows us to look outside the usual boxes, to revise the roles of the stakeholders, to apply original thinking and learning, and to develop effective modes of communication.

To make the different forces at work more tangible, they need to be labeled. Once identified, these tensions enter the conscious domain, where they can be faced and incorporated into our communications with others. Left in the unconscious domain, they will remain out of balance, driven by habit, fear, or hope.

Conclusion

Mediated modeling is a tool for overcoming some of the problems inherent in linear thinking and compartmentalized, nonparticipatory decision making. In contrast to an expert dispensing "answers," or a discussion about the perceptions of a group of stakeholders, mediated modeling aims for a collaborative team learning experience to raise the shared level of understanding in a group, as well as fostering a broad and deep consensus.

In mediated modeling, system dynamics thinking and supporting software

are used to construct computer-based simulation models at the "scoping level." The dictionary defines *scope* as "the range of one's awareness, thoughts, or actions"; "the space or opportunity to function"; or "the area covered by a given activity or subject." In a scoping model, a group of stakeholders interactively scopes out a complex problem. Such a model serves to increase the understanding of the dynamics at play rather than predicting a precise outcome.

The learning of the group and a set of consensus-based conclusions are important end products of the modeling process. The process of model construction structures the discussion and the thinking of a stakeholder group and fosters team learning. The resulting model serves as a vehicle to convey the consensus of the group to a larger audience and to formulate better research questions or management options.

Scoping also refers to the first step in a three-step modeling process (Costanza and Ruth 1998) in which the goal is to develop a high-generality, low-resolution scoping and consensus-building model. Exploration of the system dynamics involved is usually the goal. This step requires a broad representation of all the stakeholder groups affected by the problem. The scope of the participants is widened by new ways of thinking about a problem.

This first-stage scoping model can be used to answer preliminary questions about the dynamics of the system. The areas of sensitivity and uncertainty and the gaps in information become clear. The research agenda for the second stage and the management agenda for the third stage are based on the first "scoping" step.

With research and eventually management models, the direct stakeholder involvement present during the model construction reduces gradually. Compare the three-step process to a painting: the scoping model sketches the outline, the research model fills in the details, and the management model adds the color. Sometimes a sketch is sufficient; sometimes a full-fledged painting is an appropriate use of time and funds.

All the case studies in this book are developed at scoping level—that is, the models developed during a mediated modeling process generally aim for being simple, but elegant, rather than aiming for a model high in resolution and detail.

Table 1.2, created by Guy Hager of Parks & People in Baltimore for a presentation to a group involved in "Revitalizing Baltimore," lists the benefits of a mediated modeling process.

This book is intended to be a practical, introductory guide to apply a mediated modeling approach toward realizing these benefits either for practioners considering commissioning a mediated modeling process, for modelers who wish to expand their skills into mediation, or for mediators who wish to explore modeling skills. It explains the basic mechanics of the modeling process. It also draws out the implicit choices one makes when using this process. In addition

Table 1.2.
The benefits of mediated modeling

Before Mediated Modeling	With Mediated Modeling
• Problems seem to be intractable.	• Important stakeholders are included in the process.
• Parties are often caught up in confrontational debate.	• Everyone participates in the model-building process. The modeling language, STELLA, is user-friendly.
• No way seen to bridge polarities.	
• Experts may create "solutions" but may omit stakeholders who are needed for implementation.	• Mental models are made explicit, examined, and tested.
• Models are often "black boxes" only understood by the modelers.	• The process combines the best of consensus building and team learning by using modeling.
• Lists of problems are easy to create, but priorities are difficult to see.	
• Consensus may be achieved, but solutions may not be related to reality.	• The model helps participants confront "beliefs" and "facts" and serves as a reality check.
Result: Little or no improvement	*Result: Consensus on both problems/goals and process, leading to viable policies.*

Source: Guy Hager

to explaining the driving forces behind mediated modeling, the book presents the broader framework made up of several continua or choices one needs to make when considering the use of any tool for environmental decision making or management. This framework is important in that it enables one to more readily share the experience with different forms of mediated modeling processes, discover connections with other tools, and evaluate opportunities offered by different approaches.

Chapter 2 evaluates the role of mediated modeling in the context of other tools—their overlap and complementarities. While no particular spot on these continua is per definition better than another, it is important to make conscious choices in those domains that fit a particular situation. This chapter also provides some of the history and the academic disciplines that have inspired many practitioners of mediated modeling.

Chapter 3 gives insight into the general characteristics and context of the mediated modeling process.

Chapter 4 describes a mediated modeling process as a guideline for users and providers of this tool. There are, of course, many variations on this general guideline: certain steps can be emphasized or deemphasized, depending on the situational needs. This chapter sets forth some of the practical choices that must be made in designing a mediated modeling process—for example, the level of stakeholder involvement, the level of acceptable conflict, group size—and connects examples to the case studies in this book.

Chapters 5 through 9 present five case studies.

Chapter 10 synthesizes the experience from these case studies. This chapter can be used in evaluating whether a mediated modeling process is an appropriate tool for users or consultants, or an in-house skill to be developed. Additionally, Chapter 10 can serve as a framework for discussion among mediated modeling practitioners on how to increase the usefulness of this tool. This discussion is continued in detail in Appendix 1.

2

The Role of
Mediated Modeling

As outlined in Chapter 1, mediated modeling facilitates the integration of expert information and stakeholder participation in a dynamic framework to address complex problems. It is a variation on computer-facilitated group modeling, pioneered by Royal Dutch Shell for developing business strategies involving its various departments. Rapid advances in computer capabilities, starting during the mid-1980's, made tools such as mediated modeling possible. Mediated modeling is now becoming a popular decision support tool beyond executive rooms, extending into communities, government, and academia, and beyond business strategies opening into the field of environmental policymaking. This chapter describes the intellectual roots of mediated modeling and places this approach among other concepts and tools currently available.

Participatory Modeling

Any form of participation in the modeling process could be labeled as participatory modeling. There are two important points to be made regarding participation, however. First, there is a continuum of levels of participation involved in a modeling effort. At the low end, stakeholders are individually consulted for their input in the modeling process. The high end reflects an interactive team learning situation in which a group of stakeholders is in complete control of the type of modeling they want to undertake as well as the content of the model. At this end of the participation spectrum, the model is more a by-product of the team learning. Mediated modeling is positioned at the high end of the participation spectrum.

The timing in the modeling process at which participation takes place represents a second continuum (see Figure 2.1). At the low end, participation is invited relatively late in the modeling process. Not much latitude is left at this point for any potential change of course, even if it were highly desired by the stakeholders. The purpose of a mediated modeling process could be to relate and integrate existing information. At the high end, participation shapes the modeling process from the very beginning. A group of participants ideally chooses the form of modeling and jointly crafts the model. A mediated modeling process then provides support in exploring innovative solutions.

The term *modeling* provides an opportunity to describe another important continuum. Any form of abstract representation of reality is a model. But the aid that records and reflects the model can vary over a wide spectrum. At one end of the spectrum are techniques such as participatory rural appraisals, in which originally a wooden stick was used to draw maps and concepts in the sand of a rural village. Flip charts can be used to construct conceptual models, such as causal diagrams. At the other end of the continuum are computer-based approaches to modeling. Computer capability can be a blessing as well as a burden. There is a trade-off between a high level of complexity that can be addressed with the aid of computers versus the fragility of the equipment. A

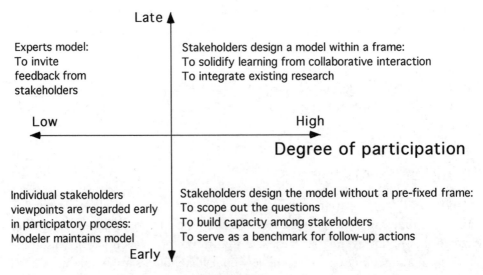

Figure 2.1.
Participatory modeling

stick in the sand doesn't fail, and a flip chart can be easily transported. A computer can fail and crash, but if it works, it works beautifully.

Mediated Modeling

A mediated modeler uses visually oriented modeling software in a series of meetings to enable diverse stakeholders to interactively and collaboratively design and construct a model of a system or a set of interlinked systems. For example, the mediated modeling process that was used to support policymaking for Banff National Park (see Chapter 7) included an ecological component, represented by wolves and elk, and a variety of socio-economic aspects, such as number of visitors, infrastructure, economic development, and employment.

A mediated model is created by a group of people with a variety of backgrounds, interests, and viewpoints. It is usually initiated when a conflict about alternative policies or management is anticipated or existing or, when an undesirable trend is noticed but no single cause can be pinpointed. Participants in a mediated modeling exercise don't need previous modeling experience or affinity.

A preliminary model may be developed before a series of modeling meetings starts. Such a preliminary model is based on individual interviews with participants and can be rejected or accepted by the group. Mediated modeling does not rely on preexisting models developed solely by expert modelers. Instead, the building blocks and assistance to put a model together are provided to jointly construct a simulation model. How the building blocks are placed and what the outcome will be is an unknown to the organizing team and the participants.

The resulting model can be used to learn about the complexity of the system's dynamics and to explore alternative development scenarios.

A mediated modeling process:

- Increases the level of *shared understanding* among the group
- Builds *consensus* about the structure of a complex topic and its dynamics
- Provides a *strategic and systematic foundation* or backbone for investigating policy, research, or management alternatives
- Serves as a tool to *disseminate insights* gained by the participants

Mediated modeling is a process for involving stakeholders in the conceptualization, specification, and synthesis of their knowledge and information into dynamic computer-based simulation models. The process is detailed in Chapter 3, but for the time being it is important to know that it helps to integrate different aspects, such as ecology and economics, for understanding the dynamics of complex systems. The goal is to increase the effectiveness of decision making by considering decision making to be a part of a team learning effort. The core of the learning experience lies in the achievement of stakeholder-specified goals by means of a better, shared understanding of the system dynamics. As shown in Figure 2.2, it combines the positive attributes of expert modeling and facilitated discussions.

The added value of mediated computer modeling with stakeholder participation versus a mediated discussion without modeling, or versus modeling without stakeholder participation, is also illustrated in Figure 2.2. A distinction is made between "consensus among stakeholders" and "understanding of the system dynamics." Some effective form of interaction and discussion among stakeholders may presumably achieve consensus among stakeholders. But consensus among stakeholders does not necessarily mean that the shared understanding of how the system works has improved. The consensus may be based on wishful thinking. For example, groups may achieve consensus on goals and visions for the system or on the relative risks of various activities, but they may not fully appreciate the dynamic links between the variables. While envisioning exercises such as "Future Search" (Weisbord 1992; Weisbord and

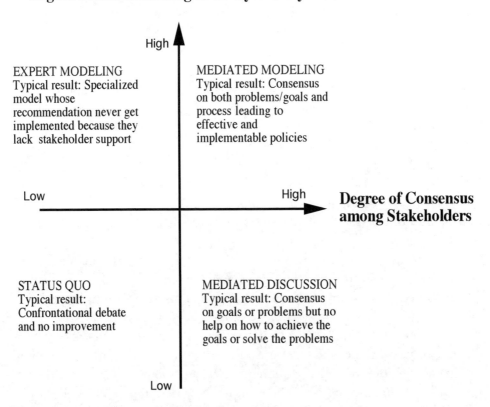

Degree of Understanding of the System Dynamics

High

EXPERT MODELING
Typical result: Specialized model whose recommendation never get implemented because they lack stakeholder support

MEDIATED MODELING
Typical result: Consensus on both problems/goals and process leading to effective and implementable policies

Low   High   **Degree of Consensus among Stakeholders**

STATUS QUO
Typical result: Confrontational debate and no improvement

MEDIATED DISCUSSION
Typical result: Consensus on goals or problems but no help on how to achieve the goals or solve the problems

Low

Figure 2.2.
Increasing shared understanding versus building consensus

Janoff 1995) can be very empowering, they are not geared toward improvement of the shared level of understanding of the system dynamics involved.

With the use of computers, the system dynamics component can be enhanced and strengthened. Even though the resulting model may be less elaborate than if it were merely constructed by modeling experts, its important advantage is that it generates stakeholder consensus about how the system works and how stakeholders would like to see it work. Stakeholder consensus greatly improves the prospects for implementation of the model's results. Vennix et al. (1997) states that "studies of the impact of computer models on policy making having convincingly revealed two things. First, in most cases the impact is conceptual (i.e., people learn from it), rather than instrumental. Second, most learning takes place in the process of building the model, rather than after the model is finished." However, a modeling effort does not have to stagnate at scoping level where stakeholders are heavily involved. There is most certainly a legitimate place for well-anchored expert models.

Costanza and Ruth (1998) promote a strong stakeholder involvement at the front end of a three-step process in which model building progresses from simple but elegant scoping models toward research and management models. However, the development of a model at scoping level geared toward a team learning experience among stakeholders (including scientists) is all too often skipped.

Mediated modeling is an improvement over discussion alone because it forces a confrontation with facts. Based on the way humans construct a social reality, one can argue that there is no such thing as an objective "fact." What is perceived as real by individuals is partially influenced by what others in our environment think (Berger and Luckmann 1966). Science has developed specific methods and peer review processes to maintain as objective a view as possible, but in other environments this conscious effort is often lacking. Even within the academic community, the disciplines often don't expose their ideas to the other disciplines and consequently run a risk of becoming myopic.

Hogarth (1987) states:

> It has been suggested, for instance, that illusory correlation persists in situations where people do not receive good feedback concerning their judgments and where others share the same illusions. Thus instead of feedback concerning actual outcomes, each person both reinforces and is reinforced by the illusions of the others.

Sharing different viewpoints, separating beliefs from facts, and connecting the potential outcomes of current actions with future outcomes all can be explored by means of mediated modeling. System dynamics software can be tremendously helpful in this process.

A potential pitfall in a mediated modeling process—which relies entirely on the input from the participants—is that the positions of groups may be based on a selfish perception of their own interests. Potential participants may be uninterested in a learning experience by sharing information or in looking at the system under study in a more objective way. Commitment to personal interests may prevail, and some stakeholders may be present only to obstruct a positive attempt to get at the problem.

The mediated modeling process is based on a voluntary commitment of participants to collaborate, usually without monetary compensation. It should be agreed by the group at the outset that the question, What is equally good for all? (Habermas 1992) prevails throughout the process. A self-selection of participants with a relatively positive attitude toward cooperation for the mediated modeling process may thus be expected.

Are the most skeptical participants likely to take the time to participate just to sabotage the process rather than ignore it? Since mediated modeling aims at a relatively low-resolution scoping model, it may be expected that the real obstructionists will wait to dig in their heels until specific measures evolve from the process. If the process picks up momentum and produces concrete measures, hopefully the collaborative process has included or reached a broad enough public to become appealing to any uncooperative interest groups.

Mediated modeling thus helps accomplish three things that people of diverse background need to jointly produce measurable results:

- *Mediated modeling helps to structure a group's thinking.* A group is systematically asked at times to focus on a future vision, and at other times to focus on observed past behavior of problem-related aspects. Step by step, past observations, past information, and aspirations for the future are integrated in a simulation model designed by the participants. Multiple elements may influence each other to the extent that this influence may be difficult to keep track of. Counterintuitive behavior and the dynamics of interlinked systems require a systematic, structured, and logical examination. Based on the understanding of the dynamics of the underlying system, participants can develop short-term recommendations and an action plan. Using a computer model to record the discussion helps to structure the thinking.
- *Mediated modeling helps to structure a group's discussion.* When a group designs a frame—represented by the "model sectors" discussed in more detail in Chapter 4—for their complex challenges and fills that frame of model sectors with knowledge, experience, and information, most important parts find their rightful places. Addressing a higher conceptual level by means of a frame of model sectors before turning to specific challenges allows for openings toward innovative solutions. Starting with a conceptual frame helps in maintaining a more balanced course during the discussion. For example, when a participant presents a

specific point of view, the facilitator and the other participants help to interpret how this point of view can be reflected in the evolving model. Tailoring a discussion around a modeled problem helps to keep a discussion structured and connected.

- *Mediated modeling stimulates joint learning among a group of individuals with varying backgrounds.* Stakeholders can become relatively myopic in assessing a (potential) conflict, especially when they do not meet regularly. Workshops geared toward addressing a common challenge may help to widen the scope of individual participants. They learn specific information from each other, build a better understanding of each other's viewpoints, and learn how they may be interconnected in the larger picture in a variety of ways.

As will be shown in the case study chapters to follow, mediated modeling has proven effective in resolving existing or anticipated conflicts among community members in a wide range of settings. It can function as an integrative tool for extensive research programs. In a two-way exchange, mediated modeling has also been used to invite stakeholder input into an extensive research program and, alternatively, to provide research results to a variety of stakeholders.

Intellectual Roots of Mediated Modeling

An interesting journey never follows a straight path. There is no straight path or discipline that leads directly to mediated modeling. The mediated modeling process is a transdisciplinary approach. Inspiration for this approach has come from a wide variety of sources.

Mediated modeling is an applied approach that allows for action research (Allen 2001), also referred to as design-oriented research. With every application, our understanding of the mediated modeling process improves. First describing the baseline situation in each case, then identifying what happened during the mediated modeling process, and finally comparing the results of the process to the baseline achieve this development in understanding (see Chapter 3 for a more detailed description of action research). The Upper Fox and Ria Formosa case studies (Chapters 5 and 9) are explicit examples of action research, because surveys both before and after the mediated modeling process were used to establish a baseline and a result. Analysis of those parts that have succeeded and those that have failed provides a basis for improvements in the design of following studies.

The intellectual roots of mediated modeling are many and varied, and it would be impossible to trace all the threads comprehensively. Several of the most important direct antecedents are briefly described below, with the recognition that not all antecedents may have been included. Major contributing fields include ecological economics, system dynamics, organizational learning, and social psychology.

Ecological Economics

Ecological economics addresses the relationships between ecosystems and economic systems in the broadest sense (Costanza 1991). Its core issues include the sustainability of interactions between economic and ecological systems, the social fairness of resource distributions, and the allocative efficiency of the economy when natural capital, fairness, and sustainability are taken into account. Ecological economics thus involves issues that are fundamentally cross-scale, transcultural, and transdisciplinary, all of which call for innovative approaches to research, policy, and social institutions (Costanza and Daly 1987; Costanza, Cumberland, et al. 1997).

Ecological economics is characterized by a holistic "systems" approach that goes beyond the normal territorial boundaries of the academic disciplines. It aims for a high level of stakeholder participation in decision making and advocates "strong democracy" as a formal governance regime (Prugh et al. 2000). Mediated modeling shares the transdisciplinary, multiscale systems approach of ecological economics. In fact, one could argue that mediated modeling is a fundamentally ecological economics approach to modeling.

System Dynamics Thinking

Jay Forrester initiated the field of system dynamics when he applied feedback theory to industrial systems (Forrester 1961). System dynamics has two important features that may seem obvious but which require conscious effort to apply. First, system dynamics practitioners are interested in the interrelatedness within and among systems. Second, the time span of interest is such that patterns have a chance to become clear.

System dynamics thinking studies the changes in systems over time that emerge from the interrelatedness of the parts. A change to a part can ripple throughout a system in unexpected ways. Systems are not expected to maintain equilibrium—in fact, they very seldom do. Figure 1.1 illustrates the basic difference between linear and systems thinking. The impact of a particular element on another may lag in time, thereby causing a pattern of growth or decay. Alternatively, elements may be interrelated in a way that causes a feedback from one to the other. Over time a feedback loop can also cause a specific pattern.

When time lags and feedback loops simultaneously exist in a system, patterns of accelerated growth followed by accelerated decay (depicted as S-shaped curves when plotted in a graph) can provide the basis for unexpected behavior in a system. For example, multiple nonlinear feedback loops present in social systems often lead to counterintuitive, nonequilibrium behavior (Forrester 1969).

Many large cities have experienced a period of rapid growth followed by a period of rapid decay. The model Forrester presents in *Urban Dynamics* portrays a city as a system of interacting industries, housing, and people. At the onset, the model simulates a city that grows rapidly. However, as its empty space fills, the simulated city becomes relatively full, growth stagnates, and decay in the form of aging housing and industry resembles the unfortunate reality many large cities face.

Forrester simulated popular revitalization initiatives, such as the construction of premium housing, and discovered that this scenario would fill the available land area even faster, leaving less space for new industry and starting the stagnation at an earlier point in time. Alternatively, his model simulated that removing old houses and creating space for new industry could invite a more balanced mix of new industry, housing, and people. The conclusion of this model ran squarely against the conventional wisdom of planners at that time and could be considered a counterintuitive result.

System dynamics modeling is helpful in examining the gap in time and space between decisions, actions, and results. Results are produced in the form of comparative scenarios, their relative differences, and their trade-offs.

Thinking in dynamic systems does not necessarily come naturally to people, since, from an evolutionary perspective, we did not have to rely on this skill for survival in a relatively empty world. Now that we are part of a relatively full, complex, and interconnected world, it has become essential to develop this skill. Developing thinking in dynamic systems starts with examining the readily available beliefs we all hold, followed by a willingness to break with habitual thought patterns and examine new alternatives. When facts and beliefs are separated, hopes and aspirations in the form of future visions can take their rightful place. Uncertainties can be acknowledged, and learning from a system dynamic perspective can occur.

In a system dynamic environment, decisions and their consequences are more easily examined. The linking of past and future allows insights to be generated. Simulation with system dynamic models enables decision makers and stakeholders to learn and include non-linear and lagged feedback mechanisms in decision-making experiments (Kleinmuntz 1985; Brehmer 1989; Sterman 1989). System dynamics modeling is the fundamental approach to the process employed in mediated modeling.

Organizational Learning

Partly inspired by system dynamics, the field of organizational learning emerged in the business community in the late 1980s. Organizational learning puts people, their state of "being," and their ability to learn as individuals as well as a group in the center of organizations.

Learning is a prerequisite for productive decision-making and goes far beyond training. Since many people learn more effectively from experience than through the use of conventional teaching techniques, it makes sense for relevant stakeholders to learn by experiencing the decision-making process and working through their differences in a group setting (Chawla and Renesch 1995).

The goal of a learning organization is to create an adherence among several far-reaching concepts. For example, knowing the rules, checklists, and procedures and acting accordingly is not enough for people working in a learning organization. *Understanding*—that is, perceiving and comprehending the nature and significance of something—is necessary. Understanding reflects the ability to see through the surface, to perceive the essentials, and to sense how facts hang together. Thus, in a learning organization the focus is on synthesis of the most important elements beyond analysis. There is a self-organizing drive rather than a reliance on command and control. There is a sense of purpose, and workers find meaning in what they are doing and the way it is done (Morris 1995).

Learning organizations are firmly embedded in their surrounding environment. They must therefore develop a form of interacting—not only with clients but also with affected communities—that creates consensus beyond just "coming to agreement." The development of alternative scenarios can be an important tool in understanding the driving forces in the way the world works.

Scenarios can be developed in a passive manner, in which the writers of a set of scenarios see themselves as incapable of influencing any aspect that creates the scenarios. From this point of view, a scenario plays out because there is uncertainty about several interrelated driving forces in a system.

Scenarios can also be developed in a more active manner, in which the writers of the scenarios see themselves as capable of influencing how scenarios play out. However, the developers of these scenarios do not feel that they can predict the world or are capable of controlling uncertainty. Rather, they recognize that humans are interconnected on a spiritual level. Adam Kahane (2000) sums up this state with the term *holistic listening:* "Each story reflects the whole, rather than merely contributing a piece to the puzzle." Holistic listening "opens up the possibility of communion and oneness of transcending history to create a new future."

Peter Senge (1990) promotes the use of a shared vision and the creative tension that results from the realization that there is a difference between the current reality and a desired vision. Creative tension can be the motivation to initiate or pursue action.

A common insight from a mediated scoping model is that even though we are content with where we are now (current reality), the trend is toward an undesirable situation. The tension between the preferred future vision and the understanding of where we have been, where we are now, and where we are going is essential for sustainable development. Once some consensus on reality and on the preferred vision has been achieved, one can judge alternative scenarios according to their effectiveness in moving the current world toward the desired world.

Within the field of organizational learning there is an emerging concentration on modeling for learning organizations. Morecroft views models as maps that capture and activate knowledge, as frameworks that filter and organize knowledge, and finally, as microworlds for experimentation, cooperation, and learning (Morecroft and Sterman 1994). This work and contributions from Vennix (1996) and Akkermans (1995) served as important sources of inspiration for mediated modeling. However, the literature of modeling for learning organizations concentrates primarily (but not exclusively) on existing organizations in which representatives of departments provide the variety of viewpoints. Mediated modeling broadens this participation to society as a whole and to merging organizations. The applications in this book focus on environmental challenges in particular.

Social Psychology

Social psychology is the science of social and mental processes that determine people's behavior. For example, social psychology encompasses such subjects as leadership, persuasion, and collective behavior. Of specific interest for the context of this book is the field of group dynamics. Group dynamics examines the behavior in a group (intra-group behavior) as well as behavior between groups (inter-group behavior) and gives insights in how people connect and negotiate reality with others.

Group dynamics research mainly operates in controlled laboratory settings, but informative insights can be gained for the very practical circumstances under which groups using mediated modeling operate. Of particular interest for mediated modeling is characterizing what defines a "group." Hare et al. (1994) ascribes the following characteristics to a group:

- Group members have a set of shared values that help them to maintain an overall pattern of activity.
- They acquire or develop resources and skills to be used for their activity.
- They conform to a set of norms that define roles to be played in the activity and have a sufficient level of morale to provide "cohesiveness."
- They have a specific goal or set of goals that they wish to achieve and

the leadership necessary to coordinate their resources and roles in the interest of the goal or goals.

Alternatively, Brown (1988) evaluates the level of "groupiness" on the basis of the following five characteristics:

- The individual members perceive they are part of that group and outsiders perceive they are not part of the group.
- A group is oriented toward a common goal.
- Interaction between group members exists.
- A realization of interdependence is present.
- There is a structure of roles/status and norms.

Analyzing a group according to a set of characteristics is relevant because defined characteristics can assist in the evaluation of the effectiveness of an ongoing group modeling process. An evaluation before a group process establishes a baseline that can be compared with an evaluation of the same characteristics after a specific group process has taken place.

Even though lists of defined characteristics contain somewhat static representations of groups, they can be helpful in determining whether a group is moving toward a more or less cohesive state over time. Such a determination is of importance for groups that use mediated modeling because often these groups are emerging, self-defined, and brought together to catalyze positive change in a community. Defining the characteristics of a group and how they change over time is a stepping stone toward establishing whether group learning has taken place as part of an ongoing dialogue.

It is interesting to note that some of the insights within the field of social psychology have a remarkable resemblance to insights developed in unrelated fields. For example, Levi and Benjamin (1977) developed a dynamic model for conflict resolution that shows much similarity with adaptive management as presented by Holling (1978). Parties repeatedly decide to focus on "new solutions, ratings, redefining the conflict, gathering more information, and attempting influence" (Hare et al. 1994). This can be interpreted to mean that the appreciation of dynamics is increasing across the borders of different fields.

Other Concepts and Tools

A variety of concepts and specific tools is available to environmental professionals to design a comprehensive environmental management or policy program. Mediated modeling can help these professionals advance a number of invaluable approaches, such as integrated assessments, ecosystem-based management, adaptive environmental management, collaborative management, collaborative learning, and the mutual-gains approach to negotiation.

INTEGRATED ASSESSMENT

Studies assessing the combined influence of multiple systems qualify as an integrated assessment. By nature, integrated assessments have an interdisciplinary character and usually a decision support aim. According to the taxonomy for integrated assessment studies provided by Van Asselt (2000), mediated modeling qualifies as a demand-driven, participatory modeling method, generally but not exclusively with regional or theme-specific focus.

ECOSYTEM-BASED MANAGEMENT

Ecosystem-based management suggests management in harmony with ecological principles focusing on a goal of sustainability. Rather than focusing conservation management on single species, ecosystem-based management focuses on multiple interdependent species and their habitats. Ecosystem-based management takes into account multiple geographic scales, interactions among species, and ecological relationships.

Yaffee et al. (1996) provide an excellent assessment of ecosystem management in the United States. For example, when a watershed is under study, political jurisdictions tend to overlap. The time frames of political, scientific, and cultural aspects of the watershed are not well connected. In addition, the people who reside in and use the watershed have a more personal and intimate knowledge of the system. Scientists may have a thorough understanding of the hydrology, biology, and chemistry of the system or a formal knowledge of the aggregated sociocultural or economic picture. However, they need to make sure this picture connects to the practical needs of residents, users, and politicians. Mediated modeling can be helpful in searching for the most important aspects of the ecosystem under study.

ADAPTIVE ENVIRONMENTAL MANAGEMENT

Adaptive environmental management is emerging through the integration of ecological and participatory research. This approach suggests an iterative process of "learning by doing" and attempts to make a closer connection between science, management, and policymaking. In this view, policy is regarded as an experiment (Holling 1978; Lee 1993). The implemented recommendations are followed by monitoring, assessment, and possible adjustment of the course set. Monitoring is not limited to monitoring ecological data but may include social, economic, and cultural values as well.

Adaptive environmental management started with quantitative modeling workshops wherein scientists and resource managers collaborated in developing and evaluating alternative options. In the process of adaptive management, integrated modeling and consensus building are both essential components (Gunderson et al. 1995).

Adaptive management is currently finding a more prominent role in social learning (Dovers and Mobbs 1997).The adaptive management process may strengthen institutions; it can also empower individuals to regain a sense of control over their lives and confidence in their ability to give direction toward a preferred future.

Mediated modeling is a suitable tool for adaptive environmental management, which is adopting a stronger emphasis on collaborative management. Mediated modeling can be helpful in joint fact finding, in developing recommendations, in creating a monitoring program from a dynamic perspective, and in comparing the assessment with the previous model. The model is flexible and relatively inexpensive to adjust in designing the next generation of policy or management recommendations.

COLLABORATIVE MANAGEMENT

In accordance with the course of adaptive environmental management, the collaborative aspect of mediated modeling emphasizes:

- *Participation in a broad sense.*"Fostering discourse between divergent groups, allowing for the productive interaction of different types of knowledge" (Blumenthal and Jannik 2000).
- *Institutional analysis.* The success of a mediated modeling process depends in part on a thorough institutional analysis including: "(1) a well-defined group of stakeholders, (2) a balance of power among stakeholders, (3) financial resources to sustain the institution, (4) sanctions to encourage cooperation once decisions have been made, (5) mechanisms to resolving conflict" (Blumenthal and Jannik 2000).
- *Simplification.* Simple but elegant models are aiming at the development of a common understanding among a group of stakeholders. The emphasis to understand the behavior of systems is also inherent in the adoption of system dynamics thinking.

Historically, adaptive environmental management has focused on ecosystems bounded by their natural function, such as watersheds or forests. Recently, the focus has been expanded to include larger scales, such as regions or issues at global level. This expanded focus makes collaboration more difficult, but also more necessary.

At larger scales, the diversity of ecosystems, the number of stakeholders, and the options for managing a large-scale area increase. At larger scales, mediated models rely on generality—the level to which a model could apply to other systems as well. However, one may expect models at larger scales to concentrate on realism—the structure of the model mimics the real world relatively well, and the output is realistic.

The precision of a model in terms of predicting an outcome somewhat accurately gains importance at larger scales. This added importance does not imply that the focus of understanding systems needs to shift toward prediction of outcomes. Although all three characteristics of generality, realism, and precision are important there are fundamental trade-offs as discussed in Appendix 1. At larger scales, the stakeholders and therefore the participants in a mediated modeling process may be expected to be well connected in the institutional setting—to the extent that these representatives may make a difference in altering a trend at large scale. The topic of stakeholder involvement is discussed further in Chapter 3.

In mediated modeling, the option for an explicit visioning component (see Chapter 4) is added to the traditional adaptive environmental management framework to encourage a stronger connection with participants' deeper motivations. Both the intellectual understanding of a system and the emotional connection of a participant strengthen the social fabric that is required to induce a positive institutional change.

COLLABORATIVE LEARNING

Collaborative learning (Daniels and Walker 1996, 2001) is an intervention process to facilitate learning among stakeholders, who often have conflicting views and interests. The collaborative learning approach is grounded in theoretical work on soft-systems methodology (Checkland 1981; Checkland and Scholes 1990; Wilson and Morren 1990; Flood and Jackson 1991) and alternative dispute resolution (Moore 1986; Susskind and Cruikshank 1987; Gray 1989; Fisher, Ury, and Patton 1991).

The concept of soft systems—as opposed to hard systems, represented by information and technology—emerged in the beginning of the 1990s, when the need to involve multistakeholder parties became evident. Soft-systems methodology builds on the theoretical work of systems analysis (Senge 1990) and experiential learning (Kolb 1986). The basic assumption in soft-systems methodology is that management of complex problem situations ("fuzzy" or ill-defined problems) demands a focus on process and attaches maximum importance to learning. Instead of the hard-systems emphasis on problem solution, the soft-systems approach focuses on "situation improvements" that can result from active learning and debate.

Checkland and Scholes (1990) argue that soft-systems methodology is best suited for situations in which the problem itself is ambiguous and subject to different interpretations. Management of ecosystems, particularly the issue of non–point source pollution, is precisely the type of situation in which problems are often characterized by a high degree of uncertainty and equivocality.

Collaborative learning calls for modeling efforts but stops short of describing modeling efforts in detail. Mediated modeling can be considered a form of collaborative learning that expands toward the use of modeling techniques. As an example, the San Antonio case study in Chapter 6 was performed on the basis of the collaborative learning approach.

The collaborative learning process also promotes development and identification of stakeholder concerns and underlying interests. Recent theory and research on negotiation and mediation has adopted an interests-based approach. One viewpoint (e.g., Fisher, Ury, and Patton 1991; Bazerman and Neale 1992) maintains that traditional positional approaches to negotiation may be inefficient because stated positions taken by parties in conflict are often extreme and obscure the underlying interests (i.e., needs, concerns, values) that parties are trying to advance through negotiation. The structured set of collaborative learning activities is designed to move participants away from positional bargaining strategies and toward the identification of mutual interests and joint gains from collaboration. Moreover, the presence of outside facilitators during collaborative learning sessions permits the use of effective principles derived from mediation theory and research (Moore 1986; Gray 1989).

THE MUTUAL-GAINS APPROACH TO NEGOTIATION

The mutual-gains approach to negotiating environmental agreements aims at a facilitated or mediated process as an alternative to litigation. This approach rests on the basic assumption that conflict resolution or problem solving benefits from a willingness by affected parties to look at the bigger picture in order to "enlarge the pie" or "create value" before "dividing the pie" or "claiming value" (Raiffa 1982; Lax and Sebenius 1986; Susskind et al. 2000). This approach usually takes place in situations with relatively high levels of conflict.

Exploring the possibilities is a separate activity from committing to a package (Fisher et al. 1998). Mediated modeling can add strength to the first two stages—preparing and creating value—of the mutual-gains approach. It not only helps the parties to think through what their interests are but also helps them to outline the system in which the interests are embedded and connected to other interest groups.

Decision Support Tools

Mediated modeling is a tool that allows the leadership of a research team, community organizers, governmental agency, nongovernmental agency, or all of the above to integrate a larger set of tools into a conflict resolution, or a policy- or decision-making process. A few specific decision support tools—statistical models, geographic information systems, microworlds and games, and role play—are particularly relevant for mediated modeling and deserve to be highlighted. Any of these tools can be incorporated into a mediated modeling process. Alternatively, a mediated modeling process can proceed, enhance, or follow after some decision support tools.

Statistical Models

Standard statistical models (such as multiple-regression models) are widely used. These models incorporate empirical, data-driven approaches and are generally limited to one or a few links in a complex, dynamic system. They can be quite useful in quantifying parameters or upper and lower limits for parameters. In addition, statistical methods can be useful to establish relationships among parameters in a larger system dynamic model.

Statistical models are sometimes used to predict how a person in a specific situation will respond. In mediated modeling we would be more interested in including the "subjects," having them interact, and evaluating the system and scenarios under which certain responses would be evoked.

Geographic Information Systems

Geographic information systems (GIS) are a tool for integrated analysis of a variety of spatially explicit information that can be expressed in the form of maps. GIS is, in many respects, one of the most complex multidisciplinary approaches used to develop an abstract representation of reality. GIS can include multiple data layers describing physical, ecological, and human systems. The complexity of such systems manifests itself not only through the interactions among systems but also among scales. Any changes in driving forces are experienced at all scales from global to local, and the interrelationships are characterized by numerous feedback loops.

To be usefully understood and applied, geographical systems must be treated as an integrated whole, but detailed consideration must also be given to their parts, since many of the most important interactions among their components take place locally. To capture these interactions and the response of a spatially explicit system to factors like population growth or climate change requires that all important components be modeled, as well as the links among components.

To capture temporal changes in the systems, the GIS might be linked to a dynamic modeling of the processes. Multiple layers of spatial information can serve as the summarized input usable in a dynamic model.

An emerging field is spatial dynamic modeling, in which spatially explicit maps change gradually over time (Costanza et al. 1990, 2002). The complexity of these models is much higher than the spatially homogeneous scoping models that are often produced through a mediated modeling process. The spatial dynamic models traditionally have been difficult for stakeholders to access. The scoping models developed as part of a mediated modeling process can provide a more thorough foundation for spatially explicit dynamic modeling efforts and serve as a stepping stone toward the more complex spatially explicit dynamic models. Alternatively, a scoping model can be transformed into a "summary" model in which the outcome of a spatially explicit model is summarized and interpreted.

Microworlds and Games

Microworlds and games—such as Fish Banks (Fish Banks Ltd.), SIMEARTH (Electronic-Reference Arts Inc.), and SIMCITY (Electronic Arts Inc.)—have successfully engaged stakeholders in role play that simulates "what if" scenarios (Johnson 1995). After the first microworlds and business "flight simulators," simulation games have developed into computer-based learning environments (CBLEs) or interactive learning environments (ILEs). Even though learning is at the heart of the design of all the games, the CBLE and ILE games have a greater emphasis on the learning experience. Different layers of knowledge about the model's structure can be disclosed to the users.

While role play informs users about the ways in which they are linked with the system on an input and output level, the model itself remains a "black box"—that is, the players know the variables that go into the model and they know the outcomes, but the underlying understanding of the system is known only by the expert modelers who constructed the game. The mediated modeling process differs in a significant way from such games in that the users actually construct the model.

Although informative, the relationships built through playing with a pre-constructed model are not as thorough as the team learning relationships developed through a mediated modeling process. For one, the time stakeholders spend interacting is much longer and more profound during a mediated modeling process. Even when the models in CBLEs are not black boxes and are available for the users to explore, they differ from mediated modeling in that in the mediated modeling process the team of users also actively constructs the model.

There simply is more latitude for creative energy toward designing innovative solutions when a group designs its own model rather than executing a preexisting model. The learning experience may be more profound within the teams that extensively build the model, independently of the disclosure of the model's structure to the users. It's a matter of *learning by building* a model versus *learning by experimenting with* a model.

Role Play

Role play has been used as a way to elicit information about a complex dynamic problem from stakeholders. Sometimes the roles are based on carefully crafted scripts. The participants are than asked to play their roles with the goal of reaching a certain outcome. Sometimes the roles are left to the imagination of the participants, allowing them to play out their worst fears or most glorious hopes. The goal of role play is to generate insights on a particular problem and to develop understanding for the perspectives of the positions held by stakeholder groups (also referred to as "agents").

In Zimbabwe, researchers used the results from a role play with local non-modeling experts to adjust a previously developed agent-based model. The adjusted model simulated scenarios requested by the participants in the role play (Lynam et al. 2002).

Role play can be used during a mediated modeling process to look at a model from a new perspective, as in the "game of mistaken identity" described in Chapter 4.

Decision-Making Tools

Decision-making models are constructs in which the decision-making process is modeled. These tools differ significantly from decision support tools, such as mediated modeling, in which the objective is to involve decision makers in modeling the system they are supposed to make decisions about.

Bayesian or belief networks are one type of decision-making model. Other static decision-making models include ecological risk assessment (ERA), ecological stressor interactions (ESI), and a family of multicriteria decision-making procedures. However, these models are sometimes constructed with the aid of interactive processes and incorporate multiple stakeholder perspectives.

Ecological Risk Assessment

Ecological risk assessment (ERA) is a methodology designed to identify and assess those factors (called stressors) that cause the greatest stress to ecosystems. *Stress* refers to external forces that threaten an ecosystem's vitality or integrity—that is, its ability to maintain its organizational structure and function.

In a specific ERA approach developed by Harris et al. (1994), the first step is the identification of a set of stressors that clearly affect the ecosystem under study. A specific set of attributes determines the ways in which stressors contribute to the potential decline in the vitality of an ecosystem. These attributes are referred to as ecosystem values, a term intended to connote a value system that associates value with natural systems, thereby expanding on the more limited view that all valuing is human centered.

The identification of both stressors and ecosystem values is accomplished most effectively through a group process in which the participants possess knowledge or expertise pertaining to the ecosystem. Once the sets of stressors and ecosystem values have been agreed on, expert judgment is employed in completing a stressor/value matrix. Utilizing techniques based on fuzzy set theory, the data contained in the stressor/value matrix can be used to rank the stressors, thus identifying those that are most likely driving the ecosystem toward an undesired state or are most responsible for having brought the ecosystem to an impaired state.

By extending the basic analysis of the stressor/value matrix to include multiple management and time-scale perspectives, opportunities for management strategies leading to ecosystem risk reduction can be identified. This information can be used as the starting point for a mediated modeling process. Alternatively, an ERA could strengthen the outcome of a mediated modeling process by prioritizing the outcomes in a more rigorous way.

Ecological Stressor Interaction

Ecological stressor interaction (ESI) is designed to analyze the interactions among ecosystem stressors (Wenger et al. 1999). This modeling approach can provide additional information and insights concerning the way stressors impact an ecosystem. The following types of questions can be answered with ESI:

- Are there subsets of stressors for which a case can be made that they should be dealt with or managed as a group?
- Are there interactive paths or loops among the stressors that have significant management implications?

To analyze these questions, the relationship between each pair of stressors in an agreed-upon list of stressors—usually the same list as used in the stressor/value matrix—must be delineated. This tool is based on elementary concepts in the mathematical discipline of graph theory. Like ERA, it can be a valuable input to a mediated modeling process.

Multicriteria Decision Making

Multicriteria decision making (MCDM) encompasses a large variety of decision-making methods, chiefly multiattribute utility (MAUT), multiattribute value theory (MAVT), analytical hierarchy process (AHP), outranking methods (PROMETHEE and ELECTRE), compromise programming (CP), and goal programming (GP). Current research in this field strives to incorporate multiple decision makers in the decision-making process, as well as to integrate uncertainty and imprecision into the analysis.

Stakeholders and decision makers come together to decide on (1) the decision problem, (2) the alternatives or "solutions" to the problem, and (3) the criteria on which the alternatives will be judged. The methodology and theory behind various approaches differ; however, the end result is a rating or ranking of all alternatives based on all preagreed criteria. These criteria can be qualitative or quantitative.

Current research is also looking at the ways in which MCDM and geographic information systems can be integrated to present decision issues in a spatial framework.

Although stakeholder participation in MCDM is certainly common practice, I do not know of any currently existing work that used MCDM in conjunction with a mediated modeling process. An MCDM approach is a relatively static method, as are ecological risk assessment and ecological stressor interaction. *Static* in this sense means that these techniques usually provide a snapshot in time. Alternative solutions and the criteria for judging alternative solutions are generated before a group of stakeholders (including decision makers) have had a chance to learn more about the system and its dynamics and to integrate the varying interests. Mediated modeling could therefore add a dynamic component, and—like ERA and ESI—MCDM could be used to strengthen the resulting priorities.

Mediated modeling can be used as the backbone of a decision-making process evolving from joint fact finding to collaborative learning and decision making. The goal is to create common knowledge, explore common goals, and understand the views, interests, and rationale of opposing parties (Susskind et al. 1999). Scientific experts are encouraged to participate as stakeholders during part of the process, rather than as outside experts hiding behind a veil of "objectivity" (Ozawa 1991). The objective is to formulate the questions without ambiguity to all stakeholders so that the answers can be interpreted accordingly and placed in a context understood by all participants.

Deliberation Tools

Besides decision support and decision-making tools a suite of tools is available to help groups deliberate. Webster defines deliberation as a "formal discussion and debate of all sides of an issue." Two tools on the ends of a deliberation continuum are presented here. Future Search is an example of an envisioning process with a group, for the benefit of that group. On the other end of the continuum, focus groups are geared toward eliciting information from groups, but not necessarily for the explicit benefit of the members of that group.

Future Search

A future-search process is a three-day envisioning exercise designed to discover common ground. Weisbord and Janoff (1995) describe this process as "bring[ing] people together to achieve breakthrough innovation, empower-ment, shared vision and collaborative action." Similar to a mediated modeling process, a future-search process strives for the creation of self-organizing sys-tems and accepts the dynamics of nonequilibrium situations.

In future search, structure is created as a chaotic situation is allowed to un-fold, and order is found in information freely generated and shared among participants. During a future-search conference several methods are used to record and stimulate the generation of information. Weisbord (1992) states that "tasks that are open-ended, global in context and voluntary go a long way . . . while reducing anxiety to manageable levels" and that "when we get past forums and formats the shortcut to common ground starts with accepting each others' opinions." A *search conference* is an earlier variation of future search (Emery and Purser 1996).

The most obvious difference between future search and mediated model-ing is that future search is more open-ended, whereas mediated modeling pro-vides more structure to the process. Within certain limits, a future-search process can be an integral component of a mediated modeling process. Alternatively, mediated modeling can be seen as taking a future search one step further so as to better assess the paths to achieving the preferred vision established during the future search.

Focus Groups

A focus group is usually composed of seven to ten participants selected because of certain characteristics. Focus groups have been used extensively in private-sector marketing research and have only more recently been used by social re-searchers (Krueger 1994). The participants are screened from a randomly selected population, and the conversations are systematically analyzed. A focus group process is usually repeated several times with different participants.

The focus group approach is intended to look carefully into the perceptions of participants, which are elicited in a friendly environment encouraging inter-action. Such focus groups often provide new ways of looking at an issue under investigation that are superior to the insights gained through an individual survey. Benefits from a more open-ended approach were realized as early as the 1930s and included identifying participants' appreciation or dislike of attributes of a product that were not anticipated by the marketers.

The objectives of the focus group approach and the mediated modeling ap-proach are quite different. The focus group approach is designed not to build consensus on a product, concept, or project but rather to learn from the groups. A mediated modeling process is organized to foster learning within a group. Recently though, focus groups have been used in a collaborative manner.

A mediated modeling process benefits from focus group research's early recognition of the usefulness of an open-ended approach. However, the focus group approach uses several parallel groups to investigate the same topic. In contrast, there is usually only one mediated modeling process with respect to one topic. However, the value of multiple parallel processes is briefly discussed in Chapter 3.

In addition, the criteria for stakeholder selection for a mediated modeling process differ from the criteria for a focus group. In preparing a mediated modeling process, the aim is to identify crucial stakeholders so as to move a decision-making process forward. A focus group usually relies on a random sample of participants who fulfill certain criteria.

Mediated Modeling as a Starting Point or as a Complementary Tool

A mediated modeling process can be used as a starting point to design a research, management, or policymaking process. It can also be a complementary tool in a program in which different attributes are valued than the ones offered by the prospect of mediated modeling.

Consider four attributes for a group with participatory objectives:

- Level of understanding
- Level of consensus
- Level of participation
- Timing of participation

Figure 2.3 plots these attributes, ranging from low in the center toward high at the outer points. Timing of participation is plotted from late in the center toward early at the end of the arrow. The strengths of different tools can be easily compared using this diagram.

Mediated modeling is expected to score relatively high on the first three aspects—understanding, consensus, and participation—and it is useful (although not mandatory) to start a mediated modeling process early in a participatory process. A mediated discussion also displays strengths in getting stakeholders involved at early stages and may be expected to score high on consensus building and perhaps even higher on level of participation when a process is designed with an open access for new stakeholders.

On the other hand, even though the option for open access may improve the level of participation in a quantitative manner, the quality of participation may decrease beyond about thirty participants, for reasons explained in Chapters 3 and 4. Nevertheless, an open-access process may be more suitable in certain situations, especially if the level of joint understanding can be sacrificed.

Alternatively, a particular challenge may benefit from an increased level of understanding resulting from the construction of high-resolution computer

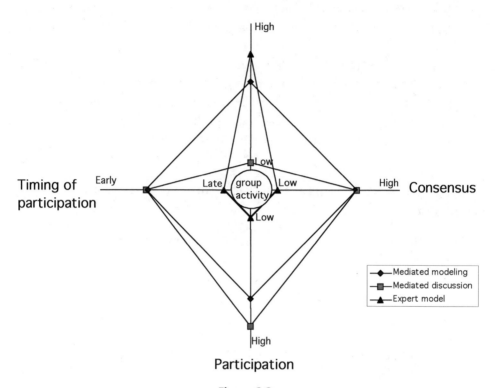

Figure 2.3.
Tools for different situations

models by experts. Generally, however, computer-assisted model building at that level is not very transparent for nonmodelers.

The choice of a tool for addressing a complex environmental problem depends on the nature of the problem, the situation, and the means and goals of the stakeholders. Mediated modeling can provide a useful starting point for leading an integrated stakeholder-involved learning venture. It also has the potential to remain the backbone of an extended program in which more specialized tasks are added to a regime leading toward solutions of environmental problems.

As noted earlier, Costanza and Ruth (1998) advocate a three-step modeling approach in which the first step is the construction of a scoping model similar to the type of models generated through a mediated modeling process, followed by a research model and a management model.

Conclusion

Mediated modeling is a sign of the times. Complex environmental challenges require a broader involvement by stakeholders and a broader range of academic input by integrating relevant disciplines. A variety of academic disciplines and business consulting techniques has inspired the development of mediated modeling.

The following approaches—based on a research and development model by Jiggins (1993)—provide the basis for features of mediated modeling as a tool:

- Process-based management and policymaking geared toward learning (adaptive environmental management)
- Ecosystem-based management on increasingly larger scales, without losing the connection to smaller scales
- Facilitation of the social processes and organizational capacity to accomplish these (collaborative and organizational learning)
- Methods for bringing about capacity for action among multiple agencies and actors, often with conflicting views and interests

Mediated modeling connects very well with some of the most promising contemporary approaches to environmental problem solving. Many practical tools are available for developing the most comprehensive and appropriate approach for a particular situation. Mediated modeling contributes to these possibilities, especially those incorporating current computing capabilities. Chapter 3 gives a generic overview of the basics of the process and Chapter 4 offers a step-by-step guide to mediated modeling. The practical experience of some practitioners who have applied this tool in complex environmental problem-solving situations is summarized in Chapter 10.

3

The Mediated Modeling Process

A common reaction from groups considering initiating a mediated modeling process is, "We have to wait until we have figured out how we want to solve the problem before we can engage in a modeling project." The whole idea behind mediated modeling is that it assists in figuring out why a certain problem exists and in developing innovative ways for addressing it. This idea is inherent to system dynamics thinking but isn't always recognized as such.

For example, a mediated modeling exercise in Patagonia was undertaken to integrate the results of three years of research activity and data gathering (van den Belt et al. 1998). However, because mediated modeling was initiated after the research activities and data gathering phase had occurred, the individual research projects within the wider program did not necessarily lend themselves well to an integrated picture. Many pieces of information that were missing could have been available if an integrated model had been developed from the beginning. The model could then have been refined as the data were gathered. A goal of a mediated modeling project is to learn what kind of information is available and what additional information should be gathered to answer the relevant questions.

This chapter describes the mediated modeling process and puts it in its real-world context. It also answers following questions:

- Why should a mediated modeling project be undertaken?
- What can be regarded as a successful mediated modeling process?

- What can and cannot be expected from this process?
- What can be done with the results?

A mediated modeling process is shaped by the interaction among stakeholders. The chapter therefore continues to discuss considerations as to who should or should not be taking part in a mediated modeling, the roles of the participants, and that of the expert mediated modeler.

Why Should a Mediated Modeling Project Be Undertaken?

There are several types of problems that are particularly amenable to mediated modeling, as discussed in the following sections.

1. The challenge is a complex one with several dimensions.

A complex problem is characterized by several interconnected subproblems rather than one isolated problem. For example, on a global scale, local, national, regional, and global problems are interconnected, although the pattern symptomatic for a problem may be more evident on one particular level. Only by asking certain questions with respect to a global level, for example, does it become clear that the abundant emissions of greenhouse gases are a problem.

In addition, a problem may occur in different forms when one looks at it from the perspective of different temporal scales (seconds, days, months, years, centuries). For example, the negative impact of greenhouse gases may not become clear from the perspective of a few days, but it most certainly will become clear from the perspective of centuries.

On a socioeconomic scale, a complex problem can be addressed by different academic disciplines or from different professional orientations. For example, the answer to what to do about greenhouse gases depends a lot on whether you ask a representative from the oil industry or a representative from an environmental nongovernmental organization.

Finally, interaction among the different scales is required to achieve an understanding of the complex problem (van Asselt 2000).

Complex problems are often open-ended and poorly defined. In addition, they are usually embedded within systems whose boundaries are unclear. Solving problems of this type requires a different approach from those typically used when solving well-defined problems. For example, the "menu" approach often used in solving engineering problems may work well in achieving widely accepted, utilitarian outcomes. However, when interested and concerned parties focus on a single dimension of a complex problem, conflicts may arise and a tug of war may develop. The resulting impasse may be broken when a single dimension of a problem is placed in its larger context. When disputants discover this context together, they can often then find innovative solutions.

Consider, for example, a case in which a commercial agriculture firm proposes a factory farm adjacent to a small town. The proposal has drawn opposition from a significant proportion of the townspeople. A public hearing has been held to grant or deny a variety of permits, but the opposing arguments lack coherency. The townspeople present their individual concerns separately and are not organized. In addition, there are several different permitting processes to certify different aspects of the proposed factory farm. The opponents' concerns include stress to water wells, air pollution, excessive flies, and runoff of nutrients, as well as impacts upon the town's social and economic structure.

The permit-driven deliberative process does not necessarily provide a way to integrate these concerns into the larger picture, and the opponents have a difficult time organizing their issues into a coherent whole. The agribusiness is thus unable to find ways to address those concerns within a coherent overall business strategy or permits may be granted for suboptimal operations.

2. A potential conflict is anticipated, or a collaborative climate for team learning to understand and/or solve the problem is present or desired.

It is easier to engage representatives from a variety of social and professional groups in an anticipated problem than in a more pressing acute or long-standing conflict. A characteristic of more entrenched, high-intensity conflict is that the stakes are often described in narrow terms (e.g., George W. Bush's polarizing statement that "Either you are with us or against us"). Not much room is left for dialogue. Because the parties generally have chosen a position and are seeking to divide a pie rather than enlarge it, it is difficult to change the parties' understanding of the problem.

In low-level conflict, parties are more willing to maintain a discussion after a problem is perceived and defined, and before solutions are carved in stone. Before settling on a solution with irreversible consequences, there is a window of opportunity to (1) examine the problem from different sides; (2) understand the complexity of the problem at different scales (geographic, temporal, economic, and sociocultural); (3) hear different opinions; (4) foster mutual learning among a variety of stakeholders and develop a more accurate understanding of the true problem; and (5) determine the uncertainties and risks involved.

In high-conflict situations, it is especially important to engage in a discussion that incorporates the goal of learning from different parties and that defines "the pie" that is to be divided (Susskind et al. 2000).

3. An increased level of shared information among a group of stakeholders is desired.

A range exists between those who feel that conflict is endemic and those who are more optimistic that conflicts can be resolved. Conflict can be considered as an unorganized form of competition. The question then becomes, Should competition be managed or not? Should the players come together to establish the rules of the game? A tool such as mediated modeling may be considered too time consuming, risky, or costly for those who feel conflict is bound to exist or for those with a winning hand in the unorganized competitive situation. Although there are good reasons to work toward a shared understanding among stakeholders, some encouragement for collaboration is often required (Stern and Hicks 2000).

4. A system dynamics approach is likely to be helpful.

Understanding the system is often a more important goal than predicting the future accurately. Senge (1990) distinguishes between "detail complexity" and "dynamic complexity." If a prediction about what will happen under the status quo is required, tools for forecasting and analysis that are geared toward handling many variables are used. This is referred to as detail complexity. However, when cause and effect are subtle (because of the presence of feedback loops) and effects over time are not obvious (because of time lags), dynamic complexity is at work. Such situations occur in most real systems.

In order to understand such dynamic complexity, identifying the interrelationships among variables is more important than accurately quantifying linear cause-effect relationships. Emphasis on the process is more important than snapshots. Defining the gaps between "what is desirable" and "where we are" is instrumental for a start in identifying patterns. A system dynamics approach can help to define this gap by thinking through the structure of the system, how it arrived at its current state, and what variables can be changed to make the system function more desirable.

The system dynamics approach connects well with the idea of adaptive environmental management (Holling 1978). Rather than a static solution, a policy or management plan is considered as an experiment. Its impacts are monitored and assessed by comparing where we came from, what is desirable, and where we currently are.

5. Fostering a vision for the future is desired.

A vision deserves attention and is worthwhile to pursue to the extent suitable for a particular group. Donella Meadows states (in Costanza et al. 1996, p. 6):

> A vision is about what one really wants, not what one would settle for. For example, we really want self-esteem, but we settle for a fancy car; we really want health, but we settle for medicine; we really want human happiness and we settle for Gross National Product (GNP); we want permanent prosperity but settle for unsustainable growth.
>
> - A vision should be judged by the clarity of its values, not the clarity of its implementation path.

- Responsible vision must acknowledge, but not get crushed by, the physical constraints of the real world.
- It is critical for visions to be shared because only shared visions can be responsible.
- Vision has to be flexible and evolving.

By making ideals verbally explicit, current constraints must give way for a moment so that creativity may start to flow. Peter Senge (1990, p. 206) describes shared vision as

> a force in people's hearts, a force of impressive power. It may be inspired by an idea, but once it goes further—if it is compelling enough to acquire the support of more than one person—then it is no longer an abstraction. It is palpable. People begin to see it as if it exists. Few, if any, forces in human affairs are as powerful as shared vision.

Senge's work provides the insight that a shared vision of the future is crucial in maintaining "creative tension" in the present situation that fuels a commitment for future change.

Nonetheless, some observers feel that a pursuit of a shared vision may be a waste of time at best (Daniels and Walker 2001) and undesirable at worst, while others advocate it (Senge 1990; Costanza 2000). These ideas are not necessarily in opposition but rather suggest different emphases on where to focus limited time, energy, and resources. These differences may also be due to the interpretation that the sharing of visions means that worldviews have to be identical or that there is a desire to make the worldviews identical.

Those opposed to pursuing a joint vision seek to acknowledge and learn from existing differences in values and worldviews and to then generate implementable improvements. Advocates for envisioning would not disagree with this goal, but they claim that the overlap in values and worldviews (rather than differences) is more useful to emphasize as a basis for group action.

6. Fostering consensus on the way the world works is desired.

Not only is it important to have common goals or a shared vision, it is also paramount to create a shared understanding of where we currently are and how we got here. Such an understanding gives us insights on the most important relationships that drive a system—for example, whether a slow growth in a system may be the result of a primarily positive feedback loop, tapered by a negative feedback loop.

From a systems perspective, rather than from a personal spyglass perspective, we can ask the questions, What has happened? and Why did it happen? When we follow that line of thought with, Where will it lead to? and Do we want to go there? there is a better common foundation to ask, What can we try to do differently to alter our course?

7. *Fostering consensus on a decision and a commitment to the decision are desired.*

Not all situations require a formal consensus-based decision. When decisions fit into an overall consensus-based frame, there is no need for an explicit consensus-building process for individual decisions. However, when, as described in Chapter 1, numerous small-scale decisions develop broader-scale trends with undesirable consequences, it may be wise to create a consensus-based frame to support these decisions with the potential capability to alter a negative trend into a more positive one.

For example, the participants in the Upper Fox case study (Chapter 5) are facing a trend of urban sprawl. Originally, the expansion of real estate into the western part of the watershed generated positive income for the area. Currently, urban sprawl is at the point where it may suffocate itself. The natural and rural agricultural qualities that originally attracted residents are being negatively affected.

A consensus-based decision is more likely to be implemented because of a naturally motivated commitment than because of a negotiated decision in need of enforcement (as discussed in Chapter 1 [Table 1.1]). Vennix (1996) proposes the idea that consensus fosters commitment to see the implementation of a decision through. In a mediated modeling process, individuals are given a chance to participate. Participation is an important prerequisite for consensus; however, participation is not a sufficient condition for consensus.

Ownership of a model by the participants is a goal for a mediated modeling process. Ownership of the outcome reinforces the commitment to the course of action. Then again, in some cases it may be unrealistic, undesirable, or unnecessary to aspire to consensus over a negotiated outcome, and to commitment over enforcement.

Outline of a Mediated Modeling Process

Chapter 4 offers a practical guide to the steps of a mediated modeling process, whose steps can be summarized as follows:

- *Step 1: Preparation.* Relevant stakeholders are selected and invited. Baseline information is established about the group and the perception of its individual members with respect to the issues. This information can be gathered by means of a survey or questionnaire. A preliminary model may be developed to serve as a starting point for the workshops.
- *Step 2: Workshops.* A series of meetings are held, aimed at fostering

learning among stakeholders. With the assistance of a mediated modeler the participants develop a problem definition—a qualitative model that evolves into a quantitative simulation model. The participants run "what-if" scenarios during the scenario evaluation phase.

- *Step 3: Follow-up.* With assistance of the jointly constructed model, the participants practice communicating the results to a wider audience, make plans to disseminate the results, and prepare for implementation of the results. A survey or questionnaire reveals what improved or did not improve in relation to the baseline information. The model and accommodating reports are prepared for wider distribution.

Adaptive and Collaborative Management

Mediated modeling acts as a participatory tool for adaptive and collaborative management to the extent that initially a group of up to thirty participants (a representation of relevant stakeholder groups) can directly participate in the group learning process. The model produced by the mediated modeling process is accessible to a larger public because the software and the model are relatively user-friendly and can be easily explained to a larger audience by those who participated in its construction.

A process-based instrument such as mediated modeling serves well as a backbone in a complex, dynamic institutional setting. A mediated modeling process can be extended not only to incorporate horizontal integration among institutions but also to encourage vertical integration of a wider variety of unorganized stakeholders, given enough time, funds, and commitment.

Mediated modeling can also be helpful in designing management processes on larger scales. For example, at the global scale, experts have developed many well-recognized and very detailed global models of climate change. Even though these models all suggest that the global climate is changing, there is enough disagreement among them with respect to the extent of the change, with respect to how global climate change may manifest itself, that the results leave a lot of room for disagreement as to what should be done to address the issue.

An extended mediated modeling process might be used to bring groups of stakeholders (horizontally and vertically anchored) together to participate in addressing the policy implications of global climate change. Such an exercise would not just add another model to those already in existence. The existing expert models on global climate change would, in this case, be a source for information in regard to questions the broader stakeholder community would consider of interest.

The preceding example describes a situation in which detailed models about a complex problem are available but in which there is a poor link between the models and what society can actually do with the results. In fact, a situation like this almost requires a reversed three-step modeling approach (Costanza and Ruth 1998). It is as if the stakeholders in global climate change cannot hear the results of the expert models. They are too far removed from the issue, and they cannot find their legitimate place because it is not clear how the overall system hangs together.

Mediated models are usually spatially homogeneous, especially at the scoping stage. A three-step modeling approach can be used to increase the spatial resolution, beginning at a scoping level, expanding to a research model, and then ultimately arriving at a model that can be used as part of an ongoing management program.

Adaptive management aims at a recurring cycle of "policymaking as an experiment" or "learning by doing." Table 3.1 provides an overview of the classic elements of adaptive environmental management: vision, assessment, information collection, planning, implementation, and monitoring. The added emphasis on the human aspect of this process, in the form of expanding toward collaborative management, is described in Chapter 2 and is reflected by an envisioning step within the adaptive management cycle.

Table 3.1 explains the role of mediated modeling for each step, thus helping to clarify the strengths as well as the weaknesses of a mediated modeling process as a tool at each step within an adaptive environmental management cycle.

Participants and Roles

Anyone involved in preparing, supporting, or making environmental decisions can initiate a mediated modeling process, whether that person is in government, an affected business, or an NGO, or is simply an affected citizen. The person has to have been exposed to the concept of mediated modeling, must recognize its potential with a specific situation in mind, has to champion the dissemination of information, and must work to create a vision of a potential future project.

More importantly, anyone wishing to initiate a mediated modeling process needs to enlist a sponsor—usually a government agency, foundation, or association—or a contribution from participating stakeholder groups. Ideally, several sponsors among the stakeholders will be found, but a great deal of consensus building will be needed for stakeholder sponsors to agree that the mediated modeling project is the key to finding a solution.

If sponsors are not part of the workshop activity, they may lack appreciation for the process and may view the work as just the final model. The overriding purpose of a mediated modeling project is to generate a shared level of information among participants and team learning as a (emerging) group. The

Table 3.1.

The role of mediated modeling within cycles of
adaptive environmental management

Cycles of AEM	Target	Role of mediated modeling
1st round	Vision	Envisions what kind of future we want, instead of what kind of future we would settle for. A vision is not a static picture but a process that gets refined over time.
	Assessment	Mediated modeling can be used for "scoping" purposes and for assessing the past, current situation, and possible future scenarios by a group of relevant stakeholders. The links between ecology, economics, and the social aspects of a system are explored by explicitly defining the most important pathways.
	Information collection	Involved participants collect and summarize information and place it in a larger picture with the aid of computer software and a facilitator. Data gaps are identified in the course of the mediated modeling process.
	Planning	If consensus can be reached, an action plan is developed. If no consensus is reached, a research plan is developed to gather the data and information required to substantiate the model.
	Implementation	Each participant can use the scoping model to convey the background of an action or research plan to a larger audience. Its relative transparency enables the modelers to show what is or is not in the model and thus to build trust with the larger audience.
	Monitoring	Results are measured according to agreed-upon indicators. These indicators are based on the scoping model.
2nd round	Vision	Refines the vision of the preferred future, perhaps addresses the feared future. The scoping model can support the vision discussion by running scenarios.

Table 3.1. (Continued)

Cycles of AEM	Target	Role of mediated modeling
	Assessment	The scoping model can be compared with the real-time results and calibrated and adjusted to match the new information.
	Planning Implementation Monitoring	The same principles as the first round apply. However, the scoping model is becoming the backbone that keeps several initiatives integrated in a simplified manner. The model becomes a summary model in the final stage.

final model itself is of secondary importance and functions mainly as an information dissemination tool to persons not initially part of the collaborative model building process. At a minimum, it is important for a sponsor to take part in the problem definition phase and the scenario evaluation phase.

Someone who commissions a mediated modeling process could be a decision maker or leading professional who is looking for a well-informed basis for a decision or course of action. Users could also be groups entangled in an acute conflict and wishing to "enlarge the pie" by generating more knowledge about the larger picture, including all viewpoints, and by creating the space to generate an innovative solution (Susskind et al. 2000).

Chapter 10 provides an in-depth discussion of the strengths and weaknesses of the mediated modeling approach.

The Mediated Modeler

In mediated modeling, an individual functions as facilitator, mediator, and modeler who prepares the meetings, guides the discussion during the meetings, filters out the dynamic thought patterns, and simultaneously translates the results into stocks, flows, and functional relationships on the projected computer screen. The participants give immediate feedback to the suggested changes or may request an elaboration or explanation. The screen is visible to everyone in the room, and the participants should all be comfortable with the changes made.

Richardson and Andersen (1995) provide five distinct roles for a support team of a group modeling process; facilitator, modeler/reflector, process coach, recorder, and gatekeeper. They write: "We hypothesize that some of the five roles may be combined, or distributed among the consultants and the clients in a group model-building project, but that all five roles or functions must be present for effective group support. We further hypothesize that group modeling efforts can be significantly accelerated by explicitly recognizing the five roles and deliberately assigning them to different skilled practitioners." (p. 115)

The first hypothesis of the distinct aspects of a group model-building project has, over the years, proven very useful and reoccurs in different forms throughout this book as the conscious differentiation between interpersonal aspects and group dynamics (represented by the roles of facilitator and process coach) on one hand and model building and system dynamics (represented by the roles of modeler/reflector and recorder) on the other hand. However, the second hypothesis has proven more cumbersome in practice and, in my view, tips the efficiency scale the wrong way. Perhaps, ideally it would be wonderful to have skilled specialists collaborating effectively and have the means to employ them. An extensive support team, when affordable, must have the capacity to work together seamlessly, or information and time may be lost when multiple individuals with different tasks are involved. The underlying assumption of striving for this ideal must be that the process and product aspects benefit from being kept separate and in-depth specializations. However, I would argue that, after having achieved a certain level of competency, it might be more efficient if members of a support team expand their skills into synthesizing and acquire the full breadth of facilitation and modeling skills, because these aspects are inseparably intertwined. Richardson and Andersen (1995) recognize the need for knowledge of system dynamic modeling to some degree for all five roles. It is not just a matter of eliciting information from a stakeholder group and being able to present a model back in the shortest amount of time among a relatively small group of people. As stated by Vennix, Andersen, and Richardson (1997) the learning takes place during the model building process. Part of learning is to work through conflicts (Wondoleck and Yaffee 2000), which, in my mind, tips the balance more toward process aspects than was recognized by Richardson and Andersen (1995) and therefore increases the need for combined and balanced skills of facilitation and modeling in each support team member. With an increased emphasis on process and multi-stakeholder aspects of environmental consensus building, this book presents experience suggesting that it may be equally or more efficient for one person to take the lead in both facilitation (and mediation) and simultaneous modeling. In this case, the facilitator/modeler/reflector roles have merged and keep pace with the speed with which a group reaches a shared level of understanding and a productive level of consensus. Similarly, the tasks of the process coach and recorder may be dual as well, however, recognizing that they both are equally important, but approaching these tasks from a more holistic perspective. In fact, mediated modeling processes may very well be initiated by one gatekeeper and one mediated modeler, expanding the team in breadth and depth as the resources allow.

The "gatekeeper" is described in Chapter 4 as the "champion." Without this initiator and promoter, for both the human and the technical aspects, these projects don't materialize. There is ample opportunity to fortify the process with assistance from individuals with specific tasks relating to the computer model or facilitation and mediation within the group. For example, an assistant can provide input to the process during breaks when the participants are engaged in small-group activities or via some predesigned mechanism during the sessions. Alternatively, separate modelers can insert their expertise in between group meetings to provide modeling advice.

It is crucial that an assistant facilitator have a good understanding of modeling, so as not to divert the discussion too far away from what happens on the screen.

Another assisting role is that of a "recorder." Videotaping a conference may inhibit the freedom of participation, and voice tapes are cumbersome and not very instructive. A "recorder" in this case would be a project team member who is not participating in the modeling directly but who is observing (as objectively as possible) what is happening in the room. The recorder can note signs of conflict, rate of participation, level of consensus, general motivation, and ideas that were not fully explored. Especially in a multicultural setting, an assistant facilitator may be helpful in moderating interpersonal conflicts or difficulties arising from language or cultural differences.

At all times, the goal should be to use the time of the participants effectively. If modeler and facilitator are separate individuals, there must be adequate cooperation and communication between them. Modelers and facilitators don't necessarily meet in the middle if both are left to their natural inclinations. It requires hard work for them to reach agreement on how they will work together, just as it requires hard work for one person to develop both skills.

Following are the distinctive roles incorporated into the job of a mediated modeler:

- *Facilitator:* A facilitator is an impartial party who manages meetings as part of a collaborative process. A facilitator's tasks include preparing the meeting and guiding the discussion during the meeting so participants can devote their energy to the goals they have chosen to address. A facilitator summarizes the ongoing discussion and brings closure. In mediated modeling, the discussion is summarized on a projected computer screen in the form of a system dynamics model (as will be further detailed in Chapter 4).
- *Mediator:* A mediator is an impartial party who intervenes in a negotiation. A mediator plays the role of a facilitator when a group meets. When a group breaks up, the facilitator's job is usually over, but a mediator is still involved in shaping the process through meetings with small groups or individuals in between plenary meetings.
- *Modeler:* In general, a modeler tries to create an abstract, simpler

representation of reality. As discussed in Chapter 2, the modeling medium used can vary from drawing pictures or a map of activities in a rural African village with a stick in the sand (rapid rural appraisal), to a flip chart, to a computer equipped with system dynamics software, as is the case with mediated modeling.

Between workshops, the mediated modeler cleans up the model and may meet with small groups, individuals, or outside experts that the participants have agreed should be consulted. When making changes to the model, the modeler must not go beyond agreements derived from the group. Emerging modeling solutions to agreed-upon modeling problems should be briefly presented to the reconvening participants for approval or a chance to raise objections. A model should not become the modeler's model but should reside in the public domain of a group. Otherwise, loss of ownership among the participants over the model may result.

To make the most effective and efficient use of the valuable time of the participants, a mediated modeler must remain focused on the deliverable objectives and be flexible about how to achieve them. Scripts can be used to aid in keeping track of the deliverable objectives at different stages of the process (Andersen and Richardson 1997). The description of the steps in a "generic" mediated modeling process, as presented in Chapter 4, offer some considerations in developing a personal script.

Certain attitudes will increase a facilitator's effectiveness in applying mediated modeling. I agree with Vennix (1996) that there are several important basic attitudes: a helping and inquiring approach, authenticity and integrity, and neutrality. Each of these attitudes require a mediated modeler to make a thorough and constant self-examination in the face of numerous challenges, as the facilitator is an important model of behavior for the group.

For example, a helping attitude does not mean that the facilitator fixes problems for the group; rather, the facilitator engages in a process of joint thinking about the problems with the group. A helping attitude stimulates an attitude of inquiry in which questions are welcomed.

Authenticity and integrity are required for building trust, which in turn is a prerequisite for group members to remain committed to a collaborative process. Lastly, a mediated modeler can be considered as the process coach and does best to remain neutral where the content is concerned.

In addition to the aforementioned personal attitudes, certain skills, such as conflict handling and communication, can be developed by practice. It helps to develop a keen sense for the basis of the existing conflicts. For example, conflicts may arise from clashes of personalities or be based on fundamental differences in worldviews. In general, the way to resolve unproductive conflicts is to get to the underlying reasons. This can be a delicate and uncomfortable process, with much to gain but also much to lose. However, stimulating conflict can be a great source of creativity, especially in groups of very like-minded individuals with a group culture of compromise and concurrence.

Communication skills are essential in mediated modeling. Two elements of communication stand out: on the one hand, the skill of active and open listening; on the other, the skill of conveying a message precisely (perhaps in several different ways). Listening and conveying are obviously connected, and it is crucial to request feedback to confirm that a message has been properly received.

A group that starts to work with a mediated modeler needs to have some sense of the role of the mediated modeler as a process coach, rather than as the "fixer of all problems." The ground rules outlined in Chapter 4 reflect some of the basic behavioral guidelines, consensus-enhancing procedures, and/or conflict-handling strategies that can be laid out for a group at the onset of a mediated modeling process. The ground rules may help clarify the role of the mediated modeler at the onset of a modeling process; however, the actions of a mediated modeler will quickly determine how participants perceive that role.

Action Research

A mediated modeler falls under the definition of action research: "Critical collaborative enquiry by Reflective practitioners, who are Accountable in making the results of their enquiry public, Self-evaluative of their practice, and engaged in Participative problem solving and continuing professional development" (CRASP) (Zuber-Skerritt 1992). A mediated modeler must maintain a constant inner dialogue concerning the process as well as the product. He or she must keep the objectives in mind and listen for the most important pieces of information as well as identify the vision that makes people tick. In addition, a mediated modeler must advocate and encourage the use of procedures that enable the participants to function as a group and must invite the group members to move into a space in which creativity and authentic learning are possible.

Bunning (1995) describes the profile of an effective action researcher as a person who is:

- Inner-directed—tends to independence of thought and expression
- Developmentally oriented—busy, but always open to something new
- A reflective philosopher—willing to step back and reflect on things
- Effectiveness-oriented—interested in strategic issues

Time Frame

Mediated modeling projects tend to take about forty to sixty contact hours or five to seven working days of interaction among participants. Naturally, the speed at which a group works through the program depends on the group dynamics, the task, and the funding available to support a genuine consensus-building effort.

In complex environmental issues with multistakeholder participation, it generally takes about three days to develop a conceptual or qualitative model that sets out the way in which ideas and issues relate to each other. One day should be reserved for developing a list of data requirements and dividing this list among participants who are charged with the responsibility for obtaining the information (if it exists). Ideally, the participants spend about a day incorporating the data in the model. However, most groups entrust the data incorporation to the mediated modeler, for reasons that will be discussed in Chapter 4. Around two days are spent on discussion of model simulations of different scenarios, and, finally, a hands-on tutorial gives participants a chance to practice relaying the insights gained to others.

Give or take a day, this process adds up to about seven days, which can be spread over a period of time ranging from a week to five years, depending on the goal of the project. This projection excludes additional collaborative efforts that occur between modeling sessions among individual stakeholders or small groups of stakeholders.

For example, the development of the Patagonia Coastal Zone Management Model (van den Belt 1998) took one month and mainly involved the integration of data and the discovery of important missing pieces. Some of the industrial projects reported in the literature took a month; however, the results were mainly qualitative maps rather than quantitative running simulation models. Both the Ria Formosa and the Upper Fox projects (Chapters 5 and 9, respectively) had a duration of about four months and were very comparable in scope. In the Banff case study (Chapter 7), a form of mediated modeling process guided the development of the Banff round table over the course of two and a half years. The San Antonio Urban Watershed and the Sage Grouse case studies (Chapters 6 and 8, respectively) spanned a time frame of about one year. One current project, "Socio-economic Impacts of UV-b Radiation" (van den Belt, in preparation), will span five years and will be completed in 2005.

What Results Are to Be Expected?

Expected results for the participating groups or communities include the following:

- *Team building and learning.* The group becomes more cohesive and develops a higher level of shared understanding.
- *Consensus.* A successful process generates a workable level of consensus. Ideally, every participant is equally enthusiastic about the resulting recommendations. Strong consensus is the goal; however, a situation in

which everybody can "live with" the recommendations can still be considered a success, as discussed in Chapter 1.

- *Communication tool.* Every participant will be able to operate the final model. The resulting model can be used as a basis for discussion with remote stakeholder groups and as an educational and communication tool.
- *Decision support for policy and management.* A basis for more equitable, resilient, and sustainable policies and management options is established because stakeholders have been effectively involved.
- *Adaptive management.* The resulting model is flexible and can be updated and changed as new information is available owing to monitoring and assessment of the implemented recommendations.

Defining Success

Because mediated modeling is a process-oriented tool, its success or failure must be measured in process terms as well.

In the *short term,* a mediated modeling project is successful when a group of about thirty diverse stakeholders have a better-shared understanding of a complex problem and reach consensus on a course of action to address this problem. Individuals in the group become aware of the interdependency among group members and between economical, ecological, social, and/or other relevant aspects. They develop a greater appreciation for the roles played by the other members of the group and an improved sense of how common goals can be achieved.

Sustained interaction among the group members to collaboratively implement, monitor, and assess the recommendations is a *medium-term* sign of success. The group has formed new working relationships among its members that are likely to change the way decisions are made in the future. Decisions are evaluated on their cohesiveness concerning short-, medium-, and long-term impacts from a dynamic perspective and are forged from a shared vision. At this level, a result is evaluated in gradations according to its position on the spectrum between "where we are" and "where we want to be." If the gap is closed, the problem is "solved"; if the gap becomes smaller, the situation has "improved"; and if the gap is unaffected or widens, "insights are gained."

A *long-term* success is characterized by the ability of the model-building process to incorporate newly gained information as it becomes available over time and to function as the backbone of the stakeholder-involved collaborative learning process. However, a model should be abandoned when the reason for building it is accomplished. Hanging on too long inhibits innovative thinking and learning.

Mediated modeling is still a relatively new tool, and very little information is available regarding the long-term results of mediated modeling processes.

Therefore only the short-term achievements can be discussed here. Success of a mediated modeling process is heavily dependent on the starting point. As part of action research, surveys before and after the series of workshops establish what has occurred as a result of the meetings in terms of (1) the model as the product; (2) the effectiveness and efficiency of the process; and (3) group coherence and group functioning as a basis for sustained collaboration.

Following are some suggestions for domains that may be included in a survey administered at the conclusion of a series of meetings:

- Did the participants establish or reach common goals?
- Do the participants indicate that learning did occur?
- Has the group achieved sufficient substance through its work that the outcome is recognized as an important contribution by parties that have participated only indirectly or not at all?
- Did the team members contribute their knowledge and creative thinking toward innovative solutions? Is there a sense of ownership of the process and the model?
- Are the participants committed to function as leaders in the dissemination of the results and insights gained during the process? Do the participants expect that the model will assist in the dissemination of these results and insights?
- Is there an increased sense of interdependence among the team participants?
- Has a collaborative climate emerged or improved?
- Does the group continue to exist after the first round in the mediated modeling process? Are new initiatives implemented, monitored, and assessed? During a second round, is the updated model based on the newly available information?

One can hardly expect statistically significant results from these surveys, since the group is relatively small from a statistical point of view. In addition, it does happen that the participants who start the process are not necessarily the same as those ending the process. However, the surveys provide very useful insights for the organizing team to use in improving the process; the surveys also provide information to the commissioning agencies, whose personnel may want to replicate the process in other areas.

If at all possible to administer them, surveys conducted in person are preferable.

Accumulation of results in the above-mentioned domains may over time provide a more general insight into the strengths and weaknesses of group modeling processes (Rouwette et al. 2002).

Disseminating Results

The fact that the number of direct participants is limited to about thirty (perhaps forty in a very positive and cooperative group) may be problematic in certain situations. However, the process can be designed in a flexible manner so that it can be stretched to incorporate additional individuals. For example, between workshop sessions, participants are actively encouraged to relay the train of thought to others and to discuss with them the evolving model structure. Feedback from these discussions should help the participants identify what should be expanded, simplified, highlighted, or altered at the next meeting. Apart from discussions with the groups the participants represent, these discussions can be extended to non-participants who may have access to crucial viewpoints or information. Some non-participants involved in those discussions may become interested to the point where they may wish to participate in the ongoing sessions.

At the end of the series of workshops, participants receive a tutorial in which they practice presenting the recommendations based on insights gained from the model. The software is relatively user-friendly, so each motivated participant should be capable of using the model for information dissemination. If the model has sufficient substance and the participants feel enough ownership of the model, they will be motivated to use it for disseminating the results and to explain the process by which the team arrived at these results.

Over time, reliance on the model will taper off as recommendations based on the model are implemented, monitored, and assessed. If the model was useful, it may gain renewed interest when new information becomes available. In this way, the model remains a flexible and relatively inexpensive backbone of a stakeholder-involved collaborative learning process for assisting research, policymaking, or management.

Conclusion

Stakeholders have mental models of reality, and the data that support those mental models are the basis of data gathering for the group model. The participants, or the experts that they decide to invite or consult about specific sub-problems, then generate the actual data for the model. However, the data may not support mental models. Beliefs and facts are confronted, thereby presenting an opportunity for learning. In addition, new opportunities for addressing problems may reveal themselves, and it may be necessary to initiate new research. In this case, a mediated modeling process may support the ongoing activity of joint fact finding and can become the backbone of an adaptive management program.

Initially, mediated modeling can be helpful in the planning stage. As an action plan is implemented, monitored, and assessed, the initial model may be updated and adjusted to support the next generation of action plans. A mediated model should remain simple but have the capacity for incorporating summarized information from highly specialized analytical research as it becomes available from a variety of disciplinary sources.

In general, it is best to initiate a mediated modeling process at the scoping level, when a problem arises, or as a way to support an ongoing research program. It may provide a flexible backbone for a management, policy design, or research program at relatively low cost. Chapter 4 provides step-by-step guidelines to design a tailored mediated modeling process.

4

Conducting a Mediated Modeling Process

The steps of a "typical" mediated modeling process include preparation, introductory interviews, preliminary model development, actual workshops, and tutorial. It is important to note, however, that there is no cookbook recipe for a mediated modeling process, and (un)common sense and flexibility are necessary. There is always the danger that when one has a hammer, everything begins to look like a nail. This chapter explains when the mediated modeling "hammer" is appropriate and how it can be combined with other tools in solving complex problems.

Andersen and Richardson (1997, p.107) "initiated a larger discussion of shared scripts and techniques for group model building." The scripts they present are developed for one- or two-day conferences for relatively small groups and their work lies as the basis of the expanded guidelines for a mediated modeling process as discussed here.

Some steps in the generic mediated modeling process described in this chapter can be expanded and elaborated or, perhaps, abandoned. The goal is to provide a starting point for aspiring mediated modelers and a basis for discussion by those working in this field. Environmental professionals who contemplate whether a mediated modeling process could be an asset to their programs would gain insight about the possible steps that could be taken, as well as which steps should be emphasized and which deemphasized. Informed professionals make better partners in commissioning and designing a mediated modeling process.

No two mediated modeling processes can be exactly the same. Complete overlap is by definition impossible because the participating stakeholders are different people, participating in different situations or at different points in time. In addition, even though a mediated modeler tries to remain as impartial as possible, the outcome of a mediated modeling process is heavily dependent on the modeler's attitude, skill, experience, and personal style. The procedural aspects and personal interactive aspects cannot be separated (Nothdurft 1995).

Nonetheless, as mentioned in Chapter 3, there are certain elements common to most mediated modeling projects, and a sequence in which they should be pursued:

1. Preparation
2. Workshops
3. Follow-up and tutorial

What each of these elements entails will differ from project to project, and the mediated modeler will have to adapt them to the situation as it unfolds. The generic procedure described in the remainder of this chapter is based on the accumulated experience of some mediated modelers up to the present time. Every new project provides an opportunity to test, compare, and improve the generic methodology.

Step 1: Preparation

In preparing for mediated modeling workshops, the organizing team must first take careful account of the history of the problem to be addressed, as well as the social, psychological, and cultural characteristics of the groups who will be involved in the process.

Cultural undercurrents in particular can cause friction during the process. For example, Canada has a long record of round table involvement of stakeholders. Therefore, the futures modeling project in Banff (see Chapter 7), which was based on a round table, was culturally appropriate. It is not surprising that many group modeling projects have been performed by consultants from the Netherlands, a country with a history of "consensus covenants."

In Argentina (Patagonia), the lingering sentiments after a period of autocratic military government and the associated mistrust were an obstruction to open discussion. Similarly, Portugal (see the Ria Formosa study in Chapter 9) was a dictatorship in the relatively recent past, and a culture steeped in hierarchical decision making does not necessarily foster collaborative processes.

The United States has a rather legalistic, confrontational, and result-oriented attitude in its culture, which sometimes hampers non-result-oriented exploratory discussions (see Chapter 5, Upper Fox Case Study).

Cultural differences like the aforementioned are something to be aware of, if you are to deal with a group respectfully.

A historical description of the issue is useful in terms of what has already been attempted to address the problem under discussion and, alternatively, what has been done that exacerbated the problem. For example, the Ria Formosa case study (see Chapter 9) describes a history of overlapping jurisdictions in this national park that may have contributed to a situation in which problems were addressed from an end-of-pipe perspective rather than a systems perspective.

However, in some situations it may be wise for a mediated modeler not to get too deeply involved on a personal level in the history of a problem. Ignorance can be a blessing in terms of maintaining an unbiased point of view. Suzuki Roshi points out in *Zen Mind, Beginner's Mind* that "if your mind is empty, it is always ready for anything; it is open to everything. In the beginner's mind there are many possibilities; in the expert's mind there are few."

Social networks can play an important role in creating functional links across scales and can tighten feedback loops in socio-ecological systems. The effective use of social networks for ecosystem management may be of vital importance in adaptive co-management and successful self-organizing groups (Folke et al. 2002, 2003). A form of institutional analysis and development framework (Imperial 1999a, 1999b) can provide a strong platform from which to organize and manage a mediated modeling process.

Research has shown that people moving from one area to another can easily gain detailed knowledge of particular resources and species, but that knowledge of processes and of the functions of the underlying ecosystem that sustain those resources takes a much longer time to develop (Muchagata and Brown 2000). Spending extensive periods of time in a specific place may be crucial in generating understanding of ecosystem dynamics and sustainable management practice (Nabhan 1997). Acknowledging the value of the evolution of socio-ecological networks, mediated modeling can be helpful in tightening the fabric of the networks and in explicitly addressing the process aspect of knowledge accumulation in a group.

A pitfall for an existing network is that questions are sometimes ruled out immediately because "it has already been tried and did not work"; however, because the circumstances may have changed, some of these questions may be worth reconsidering.

Also, for information to be understandable by all participants, experts in a group should be able to communicate clearly enough to convince the mediated modeler of the points they wish to make.

A mediated modeler should be able to prepare for meetings with a focus on the process rather than on the predetermined specifics of the problem. The contribution of the mediated modeler is that of a coach in process matters.

Having addressed these questions, there are four specific tasks a mediated modeler and/or organizing team will have to undertake in step 1 of the mediated modeling process:

1. Identify the stakeholders.
2. Set the participant group.
3. Conduct introductory interviews.
4. Prepare a preliminary model.

Identifying the Stakeholders

Whoever is present at the meetings will shape the process and the outcome. Therefore the identification of stakeholders is a very important step in the initiation and preparation of the mediated modeling process. A narrow definition of a stakeholder limits stakeholders to those who have legal and presumed claims. A broader definition includes anyone who can influence a process—the direction, speed, and depth of it.

A stakeholder with a direct or indirect "stake" bears a certain risk. The magnitude of the risk and the uncertainty surrounding the risk attach an urgency to a stakeholder's participation. For example, in the Ria Formosa case study, the industries of tourism, fisheries, and salt making responded favorably to an invitation to the mediated modeling process. The harbor authorities and the army did not feel a similar sense of urgency in the first round but showed more interest in the second round of activities, when the first-mentioned group had laid a productive foundation for addressing important problems in the Ria Formosa.

A wide variety of stakeholders fosters a more diverse input of ideas and worldviews and is therefore a source of creative solutions. Often the fear of differing views or conflicts means that essential and valuable stakeholders are ignored.

A mediated modeling process is generally initiated to bring relevant institutions and stakeholders together to understand acute or anticipated challenges. These challenges, whether they are acute and apparently short lived or anticipated and longer lived, usually don't appear in isolation. An intricate web of issues may link the identified stakeholders into a network that could be very helpful in the face of a changing environment and the accompanying responses those changes require from "the network."

Therefore, rather than limiting the focus to a specific challenge, the secondary objective of a mediated modeling process could be to form long-lasting formal or informal relationships that leave a network better equipped and positioned to address unforeseen challenges.

Horizontal integration of connections among representatives of institutions, organizations, and agencies is often easier to achieve, especially when the agencies are operating at a similar or overlapping geographical scale. More difficult is the enrollment of nonorganized but affected citizens. Similarly, it is more challenging to integrate institutions operating at higher scales—referred to as vertical integration.

Recent research underscores the contribution of the institutional and organizational landscape to the resilience of socio-ecological systems (Folke et al. 2003). There is some evidence that socio-ecological systems become more robust and are better equipped to adapt to ecological challenges in a self-organizing matter when the emphasis on knowledge of structure extends toward the knowledge of process (Berkes et al. 2003). Practically, this calls for

> vision, leadership and trust; enabling legislation that creates social space for ecosystem management; funds for responding to environmental change and for remedial action; capacity for monitoring and responding to environmental feedback; information flow through social networks; the combination of various sources of information and knowledge, sense-making and arenas of collaborative learning for ecosystem management. Such knowledge is seldom generated in a social vacuum but tends to evolve with working rules and organizational dynamics. (Ollson et al. 2003).

Sometimes these networks exist in an informal way. All that may be required is to interview and trace back the lines of communication among institutions and stakeholders and bring them together at a specific time and place.

If a formal stakeholder group does not yet exist, or if an existing group wants to evaluate its members, a useful process for identifying stakeholders is a referencing method. An initial small group of people is asked to list names and organizations that they feel should be invited to a proposed mediated modeling project. Recommendation of the same organization or person by different people indicates that this may be a good person to invite and/or to add to the group of people, who are then asked to submit further suggestions of people to invite. One has to pay close attention to those who are asked to provide names because a self-referencing element may be hard to avoid.

It is not unusual for identification and selection of stakeholders to take about a year, but a satisfactory stakeholder list can unfold within a month as well. The San Antonio case study in Chapter 6 describes the stakeholder identification process at great length.

Stakeholders can take on a variety of roles. Gunderson et al. (1995) summarize what they learned in the process of "exploring ways for active adaptation and learning in dealing with uncertainty in management of complex regional ecosystems" (page ix). They identify six roles that individuals can play in shaping a constructive adaptive management or policymaking process (p. xii):

- The creatively destructive role of public interest groups
- The alerting role of loyal heretics within agencies

- The importance of "gray eminences"—respected, wise individuals who synthesize, integrate, and communicate information
- The redefining role of informal collegia of natural scientists, engineers, and social scientists operating outside formal institutions
- The strategic design and research role of adaptive council in systemwide governance
- The democratic political role of citizen science

Setting the Participant Group

At this point we have identified the parties that should ideally be included, and we proceed with the design of a specific participant group. A participant group can be an already existing group, a selected group, or a self-selected group, or it can be determined in some other way.

The optimum number of participants for a mediated modeling process is about 20 to 30, with no less than 10 and no more than 40 participants. This recommendation is based on personal and practical experience rather than on any objective criteria and may vary from facilitator to facilitator. For example, others consider a group of 5 participants small but effective, while 10 to 12 is an upper limit.

The reasoning for the lower limit is that a certain number of participants are needed to fuel creativity, provide a broad knowledge base, and have access to a wide enough network to propel change. The upper limit is set by the number of people who can be effectively facilitated as a group in which the input of all participants can be acknowledged. In a strong collaborative atmosphere, more people can participate effectively. In a highly contentious atmosphere, a smaller group may be more effective.

Research is rather undecided about the optimum group size because of the varying forces at work. Vennix (1996, p. 113) summarizes these forces as follows:

- Increasing the group size will be beneficial in creating a larger organizational platform for change and commitment with a decision but simultaneously decreases participation and the satisfaction of group members.
- Increasing the group's diversity will be advantageous with regard to the model's quality but might at the same time create more tension within the group, which in turn reduces group performance.

The upper limit is also set by the number of participants who can be accommodated without fostering a "free rider" attitude in face-to-face interactions. The skills and experience of the mediated modeler with respect to facilitation play an important role here. Ample opportunities need to be provided, especially for the least dominant participants, to contribute to the discussion and to the product.

As stated earlier, the perceived level of conflict is an important factor in how many participants can be facilitated effectively. In each group there is a perceived level of conflict or absence thereof. The lower the perceived level of conflict, the easier a group can be motivated to collaborate.

- When participants are not aware of potential conflicts, the level of conflict is considered low, and collaboration may be welcomed.
- A medium level of conflict reflects a situation in which the potential for an escalating conflict is present but the consequences are still remote enough in time that a meaningful dialogue and collaboration are possible, especially when the common goals are explicit. The conflict has not developed into an acute conflictive standoff but has the potential to escalate.
- An acute conflict to which a solution has to be found in a short time span is considered a high-conflict situation. It takes much effort to curb such situations into a collaborative effort.

An identified stakeholder group can send a representative as a participant. Preferably, this person has received a positive mandate from his or her organization and is committed to the process on a personal level. Lawyers hired by a specific group to observe the possibilities for legal arguments just in case something evolves from the process are not particularly helpful (and, in fact, can be quite detrimental).

The inclusion of participants with decision-making power in a mediated modeling project is desirable, since such individuals can be helpful during the implementation phase. However, decision makers are often not up to date with specific quantitative data/information and are often unable to commit to full participation. As a second-best alternative, decision makers attend during the problem definition and scenario analysis phases of the process, while their technical representatives or collaborators participate during the entire process, again with a positive mandate. This is why the mediated modeling approach is often classified as a decision-support or decision-aiding tool.

As argued in Chapter 1, scientists are stakeholders as well. Scientists have specific information to contribute to the larger picture and can communicate the uncertainty surrounding relevant information. Scientists can also learn from the mediated modeling process about the practical questions that other stakeholders face, which can help them in designing research programs that address these problems.

Larger audiences, beyond the number of participants that can be effectively facilitated, can be involved in a networking mode. Preferably, individual participants engage their networks in the discussion and gradually develop the model or spin-off products. The Banff case study (see Chapter 7) provides an excellent example of how a mediated modeling process was embedded in a larger network. A similar approach was used by Stave (2002) in a process with the Regional Transportation Commission of Southern Nevada. Stave paid particular attention to the horizontal and vertical integration of the stakeholders involved. It proves more difficult to satisfy vertical integration of stakeholders and to invite those keystone participants.

An alternative way to involve larger audiences is to perform several mediated modeling exercises with the same starting problem but with different groups of participants. The opportunity to compare results from different groups could be a real advantage and would be an interesting scientific exercise. In practice, it is often hard enough to find funds for just one process. However, as problems at larger scales, such as regional and global issues, are explored, this option may become necessary and feasible.

Within the framework of mediated modeling, a group commits itself to a certain process designed to achieve a specific outcome within a certain time frame. A mediated modeling process is thus different from a collaborative learning process, in which the design of meetings is more open and a follow-up meeting takes place only if the former one was a success.

The goal in a mediated modeling process is to maintain a relatively stable number of participants, at least until the first round of consensus-based conclusions has been completed. In certain situations it may be crucial that newly identified stakeholders participate as freely as they like. Those situations will benefit from a collaborative learning process without a limit on the number of participants.

It is best to evaluate the need to expand participation to new participants only before and after each completed round of model building or updating. No matter how thorough the stakeholder identification process may be, important stakeholders are sometimes overlooked or initially decline participation. However, the arrival of newcomers can be very disturbing to the mediated modeling process. Newcomers may reopen questions that the group may have just brought to a closure, without adding any new perspective. Often these questions only create uncertainty about the process, and little constructive input is gained from the new stakeholder.

It takes time to bring a newcomer up to speed in the group, even if the facilitator or a seasoned participant briefs the newcomer. However, sometimes a new participants blends right in. A highly motivated volunteering participant with a unique perspective may be worth a lot to the group. Even a defiant personality with a specific perspective and access to a crucial network of interests may still be worth the trouble of integrating into the emerging group.

The potential costs and benefits of adding new participants need to be weighed on a case-by-case basis. Generally, late integration can be avoided by adequate preparation prior to the start of the project.

Introductory Interviews

When the participants are selected and funding is secured, they can be interviewed to set the stage for the series of mediated modeling meetings. It is useful for the lead mediated modeler and/or an assistant to spend about a half hour to an hour with each of the participants to achieve the following goals:

- Introduce the mediated modeler and/or the mediated modeling team
- Answer any questions or address concerns a participant may have about the upcoming mediated modeling process
- Get a feel for the perspective of each participant concerning the problem he or she perceives
- Establish a baseline with respect to the relevant aspects of the problem, the functioning of the group, and the anticipated process.

This information can be used to generate a relevant introduction regarding the contribution of mediated modeling as an integrative and collaborative tool and to kick off the modeling meetings.

During these interviews, a questionnaire can be used to uncover the initial perceptions and expectations of the individual participants and to clarify any questions that participants may have about the modeling process. For example, in two of the case studies presented here, participants were asked at the beginning of the interview whether they understood the purpose of the project. At the end of the interview, they were asked to rate the confidence they had about the task ahead. When the responses to these questions were compared, it was observed that the participants had gained some additional understanding or confidence during the course of the interview. The number of participants confident about the task ahead at the end of the interview process was larger than the number who said they understood the purpose of the project at the beginning of the interview process.

During introductory interviews, committed participants are asked about their perception of the problem within the scope of the project. These perceptions can be elicited in an interactive discussion involving the following components:

- Introduction to the questions—for example: "The subject of the mediated modeling workshops is the linkage between ecology and economics. Within this wide area a problem definition needs to be developed that the model should solve. What is or are, in your opinion, the main problem(s) right now?"
- What causes the problem(s)?
- What are the main effects of these problems?

During the interview a causal diagram can be sketched to help elicit the perspective of each individual participant. A causal diagram shows the direction of causality between variables. Each variable is connected with arrows to other variables. A positive (+) or negative (–) sign indicates the nature of the causal relationship. A feedback loop may become clear when an effect can be linked to a cause of the problem. For example, a region copes with urban sprawl, which is in part caused by the attractive nature of its open space. However, the effect of sprawl is a reduction of open space.

Based on the individual perspectives, the modeler may prepare (1) a preliminary model of the situation and (2) a situational context of the group, including such aspects as the perceived level of conflict, perceived goal orientation, and perceived level of interdependence.

Preliminary Model

On the basis of the preparatory interviews, the mediated modeler can construct a preliminary model. Such a preliminary model doesn't have to be very elaborate and the construction of it doesn't need to take much longer than a few hours to a day. A preliminary model addresses four goals:

1. To establish a point of reference by presenting an interpretation of the interviews with the participants. As a point of reference, a preliminary model should give all participants a sense of inclusion; each participant should recognize at least one aspect of the preliminary model as part of their view, even though that one aspect may be upgraded to a higher conceptual level.
2. To demonstrate the type of output that can be obtained from a model structure. Until a preliminary model is shown, many participants may never have seen a simulation model before.
3. To function as a starting point from which the discussion takes off during the first meeting, if a group wishes to do so.
4. To reduce the risk for both the mediated modeler/team and the group. There are good reasons for development of a preliminary model by the mediated modeling team to be shown at the first meeting, but if time is scarce, this step may be eliminated. Eliminating the construction of a preliminary model by the mediated modeler may increase the risk considerably for the mediated modeler as well as for the group. The experience of the mediated modeler is crucial in facilitating an unexpected contentious discussion at the first meeting—while translating the issues into a model—tasks that require a variety of strong skills and experience. A sudden outburst of contentious speech is to be avoided at the onset of the first meeting. A preliminary model may help to ease a mediated modeler into a contentious discussion and thereby reduce the risk of making irre-

versible mistakes. The risk of an outbreak of an uncontrolled contentious discussion for the group is that participants may withdraw from the group process because of the perceived failure at this stage. The resources devoted to preparation therefore depend on the experience and capacity of the mediated modeler and the organizing team as well as on the characteristics of the group they are working with.

If the resources are invested by the mediated modeler in the development of a preliminary model based on the interviews before the first meeting, the result will be presented to the participant group at some point during the first meeting (see Step 2: Workshops). It may be accepted as a starting point, alternatively, it may be rejected by the participant group. A reason to reject a preliminary model as prepared by a mediated modeler often indicates that a group is just starting to think about a particular problem. The participants are not ready to commit to an outline as proposed in the form of a preliminary model by the mediated modeler. Especially emerging groups seldom end up pursuing a preliminary model developed by the mediated modeler. It often signals the importance to allow adequate time for "venting positions" toward establishing a problem definition as outlined in "Step 2: Workshops." Often there is a great desire to express strongly held opinions and stake out interests, before participants show a willingness to actually use their brains and think about the issues in an original way.

When a group prematurely accepts a preliminary model, there is a risk that ownership over the model may get lost and the participants don't vest as much interest in the process as they could. However, in comparing rejected preliminary models with the final model as developed over a period of time by participant groups, many similarities between the rejected preliminary models and the final models can be identified. The difference is that the group model is *their* model, whereas the preliminary model was still too much of the *modeler's* product.

Step 2: Workshops

A series of workshops covers a logical sequence:

1. Introduction
2. Problem definition
3. Qualitative model building
4. Quantitative model building
5. Simulation

However, it is virtually impossible to provide a schedule one can adhere to. As discussed in Chapter 3, the mediated modeler must have a relatively detailed but flexible set of scripts. Scripts are written for the workshops and provide some structure to an otherwise flexible process (Andersen and Richardson 1997). The "structure" comes from certain outcomes that need to be achieved in order to take the next step in the process. The "flexibility" lies in how these outcomes are achieved.

Even the sequence of the steps may be altered as the need arises. For example, if a participant brings up a certain issue out of context or out of flow and it seems manageable for the facilitator/modeler to give it a place within the process, it may be a good idea to pursue the issue to see where it leads, without losing track of what needs to be achieved. For instance, at the very beginning of the first meeting a skeptical participant may raise a concern about personal interactions. As a response, the mediated modeler may bring the "ground rules" to the forefront, rather than saying, "After the demonstration of the preliminary model, we will discuss the ground rules."

It installs trust in the process (and in the mediated modeler) when concerns of the participants are addressed as promptly as possible, without losing the flow of the process. This is especially true during the actual model building. The mediated modeler must have a mental "grip" on the entire model at all times in order to interpret the discussion and suggest additions to or subtractions from the model.

Every group has different needs, and every process develops in a unique manner. However, it is convenient to have a few strategies available to break an impasse or to shorten or delay a certain step. Sometimes issues just need to be rephrased or looked at in a different light. Sometimes going off on a slight tangent can be helpful. For example, an envisioning exercise may improve the quality of the "questions the model needs to address."

Alternatively, a "game of mistaken identity" may lift a group over a lull (like the one that often happens toward the end of the construction of the qualitative model). In this exercise, participants are asked to place their name tags with affiliation in a basket and randomly select a new "identity." The model is then examined once more through the assumed thought process of the person whose name tag was selected.

In all cases, it is important that a group move as a whole and that the interest, motivation, and opportunity for contributing and learning of all participants are cultivated.

Meeting Space

Ideally, a meeting space is free of environmental "stressors" such as noise, heat, cold, pollution, crowding, and density: "Stressors that are intense, prolonged, unpredictable, and uncontrollable are particularly distressing and debilitating" (Hare et al. 1994). The goal is to create an environment that allows for the maximum use of creative energy by the participants.

A meeting room where the tables and chairs can be moved around is often best. If the space allows, place the tables and chairs in a half circle so that the participants have a good view of the projection screen as well as of each other. The mediated modeler has a computer and a whiteboard located near the projection screen. Ideally, one or more small rooms should be available close by for small-group sessions and/or coffee breaks. Alternatively, the furniture may be moved around for the small-group activities, but doing so can be a noisy distraction.

Workshop Stage 1: Introduction

Every workshop starts logically with an acknowledgment of the presence of each participant and a brief statement of why the workshop is taking place. This is also an opportunity for a (sponsoring) official to place the project in a practical context by expressing excitement about the recommendations that may result from the meetings. Ground rules are proposed, possibly adjusted, and accepted. Finally, system dynamics principles and system dynamics software are introduced. More details can be found in the following sections.

NAME GAME

It may be helpful to take five to ten minutes to play a game that will ensure that people know each other's names. For example, ask one participant to say his or her name. The following participant repeats the name of the first participant and add his or her own. The third repeats the first two and adds his or her own, and so on. Many people initially feel this is an impossible task and become somewhat self-conscious, but usually participants (with a little friendly help) accomplish the undertaking with grace. The mediated modeling team is the last in line in this game.

The facilitators of the San Antonio case study (see Chapter 6) describe a more elaborate exercise that had the purpose not only of learning each other's names but also of learning more about the watershed.

GROUND RULES

It is important to establish several ground rules at the beginning of the first meeting. Such ground rules lay out:

- The rights and responsibilities of the participants and the facilitator/modeler
- Behavioral guidelines
- Consensus-enhancing procedures and/or conflict-handling strategies
- Modeling guidelines

Ground rules help to maintain accountability during an otherwise flexible process (Wondolech and Yaffee 2000).

Ideally, participants would generate their own ground rules. In the interest of time, however, most groups opt to follow suggestions from the facilitator and may change or expand them as the need arises. For example, when the first round of a mediated modeling process is completed and a group has the intention of continuing its engagement toward future implementation, monitoring, and assessment, the ground rules could be revisited to examine whether they suffice for the tasks ahead.

The following discussion of the aforementioned ground rules is by no means a generic set of guidelines but offers examples that have worked for us.

Rights and Responsibilities

All participants' rights and responsibilities should be defined at the outset. Any right is always coupled with a responsibility. Here are several key principles to follow in defining these rights and responsibilities:

- It is each participant's right and responsibility to be unique. Each participant should be respected for the perspective he or she brings to the table. Participants also have the responsibility to communicate their perspectives as concisely and clearly as possible. Hiding behind a veil of expertise is not constructive.
- Nobody knows everything, but together a group knows more than anyone alone.
- Ideas generated in the group belong to the entire group, not to any specific individual.
- Assume that all those present are the right persons for the group's chosen task. Differences in status or rank are to be disregarded. The group should realize that present participants compose the group that will perform the work. Once the group has decided that the participants present are adequate for the goal, it is counterproductive to begin second-guessing on an individual basis about who else should have been included or which of the current participants should not have been included. However, when the group as a whole decides that crucial representatives are missing, the group as a whole may decide to invite those representatives or to consult experts.

Behavioral Guidelines

A group that has committed to take on a mediated modeling process as a way to work through a conflict or anticipated challenge can be expected to bring a variety of knowledge as well as emotions to the meetings. Participants often bring an enormous energy, passion, and sometimes hurt feelings, and it is the facilitator's role to guide their precious time and energy in constructive ways.

Conflict resolution literature is available, ranging from entertaining to serious and inspiring, with titles such as *Managing People Is Like Herding Cats* (Bennis 1994), several headings on *How to Deal with Difficult People* (Bramson 1981, Weiss 1987, Soloman 1990, Markham 1993, Lundin 1995, Pike 1997, Toropov 1997) to *Emotional Intelligence at Work* (Weisinger 1998) and *Resolving Environmental Disputes* (Bingham 1986).

By providing some behavioral guidelines, a facilitator presents his or her view of the characteristics that constitute an orderly and productive discussion. When undesirable situations occur, it is more prudent to refer back to earlier stated guidelines than to single out a specific participant's behavior.

The following guidelines are personal favorites of mine that prevent dominant personalities from monopolizing a meeting and which provide space for more timid people to be heard:

- *Everyone has two ears and one mouth . . . use them in the appropriate ratio.* The goal is to restrict speeches of the participants to a maximum of two minutes per intervention. Everybody should get the chance to contribute his or her share. When this rule is clearly stated at the beginning, the mediated modeler can more easily cut off extended monologues without loss of face to the participant.

- *Creativity can flow only when destructive criticism is withheld.* Withhold judgment until a participant has made him- or herself understood. Allow ideas to exist and grow, take them in, actively listen, listen for possibilities, and allow for the possibility of being inspired, even when you would prefer to shut out certain ideas immediately on the basis of your own rationale. Sorting through the options presented will be done in due time. Ask questions for understanding rather than for the purpose of invalidating a contribution.

- *Disagree without being disagreeable.* Emphasize the situation rather than the people involved. Don't become personal in disagreements. Maintain a focus on a logical train of thought rather than making "You are wrong." statements. Such statements will invoke a request to substantiate with "evidence" to the group. Instead, encourage participants to feel competent and to value disagreements as a source of creative ideas.

- *Maintain a focus on what is equally good for all.* This goes back to "increasing the pie" before "dividing the pie." Often there is an intricate ongoing tension between "what is best for the overall objective" versus "what is best for me or the group I'm representing." A focus on the latter is naturally present. The challenge is to allow a focus on "what is best for the overall objective" to coexist. In addition, "what is best for me" is often relative to the extent that other stakeholders' needs are satisfied. One way to open the pathway toward "what is best for the overall objective" is to concentrate on underlying concerns and interests rather than on stalemate positions. Another way is to emphasize future improvements rather than dwelling on the past.

- *There is no need to impress others.* It is useful to emphasize that the ability to explain complex information in lay terms is more valuable than confusing people with expert language.

Consensus-Enhancing Procedures and Conflict-Handling Strategies

As described in Chapter 1, mediated modeling is based on the assumption that consensus building as a means of making decisions and solving problems is preferred over the pursuit of narrow individual goals. However, consensus building is not a quick fix, and sufficient time must be allowed for the process to unfold. In addition to the help offered by a competent facilitator or mediator, group members committed to a consensus-building process may feel more comfortable if they have a set of agreed-upon procedural and behavioral guidelines. Susskind et al.'s *Consensus Building Handbook* (1999), consisting of over a thousand pages of useful information and ideas for consensus building, offers a practical road map.

Following are just a few of the ideas we have found useful in facilitating a consensus-based process such as mediated modeling:

- *Free discussion geared toward creativity is the primary goal.* Consensus is never a requirement but is rather a secondary goal as the crucial aspects of an issue are systematically lifted out of the free discussion and narrowed down to consensus (Susskind et al. 1999).
- *A request for a show of hands is useful in identifying the group's perceptions about a specific issue.* Even though not every participant may be equally happy with a specific solution, it may be necessary for everyone to "live with" the proposed step. This procedure may generate a temporary verdict that usually has some participants studying the subject to defend their beliefs and to provide the group with facts. Interestingly enough, the "voting" procedure is usually not required when addressing qualitative matters but is rather mainly reserved for quantitative manners.
- *Consensus is achieved in the absence of "reasoned and paramount objections"* (Endenburg 1998). In mediated modeling, a group will seek unanimity; however, an absolute consensus on every issue brought up during the entire modeling process is impossible. In the interest of time, groups may choose to continue if there is "no reasoned and paramount objection." However, when turning toward the absence of reasoned and paramount objections too early, the group runs the risk of ending up with solutions that all can live with, but the solutions may lack teeth and therefore may not be useful. A status quo prevails.

- *Plenary sessions alternate with small-group sessions during the entire mediated modeling process.* The plenary sessions are appropriate when the agenda is set for the next step or the results from the small groups are incorporated in the model. The small-group sessions are used initially to establish trust in the group. Often small-group exercises produce similar suggestions, thereby boosting the confidence. With this confidence, small groups can then be used to solve limited problems or develop parts of the model to save time. The small-group findings are presented and discussed in a plenary session and simultaneously introduced in the model. It may be helpful to have a facilitator in every small group, especially when the level of conflict is high or when the participants are not accustomed to working in this way. The plenary sessions are crucial in keeping everybody engaged and connected.
- *Ad hoc meetings with individual participants, groups of stakeholders, or experts may occur as the need arises between the workshops.* In the data-gathering and quantification stage, ad hoc meetings with specific small groups are often required to figure out specific problems or to determine the most elegant reflection of a specific discussion. By this point, the whole group has identified these specific problems and is looking for an answer either from a group member or subset, alternatively, from an outside expert. It is important that small steps are taken, both during these ad hoc meetings and between the meetings of the larger group, in order to retain the cohesive understanding of the ``participants.

Modeling Guidelines

The word *modeling* means different things to different people. We have found the following guidelines helpful in establishing a context for, and maintaining a perspective on, the type of modeling applied in a mediated modeling context:

- *The final model is a joint product of the team learning experience.* The team learning is as important as the model as an end product. The final model itself serves as a vehicle to transfer the insights gained to others.
- *A model is always an abstraction of reality.* A model can be evaluated only for the purpose for which it was designed.
- *Synthesis is the art of leaving things out.* A minority of the variables that could be chosen should explain the majority of the system's behavior. A relatively small number of all possible variables that could be incorporated in a model are chosen to explain the behavior of the system. This means that those constructing a scoping model should aim for simplicity and elegance.

INTRODUCING SYSTEM DYNAMICS THINKING

As discussed earlier, system dynamics is the guiding modeling approach for mediated modeling. The importance of system dynamics thinking over linear thinking is explained in Chapter 1. Chapter 2 introduced important principles of system dynamics thinking, such as feedback loops and time lags, that can result in counterintuitive behavior of systems. Workshop stage 3 delineates approaches to addressing these principles within a group.

The principles of system dynamics thinking and the software can be introduced along a continuum of effort during workshop stage 1. On the "low end" of this continuum, system dynamics thinking and the software can be introduced simultaneously by an illustrative example. About half an hour is needed to accomplish this task. The objective is not to fully educate participants in modeling or to improve modeling skills (although some participants may develop a lasting interest and seek to develop this skill), but rather to provide enough understanding of the icons used in the modeling software, the possibility of using graphs and slide bars to advance a discussion, and to illustrate the output in the form of sequential graphs. Feedback loops and time lags are briefly touched upon. Other participants naturally shy away from anything computerized, and that is fine, too. Both types of participants, and all those in between, are equally valid participants in a mediated modeling process. During the process the mediated modeler will continue to ask questions to understand the causes and effects of problems, thereby jointly exploring the system dynamics of an issue with the participants. The participants will learn some system dynamics by doing it.

The Upper Fox case study (see Chapter 5) is an example of a case on the low end of the effort put into modeling skills continuum and focuses entirely on the learning (by doing) and consensus building within the group. System dynamics principles and the use of the software are learned by using them; they are highlighted by the mediated modeler when an appropriate occasion arises. However, even during the process in the Upper Fox, at least one participant developed modeling skills to the extent that he could pursue adjusting the Upper Fox model to strengthen the county conservation management plan.

On the "upper end" of the effort put into modeling skills continuum are those mediated modelers who put more time and effort into explaining the system dynamics principles and software. This kind of introduction may take as long as two days before the actual problems are addressed. An example of this end of the continuum is provided by the Sage Grouse case study (see Chapter 8). The process used in the Sage Grouse case study included the goal of training participants in modeling in addition to scoping the impact of grazing by sheep and the impact of fire regimes on sage grouse habitat.

At a minimum, participants should understand the following system dynamics principles:

- The emphasis is on the relationships within a system or between different subsystems.
- Feedback loops and time lags are critical in understanding behavioral patterns.
- Understanding patterns rather than creating accurate predictions is often the primary objective, at least at the initial scoping stage.

INTRODUCING THE MODELING SOFTWARE

Several system dynamics software packages are available on the market. All of the cases reported in this book have used STELLA, a relatively user-friendly dynamic systems modeling software package (Richmond and Petersen 1994). Other software packages suitable for purposes within the scope of this book would be Powersim and Vensim (see Appendix 2).

The introduction of the system dynamics software starts with a brief overview of the basic model components of stocks, flows, auxiliary variables, and functional connections (see Figure 4.1). A detailed explanation of the basic model components follows later, under "Workshop Stage 3: Building the Qualitative Model," where participants are asked to actually use these four icons.

Figure 4.2 shows the three communicating layers of the STELLA software's modeling environment. The model icons (presented in Figure 4.1) are used in the middle layer of a model constructed with STELLA (see Figure 4.2). When the icons are selected and placed in the middle level, the software

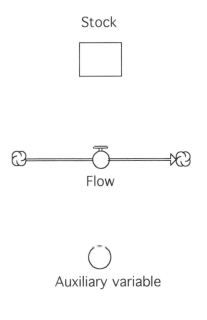

Stock

Flow

Auxiliary variable

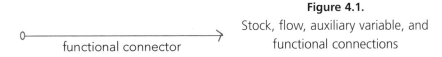

functional connector

Figure 4.1.
Stock, flow, auxiliary variable, and functional connections

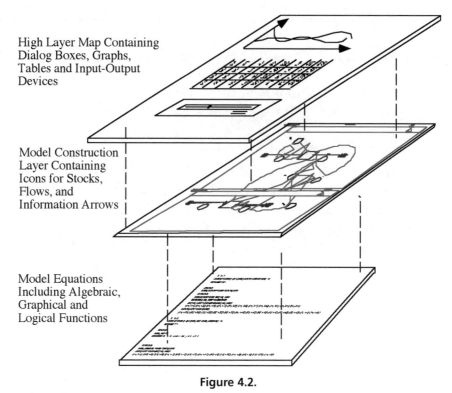

High Layer Map Containing
Dialog Boxes, Graphs,
Tables and Input-Output
Devices

Model Construction
Layer Containing
Icons for Stocks,
Flows, and
Information Arrows

Model Equations
Including Algebraic,
Graphical and
Logical Functions

Figure 4.2.
STELLA modeling environment. Source: Costanza and Ruth 1998.

translates these icons into difference equations visible at the lowest level. Alternatively, modelers may write the difference equations at the lower level and those then translate into a model structure visible at the middle level. However, the latter is not to be recommended when working with a group of nonmodelers. The graphic representations of these model icons are connected and manipulated to build the basic structure of the model. This process is made transparent to a group by projecting the computer screen onto a wall. Participants can then both follow the model construction process and contribute their knowledge to the process. Examples of model structures at the middle level can be found in the Upper Fox case study (Chapter 5).

The middle layer of the model is displayed during the construction phase. Icons represent the basic structure of the model and provide an input pathway for subsequent data. Once the basic structure of the model is laid out, initial conditions, parameter values, and functional relationships can be specified. Input data can be entered in graphical or tabular format.

The highest layer is the "user interface." In the final stage, users can easily access and operate the model from this level. Slide bars allow a user to immediately respond to the model output by choosing alternative parameter values as the model runs.

The model output can be generated in tabular or graphical form. The modeling approach is dynamic with respect to the behavior of the system itself and with respect to the learning process of the participants. The modeling process can lay out and address contentious issues, identifying uncertainty due to insufficient knowledge or data gaps and synthesizing and integrating ecological and economic disciplines through use of common units and categorical data. Appendix 10 contains an example you can use to introduce STELLA software to your group.

Workshop Stage 2: Defining the Problem

There are many different ways to help a group define the problem at hand, ranging from a brief discussion to define the scope to more elaborately structured methods such as an Ecological Risk Assessment (ERA). In the case of the Upper Fox, an ERA was applied parallel with the problem definition phase. However, an ERA as a formal element of a mediated modeling process requires planning. Simplified envisioning exercises can be used in a more flexible manner on an ad hoc basis as the need reveals itself. Time constraints as well as the needs of the group dictate how to go about the development of a problem definition. The result of the problem definition phase should include, at a minimum:

1. a reference mode of behavior or, alternatively, a set of issues or questions that the model will address or explain. It is important to note that a model is useful only to the extent that these questions can be answered, explained, or generally better understood, and;
2. a definition of scale in terms of system boundaries, time horizon, and time step.

REFERENCE MODE OF BEHAVIOR

The statements or questions that need to be addressed often include specific problems and their trends. In case specific data are available about a desirable or undesirable trend, the model to be constructed will most likely include this trend as part of a system of driving forces that explains the resulting trend. Using a trend as a starting point for model construction is called the *reference mode of behavior* (Vennix 1996). An example of a reference mode of behavior can be a certain fish population that has been monitored and which has declined over time. If a group has to develop a broader list of questions and observations, the progress during the problem definition phase may stall. Then an ad hoc envisioning exercise may help to discover commonly held values.

When historic data are not available to provide a starting point, a set of statements or questions the model needs to address still must be developed to give direction to a modeling process. This starting point will be revisited frequently during the modeling process. At the end of a modeling process the reference mode of behavior functions as the baseline in the evaluation of the progress made.

ENVISIONING

An envisioning exercise offers the opportunity for participants to develop a personal vision of the question, How does the world look when it is perfect? When participants share the images that surface in answer to that question, they make a connection at the vision level. At this level, a tremendous amount of creative energy is released that inspires the group. The images that surface during an envisioning exercise also inspire development of the questions that the model should answer. Often these images are the basis for innovative experiments geared toward solving a complex problem.

Envisioning can be done at different levels of intensity. One type of envisioning exercise is a "future search," an intensive three-day group activity for developing a vision for the future (Weisbord and Janoff 1995). The premises of a future search correspond closely to those that underlie mediated modeling. Ideal future scenarios provide a starting point that can be used as a reality check for developing an action plan.

Within the scope of a mediated modeling project, a three-day envisioning exercise is usually not feasible, but even an hour devoted to envisioning can release substantial creative energy. Be sure to capture this energy. It is very frustrating when participants view a positive image for the future during an envisioning exercise but are not provided an opportunity to express it, and have other participants connect with that positive image and build on it. As long as there is excitement in the group resulting from this exercise, use it! Reconnect with the vision at every opportunity during the model construction.

Another type of envisioning exercise is a "strategic forum." In a strategic forum, the past, a future vision, and steps that can be taken now are addressed sequentially and revisited at different times (Richmond 1987, 1997). Figure 4.3 shows these elements in the context of mediated modeling. With a better un-

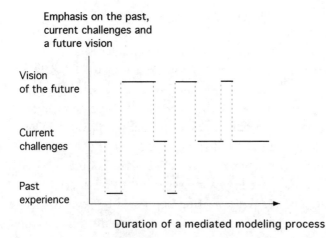

Emphasis on the past, current challenges and a future vision

Vision of the future

Current challenges

Past experience

Duration of a mediated modeling process

Figure 4.3.
Maintaining tension between future, past, and current challenges

derstanding of the past, we can acknowledge it and learn from its positive and negative aspects. Then we leave the past and revisit the vision for the future (How does it look when it is perfect?). Then we let ourselves be inspired to design innovative ways to address a specific challenge by taking action now.

This cycle of changing focus between the past, present challenges, and a future vision is repeated many times during a typical mediated modeling process. At the beginning of the process, there is some logical sequence of emphasizing the past, current challenges, and a future vision. Also, initially, the group may look to the mediated modeler for guidance since the modeler has experience with this approach to collaboration and conflict resolution. And, initially, the group usually accepts the script of the mediated modeler as to how to divide their time between past, present, and future. However, once the rules and the tools of the mediated modeling process become clear to a group, the attention and emphasis may shift more randomly among the past, present, and future as the group process dictates.

The time division between past, present, and future is never right or wrong. However, observing where the group puts its emphasis and how the transitions in emphasis occur may give some insight to a mediated modeling team on how to best serve the group.

ECOLOGICAL RISK ASSESSMENT

An ecological risk assessment (ERA) is a statistical method for identifying and ranking ecological stressors by a group. The ERA is a static approach assessing perceptions at a certain point in time as explained in Chapter 2.

The most important stressors can function as a starting point to build a mediated model. If the ecological risk assessment is done first, the project participants have the opportunity to identify important ecosystem issues and elements before undertaking the more extensive mediated modeling exercise, in which the elements of the ecosystem can be structured quantitatively and analyzed dynamically.

On the other hand, since the mediated modeling process is a learning process, the ERA could also be performed when the model construction is finished. The ERA then functions as a way to firm up conclusions drawn from the mediated modeling process.

In the Upper Fox case (see Chapter 5), an ERA was performed simultaneously with the problem definition phase of the mediated modeling process. The problem definition phase of the mediated modeling process generated priorities similar to those identified in the ERA.

SCALE ISSUES

Three dimensions of scale are related to modeling: time, space, and complexity. In addition, there is a social dimension of scale. The social dimension is addressed during the preparation phase in terms of stakeholder selection. The social dimension is a given during the workshops. Furthermore, there are two important aspects of scale: extent and resolution. The extent is the magnitude, range, or size of the dimension. The resolution refers to the fineness of detail that can be distinguished.

Table 4.1 illustrates how extent and resolution apply to the dimensions of scale, using as an example a model in which the time frame extends from 1970 to 2020, with a time step of one year. A time step refers to the interval at which a model calculates the next value. The geographic space in this example addresses a spatially nonexplicit (homogeneous) watershed. In this watershed, ecology and economics are described with 10 state variables, 25 auxiliary variables, and 52 parameters. With respect to social scale, there are 23 people directly involved from 8 institutions. The networking is limited to inter-institutional relationships. The process does not formally reach out to people outside the institutions involved.

The choices for the dimensions of scale have consequences:

- The time horizon and the magnitude of the time step will lead the participants to focus on some questions and trends while ignoring others. For example, a time horizon of 50 years with a 1-year time step means that most geological changes will be left out or considered static in this model.
- The geographic boundaries of the area under study are often, but not always, already determined before the stakeholders are formally invited to participate in a mediated modeling process. This doesn't mean that

Table 4.1.

Issues of scale in modeling

	Time	Space	Complexity	Social
Extent	Time horizon—e.g., 1970–2020	Global, regional, local—e.g., a watershed	Diverse issues included—e.g., ecology, hydrology, biology, economy, sociology, culture	Horizontal and vertical integration—e.g., interinstitutional emphasis
Resolution	The time step—e.g., 1 year	Level of spatial explicitness, number of pixels—e.g., homogeneous	Number of model icons—e.g.,10 state variables, 25 auxiliary variables, 52 parameters	Number of people involved, institutional networks accessed—e.g., 23 people from 8 institutions

major influences from beyond the area under study cannot be considered. Many scoping models are spatially homogeneous and do not address spatial patterns in an explicit manner. For example, in a spatially homogeneous model, land areas are summarized as percentages of the total area, without specifying where exactly they are located within the area under study. The rapid developments in computing technology may very well provide the capability to make more direct use of geographic information systems in the future.

- The level of complexity of a scoping model produced through a mediated modeling process can be expected to extend into several variables but remain relatively low in resolution.
- Depending on the situation, a modeling process can be designed to be narrow or broad in its inclusiveness of social networks. However, there are a maximum number of people that can directly be involved in the formal modeling. Mediated modeling has demonstrated its strengths in the horizontal integration among institutions. The extent can be broadened to address vertical integration of nonorganized stakeholders, but that may require adding a tool to a program to achieve this goal. How to achieve vertical social integration is not within the scope of this book.

A useful exercise is to assess whether approaching the same "questions the model needs to address" would yield different answers at different scales. For example, would the answers to the questions posed have been different if the spatially explicit route were chosen?

In both the Upper Fox and Ria Formosa case studies (Chapters 5 and 9), it turned out that information about land use was scarce and that some of the issues addressed are explicit spatial problems. For example, 90% of the releases of sediment from agriculture are localized in a specific area in the Upper Fox. In the Ria Formosa, the purpose of dredging dictates the location of the dredging activities. However, these issues came up during the scoping process, and the stakeholders now have the option to pursue spatially explicit research in the identified direction. The results of such research can provide answers with which to update the scoping model.

Spatially homogeneous scoping models are complementary to spatially explicit models, rather than a substitute. They can provide a better basis for building more complex models in a three-step modeling process (Costanza and Ruth 1998).

Workshop Stage 3: Building the Qualitative Model

Armed with a reference mode of behavior in the form of specific historical data or a set of open questions the model should address as well as a sense of scale, a group is now ready to begin working with the system dynamics software.

The end product of this stage using STELLA software is a conceptual model constructed with stocks, flows, auxiliary variables, and information connectors, all within model sectors.

If one looks at a finished qualitative model structure in STELLA, such as those presented in Chapter 5, the image of "spaghetti and meatballs" immediately comes to mind. The distinction between the meatballs (or the stocks) and the spaghetti (or the information connectors) provides a basis for a continuum on how one approaches model construction.

Focusing on the "spaghetti," one can start with describing an existing problem in terms of interconnected information—one or more feedback loops in the form of a series of auxiliary variables interconnected by information arrows. This process results in the identification of an appropriate stock, which can represent an indicator or a physical quantity. To stick with the metaphor, one starts with the spaghetti and adds the meatballs.

Alternatively, one can start with the meatballs by identifying the stocks, and then add the spaghetti to explain how the meatballs are interconnected. In a business context these alternative approaches are described as the "feedback loop approach" and the "modular approach" respectively (Wolstenholme 1982, Wolstenholme and Coyle 1983, 1990).

The appropriate starting point depends on where a group is with respect to how a problem is perceived. For example, when a participant group has indicated an obvious dynamic trap as a central problem, the auxiliary variables and information connectors provide the more appropriate starting point for a qualitative model structure (the spaghetti approach). If, on the other hand, the group has indicated the status of several key stocks (e.g., water quality or land use) as the central problem, identifying stocks first and then linking them (the meatball approach) would be more appropriate.

These two approaches are part of a continuum, and a mix can easily develop. However, during the preparatory interviews with the participants it often becomes clear that causal diagrams are difficult to elicit, as exemplified especially by the Upper Fox and Ria Formosa cases (Chapters 5 and 9). No obvious feedback loop is present at the outset, and the construction of a model more readily follows the "meatball " approach. This approach is described in more detail in the remainder of this chapter.

SECTOR DEFINITION

To begin work on the group's qualitative model, the participants first define a few sectors that encompass the major aspects of the problem. During this process, the group keeps in mind the previously developed reference mode of behavior or "questions the model should address." For example, a group with the objective of examining "linkages between ecology and economics" may choose "natural capital" and "ecosystem services" as one sector in which the ecology-related aspects will be described. They may choose "socioeconomics" as another sector.

The model sectors serve as a framework or outline for the model. The purpose of sector development is to guide thinking along several main directions. By developing the model sectors first, a group is less likely to take off on tangents or dig into details. They are more likely to give equal attention to other important issues in this multidisciplinary exercise.

It is recommended that the number of sectors be limited to about four during the initial stages of the modeling process. More may be added later for the purpose of balancing the thinking, but preferably not for the purpose of increasing the level of detail.

Focusing attention on the overarching, systemwide level of the problem allows the participants to start working as a team, leaving behind individual interests for a moment and instead maintaining broader perspectives.

The creation of model sectors is also useful during the process because it may highlight problem areas. For example, an empty sector indicates that the subject of this sector has not yet entered into the discussion. Alternatively, an empty sector may signal that the appropriate knowledge is not available in the group, even though the group has acknowledged that the subject plays a crucial part in addressing its challenge. Or perhaps an empty sector may simply suggest that the time has arrived to reevaluate the essence or the reason for existence of the sector.

Model sectors help in structuring the discussion and in maintaining an appropriate overview. During the quantification phase, model sectors provide a practical reference point for debugging a model.

STOCKS AND FLOWS

When the group has chosen the model sectors, the participants can be split up into small groups for one or more short periods of time to discuss what stocks should be included in a particular model sector. Short sessions of fifteen minutes to half an hour are recommended to keep in touch with the progress the groups are making. For example, the assignment may be unclear, or the concept of a "stock" may be too complicated, or communication may not develop well in some of the small groups. Reconvening in a plenary session is more appropriate than muddling through and wasting precious time.

A *stock* is a variable important enough to be explained within the model. A stock represents a state variable that embodies an aspect of the system under study. Usually it is a quantifiable, measurable unit.

An initial maximum of about four stocks in each sector is recommended to keep the model at a manageable size for its identified purpose. A few more (or less) stocks are not necessarily a problem, but initially a group needs to stay focused on behavior patterns and limit itself to a small number. When left with an open number of stocks, groups have a tendency to add all possible items and to analyze details rather than select the most important ones and synthesize the broad lines. The purpose is not to describe the system as exactly as possible with as many variables as possible but rather to find the main variables that define most of the system behavior.

Choosing the sectors and the stocks is often the only formal assignment in which the participants are asked to choose specific icons—for example, as part of a natural capital sector, participants in the Upper Fox case chose "wetlands," "forest," and "grassland" for stocks. After the stocks are in place, the flows, auxiliary variables, and information connectors are added based on a content-driven discussion within the group. For example, a stock of wetlands (in hectares) in Upper Fox watershed is expected to decline. While the creation of new wetlands (inflow) is negligible, the destruction of wetlands (outflow) is caused by several activities, which can be represented by auxiliary variables.

Until this point in the process, the mediated modeler provides most guidance in the form of providing a new tool. From here on, the participants own the tool and lead the process. By now, the four model icons—stocks, flows, auxiliary variables, and functional connectors—are part of the new vocabulary the group is using to further discussions by the group members.

With the newly acquired language, the level of chaos often rises. The mediated modeler assists in summarizing the discussion and in translating it into model language and keeps the anxiety and frustration with the chaos manageable.

Small-group sessions tend to be geared toward discussion and solving specific problem points, such as how one problem is linked to another and what mechanism expressed in model icons would best express that train of thought. The plenary sessions are reserved for making any changes to the model and maintaining a focus on the larger picture. Every participant should have a chance to understand and comment on the latest alterations or additions.

As a model structure unfolds, the level of chaos reaches a maximum. Invariably, every process builds up to a higher level of chaos relative to the onset of the process before things start to fall into place. The participants are still confused, but on a higher level than when they started the process. At this point, participants have exhausted their usual ways of thinking about the problem. Now it is time to use both their intuitive and logical brain capacity to apply some original thinking.

It is important that the facilitator/modeler has the faith that the higher level of chaos is productive. He or she should not attempt to interfere in the dialogue or to insert more structure to reduce the chaos any more than is absolutely necessary to maintain manageable interactions that will result in a productive outcome. Some participants may be pushed past their cognitive comfort zone and may need some respectful assistance. This is where experience comes in. Even when someone knows the steps in the process, it is helpful to be present in at least one mediated modeling process to see a relatively chaotic process unfold into a new, often satisfying, and innovative product.

As the participants are brainstorming about relationships and new variables to include, a "ghost" option (see Appendix 10) can help keep the model graphically organized. A ghost allows an icon to be used in a part of the model other than where the original icon was defined instead of using an information connector. This allows sectors to share variables without the use of long information connectors that can make the model appear cluttered.

In addition, the "document" option for each icon is a very important housekeeping tool during the modeling process. A document describes the sources or assumptions on which the values and relations are based. As the discussion among participants develops, pieces of information are volunteered, and background information supporting particular decisions is supplied. All this background information can be stored in the document of the icons.

SMALL GROUPS VERSUS PLENARY SESSIONS

The mediated modeler's good judgment is required to find a balance among the factors that need to be considered when deciding whether breaking into small groups to work on specific tasks is an option. For example, if participants have not yet established enough trust among themselves, they will have very little motivation for small-group work that focuses on complementary tasks, such as identifying stocks for the various model sectors. Alternatively, having all the small groups focus on one identical task can enhance trust if the small groups come up with similar lines of thought that build onto each other when presented at a plenary session. If the small groups don't come up with similar lines of thought, the plenary sessions are extended.

For trust-enhancing purposes, developing model sectors or choosing stocks for the sectors are appropriate tasks for the first small-group sessions. When building the qualitative model is well on its way, small-group sessions are used mainly for complementary tasks, during which small groups discuss specific parts of the model. The small groups report back during a plenary session, at which time the results of the small-group discussions are incorporated into the model.

Larger groups engaging in a mediated modeling process may be in more need of structure to be effective and may require breaking up into small groups more frequently. The purpose of the plenary sessions is to try to keep all participants connected. All participants should have a clear understanding of how the discussion has been summarized and of the results included in the model.

FEEDBACK LOOPS AND LAG TIME

Dynamic systems are characterized by nonlinear behavior patterns. There are a few classic patterns, such as exponential growth and decay, and oscillation (Ford 1999).

As an example of a general example of nonlinear behavior, the concentration of a pollutant in a lake may not noticeably affect a fish species in the short run, but as the pollutant reaches a certain threshold, the direct impacts become evident. This behavior might produce an S-curve, which involves exponential growth and decay rates at different points in time.

In a truly dynamic model, several nonlinear behavior patterns may be interacting. Feedback loops and time lags are important generators of nonlinear behavior in dynamic systems. Therefore, feedback loops and lag time between different variables must be thought through carefully. It is easy for most people to continue to think linearly and leave out the feedback loops and time lags. One would not need dynamic systems modeling for a linear problem.

At some point during the modeling process, the qualitative model satisfactorily includes the dynamics of the system under consideration, based on the discussion among the group members. New angles to the problem have emerged, and some latitude for innovative solutions seems to exist. There is a tendency to add more details and make the picture more precise. This is a good time to move on to the quantification stage of the process.

Workshop Stage 4: Building the Quantitative Model

The term *modeling* is used for both qualitative and quantitative modeling—a situation that can raise confusion when comparing group modeling efforts. Qualitative modeling is always a prerequisite for quantitative models, whether performed on a flip chart or on a computer. A quantitative model is a prerequisite for simulation of "what if" scenarios. All of the cases presented in this book are quantitative models, and simulations have been performed.

The extra step toward quantification adds an opportunity for learning. A group may agree on common goals or on a certain direction for action, but controversy may still exist about the order of magnitude of different variables. However, as with everything else within the scope of this book, the extra step toward quantification may not be a cost-effective one for a specific situation. For example, one can imagine a situation in which the conceptualization of a system alters the perception of a problem in a group enough to move forward in a positive direction.

An often-heard argument against quantification is that the problems of a poor conceptual model will be exacerbated when that model is being simulated quantitatively—that is, "garbage in, garbage out." On the other hand, the quantification stage may serve as a check for a conceptual model, and it can be argued that full understanding of a dynamic problem does not occur until it is quantified. Once a model can be simulated and odd or undesirable behavior of the model becomes apparent that cannot be attributed to model-building errors, the conceptual structure must once again come under scrutiny.

When mediated modeling is used in an exploratory mode for a poorly defined problem, the data may be scarce. As mentioned earlier, scarcity of data is not necessarily a valid argument to abandon quantification of a conceptual model, because it still adds to the understanding of what data are actually lacking, it often provides a concrete insight into what data would be useful to further the learning process of a group, and it provides an opportunity to develop a working hypothesis for the group within an agreed upon ball park.

At this stage, a group has developed a good sense of how a system under study behaves in a qualitative way. The goal of building the quantitative model is to arrive at an operating simulation model.

QUANTIFICATION AND DATA GATHERING

The first thing to do in building a quantitative model is to develop a list of time-series data requirements. This list contains most of the parameters in a model. Most participants are willing to provide data on the topics that are of greatest interest to them. Sometimes experts are invited to contribute a set of values, to explain the proper context for them, or to share insight in how variables relate to each other.

Some of the data are used directly in the model. However, the time-series data are used mainly to calibrate the model. Usually, most participants are not interested in the development of model equations. However, participants often find the possibility of relating two variables in graph form very useful, as explained in Appendix 10 (Andersen and Richardson 1997; Richmond 1997; Ford and Sterman 1998).

Between modeling workshops, the mediated modeling team works on the model—and with individual participants or small groups, if necessary—to come up with the most elegant ways to represent the discussion of the group and to incorporate the data.

When quantifying the relationships in a model, the units for the parameters must be consistent (Meadows and Robinson 1985). Opportunities for learning present themselves during the process of synchronizing parameters. A relationship between two entities may seem simple, but when one tries to capture this relationship in quantities, several conversions may be needed and additional relationships may be drawn into the picture. The participants don't always delve into the modeling to this extent and the mediated modeler resolves some of these issues between workshops. However, valuable insights sometimes reveal themselves through these modeling details.

Box 4.1 offers some quotations relevant to modeling. The modeling team may want to share these with participants at some time in the modeling process, to help them to maintain a proper perspective.

CALIBRATION

Calibration is "tuning" a model by manipulating independent variables and model parameters to obtain a reasonable match between observed and simulated

---

Box 4.1.
Some Quotes Relevant to Modeling

All models are wrong. Some models are useful.
   W. Edwards Deming

The best explanation is as simple as possible, but no simpler.
   Albert Einstein

Perfection is attained not when there is no longer anything to add, but when there is no longer anything to take away.
   Antoine de Saint-Exupéry

Seek simplicity . . . and then distrust it.
   Alfred North Whitehead

Models can easily become so complex that they are impenetrable, unexaminable, and virtually unalterable.
   Donella Meadows

---

values of the dependent variables. The observed values preferably are available in a time series. If the model generates a data pattern similar to an observed data pattern over a past time period, the confidence in a model is enhanced.

Different scenarios and extreme values are used to find unacceptable errors in a model. An example of such an error would be when the extreme settings of parameters produce undesired behavior of the model as a modeling artifact and cannot be explained by the behavior in the system.

A reasonable match between observed and simulated values can be established by eyeballing the comparative graphs. A more precise and relatively quick method to apply is the R-squared statistical procedure. R-squared statistic is based on the sum of the squared error and gives a measurement of how well two graphs correlate as a percentage. See Appendix 11 for a template of R-squared procedure in STELLA icons for observed and simulated dependent variables.

Workshop Stage 5: Testing, Scenarios, and Conclusions

At this stage, the final model is tested, presented, and analyzed; conclusions are drawn; and follow-up action is discussed.

VALIDITY AND USEFULNESS OF A MODEL

In the scientific community the "validity" of a model is often questioned. Andrew Ford (1999) emphasizes that the important question is not, Is the model valid? but rather, Is the model useful?

W. Edwards Deming observed that "all models are wrong; some models are useful." All models are wrong, because by definition, a model is a simplified representation of reality. The contribution of a model can be evaluated by explicitly addressing the purpose of both a model and the model-building process. In the context of mediated modeling, measuring the performance of a model is just one aspect embedded in the performance measurement of a model-building process. A performance measurement of a model calls for an evaluation concerning its contribution toward a specific goal and can have multiple dimensions. Greenberger et al. (1976) observe that *useful, illuminating, convincing,* or *inspiring confidence,* are more apt descriptors applying to models than *valid*" (quoted in Ford 1999, p. 289).

Two dimensions of confidence can be applied to mediated models. The first is the fit of the model with historical data; the focus in this dimension is on the model. The second dimension is the buy-in, or applicability to a specific practical problem; the focus here is on the model-building process. These considerations, in effect, are very similar to the discussion in Chapter 2 concerning the purpose of model building for increasing understanding versus striving for consensus among stakeholders.

Scientists (including modelers) and stakeholders may base their confidence in the models on different criteria. Applied research such as mediated modeling will have to withstand the test by both scientists and practical users. For scientists to feel confident, the model should be based on analytical and peer-reviewed research and data. Preferably, the experiments generating the data should be replicable. The research drawn upon should ideally be tailored to the specific question it needs to answer. In the classic research model, any form of extrapolation, upscaling, or summarization is to be avoided.

Scientists (and modelers) tend to appreciate the fit of a model with historical data. However, for stakeholders and professionals to feel confident, research (including a model) has to be practical. For them, a model has to be applicable, and—especially important—the model-building process has to be useful.

Experience with the case studies presented here has shown that, in practice, stakeholders are much less preoccupied with the specific data and relationships in the model. Most participants base their confidence more on the overall model behavior than on the way the equations are structured. In other words, if the modeling process is transparent and the model performs in a way that reasonably corresponds to participants' experience of how the real system functions, they then have confidence in the results and future scenarios, regardless of the exact functional forms of the equations.

It must be emphasized that the interest in overall model behavior exists in a situation in which the stakeholders have participated in the construction of the model. After involvement in the model-building process, they are more interested in the overall model behavior, the insights it provides, the usefulness of the model in helping them communicate certain issues to constituencies, and the consensus-based conclusions.

In practice, many, if not most, decisions are made in the absence of scientific data and models, and largely for political reasons. This is a difficult fact for many scientists to accept. Collaborative approaches try to provide platforms to bring science and decision making closer to each other.

To make the most of collaboration between scientists and other stakeholders, the role of scientists needs to be redefined toward "scientists as stakeholders and participants," as has been suggested by Connie Ozawa (1991) rather than scientists as "an objective third party." Both groups have strengths to add to the confidence that can be placed in a model and the model-building process. These two perspectives could gain from each other. Researchers can view and present themselves as stakeholders in a mediated modeling process on an equal footing with other stakeholders. They contribute as resources for information and help with the construction of equations in order to reflect the data as accurately as possible.

Researchers can benefit from the practical experience of other stakeholders. On the other hand, stakeholders can benefit from the knowledge the researchers bring to the meetings. However, stakeholders should not be put into a situation in which no action at all can be taken until the "perfect" research model is developed. When scientists dominate in a group of stakeholders, a tendency toward a data-driven model often arises—that is, models are constructed to fit the available data. Ideally, participants should focus on the problems the practical model should address and use the model-building process to generate innovative solutions. However, when scientists are excluded, a wealth of knowledge about possible useful data is missed.

Modeling experts know that a small change in a model parameter or structure can alter the outcome of simulations tremendously. Finding the "right" equations for a particular model is a daunting task occupying many scientists. In mediated modeling one accepts that there is no right equation. Equations should be kept as simple as possible while reflecting most of the behavior of interest to the participants. The output from the model should assist the thinking about a complex issue.

Again, a model can never be perfect, because a model is by definition an abstraction of reality. Alfred North Whitehead observed, "Seek simplicity and then distrust it." The strength of a scientist and modeler is to distrust models, while a practitioner appreciates simple and workable concepts.

Most scientists (including modelers) are not usually trained in mediation, facilitation, or group dynamics. In mediated modeling, the model is a vehicle to structure the discussion and the thinking in a group. Many scientists accept this notion on one level but quickly revert to focusing on the model as a final product—an attitude that is helpful in making sure that a model does not produce a conclusion based on a faulty scenario owing to a modeling error.

However, the mediated modeler's focus really should be on the process rather than on the model as a final product.

The downside of the scientific attitude may be a lack of appreciation of the modeling process, the group dynamics, the contribution of scientists to a diverse group, and the contribution of a diverse group to the work of scientists. The role of a scientist calls for a change from the Greek ideal of the "scientist as seeker for the ultimate truth" to that of the "scientist as critical assessor and thinker" (Ozawa 1991).

Most scientists are trained in reductionist analysis rather than in synthesis. While there is a time for analysis (i.e., taking the pieces apart), mediated modeling is primarily based on synthesis (i.e., putting the pieces together).

While scientists often pride themselves in being objective, stakeholders do not necessarily adhere to the ideal of objectivity. How can one be sure that the model does not paint a biased picture? This all depends on who is represented. The selection of stakeholders is critical. Once a certain set of stakeholders is invited, there must be some reliance on the critical minds and the self-assigned accountability within a group of participants. If all goes well, these qualities will keep the forces balanced.

BUILDING CONFIDENCE IN A MODEL

In general, a good model should generate enough insights to help solve a specific problem (Oreskes et al. 1994). Policy changes that can be traced back to the recommendations from a model are a greater long-term test (Vennix 1996). Meadows and Robinson (1985) have offered suggestions on ways to create a model that generates confidence. Their suggestions are discussed here for their relevance in mediated modeling:

- All elements should have real-world meaning and be consistent. The elements in mediated models should have a real-world meaning and be consistent in their units. However, not all elements have to be "real" in the sense that there are specific quantitative data to back them up. If "real" data would be a requirement, mediated modeling would be grossly inadequate as a tool to generate innovative solutions. However, all the elements should reflect the subjective but agreed upon reality of the participants.
- When modeling historical periods, the model should generate the problem it was built to investigate. The driving elements of a model should be calibrated with historical time-series data to the extent that these data are available. As mentioned before, not all elements are calibrated, nor is this possible or desirable. The goal of mediated modeling often is to look at a system and how certain issues "hang together" so that a group may operate from a common platform. A second important goal is

to generate innovative solutions. This requires that the participants not be limited to the incorporation of existing data but rather be allowed to expand their thinking and include elements that may be unknown. Therefore, the lack of existing data is not surprising.

- Extreme conditions should generate reasonable answers. At a minimum, the variables represented by slide bars in the user interface should be tested for their extremes and generate acceptable behavior at the extremes.

- The parameters that are sensitive in the model should be identically sensitive in the real world. This is the toughest requirement of all, not in the least because the experiments that would generate certain real-world data cannot be performed. However, a balanced group of stakeholders may be able to reason their way toward an acceptable range of behavior. The slide bars (which are introduced in the STELLA software example in Appendix 10) in the user interface deserve the most attention. For example, in the case studies, some slide bars are set up as on/off switches ("political will" or "licensing" in the Ria Formosa model in Chapter 9), while some can be altered along a nonlinear graph ("best management practices" in the Upper Fox model in Chapter 5).

Personalities and Confidence in the Model

Differences in personality also affect the way individuals perceive a mediated modeling process. Some people—call them the realists—naturally see "the world the way it is" and will want to use well-defined existing elements, while others (visionaries) see "the world the way it could be" and may feel more comfortable with exploring new, less well defined elements. Such personality differences also influence the level of confidence that participants or others may have in the model and underline the importance of explicitly addressing and evaluating the purpose of model building. An abbreviated version of the Meyers-Briggs personality type questionnaire (Keirsey and Bates 1984) can be used to explore individual tendencies in this area.

LEARNING FROM SCENARIOS

Scenarios are model simulations based on a set of assumptions. The results are used to identify a multitude of dynamic issues for "scoping" purposes, rather than as a predictive device for one specific situation. Thus many different scenarios can be explored. Parameters in a model can easily be altered by means of the slide bars in the user interface. A variety of scenarios under different parameter settings can be displayed.

The participants are asked to imagine the outcome of a specific scenario.

Subsequently, the model is run. When the model lives up to the expectations, confidence in the model and the conclusions based on the model are more readily established. If the model does not live up to the expectations, the reason for the discrepancy is discussed.

Perhaps an oversight in the model causes the undesirable behavior. On the other hand, perhaps some parameters within the model need adjustments. Alternatively, adjustments in the model structure may be needed to satisfy the perception of reality of the group. If the results from scenarios initially are counterintuitive and errors due to modeling artifacts are ruled out, insights can be very powerful in this phase.

If simulated behavior patterns are satisfactory, the group is likely not only to be more confident with the model results but also to be more committed toward the implementation of the model-based recommendations. For this reason it is important that decision makers participate in exploring scenarios, even if their technical staff participated in the model construction.

SENSITIVITY ANALYSIS

When participants have explored scenarios, they often are interested in how sensitive the model is to the most important parameters or which parameters have the biggest impact on a desired scenario, as well as whether the model is mostly sensitive to the magnitude of the parameters or mostly sensitive to the structure, the way the parameters are related to each other. For example, Chapter 5 discusses the sensitivity of the various aspects of urban sprawl in the Upper Fox model to population growth versus a growing gross national product.

CONSENSUS-BASED CONCLUSIONS AND RECOMMENDATIONS

Once again the questions the model was set out to address are revisited. Each question is evaluated, and a short consensus statement is developed to summarize what was learned. Based on this list, recommendations for further actions are developed. An ecological risk assessment can be employed as a tool for confirming and solidifying or critiquing the conclusions from the mediated modeling process.

Step 3: Follow-up and Tutorial

Before ending the workshop, a tutorial in which participants have the opportunity to operate the model and to gain active rather than solely passive experience with STELLA should be provided. This allows participants to link the learning experience with the confidence to actively reach out to other groups and demonstrate the model to others.

Tutorial

At some point, participants should get the opportunity to gain hands-on experience with the model. As mentioned earlier, when developing model-building skills of participants is an explicit goal, participants can be expected to run a model more easily at the end of the process. However, when participants focus on submodels, they may still need some assistance in running the composite model. When the emphasis is on group learning with respect to the problem rather than developing model-building skills, a tutorial to gain hands-on experience in running the model is an important step. Either way, the purpose of the tutorial is to support participants in using the model when communicating the results based on the model-building process.

Follow-up Interviews, Written Report, and Final Model

In a closing interview or questionnaire, the participants are surveyed again for research and management purposes. The information from the process and the evaluation is compiled in a written report, together with the final model. Especially the participants can use the model for further information dissemination purposes. A re-creation of the insights can be facilitated in an interactive manner for other groups, or, in a more extensive program, the scoping model can evolve toward a research or management model.

Implementation starts during the modeling process. It is not a separate next phase that comes after the modeling process (Roberts 1978; Lane 1992). Insights occur during the modeling process and change the way the participants think. Depending on learning and changes in attitudes, different outcomes can be expected in the implementation phase. A change in attitudes could become clear from the questionnaire.

Project Length

Mediated modeling projects vary in the length of time both the participants and the modeler are involved. First, there is the issue of the number of days that the participants are involved in an interactive group setting (workshops). How much time did the group spend together in a face-to-face situation working on a model?

Second, participants may spend time working on the model in small-group settings. For example, the participants in the Sage Grouse study (see Chapter 8) worked on submodels in small groups during the meetings. The participants in the San Antonio case (see Chapter 6) interacted in between meetings without the presence of a modeler. In the Upper Fox case (see Chapter 5), the modeler met with individuals or small groups between meetings.

Third, the number of workshops can be spread out over a variable length of time, depending on the needs of the group. A short-term project is recommended to maintain momentum and quickly move on to follow-up products based on the insights generated by the scoping model. A long-term modeling process is beneficial in guiding larger programs in which the scoping model evolves into a summary model of a program.

Finally, the facilitator/modeler spends an additional number of days to—among other activities—prepare the process, the participants, and the preliminary model; clean up the model in between meetings; find elegant model solutions or experts as requested by the group; assist the participants in fact finding; develop model equations; test the model; and provide a tutorial and written support.

Conclusion

This chapter provides a framework for designing a mediated modeling process. There is no recipe for the design of this type of process. However, experience has taught that certain elements provide a basis for a level of structure. The introduction calls for exposure of the participants to the software, agreement about the ground rules, and a definition of the questions the model is supposed to address. The development of a qualitative model benefits from a framework of model sectors that are gradually filled with model icons (stocks, flows, auxiliary variables, and information connectors). To go the extra length of developing a quantitative model provides additional opportunities for learning from simulating "what happens if" scenarios.

When the modeling process is completed, a consensus document can be drafted with the aid of the answers and insights provided by the modeling process. A training session prepares participants to demonstrate the model to nonparticipants and, in some cases, is designed to develop modeling skills. These steps give a mediated modeler a compass. Exactly how the steps materialize is unforeseeable, and a mediated modeler is wise to remain flexible during the process.

Because there is no standardized format for a group modeling effort, it is even more important to pay attention to the differences in the settings and processes used during case studies to examine where improvements to the process can be made (Rouwette et al. 2002). For example, the level of active stakeholder involvement indicates where on the continuum between an absolute participatory versus an expert model the case studies are relative to each other. Similarly, the cases are placed on a continuum concerning the period over which the meetings took place. The number of participants and the level of conflict among them influences the decisions made during the process.

All of the models in this book are quantitative simulation models as opposed to qualitative model structures, a distinction frequently confused in discussing participatory model building with environmental professionals. Some used surveys before and after model building to evaluate the process, and some used preliminary models going into the series of meetings among stakeholders. These and other aspects of group modeling processes that may be of interest in comparing the various case studies are summarized in Chapter 10 (Table 10.1) and Appendix 1.

Five case studies illustrate the suggestions presented in this chapter.

5

Decision Support for Watershed Management in the Upper Fox River Basin, Wisconsin, U.S.A.

Marjan van den Belt,

Robert Wenger, and

Bud Harris

The Upper Fox River Basin encompasses a watershed of just over 500,000 hectares in Wisconsin. The Upper Fox River drains into the Lower Fox and then into Green Bay. The quality of the water coming from upstream is therefore of importance to the receiving water body, Green Bay, Lake Michigan.

The Upper Fox River Basin in Wisconsin includes the following counties or parts of them: Calumet, Fond du Lac, Green Lake, Marquette, Columbia, Waushara, Winnebago, and Adams. Rural communities in the west, grading toward urban communities in the east, characterize the Upper Fox watershed (see Figure 5.1). Traditionally this watershed has been dominated by agricultural activities, mainly dairy farming. However, the area once used for farming is diminishing. Small family farms are being forced out of business at a rapid rate and are being converted into residential areas or amended to large-scale intensive factory farms. The disappearance of the small-farm community dramatically affects the socio-economic setting of the area.

The western part of the watershed is considered relatively pristine. With excellent streams for fishing, it is one of the important tourist attractions in the watershed. The economic well-being in the eastern counties (Winnebago, Calumet, Fond du Lac) is primarily dependent on industry. The urban communities of Oshkosh and Fond du Lac are expanding. Second-home ownership in

The Upper Fox model can be downloaded from www.mediated-modeling.com

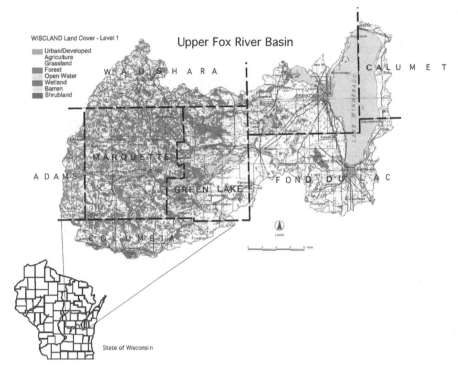

Figure 5.1.
Upper Fox drainage area

the western part of the watershed is on the rise because urbanites want to enjoy the natural and rural amenities in this region. These social pressures contribute to habitat fragmentation within the watershed and increase runoff from developed areas, but increased tourist income provides an economic benefit.

The basin is very diverse in its land use, geomorphology, and biology. The diversity of its ecosystems is largely attributable to its geomorphology. In addition, there are diverse natural resources ranging from over 80,000 hectares of valuable privately owned land and managed forest land to hundreds of kilometers of productive trout streams and warm-water fisheries to thousands of hectares of public wildlife and recreational lands. This abundance of natural resources and the accompanying range of plant and animal species are the basis for a high biodiversity level within the basin.

The Department of Natural Resources (DNR) in Wisconsin committed to an ecosystems management approach in the mid-1990s (Addis 1994). The objective was to manage the natural resources in the state using drainage basins as the management units and involving local stakeholders in developing management plans. Wisconsin was divided into twenty-three geographic management units (GMUs) on the basis of drainage basin considerations. The stakeholders who were invited to participate in the design of management plans were called geographic management unit partners (GMUPs). For a given GMU, the stakeholders were selected for membership in the geographic management unit partnership (GMUP) at the discretion of the DNR. The GMUs and their partners would decide how to proceed with the design of a management plan for their watershed.

The GMUP for the Upper Fox River Basin included a variety of local government agencies, representatives from non-governmental organizations (NGOs), farmers, real estate developers, and foresters. A total of twenty-five diverse stakeholders made up the Upper Fox GMUP. Through contacts with the University of Wisconsin at Green Bay, DNR personnel affiliated with the GMU in Oshkosh decided to offer their GMUP in the Upper Fox several options for commencing their collaborative activities.

First, the option of pursuing a traditional, more unstructured, open-ended discussion was available. An extended characterization of the Upper Fox basin had just become available in a report called "The Upper Fox River Basin," which was collaboratively prepared by a group of graduate students at the University of Wisconsin at Green Bay as part of a seminar in environmental science and policy.

Second, the option of conducting a mediated modeling process was offered. Third, at the same occasion, this group was offered the option of conducting an ecological risk assessment. The GMUP agreed to pursue both the mediated modeling and the ecological risk assessment, because these approaches can mutually reinforce each other. In the interest of the scope of this book, we focus on the experience with the mediated modeling process.

The student report was frequently used as a reference by the GMUP group. Even though much relevant information about the Upper Fox River Basin was available from this document, the data were often presented as a snapshot, rather than as ongoing trends based on time-series data. In addition, certain aspects of the data in the report were not consistently presented; therefore tradeoffs among management options were difficult to assess. For example, current population and land use information may have been presented in the report, but the mechanisms relating the two were not likely to be discussed extensively. As a result, a dynamic simulation model and the process of jointly constructing one seemed to be a needed dimension to focus discussion and promote team learning among the GMUPs.

The "kick-off" of the collaboration among the members of GMUP in the Upper Fox took place shortly after the decision was made to pursue a mediated modeling process. The participants gathered for nine workshops, each with a duration of one evening (5:30–9:00 P.M.), and an additional tutorial. The participants did not receive any compensation for their time, but dinner and refreshments were always provided at the meetings.

In the spring of 1998 the organizing team visited all the individual participants on the GMUP list. We spent about a half hour to an hour with each of them, using a multiple-part survey to guide the introductory visit. In one part, the interviewees were asked to state their perception of the problem in the Upper Fox within the scope of the project. The answers were interactively summarized in a causal diagram that evolved during dialogue. The questions were directed toward dynamic relations. The mediated modeler used the results to construct a preliminary model to be presented during the first workshop.

The problems identified by the participants were thematic and often lacked dynamic coherency. Cause and effect had to be elicited and sometimes would lead to a closed-loop relation, mostly to the surprise of the interviewee. Water quality issues were brought up as the main problem. These issues were often raised in the form of specific pollutants or problems with specific fish species.

In another part of the survey we asked about the level of satisfaction concerning the type of stakeholders on the participant list and the anticipated level of conflict among those stakeholders.

Stakeholders

When we interviewed the GMU partners, most of them had met once before, at the meeting where it was decided to use mediated modeling as a tool to assist with the development of a watershed plan. At this meeting the GMU partners had been confronted with the type of stakeholders the DNR had invited. During the preparatory interview, we showed a participant list and asked, "Are the stakeholders involved satisfactory?" Ten participants answered, "Yes," and four answered, "Somewhat." Two answered, "No," and thought that the geographic representation was out of balance and that community groups, business, chamber of commerce, and local government representatives were missing. Seven participants abstained from answering, often because they had not attended the prior meeting where the GMU partners presented themselves and agreed to engage in a mediated modeling process. The participant list did not provide enough information for them to form an opinion about the appropriateness of the stakeholders involved.

For two GMUP members, the projected burden of nine sessions was too heavy, and these stakeholders graciously declined participation from the beginning. Most GMUP members participated whenever possible. A few attended all sessions, and most attended the majority of the sessions, However, for a few, the commitment was too much, causing them to drop out during the process.

The decision was made to concentrate the mediated modeling process over a period of a few months to maintain momentum and to have the process provide the next step in the GMUPs' collaborative efforts. The evening sessions provided an opportunity for some stakeholders to participate frequently when otherwise they would have been unable to do so because of day-time work commitments.

Six representatives from the DNR were part of the group. The gender breakdown of the group was 87% male and 13% female. Ages ranged from 25 to 84, with an average age of 45. The academic or professional background of the participants was predominantly in the natural sciences. Working with STELLA was a relatively new concept for this group. With the exception of two participants, none had previously been exposed to STELLA or any other system dynamic software. The majority (19 of the 23 participants) indicated little or no experience with integrative activities linking ecology and economics.

The Upper Fox Modeling Process

The format for the Upper Fox case closely followed the generic process outlined in Chapter 4. The ten meetings are presented in chronological order and describe the relevant group dynamics as well as modeling progress.

First Meeting

The first meeting, on March 31, 1998, introduced the STELLA software and established the ground rules. The mediated modeler demonstrated the preliminary model, which was rejected by the group. The participants developed a partial problem definition.

Before the workshop sessions started, some participants had concerns about meeting in a group where some members were not disposed to cooperate because of their interest in pursuing a narrow agenda. Such a situation, they felt, would lead to further alienation and a waste of time. Under a best-case scenario, the participants hoped to establish a common goal, create mutual understanding, and learn something new.

Because of these concerns, the first evening we met a group of somewhat reserved participants. The dominant interactions took place between individual participants and the facilitator rather than among the participants. Naturally, the ground rules and basic information about the tools needed to be conveyed. The discussion of questions the model needed to address started rather tentatively. For the participants this was an opportunity to ventilate positions and opinions. For the facilitator this was a crucial point at which to enforce the ground rules.

From the information we had gathered during the visits with individual participants we had constructed a preliminary model, using less than a day's time. This preliminary model was a rough outline and demonstrated an attempt to embrace most of the viewpoints at some level. At the first meeting, we presented the preliminary model to the participants as the result of what was learned from the interviews, as well as to indicate the overarching conceptual level that needed to be addressed initially for all to "fit under the umbrella." Finally, the preliminary model gave the participants an idea of how a STELLA model might look.

Ideally the preliminary model should be demonstrated after the introduction to STELLA so the participants can understand the icons. And usually it makes sense to develop the list of questions the model should address before showing the preliminary model. Once the preliminary model appears on the screen, most groups will start to focus on this model and what is missing in it.

However, the Upper Fox group was relatively skeptical about using the modeling approach for consensus building and needed to see an example of a model early in the discussion. Demonstration of the preliminary model provided a starting point for the participants to begin identifying themselves as a group. In this case, the preliminary model also served to lift the conceptual level of focus. When the group started to focus on all that was missing, the model was deleted, and they started over to make their own.

In terms of maintaining momentum, it would have been convenient if the list of questions the model should answer had been developed before the preliminary model was shown. However, in terms of addressing the need to see a "model product," it made sense to show the preliminary model first.

Second Meeting

Two days later (April 2) the problem definition in the form of questions the model should address was finished, and the selection of model sectors began.

During the problem definition phase an attempt was made to look at water quality issues from a broader perspective. As a result, the linkages between water quality issues and land use were quickly established and accepted. In addition, the concept of natural capital was introduced—mainly because the facilitator used that term in an attempt to summarize and interpret the discussion of the group, and the group wanted to know what meaning was attached to it. The facilitator's response—that *natural capital* meant "nature as a capital from which we derive ecosystem services"—turned out to be a workable concept for the group. They gradually became more confident not only in using the term but also in working with the consequences of accepting this concept for building the model.

During the second meeting, the group finished a list of eight "questions the model should address":

1. If present economic and demographic trends continue, what are the consequences for natural capital up to the year 2020?
2. What are the trade-offs in economic terms between urban sprawl and loss of ecosystem services?

3. How can the consequences of urban sprawl be managed?
4. What are the impacts coming from outside the Upper Fox, and which of these impacts can be managed within the system?
5. Which components of natural capital can be managed?
6. Which components of natural capital, if managed properly, give the most benefit?
7. Which ecosystem services are derived from natural capital?
8. What are the economic benefits of the natural capital and, consequently, the ecosystem services derived from them?

These questions were refined somewhat throughout the process. To keep the group's perspective clear, the questions were revisited at the beginning (and often at the end as well) of every modeling meeting. At the ninth meeting, the questions were discussed, and conclusions or recommendations were based on the insights gained from them.

At the first two meetings it was especially important to allow participants to "ventilate" and establish trust, but this process cannot continue indefinitely. When the participants appeared comfortable during the second meeting, the facilitator started wearing the modeler's hat and began to actively "interpret" the discussion. We proceeded from the questions the model should answer to an attempt at defining the model sectors. The latter was done in small groups. The small groups came up with similar lines of thought that, when presented, built onto each other. This improved the trust among the participants.

The time frame to be addressed by the model was established during the course of the development of the problem definition. In a way, the scope of the questions to be addressed dictated a time frame. The participants decided to concentrate on the period from 1970 to 2020. An attempt was made to construct the model so that it would describe the observed historical behavior during the period from 1970 to 1998. Evaluated in this manner, the model would then be run based on various scenarios for the period from 1998 through 2020. The decision to start at 1970 was made because some participants felt that the 1970s provided several important data points that would be relevant for calibration of the model. It was also felt that the current trend, in which the urban area is encroaching onto the natural area, started to take noticeable form during that period.

Five model sectors were derived from the problem definition (see Figure 5.2). Information arrows relate these five sectors to each other. The exchange of information is mutual between the model sectors, and the behavior of a given sector can be reinforced positively or negatively by the other model sectors.

As explained above, "natural capital" and "ecosystem services" were introduced as new concepts for most participants during the problem definition phase. Based on that discussion, the participants initially chose the sectors

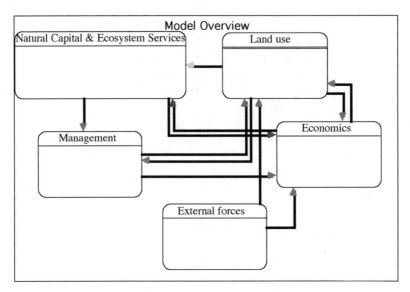

Figure 5.2.
Overview of Upper Fox model sectors

Natural Capital, Ecosystem Services, Economics and Management, and External Forces. The train of thought was as follows: There are natural areas, composed of wetlands, forest, and grassland, which make up the natural capital from which ecosystem services are derived. This concept is analogous to a bank account with capital from which one derives interest. However, when the stocks and flows were chosen to fill the model sectors, it became clear that the specific forms of natural capital deserved a place in a newly developed sector labeled Land Use. Together with an interest in area devoted to urban and agricultural use, the participants decided that it was important to understand how these types of land use change relative to each other.

This left ecosystem services and other natural aspects and indicators in one sector, renamed Natural Capital and Ecosystem Services. The Economics and Management sector was also separated into two sectors. The Management sector included different suggestions for management regimes, policy proposals, or policy evaluation. The group was interested in those measures that could make a difference in issues related to their concerns; these issues were placed in the Management sector. The Economics sector was created to keep track of the income generated by particular economic activities. The group was keen on getting a feel for the relative magnitude of the income generated by several economic activities. In addition, the economic revenues are linked to other parts of the model; thus a change in natural capital or management practices could impact economic revenue. External forces were weighted heavily from the beginning, and therefore a separate sector was devoted to them.

Third Meeting

It took four evenings (April 22, 23, 28, and 30, 1998) to construct the qualitative model structure consisting of stocks, flows, variables, and connectors. During the third meeting (April 22), the participants focused on the selection of stocks for the sectors. It took some time and effort on the part of the participants to understand the role of a stock as a state variable in the system. Since external forces are determined outside the system, no stocks showed up in this sector.

External Forces Model Sector

The "external forces" are those forces that impact the Upper Fox River Basin and, presumably, cannot be influenced by anything inside the Upper Fox region (see Figure 5.3). Originally, many participants felt that environmental problems in the Upper Fox are a consequence of factors that cannot be managed at all from within the region.

The group first identified population growth as the main external force and later elaborated on the concept with the phrase "effective population," a term that refers to both the full-time residents and second-home owners. It was estimated that about 25% of the effective population in the (urban) area also has a second home in the area. Because the period from 1970 to 2020 is relatively short, the range of population growth changes during that time was relatively small, and a constant growth percentage was assumed. Population reduction was therefore not addressed. The effective population determines how much urban area is required to accommodate population growth in the Land Use sector.

The general economic trend was considered an important external force, in part because it drives the demand for second homes. The economic trends were a combination of a long-term upward trend, on which a wave for medium-long

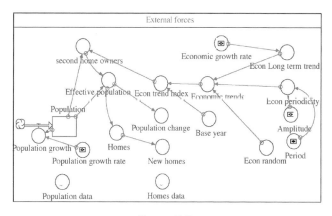

Figure 5.3.
Upper Fox external forces model sector

trends and some random noise for short-term uncertainty were superimposed. The economic trend was calibrated to mimic the resulting change in housing as observed in the data for the time period from 1970 to 1998.

Stocks were also selected for the Land Use sector. For example, the area of land devoted to agriculture was converted into urban development areas. Very quickly "flows" became part of the Land Use sector picture, and within one evening the group was comfortable pursuing the discussion in terms of model variables. The tasks were relatively nonthreatening. The atmosphere had loosened up considerably.

Fourth Meeting

The fourth night (April 23) was very pleasant. A sense of trust had been established among the participants. The participants seemed confident in discussing the issues in modeling terms and had fun building the model. We had a great time elaborating the Land Use sector.

Land Use Model Sector

Natural capital as a concept was easily accepted by the participants during the problem definition phase and initially appeared as a model sector. However, defining specific stocks of natural capital posed a challenge. This part of the process clearly showed the advantage of model construction over mere discussion.

The process of identifying stocks forced the participants to become more specific. When talking about stocks, one has to also think of the flows that alter the stock levels. This requirement forced the participants to think in terms of systems. For example, initially a stock of "clean water" was proposed. Such a label is not easily defined, however, because it has more to do with qualitative characteristics of the water than with quantitative aspects. Since the existence of natural wetlands and forest and the absence of certain polluting land use practices seemed to influence the quality of the water, this thought exercise led to stocks of wetlands, forest, and grassland on the natural side, and agricultural land and urban area on the human-regulated side. Even though water quality was an original objective, water as a stock was not placed in this model. Water quality was identified as a composite indicator in the form of an auxiliary variable.

Since the total land area is conserved at the river basin scale (area is neither created nor destroyed), the Upper Fox could be divided into the previously mentioned stocks. The discussion about the definitions of these stocks and, consequently, the flows was very instructive to the participants. What was considered urban, wetland, or forest varied from participant to participant. A middle ground was established after intense discussion, as follows:

- *Wetlands* exclude the arid wetlands, which are regions that are moist during part of the year and arid at other times.
- *Forests* are areas with trees, except where urban areas are established within a cluster of trees.
- *Grasslands* are the areas set aside as part of the Conservation Reserve Program (CRP). Natural grassland no longer exists, except for very small parcels.
- *Agricultural land* refers to land in agricultural use. The area of land devoted to agriculture use is a statistic that has been well documented over several years.
- *Urban area* refers to land with an average density of more than one house per five acres.

To reach agreement on these definitions, several parties had to make concessions. For example, the forester made many distinctions among forest types, while the environmentalist wanted to include small patches of natural grassland, even those less than an acre. Duly, a handful of small grassland patches exist within the study region. We continued this discussion until all participants could live with the outcomes.

The Land Use sector has a prominent place in the model (see Figure 5.4). The total land area in the Upper Fox River Basin is just over 500,000 hectares, divided into agricultural area, urban area, grassland, forest, and wetlands.

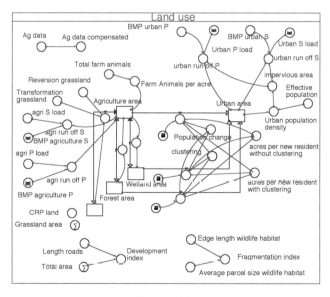

Figure 5.4.
Upper Fox land use model sector

During the quantification stage, it became clear that, contrary to the expectation of many of the group members, time-series data on changes in land use were not readily available. Time-series data on agricultural area, grassland, and forest were available, but urban area and wetlands remained open questions. It would have surprised all members of the group if urban area (whatever the definition) had shown a decreasing trend. Following the discussion about the increase in the effective population and the concomitant increase in the construction of second homes, the urban area was assumed to increase.

On the basis of the available data and owing to the fact that the total area is conserved, the area of wetlands is the main unknown in the model. The available wetland data were based on such differing definitions of wetland that a time series did not make any sense. However, the participants agreed that a decreasing trend made the most sense intuitively. In connection with the uncertainty in the area of wetlands, a hypothesis was offered that when wetlands deteriorate or die, they become open water. Since the area of open water was assumed to play no role in the land use issue within the chosen time frame, that aspect did not show up in the model. Perhaps this was a significant oversight.

Agricultural area was calibrated with a well-established set of time-series data and forms the starting point in identifying changes in land use. Agricultural area is steadily declining at the expense of increases in urban area. Until the year 2000, agricultural land was to be "rented" to establish grassland, but the funds for this program stopped in the year 2000, and the expectation was that grassland would gradually be converted back into agricultural land after this date. Very little or no agricultural area is transformed into forest or wetlands.

The stocks of agricultural area and urban area define the runoff of the main pollutants, phosphorus (P) and sediment (S). We were aware of the fact that P is often attached to S and that, as a result, some double counting may be going on. However, for the sake of addressing different managerial possibilities, this division was maintained. Several sources were consulted in determining a P loading and an S loading per hectare of agriculture area and urban area. The sources are listed in the "document" of the particular model icons and in references.

As an example, a best estimate of 1.7 lbs/acre/yr (157 kg/km^2/yr) was chosen for the P loading from agricultural areas in the model. A slide bar in the user interface can easily alter this number to examine the outcome based on other estimates of P loading.

The best management practices as defined in the Management sector (ghosts) have an impact on the total releases of the pollutants to the natural system.

The calculations of the "development index" and the "fragmentation index" are based on land use issues and therefore deserve a place in this sector. However, their impacts are felt solely in the natural system. In the model, these impacts are basically negligible (or turned off) because data were not available. Both indexes are based on hypothetical figures and deserve attention if the model is further expanded or refined.

The development index is based on the ratio of the length of roads to total area. This definition provides a logical connection to clustering in the future, since urban sprawl typically causes a high development index. The fragmentation index is calculated as the area of natural parcels divided by the length of their edges, an accepted way of defining fragmentation in landscape ecology. Both the development and fragmentation indexes are convenient ratios allowing for the use of overall percentage of areas in a spatially nonexplicit model.

Fifth Meeting

At the fifth meeting (April 28), the process ground to a halt. The group came to a total stop and did not know how to proceed. The qualitative model had become quite complex at this point, and the discussion had exhausted the readily available lines of thought. To the facilitator this "stop" or level of confusion may be a sign that the group has worked through the most obvious ideas and is now ready for some original thinking beyond what its members have already brought forth. The question then becomes, How to lead this group through this turbulent part of the process?

First, this group had gotten very involved in the modeling process and needed to be reminded that it was not the model as the end product but rather the modeling process that provided the opportunity to achieve the primary goal: group learning. The objective was NOT to produce the most complete and elaborate model possible. It was useful to revisit the "questions the model needs to answer" and important to maintain a focus on what needed to be accomplished. On the other hand, some participants became impatient. Someone said half-jokingly, "Just give us a list of right answers and we will choose one," as if the right answer were out there somewhere. This may have been a good moment to insert a "game of mistaken identity," in which the participants exchange name tags and assume a different role in order to look at the model from a different perspective.

In this case, most of the pieces started to fall in place when we took a step back and acknowledged the work the group already had accomplished and the progress that had already been made. The group then proceeded to make some major progress. For example, land use was sorted out and satisfactorily connected with ecosystem services. Also, the participants generated ideas about how to manage external forces to a certain extent. Finally, several management options were suggested to influence P and S in the streams and lakes. A discussion of the model sectors that include these ideas follows.

Natural Capital and Ecosystem Services Model Sector

Natural capital (in this case, wetlands, forest, and grassland) provides ecosystem services such as sediment retention, phosphorus filtering, and effective habitat. The participants chose these ecosystem services from a list contained in Costanza et al. (1997). The following paragraphs highlight the example of phosphorus (P), but a similar structure with different ratios was applied to sediment (S) (see Figure 5.5).

The total phosphorus filtering service of the natural areas is dependent on the natural capital available. The P filtering service provided by natural capital was expressed in comparison with agricultural land, since direct data were available only for this land use (in lbs/acre/yr). For example, the P runoff in forest is estimated to be 77% of the P runoff in agricultural lands. A study by the U.S. Department of Agriculture of the East River in Wisconsin showed that the P runoff from wetlands averages 55% (ranging from 49% to 66%) of the runoff from agricultural land. Thus, the 55% figure was used in the model; the range from 49% to 66% can be examined with a slide bar. Similarly, for grassland the runoff is 85% of that for land in agricultural use.

"Total phosphorus" and "Total sediment" depend on the releases from the urban and agricultural areas (as discussed in the Land Use sector) and on the available ecosystem services. Because natural areas have a certain capacity to retain more phosphorus than other land use areas, P runoff is decreased owing to the existence of these natural areas. The greater the amount of land devoted to urban or agricultural use, the more pollutants are released into the lakes and streams. The more natural area available, the more ecosystem services remain

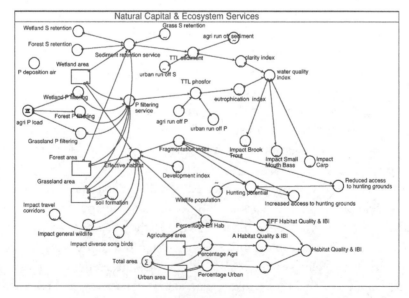

Figure 5.5.
Upper Fox natural capital and ecosystem services model sector

in effect. The base flow of 0.007 lb/acre/yr (0.65 kg/hectare/yr) was ignored. The phosphorus loading from agriculture and urban areas is due entirely to anthropogenic sources.

The total amount of phosphorus runoff affects the eutrophication of the streams and lakes, as expressed by a eutrophication index. The eutrophication index is a nonlinear function of the total phosphorus loading (in lbs/yr). It reflects the consensus by the participants that the anthropogenic activities in a river basin can release a certain amount of P into the streams and lakes without seemingly adverse consequences, but that major consequences may suddenly occur at a certain level, and beyond that point they may be dramatic and irreversible (see Figure 5.6).

It was necessary for the participants to determine where on the trophic curve (hypertrophic, eutrophic, oligotrophic) the Upper Fox was at the time. Most participants felt the Upper Fox was at the point where the graph for the eutrophication index begins to fall, but that the point of irreversibility had not yet been reached and that rigorous best management practices could reverse the trend. This subject was discussed in more detail when the scenarios were run at the ninth meeting.

In the same way that the total P was put in a dynamic perspective by means of the eutrophication index, the way in which the total amount of sediment runoff affects the clarity of streams and lakes was put in perspective by a water clarity index. The water quality index is the composite of four indices (clarity, eutrophication, dissolved oxygen, and temperature). The latter two indices were added for comprehensiveness but were not discussed by the group at great length. All indices range from 0 to 1. An index of 1 means that the maximum

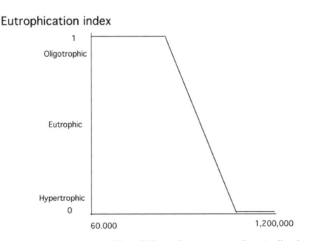

Figure 5.6.

Upper Fox model eutrophication index and phosphorus loading

achievable water quality is present. An index of 0 refers to "maximum degradation."

Water quality expressed as an index wasn't transparent to most participants. Therefore it was suggested that this notion should be linked to more tangible features of water quality, such as specific fish species. The brook trout community quickly feels the negative impact of a decreasing water quality. This change impacts the smallmouth bass community to a lesser extent. Water quality has to be quite degraded before an impact on carp becomes noticeable. Non-linear graphs were used in the model to reflect relationships implicit in this thinking.

The third ecosystem service the group considered was habitat. An effective wildlife habitat, at a maximum, consists of the aggregate of all natural areas. The aggregate of natural areas is less "effective" as wildlife habitat for a wide variety of species when fragmentation and ongoing development have occurred. However, some species (such as deer) may thrive in a highly fragmented habitat. Therefore the species composition of a diverse healthy ecosystem should be kept in mind.

As in the aquatic system, a more useful concept is "effective habitat," which differentiates between the extremes of, on the one end, a habitat functioning merely as a travel corridor for certain species and, on the other, a habitat providing nesting sites for highly fragile communities of songbirds. As levels of effective habitat decline, the songbirds will be the first to be negatively impacted, followed by general wildlife and, finally, wildlife using habitat as travel corridors.

The relation between land use and aquatic impacts is described in the model using an index based on "habitat quality and index of biotic integrity." Wang et al. (1997) derived this index for the state of Wisconsin, and it was introduced to the group by one of the participants. This index shows a relation between the area of agriculture, forest, and urban areas and the impacts to water quality, expressed in habitat quality and biotic integrity of the streams and lakes. First, the index shows that habitat quality and biotic integrity increase linearly with an increase of forest areas. A second relationship shows that the habitat quality and biotic integrity are not affected by agricultural practices as long as less than 50% of the area is in agricultural use. When more of the area is in agricultural use, moderate deterioration can be expected. Third, according to Wang et al. (1997), an area allows only 10% urbanization before the habitat quality and biotic integrity index drops sharply.

Depending on the percentage of natural, agricultural, or urban area, the impact on habitat quality and biotic integrity changes in the model. The non-linear relationship between land use and impacts in water quality became clear in this presentation. Certain thresholds seem to exist for land use levels beyond which negative impact on water quality begins to occur. The agricultural area diminished from 80% in the 1970s to about 50% in the 1990s, which would provide a small improvement in this index. The exact figure for the

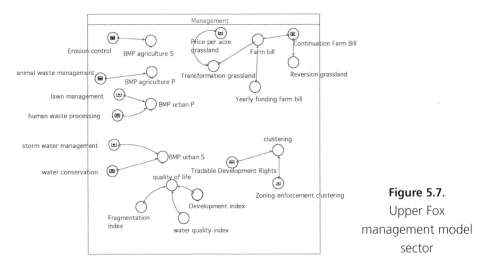

Figure 5.7.
Upper Fox
management model
sector

urban area was unclear, but when the study was conducted in 1998 it was estimated to be between 10% and 15% in the Upper Fox, right at the threshold.

Management Model Sector

The Management sector hosts a variety of decision-making formats that can be turned "on" or "off" in the user interface (see Figure 5.7). Phosphorus and sediment runoff aspects of best management practices (BMP) are incorporated for agriculture and urban areas, respectively. Erosion control and animal waste management make up agricultural BMPs. Lawn management, human waste processing, storm water management, and water conservation make up the urban BMPs. The levels of all BMPs can be adjusted with slide bars.

The BMP relations are portrayed by non-linear graphs in the model and reflect the fact that the first efforts to reduce erosion are easier to achieve than the last technically feasible units of effort. For example, if there is no erosion control, the BMP allows a maximum of 100% of sediments from agricultural areas to be released into the streams. Realistically, a best-case scenario for erosion control would involve half of the farmers reducing their erosion by 60%. This would reduce the total S output by 30%, but still up to 70% of the total sediments would be released into the waterways.

The existence of a "Farm Bill" and the available funding for it determine the amount of acreage transformed from agricultural use into grassland. The opposite effect, conversion of grassland back into agricultural land, can also occur. The Farm Bill, in effect at the time of the study, allowed the DNR to "rent" parcels of land from farmers for nonagricultural use. Usually these areas were converted into grassland.

Clustering for urban development refers to construction of homes on smaller lots, thus leaving more undeveloped space. Clustering can be achieved by the introduction of tradable development rights or by strictly enforcing zoning rules. The first option is a market mechanism that is put into effect after zoning rules are in place. The second option is a legislative alternative. The slide bars in the user interface provide an on/off switch for the clustering option. There is no "in between" option, because none of the workshop participants had any idea of how this behavior would be developed. In the model, clustering makes a difference in the area occupied by urbanization in the Land Use sector because it influences the number of hectares needed for population growth.

Quality of life is an indicator that is a key goal for management. In the model, it is based on a composite of several indexes (water quality, development, and fragmentation indices).

Sixth Meeting

The last evening of qualitative model building (April 30) was a satisfying one. This meeting was devoted to wrapping up loose ends in the model. In addition, the group took a step back and discovered that the Economics issues was virtually empty. This model sector was the least inspiring for the group to work on. Even though the participants realized that almost every proposition for action would be evaluated on its economic merits and that economics was deemed important from the beginning, only a few linkages spontaneously developed between the Economics model sector and the other model sectors.

Economics Model Sector

The Economics model sector remains the most poorly developed sector of the model. The primary objective of the original idea was to look at the relative size of the income from various economic activities. The economic activities that were to be addressed were those having a direct and significant impact on natural capital or those directly depending on natural capital. Furthermore, as a secondary objective, the original idea included the goal of surveying social impacts, such as the employment provided by these economic activities. The first objective materialized in a qualitative form, but the quantification is very weak (see Figure 5.8). The second objective was not addressed owing to a lack of time and, perhaps, a lack of interest at the time. The participants focused on the relationships between agriculture and urban areas on the one hand, and ecosystem services on the other.

The value of agricultural area is dependent not only on its market value and the number of hectares of agricultural land available but also on soil loss and soil formation. The existence of grassland is especially important in its contribution to soil formation.

The market value of agricultural land was based on prices (in 1996) in the five main counties of the watershed. An average of $1,278/acre (with a mini-

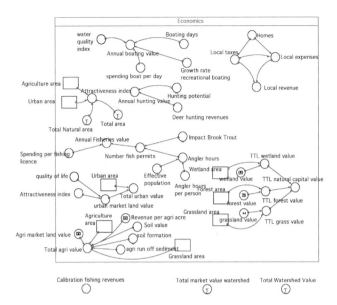

Figure 5.8.

Upper Fox economics model sector

mum of $946 and a maximum of $1,676) was used in the model, and a slide bar was added to the interface. The farming representative felt that the market value alone was not representative and that revenue per acre should be added. However, it was agreed that it was not possible to incorporate an average value because yearly fluctuations alter between profit and loss. It was decided to leave the model setting for revenue per agricultural acre at zero and to include a slide bar in the interface to vary this value. In this way, the agricultural revenue issue could be communicated to others as an unresolved issue.

When agricultural land is left as grassland, soil is formed at a certain rate ranging from 1 to 1.75 mm/yr, depending on the area of grassland available. A soil formation value of $8/ton was accepted on a recommendation from an outside expert. Sediment runoff, on the other hand, causes a loss in value. Sediment runoff from agricultural lands was discussed when developing the Land Use and Natural System sectors.

Establishing values for all economic activities that had a link to the ecosystem services was not feasible within the available time period. To incorporate a ballpark figure for the value of natural capital, general values for wetlands, forest, grassland, and lakes and streams were multiplied by the number of hectares available at each time step (Costanza et al. 1997).

The stocks in the Economics model sector were chosen in a straightforward manner and were not subject to much change over the course of the project. The following values were briefly discussed and incorporated in the model:

- The *value for urban area* is dependent on the "attractiveness index," which, in turn, depends mainly on the ratio of natural area to total land area.

- The *fisheries value* depends mainly on the number of fish permits, which is related to the types of attractive fish species that can survive in the lakes and streams.
- The *hunting value* triggered a whole new discussion at the very end of the mediated modeling project, when "hunting potential" was recognized as a potential value generator. This part should be further explored in a later version of the model.
- The *boating value* is mainly dependent on the water quality.

Finally, a discussion considering the tax base of the counties was reflected in the model purely in a qualitative manner. An increase in the number of homes in the river basin is often considered as a positive trend in terms of tax revenues. However, for every new home built, the need for local services increases expenses as well. This counterbalance may very well lead to a decrease in net local revenues, as recent evidence seemed to suggest. Although not quantified, this notion was an eye-opener to some of the participants.

Seventh and Eighth Meetings

To stay within our projected time line, the group needed to make the transition from qualitative model building to quantifying the identified relationships. This was not a popular transition. Participants had achieved a comfortable level of working together in building the model. It was generally agreed that the most important behavior was captured. There were new challenges ahead and new opportunities for learning as well. So we unraveled the model and discussed what time-series data we needed, what would be available, and who would track it down. It turned out that the participants connected to institutions had most of the available data but lacked the time to gather it. Therefore some of the noninstitutional participants (citizen groups) teamed up with the representatives from institutions to gather the data.

At this stage, the facilitator/modeler wears the modeler's hat for most of the time to help the participants gather data, sort through the data, and develop simple but elegant equations that capture the essence of what the group has discussed and agreed on. During two evenings (June 23 and 25, 1998), a list of data requirements was developed, and participants volunteered to take responsibility for those items for which they had the greatest confidence in their ability to obtain relevant information.

From the data provided by the participants, the model equations were constructed in such a way that the model behavior would reflect the historical time series as well as possible. An attempt was also made to keep the equations as simple and as straightforward as possible. Those in the group who had some specific expertise would offer to the group a particular equation form, which the other participants could then either accept or reject. In some cases, graphical relationships between variables were used so that participants could agree on the general shape of the graph.

In most cases, the facilitator/modeler developed the equations. Most of the participants were generally not interested in the equations but rather in the behavior the model showed based on those equations. When the model showed expected behavior or showed unexpected but understandable behavior, the exact equations seemed to matter less.

Some ad hoc meetings with individual participants or small groups took place to sort out the details. At this point in the process there was enough trust about the common goal that individual meetings were not disturbing to other participants. In fact, at this point, when changes in the model due to ad hoc meetings were announced, the participants would often acknowledge the people who had done the work.

Calibration of the Upper Fox Model

In preparation for the final meeting, the model was tested as much as possible. Extreme settings of the slide bars produced plausible scenarios. The model was also calibrated using real time-series data. The model was calibrated to mimic the observed population data for the period from 1970 to 1990. U.S. Census data for 1970, 1980, and 1990 were compiled by a DNR employee and showed a growth of 12.5% over this period, or an average of 0.63% per year.

An important driving force in the model is the effective population in the area, a composite figure that includes the resident population, increased by the second-home owners. The calibration of the model is a representation of population (curve 1) and homes (curve 3) against the data for population (curve 2) and homes (curve 4) is rather accurate until 1997 (see Figure 5.9). Between

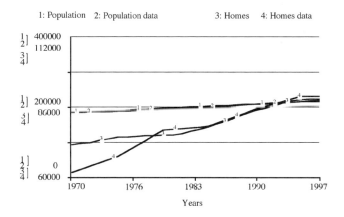

Figure 5.9.

Upper Fox model calibration of population and homes

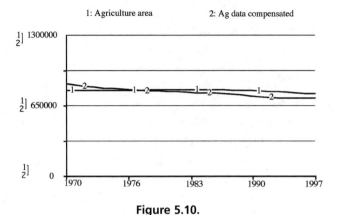

Figure 5.10.

Upper Fox model calibration of land in agricultural use

1970 and 1997 the R-squared value between model behavior and time-series data for population is 99%; for homes it is 93%. The model continues its behavior in future time under unchanged assumptions.

Effective population and homes are important driving forces for the rest of the model, and therefore it is important that the model mimic the actual data accurately over the past time period.

The same kind of calibration between the model behavior and time-series data is done for agricultural land in Figure 5.10. The R-squared value for agricultural area is 99%.

Ninth Meeting

On June 30, 1998, the participants and other interested parties were shown the final model. "What if" scenarios were requested by the participants and run, and the results were discussed. Using the model as a presentation tool and updating the model in the future with better data and new information were also discussed.

Scenarios

The graph in the user interface (see Figure 5.11) consists of several pages, allowing a user to examine the impact of a specific scenario on different aspects of the model. The following scenarios were at the core of what the participants requested. These scenarios follow more or less the pages of the graph on the user interface in the model. A selection of these pages is presented in Figures 5.12 to 5.14.

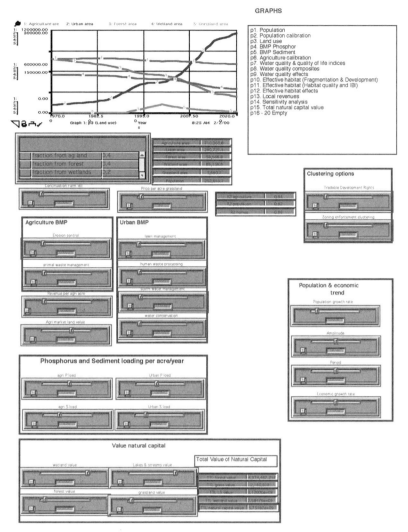

Figure 5.11.
Upper Fox model user interface

EXTERNAL FORCES

The population growth rate historically has been 0.63% annually over the past time frame of interest. The initial model construct assumes that this trend will continue. Figures 5.12a, b, and c show the effects of different population growth rates. Figure 5.12a shows the results when the population growth rate is zero; Figure 5.12b shows the results when the observed growth rate of 0.63% between 1970 and 1998 is used; and Figure 5.12c shows what could happen if the population growth rates were approximately double the observed rate (1.2%).

The slide bars under "population and economic trend" on the user interface in the model (see Figure 5.11) allow different settings of these parameters.

1: Population
2: Second-home owners
3: Effective population
4: Econ trend index

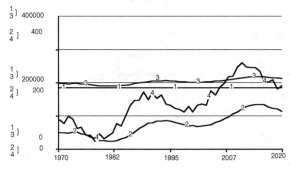

Figure 5.12a.

Upper Fox model population growth rate of zero.

1: Population
2: second home owners
3: Effective population
4: Econ trend index

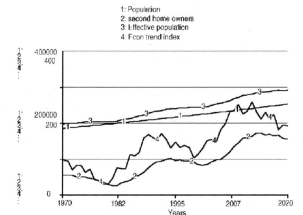

Figure 5.12b.

Upper Fox model population growth rate of 0.63%.

1: Population
2: Second-home owners
3: Effective population
4: Econ trend index

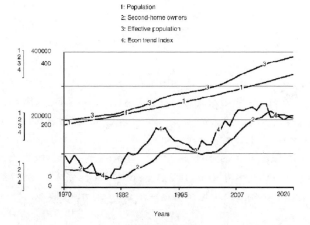

Figure 5.12c.

Upper Fox model population growth rate of 1.2%.

Table 5.1.

Effects of population and economic growth rates on the number
of homes in the Upper Fox River Basin

Population	Economic growth rate		
	0%	1%	2%
growth rate	Number of homes		
0%	190,000	210,000	230,000
0.63%	230,000	290,000	320,000
1.2%	340,000	380,000	420,000

After running the model under different parameter settings, the relevant
graph shows that population growth provides an important part of the trend
for new homes. Table 5.1 shows that the model is more sensitive to an increase
in the population growth rate than to an increase in the economic growth rate.
The economic long-term trend and the amplitude and period of the economic
cycles can also be adjusted. The initial model settings of a long-term trend of
1% growth over a period of 20 years with an amplitude of 10 were rough estimates achieved by consensus in the group.

LAND USE

The external forces (population and economic trend) have an impact on land
use mainly through their association with urbanization requirements. Urban
land use management, which promotes clustered development, has an internal
impact on the extent of urbanization. Scenarios based on land use with or
without clustering can be examined for their impacts on the area requirements
for urbanization. Figure 5.13a shows the land use scenario without clustering.
Figure 5.13b shows the scenario with clustering.

Obviously, when clustering is applied, less urban area is required; more
area remains in agricultural use and, to a lesser extent, as natural space. The
group did not have the time to fully explore the impact of urban clustering on
wildlife habitat in a quantitative manner; however, this is where an important
impact is expected to occur.

The total value of ecosystem services changes with changes in land use.
The less grassland, forest, or wetlands, the lower the remaining composite
value of natural capital in the model. The model depicts the relationship between each of these land use categories and the value of natural capital as a linear function.

Overall, the small increase in forest and wetlands improves the water quality (i.e., in terms of water clarity) when less sediment erodes into the water.
However, this improvement of water clarity, which is one component of water

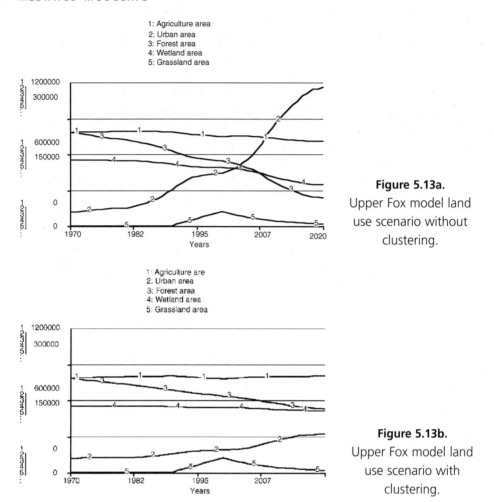

Figure 5.13a.
Upper Fox model land use scenario without clustering.

Figure 5.13b.
Upper Fox model land use scenario with clustering.

quality, is not very significant by itself when no other best management practices (BMP) on agricultural or urban areas are enacted. It becomes clear that
there is not one measurement that will solve all problems.

BEST MANAGEMENT PRACTICES

For the purpose of this scoping model (first generation), the concept of "erosion control" in agriculture areas refers to eroding sediments. Knowing that
eroding solids can have phosphorus attached, we chose to treat phosphorus independently to highlight the different problems associated with phosphorus
and sediment.

Figures 5.14a through 5.14c present three scenarios dealing with sediment
pollution. The clarity index is most sensitive to erosion control on agricultural
land. Figure 5.14a shows a clarity index of 0.1 (which indicates a relatively un-
favorable condition of water clarity) at 2020 when no BMP or clustering is undertaken. Figure 5.14b illustrates a clarity index of 0.3 after the BMP for

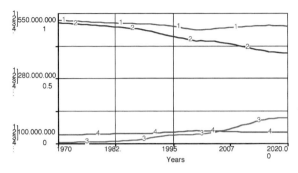

Figure 5.14a.

Upper Fox model sediment pollution without erosion control or storm water management.

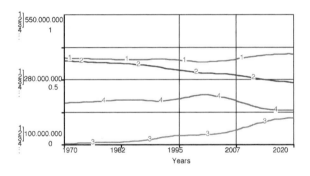

Figure 5.14b.

Upper Fox model sediment pollution with erosion control in agricultural areas.

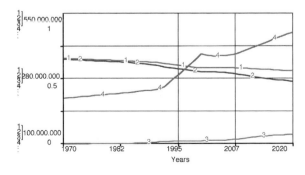

Figure 5.14c.

Upper Fox model sediment pollution with erosion control in agricultural areas and storm water management in urban areas.

erosion control in agricultural areas is explored to the extent that it makes economic sense. Alternatively, storm water management in unclustered urban areas by itself may improve the clarity index from 0.1 to 0.2 by the year 2020. However, when both erosion control in agriculture and storm water management in unclustered areas are simultaneously practiced, certain dynamic synergies come into play that could improve the water clarity index to 0.8. This is more than the sum of either BMP by itself (see Figure 5.14c).

Some measurements, such as BMP, can have a clear positive impact; however, the effect diminishes with every additional dollar spent on erosion control in agriculture. At some point it may make sense, as far as the reduction of sediment reduction is concerned, to stop investing in a BMP such as erosion control of agricultural land and to focus more on controlling urban sprawl.

Only when BMPs are explored can the clarity index of the water be brought to a point where further measures, such as clustering of urban areas, show a significant additional improvement. Clustering in combination with erosion control of agricultural areas can improve the clarity index to 0.4. Naturally, in this scenario, the effectiveness of storm water management as a BMP decreases with clustering of urban areas. If clustering takes place, the agricultural BMPs gain weight in this model.

There are, however, other considerations, such as phosphorus reduction, habitat for wildlife, and other aspects related to quality of life that interact in this complex picture.

The exercise of running scenarios with the model was insightful, especially because it became clear that no single measure was going to achieve the goals of the members of the Upper Fox GMU. Several areas of interest provided different opportunities for approaching the goals of the group.

Questions Revisited

The eight original questions the model intended to address were reviewed, and recommendations were developed.

1. If present economic and demographic trends continue, what are the consequences for natural capital up to the year 2020?

The model showed that if present economic and demographic trends continue, the urban area would increase at the expense of agricultural area, wetlands, and forest area. These trends in the model are based on the following observations:

- The *agricultural area* in the model is based on the most reliable data set. The model showed a gradual decrease in agricultural area.
- The *forest area* is based on a small number of data points, from which it was deduced that forest area gradually decreases over time.

- The *grassland area* is also based on some data points and peaks around 2000 under the Conservation Reserve Program. When this program is discontinued, the grasslands are expected to gradually disappear again.
- *Wetlands* were calibrated on the basis of the perception held by the participants; no useful time-series data were found to support this perception.
- *Lakes and streams* were considered to remain constant in the Upper Fox watershed over the period of interest. At the end of the process, the possibility for an error in this assumption was brought forward. A complicating factor in the assessment of the area of wetlands may be the fact that lakes were assumed to remain constant in area, yet wetlands may very well be disappearing into open water, which is a sign of deterioration of wetlands.
- The change in *urban area* was based on one study (University of Wisconsin 1997). The participants considered assumptions made in that particular study to be too conservative. They could not find accurate time-series data that reflected their definition of urban area (i.e., an average of one house per five acres).

Changes in urban area are more sensitive to the population growth rate than to the economic growth rate. Ten runs with incremental values from 0 to double the base case for the population growth rate showed that the urban area varies from 120,000 to 500,000 acres. When the economic growth rate is varied from 0 to double the base rate (1.2%), the urban area ranges from 210,000 to 390,000 acres. Therefore, if present economic and demographic trends continue, the demographic trend more than the economic trend could cause urban areas to expand at the expense of agricultural land and natural capital.

2. What are the trade-offs in economic terms between urban sprawl and loss of ecosystem services?

The Economics sector is the weakest part of this model. Ideally, the participants would have liked to explore the links between urban sprawl and the loss of ecosystem services in more detail, along with the relative contributions of the various economic areas in the region. Time constraints prohibited these studies. Instead, an attempt was made to quantify several economic activities in the region and to compare those with the global average values for the ecosystem services provided by the global biomes (Costanza et al. 1997). Since all natural capital items decrease slowly over the time period under consideration, this approach showed that the value of ecosystem services expressed in monetary terms also decreases over time. This monetary value is merely a starting point. It is more instructive to explore the model structure in this respect.

The model shows that on the one hand ecosystem services (sediment retention capacity, phosphorus retention capacity, and wildlife habitat) are derived from natural capital (wetlands, forest, and grassland). On the other hand, the agricultural and urban areas are net producers of sediment and phosphorus and reduce or change the quality of wildlife habitat. Natural capital provides certain resilience to the system, but when agricultural areas and urban areas reach certain thresholds, deterioration starts. This seems to be the case when over 50% of the watershed is occupied by agriculture or over 10% by urban area.

Agricultural area currently occupies about 60% of the total and the general trend is that agricultural area will continue to diminish. Less agricultural area means that a smaller runoff of waterborne pollutants can be expected. If urbanization continues and the current trend is not altered, environmental deterioration can be expected since the urban area is assumed currently to be around the 10% threshold.

3. How can the consequences of urban sprawl be managed?

Given the demographic trend, urban sprawl can be managed by governmental zoning or tradable development rights, using the market to promote cluster development. Also, best management practices for urban areas can be considered.

4. What are the impacts coming from outside the Upper Fox, and which of these impacts can be managed within the system?

Second-home owners come from outside the Upper Fox watershed; however, many are locals from Oshkosh (see question 3). In addition, the impact of a fluctuation of the general economic index is expected to have some impact on new construction. As explained under question 2, the impact from demographics may be stronger felt than the economic trend. These external pressures can be alleviated by internal management practices, such as clustering and enforcing zoning rules.

5. Which components of natural capital can be managed most effectively?

Taking into account the fact that wetlands provide highly valued ecosystem services when considered from the standpoint of global averages (Costanza et al. 1997), one could envision restoration programs to be a policy option.

6. Which components of natural capital, if managed properly, give the most benefit?

See question 5.

7. Which ecosystem services are derived from natural capital?

Sediment retention capacity, phosphorus retention capacity, and wildlife habitat are some of the ecosystem services derived from the natural capital provided by wetland, forest, and grassland.

8. What are the economic benefits of the natural capital and, consequently, the ecosystem services derived from them?

The value of natural capital is based on global averages. Time restrictions prohibited the group from exploring ecosystem service values from a local perspective. However, the DNR has expressed an interest in taking up this subject as part of a later project.

Recommendations and Observations Toward Policy Action

Based on what was learned form the model-building process, the GMUP developed a set of conclusions of its own. They provide a basis for the GMUP to construct more concrete action plans. The following conclusions (and, in some cases, proposals for follow-up action) were drawn up by the GMUP based on the mediated modeling process:

- Although population growth is an external force, internal land use management actions, such as zoning and tradable development rights designed to increase urban clustering, can reduce the impact. Follow up with clustering and tradable development rights.
- Urban sprawl: there is a demand for and a trend toward increased acreage per house.
- Smaller households: there is a trend for fewer people per house, increasing the need for living space.
- Data are available on a county basis, not on a watershed basis. An accessible conversion from county into watershed data is needed.
- BMPs can reduce phosphorus and sediment considerably.
- Sediment may be a larger problem than phosphorus. When the maximum erosion control is compared with the maximum animal waste management, a higher water quality can be achieved with the former.
- Water quality will improve when agricultural area declines.
- Water quality will degrade with more urbanization (most likely in an exponential manner).
- Under "business as usual," these water quality trends may even out. However, with BMP, strong improvements in water quality can be achieved.
- Habitat fragmentation and development may be a larger threat to habitat quality on land and to biotic integrity in the water relative to runoff issues.
- Animal waste management has a larger impact on phosphorus reduction than phosphorus reduction in urban areas, unless the urban area increases beyond the 10% to 15% threshold (i.e., urbanization without clustering).

- Erosion control in agricultural areas has a larger impact than sediment reduction in urban areas. Erosion control for unclustered urban areas may be more necessary than for clustered development.
- The model indicates that more clustering means more agricultural land with more sediment runoff than unclustered sediment runoff. This may only hold until a certain threshold is reached in land area devoted to urbanization.
- The model indicates that total natural capital decreases with every economic boom.
- Economic activities depend on, and are affected by, natural capital and ecosystem services. More research is needed to better understand these issues.

Practicing Model Presentation

Two days after the ninth meeting (July 1, 1998), a hands-on experience in running the model was provided during one evening. The goal was to provide an opportunity for the participants to familiarize themselves actively with the operation of the software and to gain confidence with the model to the extent that they could demonstrate the existing model to others.

Participants typically brought their own computers or joined someone who did bring a computer. They downloaded a "run-time-only" version of STELLA available for free from the High Performance Systems, Inc., Web site. A complementary report (van den Belt et al. 1998) to support participants in preparing their presentations of the model became available shortly thereafter. One participant became proficient enough to adjust the model for his own needs as a conservation officer. We also know of several presentations that have been given by workshop participants using the model.

Follow-up Survey

Before and after the series of meetings the participants were interviewed with the aid of a questionnaire. In some of the questions respondents were asked to rate a statement ranging from 1 (= strongly disagree) to 5 (= strongly agree). These statements are ranked in Appendix 3. Other questions were open-ended. The full answers are listed in Appendix 4. Following is an interpretation of the results.

Before the mediated modeling meetings, the participants indicated that they thought the group of participants could be important, but they did not yet believe they were operating as a group. The GMUP was more a gathering of individuals rather than "a group." Afterward, the participants thought that the modeling group had functioned relatively well as a group. "Those who re-mained interested worked well together" was a comment heard.

Afterward, the participants perceived that the Upper Fox GMUP group was relatively well-oriented toward a common goal. This perception was an im-provement in the group's orientation toward a common goal. Before the meet-ings, the anticipation of conflicting goals was relatively high. Some, but not many, conflicting goals persisted after the series of meetings.

In the "after" questionnaire, participants felt that the group had developed somewhat of a common view on how the linkages between ecology and eco-nomics in the Upper Fox system currently work, which is an improvement from the "before" questionnaire. The participants indicated a greater under-standing of linkages among stakeholders and the economic areas they repre-sented than before the mediated modeling meetings and team learning had taken place. They also indicated that they had learned about linking different pieces of information together and had expanded their causal thinking. In ad-dition, they learned that their goals were more shared by others than they had anticipated. The majority of the group members thought that interaction among the group members would be sustained. No one expected that the group would cease to exist.

In general, the composition of the group was acceptable to the participants for the goal of this project. The interactions during the modeling meetings were friendly and constructive and became more open as the process progressed.

The problem in the Upper Fox was not necessarily more complex than the participants originally thought. In the "after" questionnaire, all except one person thought that the problem the group decided to focus on was addressed satisfactorily. Useful answers to the initial questions were generated, and some workable alternatives were recommended during the mediated modeling process. Policy alternatives could evolve from the mediated modeling process. The participants felt that some indicators for sustainable development were developed.

The "after" questionnaire showed some, but not overwhelming, confidence that the conclusions would have an impact. Although some consensus on the goal for the future of the Upper Fox exists within the group, its members did not expect that such a consensus would be readily achieved. It was strongly agreed that the problem addressed by the model needs to be discussed on a regular basis across stakeholder groups. It was generally agreed that the model represents quite well the problem the group set out to investigate.

The participants felt a relatively strong ownership of the model, based on their perceived contribution to its design. They indicated a relatively strong support for the conclusions drawn from the model. The model seemed to be a helpful tool in communicating some problems in the Upper Fox.

The participants did not feel very confident in showing the model to others, although at the time of the "after" questionnaire, they had already received a tutorial on the operation of the model. This lack of confidence does not appear to be due to the model, however, because the statement "The model is of enough interest to show to others" was rated relatively high (4.1) on the agreement scale. Also, the lack of precision did not seem to affect participants' desire to show the model to others. Even though the confidence in showing the model was on the low side, people were planning to use the model in communications with others. All ten interviewees indicated that they already had discussed the model with their peers.

In the "before" questionnaire, computer modeling was expected to be somewhat helpful in structuring the discussion and in analyzing the issues involved. The verdict in the "after" questionnaire was more favorable. Mediated modeling helped in structuring the discussion and also helped in structuring the group's thinking. The facilitation was considered very effective and the meetings well-organized. All were pleased to some degree with the mediated modeling procedure in terms of the sequence of problem definition, identification of model sectors, stocks and flows, quantification, data gathering, scenario running, and drawing of conclusions.

The model was rated highest on "generality"—that is, the model could be applied to other systems. "Realism"—that is, the degree of structure mimics the real world and the output is realistic—scored lower but above neutral. As expected, the model scored below neutral on "precision"—that is, the ability of the model to predict the outcomes accurately.

The human interactions (communication) were considered to be pleasant, and the discussions during the meetings were constructive. The problem was discussed in an open fashion. The meetings were considered well worth the time of the participants. All would recommend the mediated modeling process to other groups or communities, depending on the situation. Eighty percent of the group would not hesitate to participate in another mediated modeling process if they were invited to one. The remaining 20% would consider the specific situation before making the commitment.

What Has Happened Since 1998 in the Upper Fox GMU?

Before the workshops started, the participants had concerns about meeting with a group whose members might be uncooperative and interested primarily in pursuing narrow agendas, an outcome that would lead to further alienation and waste time. Under a best-case scenario, the participants hoped to establish a common goal, create mutual understanding, and learn something new. After the workshops, most participants used the survey to express their enthusiasm for the mediated modeling approach.

Prompted by the "after" survey, the participants also provided constructive comments for improvement to the mediated modeling process. These comments indicated that some participants would have liked to have spent more time on (1) gathering information as well as on (2) learning how the model could be used to solve problems in the basin by the team members. The group could pursue these topics without the guidance of a mediated modeler, of course. Moreover, none of the fears with which the participants began the process materialized. In fact, many of their hopes for the process were realized, and the mediated modeling process proved to be a productive start of a lasting and expanding collaboration.

Soon after the modeling exercise was finished, DNR personnel demonstrated the model at several public and in-house meetings. This model has also been used in Green Lake County to document the need for riparian buffers. The Green Lake County Land and Conservation Department purchased its own copy of the STELLA software to assist with analysis of this issue and aid in the development of a county conservation plan. Some participants in the mediated modeling process have also used the model as an educational tool when addressing audiences on land use and smart-growth issues. The model is especially useful in demonstrating the interconnectedness of land use issues.

Several initiatives have been undertaken by the GMUP and DNR since 1998 on topics that can be recognized from the list of recommendations in this chapter. For example, the Upper Fox Basin Partner Team has adopted a project aimed at increasing citizen involvement in smart-growth (land use) planning. They are seeking to engage outdoor sports enthusiasts in local planning efforts to represent natural resources at planning meetings. This group of people has traditionally not been actively involved in land use issues, even though poor land use decisions often impact the outdoor sports they enjoy, such as hunting, fishing, and bird watching. They are also targeting local decision makers to help them understand the role of natural resources in their municipalities so as to be more receptive to considering natural resources as the basis for land use decisions.

On the urban side of this effort, the Upper Fox GMUP is partnering with the Urban Open Space Foundation to pilot their green infrastructure program with a few local communities. The green infrastructure approach treats all elements of green/open space as part of a community's infrastructure for trails, storm water management, wetland protection, urban forestry, park space, riparian corridors, and so forth. These landscape elements provide services to communities that have an inherent monetary value. Preserving and maintaining these elements of the landscape are to be considered the same as traditional infrastructure.

College students are involved in studying valuation of natural capital at the scale of several townships. Valuation of natural capital provides an example that could be used with local governments to illustrate the economic value of natural resources in their town(s). Also, the economic valuation of the Lake

Winnebago system fishery and recreational boating is proposed for study. It is believed that the fishery and recreational boating put multiple millions of dollars a year into the local economy, but there are no facts to back that up, as was learned during the mediated modeling exercise. The GMUP believes that if they can demonstrate that the fishery and water quality have a large economic impact on the region, local governments will be more willing to enact strong storm water management and riparian corridor protection ordinances.

At landscape scale, the Oshkosh Area Foundation is coordinating a community-based effort to put large sums of money into wise management and protection of the water resources of the Lake Winnebago system. In addition, the Upper Fox Basin Headwaters Ecosystem Inventory Project was initiated by DNR last year to categorize and prioritize rare and valuable elements of the western Upper Fox basin. This effort stalled out when Wisconsin DNR resources were heavily directed toward containment of the Chronic Wasting Disease, an epidemic affecting the deer herd in Wisconsin.

With respect to water resources, a community-based effort was initiated by DNR to develop a restoration plan for Rush Lake. The plan was developed and adopted by the community, and details for implementation are being worked out. Rush Lake is a 3,000-acre deep-water marsh. The proposed management is to draw the lake down to expose 50% of the lake bottom for a two-year period to restore the vegetative community and to kill carp over the winter through freeze-out.

Wisconsin DNR staff members are engaged with the University of Wisconsin Center for Remote Sensing and the National Aeronautics and Space Administration (NASA) in a research project to correlate multispectral satellite imaging with real-time water quality data. Initial results indicate that satellite images can be used to predict water quality with a high degree of accuracy.

Although it is impossible to trace back the exact impact of the mediated modeling process, it is clear that the Upper Fox GMUP and DNR made considerable progress toward implementation of ecosystem management. The mediated modeling process performed in 1998 provided a positive starting point toward facilitating the collaboration among an essential group of stakeholders in the Upper Fox (the GMUP). Several encouraging initiatives have been developed along the recommendations based on the modeling exercise. However, many hurdles are encountered as well.

DISCUSSION QUESTIONS

1. Is it more important that individuals with expertise on technical subjects or individuals with decision-making power participate in a project such as the Upper Fox?

2. What are the different roles for a preliminary model, and when is a good time to introduce a preliminary model?

3. What are the advantages and disadvantages of the choice of the sectors in the Upper Fox model? Was it appropriate that the group integrated natural capital and ecosystem services in one sector? What are the arguments for separating them into separate sectors?

4. How can the performance of a mediated modeling be measured more effectively?

6

Using Mediated Modeling to Facilitate Collaborative Learning Among Residents of the San Antonio Watershed, Texas, U.S.A.

Tarla Rai Peterson,

Ann Kenimer, and

William E. Grant

The sustainable use of natural resources in urbanizing watersheds of the southwestern United States poses one of the nation's most pressing environmental policy, planning, and management challenges. For many decades, these watersheds were considered unproductive when compared with those in the eastern United States because of the lack of year-round water supply. In the twentieth century, huge water diversion projects, subsidized by the federal and state governments, allowed year-round water for agriculture and community development. These projects fueled the growth of largely rural and natural resource–based economies that were focused on ranching, agriculture, and mining.

During the latter half of the twentieth century, rapid human population growth in major southwestern cities such as San Antonio has transformed these largely rural watersheds into urbanizing watersheds that are increasingly complex as socioenvironmental systems. Currently the region faces a number of unique challenges related to water resources: interdependent urban and rural uses, finite water supply, flood-prone watersheds, loss of riparian habitats, and potential contamination of water supplies. The complexities of the water-related problems that face this region present a challenge for management of complex socioenvironmental systems.

The rapid rate of urbanization in watersheds of the southwestern United States has significant impacts on water quality and water quantity. Flooding, groundwater contamination, and non–point source pollution are just a few of the problems that impact not only cities but also communities located downstream. Traditional management strategies can be inadequate in these situations when they fail to account for the systemic complexity of the environmental issues in watersheds. The scientists, managers, and planners engaged in these issues have therefore become more open to alternative management approaches, including mediated modeling.

This chapter describes how we applied mediated modeling to concerns about Salado and Leon Creeks, which are part of the San Antonio River Basin in Texas. We review the major water resource issues and socioenvironmental conditions, the activities included in our implementation of mediated modeling, and the role of our model in the dynamics of the decision-making process.

Socioenvironmental Complexity in the San Antonio River Basin

The San Antonio River Basin, located in the south-central portion of Texas, covers 4,180 square miles. It traverses at least three eco-regions in Texas: the Central Texas Plateau, the Texas Blackland Prairies, and the Western Gulf Coastal Plain. The basin's headwaters are located northwest of the city of San Antonio, Texas, and the basin extends southeast to the confluence of the San Antonio and Guadalupe Rivers near San Antonio Bay. The San Antonio basin is dominated by urban and industrial development from the city of San Antonio, but agriculture is also a major economic force in the counties through which the basin runs.

Several factors, including non–point source pollution from the urban environment, are contributing to declining water quality in the basin (TNRCC 1996, 1997, 1999). Segments of this watershed are unsafe for humans or wildlife owing to elevated concentrations of toxic metals, fecal coliform bacteria, and nutrients. These pollutants are believed to derive from urban non–point source runoff (TNRCC 1996, 1997). Water quality in these river reaches must be restored by 2003 under the Statewide Basin Management Schedule of the Texas Natural Resource Conservation Commission (TNRCC) (TNRCC 1997). Rehabilitation of the water bodies is required under the Environmental Protection Agency's total maximum daily load (TMDL) strategy for watershed restoration

The San Antonio River watershed typifies several natural resource management concerns that are becoming pervasive throughout the American Southwest. For example, human population growth has a serious impact on quality and quantity of freshwater resources. San Antonio is the only major city in the Southern Edwards Aquifer region of Texas, where the ratio of agricultural to municipal water use was 50:40 in 1990, but by 2030 is predicted to change to 30:60. Declining levels of aquifers, increased nutrient and contaminant loading of streams, decreasing freshwater inflow to estuaries, loss of endemic species, and invasion of exotic species represent human-induced ecological problems with serious socioeconomic repercussions. In 1997, municipal water use accounted for 71% of water used in the San Antonio River Basin (Texas Water Development Board 1997).

San Antonio exemplifies of a new form of American urbanism, typical of the Sunbelt (Fink 1993). Postwar public policy influenced the growth patterns of these cities by providing funding for new highways and tax incentives for single-family-home ownership (Fink 1993). Consumption of land increased and population density decreased as the single-family home and suburbia became the benchmark for success (Garreau 1991). The San Antonio River watershed has been impacted by the rapid growth of the postwar years. However, public policy has not typically emphasized the importance of urbanization on water resources.

The Clean Water Action Plan of the Environmental Protection Agency (EPA 1998) represents one of the most important benchmarks in the recognition of this environmental problem. In addition, the EPA has developed indices of condition and vulnerability for all watersheds in the United States. These indices provided a framework for involving the public in decisions regarding restoration of the San Antonio River watershed. The San Antonio River watershed has a moderate EPA indicator rating, which identifies moderately serious water problems with low vulnerability.

The sources of problems in this urban watershed are complex, and rehabilitation will require a significant effort from stakeholders in the area. The area's socioeconomic heterogeneity presents significant complications. Agriculture, which has anchored the county's economy for over a century, no longer provides sufficient focus for adequate management of the watershed. Rather, the region's economy has become increasingly diverse over the past decade. Recent estimates indicate that, although trade, government, and services provide most employment opportunities, construction, manufacturing, utilities, mining, and agriculture also contribute to the county's economy.

In addition to its economic diversity, the watershed's human population is ethnically diverse. According to recent state counts, Bexar County, through which the San Antonio River runs, was 53.9% Hispanic, 37.5% Anglo, and 6.6% Black in 1995. The fastest-growing segment of the population was located in the "Other" category and was made up primarily of Asians (Rylander 1997). Census data from 2000 indicate a demographic profile of 54.3% Hispanic, 35.6% Anglo, 7.2% Black, and 1.6% Asian (U.S. Census 2000). This watershed, therefore, represents the kind of mix of cultural groups and economic interests that tends to characterize urban areas.

Top-down autocratic resource management methods have not proven effective in protecting the San Antonio River Basin. Our research team thought that involving stakeholders in the development of a process model of the watershed could provide a high-quality public participation opportunity that would enable more effective watershed restoration by incorporating the perspectives and interests of diverse stakeholders. Upon consultation with the Texas Natural Resource Conservation Commission (TNRCC) and the San Antonio River Authority (SARA), we decided to work with stakeholders in the Leon and Salado Creek subwatersheds. Both creeks have segments that failed to meet their designated use criteria under the Clean Water Act (CWA) because of low dissolved oxygen and high fecal coliform bacteria and thus were listed by the TNRCC as noncompliant as required under the Clean Water Act (subsection 303[d]).

When the mediated modeling process began, the TNRCC was in the process of designating SARA as the party responsible for developing a total maximum daily load (TMDL) for Salado Creek. The TMDL process for Leon Creek was slated to begin soon thereafter. Because our interest in mediated modeling complemented the SARA's need to include a public participation component in the TMDL process for Salado Creek, we decided to work together.

Recruitment of Participants

Because one of the goals of our research team was to develop a group of participants that brought together the diversity among human residents of these watersheds, recruitment was a major aspect of the project. We needed people who were willing to make a year-long commitment to active participation in watershed restoration efforts. We needed to include research scientists, agency personnel, business people, and citizen groups. Because city officials assured us of their commitment to a variety of restoration opportunities for the creeks that transcended the TMDL process, and because of technical and political uncertainties associated with the TMDL process, it was important to identify the groups with their respective creeks but to avoid limiting them to the TMDL process. After consulting with personnel from the SARA, we named the groups the Leon Creek Restoration Council (LCRC) and the Salado Creek Restoration Council (SCRC).

We adopted two perspectives that are essential to understanding the recruitment of citizen stakeholders. First, we held the view that all who participate in a particular "cultural domain" are "experts" in that domain (Lindlof 1995). This perspective allowed us to be highly inclusive; virtually anyone whose life experiences included the Leon Creek watershed and/or the Salado Creek watershed was seen as a potential stakeholder. With attention to the geographical character of the two watersheds, we recruited council members from all segments of the watershed. We began by generating a list of relevant community groups and organizations. We then asked city officials and agency personnel to identify organizations and leaders with an interest in watershed management issues. We contacted community gatekeepers (Lindlof 1995) for further recommendations, and we conducted scores of personal interviews with potential participants.

Our recruitment strategy involved showing community gatekeepers that getting involved was consistent with their other commitments, such as service to the neighborhood association (O'Keefe 1990). Several individuals decided that participation in the councils would enable them to report important information back to their groups. Others, who felt they did not have time to serve on yet another committee, provided us with additional referrals.

Lindlof (1995) claims that when researchers need full participation, rather than research subjects, they negotiate access primarily as a matter of goodwill and intrinsic rewards. We were able to assure recruits that their input was important and meaningful. One purpose of our preliminary interviews was to demonstrate to potential participants that relevant management agencies valued citizen input and were prepared to act on it. Some council members had originally planned to attend only one meeting, but once they saw so many other committed people, they decided to continue participating.

We also wanted our councils to differ from most public participation venues by representing the variety of demographic categories—including race, age, sex, socioeconomic status, and education—that exist in this region. Table 6.1 reveals a general picture of the similarities and differences in demographic attributes between our stakeholder councils and the Bexar County population. For comparison purposes, the second column contains demographic data from the 1990 census. The third column presents comparable values for the Salado Creek Restoration Council (N = 60). The fourth column presents values for the Leon Creek Restoration Council (N = 35).

In respect to the general Bexar County population, council participants were older, had higher incomes, and were much more likely to have some graduate education. Women were underrepresented relative to men. Anglos were overrepresented in both councils; Afro-Americans were overrepresented in the Salado Council; Latino participants were underrepresented in both councils.

Although it was essential that we drew from active community organizations, a problem with this approach is that traditionally underrepresented groups remain underrepresented. It became apparent early on that we had primarily tapped into two groups of people. One group was composed of middle-aged, middle-class citizens, mostly Anglo, who were active in local government and community functions. A second group was composed of retirees committed to making their communities better places to live. This second group was much more racially diverse than the first. Another characteristic of the councils was that at approximately one-quarter of those attending any given ses-

Table 6.1.

Comparison of demographic attributes for Bexar County versus
Salado Creek and Leon Creek Restoration Councils

Demographic Characteristic	Bexar County 1990 Census	Salada Creek Restoration Council (N = 60)	Leon Creek Restoration Council (N = 35)
% Female	51.4%	41.75%	42.95%
Median Age	35–39 years	48 years	51 years
Median Income	$25,000–$29,000	$60,000–$69,000	$60,000–$69,000
% HS Graduate	72.5%	5.0%	3.0%
% Some College / College Graduate	41.1%	45.0%	42.4%
% Some Graduate / Master's / Doctorate	5.9%	46.7%	54.5%
% Afro-American	4.7%	20.7%	0.0%
% Anglo	49.7%	67.2%	78.1%
% Latino	33.0%	6.9%	3.1%

sion were technical experts representing agencies that were responsible for San Antonio water policy. These participants were more likely to have graduate education and were more likely to be male.

One of the racial differences can be explained by historic patterns of settlement in San Antonio. Salado Creek traverses several large communities that were traditionally Afro-American. Recruitment efforts in these communities were successful. We were not, however, successful in our attempts to recruit from the Latino population, where we encountered considerable resistance, including fear of participating in a process that involved local government officials. In this case, our success at obtaining involvement of agencies that were needed to institutionalize the groups' efforts discouraged one segment of the population from participating.

Attendance and Participation

There was a total of 35 participants in the LCRC and 60 participants in the SCRC. Approximately 20 (LCRC) or 35 (SCRC) stakeholders attended each meeting for the two watershed groups. The individual participants varied each month, with approximately 10 (LCRC) or 20 (SCRC) providing the long-term core group. Other participants circulated in and out of the meetings, depending on other commitments. Some members developed an informal alternate system that allowed them to ensure that their organization was represented even when the usual participant was unable to attend. Approximately 15 participants from the LCRC and 20 participants from the SCRC attended three or fewer meetings.

Those who attended irregularly were not excluded from any activities. For example, if they happened to attend a meeting that focused on model development, other participants invited their input and provided peer training as needed. Although unstable participation posed challenges, it was something we had expected and was one reason we had chosen the collaborative learning approach, with its emphasis on continual learning.

Given our goal of increasing the diversity among participants in local governance, we were pleased to have members for whom such processes were novel. We also had members who did not usually participate in local governance because personal responsibilities and economic necessity rarely allowed them to take time away from work. Still others were only able to attend if they were willing to ask someone to provide them with transportation. We addressed some of these issues by alternating each council's meeting schedule between Fridays and Saturdays. Agency representatives who were assigned to the councils generally preferred to meet on Fridays, while citizens who were not attending as part of their employment generally preferred to meet on Saturdays.

Although flexible scheduling enabled us to slightly stabilize participation, we were not able to avoid irregular attendance. Some stakeholders took the responsibility of requesting information when they missed meetings. Because we always provided individual notes to go with formal presentations, it was not difficult to mail this information to any member who requested it. Those who took the time to examine the information sometimes brought it with them to the next meeting, marked with questions. They then used the coffee breaks and other opportunities to ask questions of other stakeholders or research team members.

Participants maintained contact with each other between meetings and, in lieu of missed meetings, by a group e-mail list. We began the group e-mail list at the request of the members. During the second meeting, some members asked for the agenda of the third meeting. Although we were able to present a rough approximation by reviewing the feedback of the current workshop, the research team wanted to gain a better understanding of this request in order to respond more completely. During the third meeting we discussed this concern and found that, while most members simply wanted to look over the final agenda as a means of preparing for each workshop, others wanted to participate in the iterative process of agenda construction.

Since the method of contact preferred by most of the members was e-mail, we suggested that a council e-mail list would provide a simple medium for exchanging this evolving information between workshops. The membership of both councils enthusiastically used this communication tool throughout the course of the project. The approach worked for all but two active members (those who attended 50% or more of the workshops) in the LCRC and for all but three in the SCRC. Other council members took the responsibility of passing the information to these members, either by telephone or by letter. The simulation model was piloted in October 2000, with 25 (Leon) and 30 (Salado) stakeholders participating.

Level of Conflict

The level of conflict among participants was at least moderately high. In the Salado Creek watershed, conflict was acutely escalated because of a severe flood that had occurred just prior to the beginning of our meetings. Some participants' homes had been damaged, and whole neighborhoods had been destroyed. Although managing the animosity between residents who had been flooded, or who identified with those who had, and representatives of agencies they considered responsible for the flood damage was challenging, it also presented opportunities to encourage systems thinking and discussion. For example, flood victims blamed their losses on management policies that had been implemented upstream from their neighborhoods. They demanded that future upstream policies be scrutinized for possible unforeseen consequences downstream.

These demands provided an ideal opening for discussion of the complexity involved in understanding and managing the watershed. LCRC members lacked the personal experience that dramatized the links between watershed segments. Although their initial discussions were easier to facilitate, it also was more difficult to facilitate the move from discussion of individual interests to systemwide concerns. In both watersheds, management changes were imminent, and stakeholders had strong, conflicting preferences regarding these changes. The complexity associated with the conflicting perspectives regarding how best to manage Leon and Salado Creeks led us to seek an approach that emphasized learning within a systems perspective.

Collaborative Learning

Given our goals to involve a diverse group of stakeholders in development of a process model for watershed management, collaborative learning (CL), which is described in Chapter 2, provided an appropriate conceptual foundation. The CL meetings moved stakeholders through four layers of application. We designed workshops to enable stakeholders to develop and use quantitative systems simulation models, working from engagement in conceptual model formulation (the first phase identified by Grant) through model use (the final phase identified by Grant). Each new meeting incorporated information, activities, and communication processes that had been developed during previous meetings.

In the first layer of application, participants were informed about the CL process and received training in systemic thinking and collaborative discussion.

In the second layer, technical experts, panel question/answer sessions, and informal small-group discussions created a common knowledge base on the major issues affecting the watershed for participants via formal presentations. Participants began to generate specific suggestions for improvement of the current situation.

In the third layer, a series of active learning exercises helped participants to think systemically about the watershed ecosystem and enabled them to identify key issues, concerns, and interrelationships between variables affecting water quality. Participants were encouraged to refine their ideas by sharing them with other participants through structured activities that offered opportunities to articulate ideas within a modeling framework.

In the fourth layer of application, through collaborative debate with other stakeholders, a final system of improvement suggestions was organized, discussed, and refined. These suggestions were unified around flooding, which emerged as the central concern for both groups.

Although we have labeled the preceding layers of application numerically for ease of explanation, the description of specific group activities below should demonstrate that the process did not occur in such a linear manner, but iteratively.

When CL operates as it should, all participants (including scientists and technicians, decision makers and residents) become stakeholders who learn from each other. In the beginning of the relationship, the technical experts tend to act as teachers; but as all stakeholders become better informed and gain confidence in their understanding of new perspectives, the roles of teacher and student become blurred.

One example of mutual learning occurred at the end of a formal presentation in the twelfth meeting of the LCRC. The LCRC members, who had by this time conceptualized, evaluated, and used a simple model of the flow in Leon Creek, listened attentively as an aquatic ecologist presented some rather complicated results that compared observed and modeled responses of fish-performance bioassays. The ecologist used a simple simulation model to interpret the significance of his results. Stakeholders began to interrupt (which they had been encouraged to do) with questions. They were familiar with STELLA, the program the ecologist had used to develop his simulation model, and they suggested an alternative interpretation for some of his results.

The questions and related discussion caused the ecologist to reevaluate his previous interpretations. He offered to try some additional model simulations that more directly responded to the issues raised by council members. When they responded affirmatively to his offer, he constructed these alternative simulations on the spot. As he worked, he continued to project the visual image from the computer onto the large screen, explaining each step and requesting continual feedback. In this way, both the research team and members of the LCRC developed an increasingly sophisticated sense of the simulation model's capacity and significance within the watershed. Subsequently, the results from the new simulation were incorporated into later presentations, including the final report prepared for the EPA.

Thirteen CL meetings were held over a period of fourteen months, from November 1999 until December 2000. When participants first began attending meetings, each had a specific point from which they identified with the watershed. As the process unfolded over time, individual identities became enmeshed in the system represented by the entire group, which was mutually shaped by all participants. Responses of those who developed strong systemic identity through their participation indicate that, while this more systemic perspective did not minimize individual interests, it enabled members to position themselves more productively in relationship with the identities of other members.

Modeling Approaches

Within the CL framework, stakeholders participated in two sets of formal modeling exercises. Stakeholder involvement in model development varied from low for one set of exercises to moderate for the other. The first set of exercises used BASINS-HSPF, a complex, comprehensive watershed model. Although stakeholders contributed ideas to the modeling experts, stakeholder involvement in model development was minimal.

Example of a Modeling Exercise with
Low Stakeholder Involvement (BASINS-HSPF)

Geographic data was compiled from a variety of sources (USGS, TNRCC, EPA, NASA) to develop input data files for BASINS-HSPF. The San Antonio River Authority (SARA) and the Texas Natural Resource Conservation Commission (TNRCC) collaborated with modelers from the research team to calibrate BASINS-HSPF in Salado and Leon Creeks.

We introduced BASINS-HSPF and demonstrated its use to stakeholders during the third meeting. Stakeholders spent portions of the sixth and seventh meetings working in small groups to identify particularly important watershed changes, characteristics, or features affecting hydrologic response. We asked stakeholders to focus on aspects of the watersheds they considered to be most important, then identify and explain how those aspects related to each other. After they had identified critical components, flows, and relationships, they elicited mental models of the watershed.

Stakeholders were asked to graphically represent their watersheds, creating "situation maps" (Daniels and Walker, pp. 186–187), which they explained to modeling experts on the research team. Modelers developed scenarios from the situation maps and then incorporated them into BASINS-HSPF to suggest possible management alternatives, which they shared with stakeholders at the ninth meeting.

While BASINS-HSPF allowed detailed description of watershed management scenarios, the high level of model complexity prohibited hands-on use of the model. Participants reported frustration with activities associated with the BASINS-HSPF model. They stated that, although the exercises to assist them in determining what scenarios they asked modelers to run were useful in conceptualizing the watershed as a system, the presentation of those scenarios within the model framework was not helpful. The complexity of the model, combined with the fact that it was a preexisting model designed for purposes that were not clear to participants, and that the modelers were not able to explain how the information put into the model translated into final results, led to dissatisfaction among participants.

Example of a Modeling Exercise with More Stakeholder Involvement (Flow Model)

The second set of modeling exercises involved hands-on stakeholder development and use of a rudimentary, user-friendly watershed model that focused on flow. This simple watershed model was developed for the purpose of facilitating group learning among stakeholders and to enable them to share their learning with other interested parties. We developed the model in STELLA because of its relative user-friendliness. The simple watershed model allowed only two or three possible conditions for a select set of watershed characteristics. Stakeholders decided what aspect of the watershed they wanted to model, selected relevant watershed characteristics and conditions, identified stocks and flows, ran the model firsthand, and had opportunities to refine it. Thus stakeholders were able to observe changes in watershed runoff in response to watershed characteristics of their choice.

From their previous experience (both within this context and from nonrelated experiences), several participants were initially skeptical about the second approach to modeling. As they actually began to develop their own model, however, they became enthusiastic. Stakeholders claimed that the process of developing and refining a simulation model centered on flooding helped them to understand how flooding fit into the entire watershed, which enabled them to refine previously generated suggestions for watershed management. They also were pleased to have produced a tool they could use to share this understanding with others.

For example, both watershed councils were scheduled to provide the mayor with a set of recommendations for watershed management. By the conclusion of the meetings during which they piloted their flow models, they determined that they would use their models in that presentation. They planned to use some of the scenarios they found most interesting and relevant to help the mayor understand the significance of their recommendations regarding management of flow in the watersheds. Some participants also asked permission to use the model in their individual activities, which ranged from teaching an environmental ethics course to managing an online public education program to facilitating an agency's interaction with the public.

We now turn to a more detailed account of how stakeholders developed and used their own watershed models.

Mediated Modeling as a Learning Tool

We used mediated modeling to encourage more systemic understanding of the Leon and Salado Creek watersheds. Grant (1986) and Grant et al. (1997) have identified four fundamental phases in the process of developing and using a quantitative systems simulation model:

1. Conceptual model formulation
2. Quantitative model specification
3. Model evaluation
4. Model use

We spent the most time in the first phase, an emphasis that grew out of the need to ensure that our stakeholders had an opportunity to establish a common understanding of systems thinking, the modeling process, and the particular watershed prior to developing a model. The goal of this phase is to develop a conceptual, or qualitative, model of the system of interest. Using the objectives of the project as a basis, all participants worked together to decide which components in the real world should be included in our system of interest and how they should be related to one another.

The goal of the second phase is to develop a quantitative model of the system of interest. This involved translating our conceptual model, which was represented diagrammatically and linguistically, into a series of mathematical equations that collectively formed the quantitative model. This translation, or quantification, was based on consideration of various types of information about the real system, including theoretical concepts, empirical data, and expert opinion. The modelers performed this translation during the time between stakeholder meetings and then brought the results to the stakeholders for evaluation of the usefulness of the model in meeting their objectives (phase 3).

The fourth and final phase involved designing and simulating the experiments with the model that we would have liked to conduct in the real system.

During this phase, participants tried out different combinations of land use, channel condition, and rainfall to answer questions about how best to manage peak flows through the watersheds.

Tarla Rai Peterson, coauthor of this chapter, coordinated participant recruitment, facilitated workshops, and guided conceptual model formulation. Coauthor Ann Kenimer attended most of the workshops and made technical presentations regarding watershed systems and modeling. Kenimer and coauthor William E. Grant quantified the conceptual model and guided participants through model evaluation and use. We worked with other research team members for six months before stakeholder meetings began, as well as throughout the year of stakeholder meetings, to ensure appropriate delivery of information participants deemed important to their modeling effort.

We now offer a detailed description of how we moved through these phases.

Conceptual Model Formulation

The formulation of the conceptual model is very important and took up the bulk of the 14 months allotted for this project. Several activities took place before computer models were used.

GOAL OF THE MODEL

The primary goal for these models and associated exercises was learning. Both the limited participation in working with the complex watershed model and the more complete participation in developing and working with the simulation model were used primarily to enable participants to understand the impact of watershed management on hydrologic response, and to provide them with a tool to use when sharing that understanding with others. Although this goal was not achieved through the BASINS modeling exercise, it was achieved through the development and use of the flow model.

Working within the framework provided by their simulation model, the stakeholder groups developed specific recommendations for watershed restoration. Both groups used learning achieved through various workshop activities to develop and manipulate a model that allowed them to work through how their action plans could be implemented on the ground in their respective areas of the watershed. For example, because they determined that flooding was the most important issue to them, they developed a simulation model to help them understand and communicate how different intensities of land use would interact with various channel conditions and retention structures to impact the watershed's flooding regime.

SYSTEMS THINKING AND WATERSHED BASICS

Council participants agreed to attend workshops to be held on a monthly basis, for approximately one year. The first workshops were held in November 1999, and the final meetings were held in December 2000. These restoration councils convened for over forty hours during the course of a year. Participants also formed subgroups that met independently to discuss issues they did not think were adequately covered in the workshops. Following the final workshop, members from each council organized a full-day field trip that enabled members to visit sites the council had determined most important to future management of the watershed. Organizers for the Salado Creek field trip invited a newspaper reporter, who then used his article describing the field trip to begin a newspaper series about the creek. Some research team members attended every workshop, but they did not attend subgroup meetings. Peterson attended the field trips.

Although we completed basic curriculum design for the process before meetings commenced, specific content was not predetermined. Decisions regarding specific information and issues to be discussed were made by the stakeholders themselves. Because collaborative learning, which provided the conceptual grounding for our process, is grounded in systems thinking, we devoted the first workshop to this concept. We presented basic systems theory information, offered technical information on watersheds as systems, and demonstrated CL grounding in systems thinking. Members participated in exercises designed to clarify these ideas and began to identify the important relationships within their watersheds. We invited participants to comment on the systems approach, to suggest approaches and strategies for conducting the workshops, to identify questions that were essential to answer if they were to understand their watersheds as systems, and to identify additional stakeholders who needed to participate.

We also presented the councils with a highly generalized goal statement that was conducive to the public participation needs of the TMDL being conducted by the SARA (see Box 6.1).

We informed participants that the first goal—to develop a set of technically sound and socially legitimate recommendations for restoration of the entire Salado/Leon Creek watershed system—which had been shaped by the needs of the TMDL process currently underway on Salado Creek and expected for Leon Creek, would remain an objective of the group. We invited them to alter any other aspect of this statement as they desired. The consensus of the group, which included San Antonio's mayor and representatives of several agencies responsible for management of these watersheds, was to work with the goal statement, developing additional components as the group deemed appropriate.

We used feedback obtained in the initial workshop to guide continued

> **Box 6.1**
> Preliminary goals statement, San Antonio watershed
>
> ---
>
> 1. Develop a set of technically sound and socially legitimate recommendations for restoration of the entire Salado/Leon Creek watershed system.
> 2. Present the recommendation set to the appropriate city and state agencies.
>
> In order to achieve the above:
> - Develop a common knowledge base, focused on the Salado Creek watershed system (SCWS).
> - Integrate knowledge gained from multiple sources (e.g., local experience, social science research, physical science research).
> - Provide opportunities for local experience to guide further social and physical science research.
> - Incorporate the resulting systemic understanding of the SCWS into a recommendation set.

recruitment efforts and to prepare for the next workshop. At the second workshop, a research team member presented research strategies that could be used to answer the questions and clarify issues council members had raised at the first meeting. Another research team member presented technical information regarding water quality in the respective creeks (which had been requested at the first meeting). A third research team member showed how this information fit into a model of a watershed system. Members were asked to determine what information they needed to understand their watersheds sufficiently well to provide useful input to the TMDL process and to develop more extensive recommendations for future management. Throughout the year-long process, the iterative process described above determined the content for individual workshops.

ACTIVITIES

Over the fourteen-month period of meetings, we designed a variety of activities to encourage the development of systemic understanding of the watersheds. Stakeholders used these exercises to determine what material and information flows that were most critical to include in a model of their watersheds. Highlights from some of these activities illustrate a sense of the watershed as a system emerged.

At the beginning of the first council meeting, facilitators wound a length of blue fabric across the floor of the meeting room. We asked members to imagine that the fabric was their creek and to position themselves at an appropriate point along its banks. Members came forward tentatively and, by using the locator markings on the fabric (e.g., for parks, schools, and points where major highways crossed the creek), chose a position. Facilitators gave each member a lunch bag filled with objects from the creek, then pulled an empty red wagon to the farthest upstream point. They offered the handle of the wagon to the person standing farthest upstream and invited him to introduce himself, dump the contents of his lunch sack into the wagon, and then pass the wagon to the person directly downstream.

Each member followed this procedure. As the wagon filled up with objects ranging from leaves and twigs to chunks of old tires, it began to overflow and once tipped over, spilling its contents all over one stakeholder's "property." Introductions were punctuated by laughter, shouts, and groans, depending on what happened with the wagon and its contents.

The following sampling of the self-introductions by SCRC members indicates the diverse identities of group members (names have been changed to protect confidentiality), as well as the participants' tendency to think only of one aspect of the watershed.

- Because he had positioned himself at the uppermost point along the creek, Calvin was the first participant to introduce himself. He began: "I'm with the San Antonio Water System, and I didn't really know where to stand along the creek. I'm actually concerned with all the water quality along Salado Creek. My department is concerned, obviously, with water quality. We don't really care where we go; if it's dirty we help clean it up." Calvin illustrates the attitude shared by most agency participants. Although they did not identify with a particular location along the creek, they identified strongly with the aspect of the creek for which they held technical responsibility.
- Ramona, who lived near the creek and was interested in the aesthetic quality of the city, said: "I am seriously, anxiously, interested in seeing this creek reach the beautification that I know it can. It can be beautified."
- Hank, a farmer whose family members have lived on the creek since they immigrated from Italy in the 1890s, told participants, "We live up the road there on the ———— Farm. It's our livelihood. We farm there, a family farm. We are concerned about the quantity and quality of the water so we can keep the crops growing."
- Madeline, a science teacher, was "concerned about upstream development, non–point source pollution, and about truly educating our children about the tremendous value of the creek." She compared the creek to "an emerald necklace" and said she was participating because she wanted "to preserve the treasure."

- Daniel, a retired military officer, spoke about his concern with flooding: "I'm with the ———— Home Owners Improvement Association. . . . When Salado Creek flooded it came right into my house, and so I'm definitely interested in what slows down Salado Creek, and I am hoping that it won't happen again."

These individuals represent the primary motives that brought people to council meetings. People came because they had professional responsibility for the creek, wanted the creek to enhance San Antonio's aesthetic appeal and recreation opportunities, wanted to use the creek's economic potential, wanted to restore ecological integrity to the watershed, or wanted to prevent damage caused by flooding. In addition to having one of these interests, several participants also claimed a personal connection to the creek.

Following the self-introductions, the mayor expressed his enthusiastic support for the council's work and his hope that it would become a positive force for change in how the city managed creeks. Referring to the exercise, he encouraged members to think systemically about the watershed, including concerns from all reaches of the watershed in their recommendations. When the mayor told them about a political initiative he was developing that could fund some of their recommendations for creek restoration, Daniel immediately raised his hand and requested that the funds be spent to clean out the creek bed immediately upstream of, and throughout, his neighborhood. He asked that all brush and trees be removed from the creek banks, and that the creek bed be lined with concrete. The mayor responded by saying that he hoped Daniel would think about the entire watershed and would consider the needs of other council members before deciding on such a drastic course. Daniel just shook his head in frustration at this answer.

These stakeholders had not previously imagined the possibility that concerns so diverse as theirs could form any unifying motive to act. As they developed a more systemic understanding of the watershed, however, unifying motives emerged. They eventually developed a simulation model that centered on the alternative flooding possibilities associated with different channel conditions and land development patterns. They used this model internally to help refine a set of recommendations for improving their watersheds and externally to help explain the logic of that recommendation set to city officials.

Meetings generally followed a format that began with the introduction of new information stakeholders had requested. Members then broke into small groups in which they discussed how this information could be applied to improving the current situation. Finally, all groups reported back, and facilitators led a plenary discussion. At first, individuals simply reiterated their own interests, often failing to respond to information presented by other stakeholders. Our facilitation approach in these discussions was grounded in collaborative learning's emphases on mutual learning and systemic thinking.

Most of the time we allowed stakeholders to express themselves, even when the extent of their remarks threatened the accomplishment of the meeting's predetermined goals. So long as other participants appeared relatively attentive to someone's statement, we did not cut it off. We focused, rather, on guiding participants toward discussion of how individual interests and claims complemented each other and how together they defined the watershed.

Over time, participants developed an increasing desire and competence to engage in systemically grounded environmental management decisions as they began to integrate their own needs into what they perceived to be the needs of fellow council members. At the eighth meeting, subgroups were attempting to use their situation maps to develop the essential elements for building a model of the watershed, and for determining the recommendation set they would ultimately present. One subgroup, including members representing all the interests mentioned during the first meeting, reported its discussion as follows:

> Well, we wanted to protect the ecology and water quality. We felt like work needed to be done in this area that was flooded, that we have to consider protection of property and life, and that would be the driving force in that area. And what we would say is that would be the driving force, but also keep in mind protecting ecology, protecting water quality, and protecting wildlife in the area. And at the same time develop recreation facilities to serve people in that area and also all citizens so that the whole city would benefit, which would encourage spending money on the creeks.
>
> So that is what we were looking at, that protection of life and property would be in the forefront, but flooding improvements should be done in such a way to protect the wildlife and also provide recreation opportunities and other economic opportunities.

Participants were beginning to use their situation maps to specify what they wanted to model, how the components of their model related to each other, and what they hoped to learn from their model. As mentioned above, some aspects of these situation maps were incorporated into a version of BASINS-HSPF. More importantly, the map provided the basis for developing a new model that responded directly to stakeholder concerns. From this point, council members spent an increasing portion of each meeting developing and refining a simulation model that would enable them to explain the recommendations they would present to the city as a unified system for improvement. They also began discussing how to encourage implementation and enforcement of their recommendations.

Ironically, the SCRC's hard work was nearly derailed after council members assisted in obtaining sufficient electoral support for a sales tax that would provide additional funds for watershed restoration. Both councils had set aside most of their tenth meeting to make final decisions regarding the structure and components of the simulation model they would use to present their recommendations to the mayor. Extensive publicity of the new funding drew the attention of many new stakeholders along Salado Creek, and attendance more than doubled. Participants who had developed a systemic understanding of the watershed through a year of intense learning activities glanced uncomfortably at each other as new attendees vented, making such statements as:

> I know what I own and ain't no one gonna mess with it. I turned 88 last month, and I'm gonna be out there another 50 years cause Genesis 6 and 3 gives me 120 years. On top of that, you don't want to deal with my relatives. I got fifty kids. I had five, and they went out and brought home five. And that gives me ten. They gave me twenty grandkids, and they gave me twenty great-grandkids. And I got a man sitting here that is the grandfather of two of my great-grandkids. So you don't want to deal with them.
>
> You better deal with my wife of fifty-seven years and me on buying that water rights and buying that land, because other people won that land up and down that Salado and you ain't just gonna walk in and say we're gonna take it. Because a lot of them are meaner than me, and I'm as mean as a junkyard dog.

Because we had essentially turned management of the group over to local participants, we did not intervene. After listening to similar inflammatory comments for approximately thirty minutes, Cathy, one of the seasoned participants, attempted to redirect the conversation. Others, who recognized that the behaviors of the new members were threatening the attributed consensus regarding how to improve the watershed, as well as how to behave as a council member, soon joined her. They had developed these informal norms through months of difficult interaction and were not prepared to give them up lightly.

Cathy started by explaining the collaborative learning process they were using. She added that the facilitators "are here to help us make our own decisions about the creek, not to tell us what to do." She then introduced a group of people designated as "the nominating committee" (made up of participants who, at the request of the entire group, had spent the past two months developing a slate of nominees who were willing to serve as officers in a continuing council).

At Cathy's request, Hank, John, Janet, and Tina each delivered extemporaneous remarks about the work the council had done and its future direction. Janet summarized the concerns of council members when she explained, "We are concerned that we need a place at the table to spend this money. We are concerned that people will come out from under rocks to spend the money on things we don't want. We need to protect the trees. We need to help people, and we need safety and protection. We need to institutionalize ourselves."

Janet's presentation reminded everyone in the room that most council members had reconceptualized the watershed as a system, within which multiple entities held legitimate interests, and that they had worked hard to develop this understanding. It was not something to give up lightly.

Following the nominating committee's remarks, Cathy took charge of the meeting. Each time a new member attempted to return the conversation to a single interest at the expense of the more systemic perspective, she turned to an experienced member to help move the discussion back to the goal of watershed improvement.

At the next meeting, when participants piloted their simulation model, the attendance pattern changed again. The seasoned participants returned along with less than one-quarter of the new attendees. The new attendees, for whom this was only a second meeting, began accepting behavioral norms established over the past year. Each of them worked in a small group with two or three seasoned veterans who had conceptualized the simulation model they were evaluating. When the group broke for lunch, they joined in planning an upcoming field trip designed to further enhance understanding of the entire watershed.

Quantitative Model Specification

Beginning with the situation maps they had elicited, participants described their respective watersheds (Leon and Salado Creeks) by means of a series of subwatersheds and stream segments. Using information that had been presented during previous workshops, they determined that all stream segments received runoff from two subwatersheds, one located adjacent to each bank. The uppermost stream segment also received runoff from a headwater subwatershed.

Modelers worked with small groups (five to six persons) to identify critical user input requirements for modeling the subwatersheds. They decided to include precipitation depth, land use and soil type, and subwatershed area. Input requirements for the stream segments included channel roughness, channel width, segment length, and channel slope. They decided, in the interests of simplicity, to limit the model's predictive function to watershed runoff for individual storms.

Modelers were then asked to quantify the model. Data for this step were drawn from presentations that had been made in the council meetings. When additional data were required, modelers worked with council members to determine appropriate sources for these data. Kenimer and Grant quantified the model in between the tenth and eleventh workshops.

SUBWATERSHED RUNOFF PREDICTION

The SCS curve number method was used to estimate runoff from each subwatershed. This empirical procedure predicts runoff volume based on precipitation depth, land use, and soil type. The relationship takes the form (Haan et al. 1994):

$$q = \frac{(ppt - 0.2S)^2}{ppt + 0.8S}, \ ppt > 0.2S$$

$$q = 0, \ ppt \le 0.2S$$

where:

$$S = \frac{(25400)^2}{curve} - 254$$

and

q   = runoff depth, mm over the watershed
ppt   = precipitation depth, mm
S   = maximum soil water retention parameter, mm
curve = runoff curve number, unitless

Curve number values were selected from literature based on land use and soil type. Typical curve number values are widely available for common land uses and can be averaged on an area-weighted basis for watersheds with multiple land uses and/or soil types. The predicted runoff depth (q) can be multiplied by the area of the subwatershed (area) to yield a runoff volume (vol).

The curve number approach does not yield a flow hydrograph, nor does it predict peak runoff rates. Hence it has some limitations for prediction of peak flood elevations. In addition, it is not well suited for describing non–point source pollution processes, including erosion and sediment transport and fate and transport of other pollutants. However, it does provide reliable estimates of runoff volume and has been validated over many years of use, so it was selected for use in the simple watershed model.

FLOW ROUTING

Manning's equation was used to route flow through the channel system. This equation takes the form (Haan et al. 1994):

$$flow = \frac{1}{rough} depth^{5/3} slope^{1/2} width$$

where:

flow   = flow rate, m³/s
rough = Manning's roughness coefficient, unitless

depth = flow depth, m
slope = hydraulic gradient (assumed to be channel slope), m/m
width = channel width, m

Estimation of flow cross-sectional area necessitated prediction of flow depth. For this purpose, channel segments were assumed to be straight with a rectangular channel shape. Flow depth was estimated by dividing the water volume in the channel segment by the segment length and width. Further, the channel was assumed to be wide and shallow, thereby facilitating the substitution of flow depth for hydraulic radius. Predicted flow rates were multiplied by the simulation time step to determine the volume of flow exiting the channel segment.

Model Evaluation

Participants piloted their model during the eleventh meeting, which was facilitated by Grant and Kenimer. We loaded the model onto several laptops so council members could run the simulations they found most interesting and even alter basic constructs if they desired to do so.

The model provided several features beneficial for use as a stakeholder education tool. First, watershed management options were presented to the stakeholders by means of an easily understandable user interface (see Figure 6.1). The stakeholders identified model input parameters based on the different land uses (development patterns), retention structures, and channel conditions they had previously determined were possible. Kenimer and Grant had used these parameters to develop a menu of watershed characteristic options from

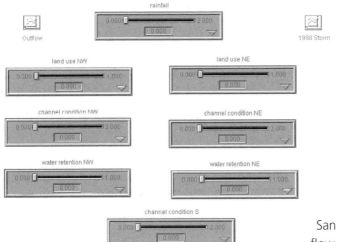

Figure 6.1.
San Antonio watershed
flow model user interface

which users could choose. Although the model was severely oversimplified, it was still a useful learning tool.

Model predictions were also easy to interpret. Each model run generated a single hydrograph showing resulting watershed runoff as a function of time. By changing watershed characteristics, stakeholders could generate several runoff hydrographs. Hydrographs for multiple scenarios could be plotted on a single graph to facilitate comparison. Sample hydrograph comparisons generated by stakeholders during this exercise are shown in Figures 6.2 and 6.3.

CALIBRATION OF THE MODEL

Flow data used to calibrate and validate the model was gathered from four USGS gauging stations located within the study area (gauging stations 08177860, 08178000, 08178050, and 08178565). Precipitation data were available from the meteorological station at San Antonio International Airport (TX007945). Periods of record selected for use in calibration and validation were chosen on the basis of completeness of the flow data record and the range of flows observed. Data used for calibration were collected during May 1992 and November 1992. Data used for validation were collected during July 1994, March 1995, April 1995, and March 1998.

Many of the model parameters were initially estimated from published values. While these published values are appropriate for conditions similar to those observed in the study watershed, they might not be an exact match to watershed conditions. Calibration allows the model parameters to be fine-tuned so that they more closely match conditions in the specific study watershed. During model calibration, input variables used in the model were adjusted until model output closely matched observed flow values recorded during the calibration periods, May and November 1992.

Model Use

The four-hour workshop began with a brief verbal description of the model given by a council member. We then asked stakeholders to divide into groups of two or three people, with each group having at least one person who had used a computer, and no group having more than one new member. Grant then showed the group what he and Kenimer had done with the group's concept. Using a copy of the same model they were working with, he walked members through the model basics, beginning with the user interface mentioned above. Members could look either at what he was projecting on the screen or at their own screens. While Grant spoke, other research team members circulated among the groups, ensuring that all groups were able to manipulate the model as directed. When all the groups seemed comfortable working on their own, we

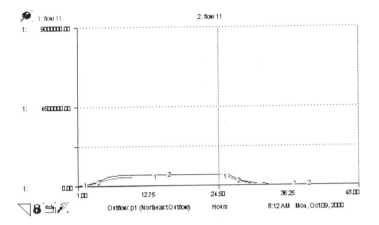

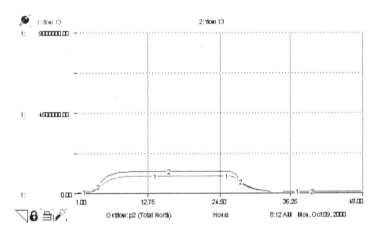

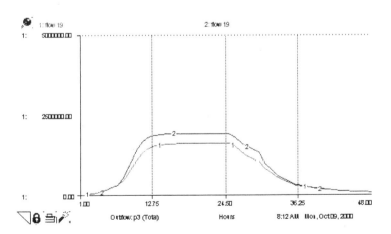

Figure 6.2.
San Antonio watershed flow model hydrograph comparisons

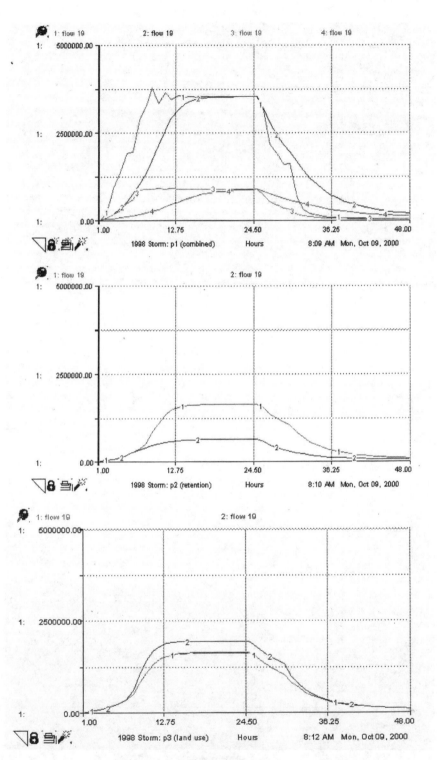

Figure 6.3.
San Antonio watershed flow model hydrograph comparisons

invited them to experiment with various scenarios. Grant joined the other research team members in roaming the room to assist when requested.

Most groups spent the remaining time running various combinations of the alternatives offered in the menu. After a short time of experimentation with the predetermined options, other groups became dissatisfied with the model's simplicity and wanted to make it more complex. For example, the model allowed only three predetermined channel conditions, and some groups wanted to change that to a continuum that ranged from concrete to full brushy understory. Grant and Kenimer assisted groups who wanted to make changes of this nature.

While all stakeholders participated (to some degree) in this evaluation activity, their participation varied. A few had never touched a computer before their participation in the councils. These members usually contented themselves with asking another group member to manipulate the model. For example, one of them asked her partner, "Let's see what happens in the hundred-year flood when we put in a concrete channel in the central segment only." Although she kept her hands in her lap throughout most of the workshop, she leaned forward, critically examining model output for each combination her partner punched in. On the other extreme, some groups wanted to make the model itself more complex. One group determined the data used to simulate the influence of retention structures were insufficient, so they sent one of their team members to his office, where additional data were available.

After allowing participants to experiment with their model for approximately two hours, facilitators asked the groups to join in a plenary discussion of what they had learned and how this could be applied to the recommendations they had prepared. Most members were eager to share their insights with others. The discussion evolved into a lively debate regarding what combination of management options the council wanted to recommend. Sometimes when teams found it difficult to explain their rationale for a particular combination of management options, they turned to the simulation model. One team sent a member to the front of the room and had him show the others on the computer that was hooked up to the projector what they meant by running a simulation they had found especially intriguing.

As the workshop drew to a close, stakeholders determined they would use their simulation models the next month when they presented recommendations to the mayor. They claimed it might help him understand why they preferred certain combinations to others. Participants spent most of the final two meetings sharing their recommendations with members of city government and relevant agencies. During these meetings, they often ran simulations to help clarify a point, or to open up a new discussion. During one of these meetings, they used their newfound skills to suggest alterations in a simulation model designed by an aquatic ecologist on the research team.

Lessons Learned

The research team left the group in December 2000, and the councils have since taken on lives of their own. One has developed into a private foundation that has won citywide awards. Electronic messages received from members indicate continuing participation in city governance issues relevant to the watershed.

Despite its loose connection with a TMDL project, the simulation model developed by these stakeholders was based on a freestanding rather than a commissioned project. There is an obvious and additional hurdle to overcome when a mediated modeling process is embedded in a freestanding rather than a commissioned project, as described in Chapter 10. In a freestanding project, it is more difficult to maintain the momentum of motivation as compared with a commissioned process.

In this case, the participants overcame the challenge of a loss of motivation and instead created a bond between themselves and existing institutions. The stakeholders were able to connect to each other and add their contribution to ongoing management debates. Because of their positive experience, the stakeholder groups have maintained themselves as self-organizing bodies, recognized and respected by existing institutions.

One of the main obstacles in moving toward sustainable, multiple use of resources is our inability to synthesize knowledge and perspectives from many distinct disciplines within a single problem-solving philosophy. Mediated modeling from a collaborative learning perspective provides a basis for sustainable, multiple resource use by facilitating multidisciplinary planning and by creating an effective communication interface between scientists, citizens, and policymakers, thus promoting identification and communication of policy options to decision makers.

The four phases of systems analysis are highly interconnected (Grant et al. 1997), and we cycled through the phases repeatedly. The simulation model evolved into the communication interface between scientists and decision makers as team members developed a sense of joint ownership of the model, thus making the modeling process more important than the model itself.

Planners, managers, citizens, and scientists have begun to consider system simulation models as tools in land use decision making, policy, and management within the complex socioenvironmental milieu of urbanizing watersheds. System simulation models could facilitate learning and communication regarding the linkage between decision making, environmental impacts, and land use planning.

Through collaborative interaction between scientists and stakeholders, we developed a system simulation model that incorporated salient water quantity and quality issues. It used iterative input from stakeholders to guide design-oriented research and restoration planning.

This case study explains how we applied this type of model to help citizens residing in the San Antonio River watershed to understand and demonstrate how different intensities of land use could impact the flooding regime of a river. This approach can also be used in any land use planning to aid the visualization of alternative schemes for watershed restoration and ecological processes at the watershed and floodplain scales.

DISCUSSION QUESTIONS

1. What are the benefits/drawbacks of contextualizing formal modeling activities within the collaborative learning framework?
2. In what situations would it be most useful to contextualize formal modeling activities within a collaborative learning framework?
3. From the perspective of a modeler, what challenges do groups such as the SCRC and LCRC pose?
4. What skills would a modeler need to work with similar groups?
5. What are the benefits/drawbacks of changing the model in between, rather than during, sessions?

7

Future Planning: Banff National Park

Laura Cornwell

Banff National Park, whose heart is the Bow Valley, is located in the Central Rockies Ecosystem of Alberta, Canada. Established in 1885, Banff is Canada's first and most visited national park and is the second-oldest park in the world. Banff is also an integral part of the UNESCO-designated Canadian Rocky Mountain Parks World Heritage Site and protects a critical portion of the Yellowstone-to-Yukon international wildlife corridor. Management decisions in Banff, therefore, set a precedent for parks in Canada as well as national heritage sites and wildlife management areas worldwide.

Owing to the high level of development in and around the park, several scientists and conservation organizations have been voicing concerns about the Bow Valley ecosystem for decades, maintaining that further compromise to natural resources cannot be sustained. Increasing public outcry and petitions to the United Nations Educational, Scientific and Cultural Organization (UNESCO) to delist the park's world heritage status were the impetus behind Minister of Canadian Heritage Michel Dupuy's commissioning the Banff–Bow Valley Study (BBVS) in March 1994. An independent task force was appointed to administer its direction, and both public involvement and input from technical experts were critical components.

The stated purpose of the Banff–Bow Valley Study was to ensure a balance between the ecological, economic, and cultural development of the Bow Valley by providing a comprehensive analysis of the Bow River watershed within

Banff National Park. The study focused on environmental, economic, and social issues within the watershed to determine the present state of the valley
and implications of further human development and use on the natural capital
and heritage resources of the area.

The major objectives of the study were:

- To complete a comprehensive analysis of existing information, and to
  provide direction for future collection and analysis of data to achieve ongoing goals
- To develop a vision and goals for the Banff–Bow Valley that integrate
  ecological, social, and economic values
- To provide direction on future management of human use and development in a manner that maintains ecological values and provides for sustainable tourism

To achieve these objectives, the task force determined that a mediated modeling process was needed that could develop potential future scenarios utilizing
several ecological, economic, and social indicators to examine various management alternatives.

This chapter describes the Banff-Bow Valley Study's Mediated Modeling
process.

Banff National Park

Banff National Park (BNP) has some of the richest habitat in the Central
Rocky Mountains Ecosystem. It contains twenty-seven areas of natural significance, with concentrations of resources that are rare or endangered and have
ecological, cultural, or scientific significance (Achuff et al. 1986). Seven of the
park's wildlife species are nationally designated as threatened or vulnerable
(Pacas et al. 1996). The park also contains important vegetation communities
that are declining in the region, such as aspen and old-growth forest (Achuff et
al. 1986; Kay et al. 1994).

The park is characterized by narrow valley bottoms and relatively rapid
vertical transitions, with 47% of its land area comprised of rock and ice or
lying above 2,400 meters (7,896 feet) and therefore unusable by most species
(Gibeau et al. 1996). Wildlife species utilizing this landscape are therefore
forced into linear corridors with few "passes" or connections between
corridors.

The valley bottoms, or montane ecoregions, are the most ecologically diverse in the Canadian Rockies Ecosystem (CRE) (Pacas et al. 1996). Much of
the vegetation mosaic in this region is dependent on frequent, low-intensity

fires (Kay et al. 1994; Achuff et al. 1996). Though making up less than 4.2% of
the study area, the grasslands, wetlands, streams and lakes, deciduous forests,
riparian areas, alluvial fans, and conifer stands of the montane ecoregion provide the highest-quality habitat in the park (Holland and Coen 1982; Holroyd
and VanTighem 1983). High-quality habitats are critical for CRE species such
as grizzly and black bear, which for most of the year are trying to meet nutri-
tional requirements for reproduction and energy stores for hibernation during
harsh and extended winters. Frequent "chinooks" (aperiodic, relatively warm
coastal air masses) and relatively low snow accumulation make montane
ecoregions important winter habitat for nonhibernating species as well, such as
several species of ungulates and the predators that depend on them (Woods
1991).

Several species in the park, such as grizzly bear and wolf, are wary landscape species that humans have been unwilling to tolerate in areas other than
national parks or designated wilderness (Paquet and Hackman 1995). These
species have large home ranges—for example, greater than 1,000 square kilometers for adult male grizzly bears (S. Herrero, pers. comm.)—and are often
dependent on seasonally specific food sources. Having access to large areas of
unfragmented, relatively undisturbed, high-quality habitat is therefore critical
to their survival.

Though ecologically significant and having national park status, the Bow
Valley watershed is also the center of human activity for the area. Banff
National Park was established after the discovery of a mineral hot springs.
Early development of the park focused on providing public access to the "cura-
tive properties" of the springs (Canadian Department of the Interior 1886, as
seen in Pacas et al. 1996). After the Banff Springs Hotel was built in the late
1800s, Banff's position as a world-class resort destination was secured. As a result, infrastructure and activities that were deemed appropriate for a national
park at the turn of the century have left a unique legacy in the Bow Valley.

The national east-west transportation corridor, including the Trans-Canada
Highway and the Canadian Pacific Railway, traverses the valley. Starting at the
east gate of the park, the highway is four lanes, and it is fenced for approximately 30 kilometers to deter wildlife from crossing the roadway. Gravel and
fill dirt for the highway are mined from sites within the park. Aquatic systems
in the Bow Valley have been extensively altered to accommodate hydroelectric
production, recreation, water supply, and transportation corridor construction
(Schindler and Pacas 1996).

Banff Townsite, an incorporated municipality on leased park land, is the
largest human development in any North American park and houses over
7,600 residents (Statistics Canada 1991). The hamlet of Lake Louise, also in the
watershed, houses over 1,500 residents (Statistics Canada 1991). These residential centers contain supporting infrastructure such as schools, grocery and
liquor stores, banks, a post office, and social services. Indeed, residents in outly-

ing areas come to the park to shop and conduct business. Infrastructure in these urban centers—including a wide variety of specialty shops and malls; a golf course; three world-class ski resorts; and more than fifty hotels, motels, and lodges—also supported the 5 million visitors that Banff National Park received in 1995. Other visitor opportunities in the park include commercial fishing and boat tours, guided trail riding, public hot springs, tennis, interpretive opportunities, canoeing, and mountain biking.

Infrastructure and human use present many problems for wildlife in the park, and prior to the study there were several indications that ecological integrity was highly compromised. The montane ecoregion not only provides the highest-quality habitat for wildlife, it is also where most of the human development and use are located. More than 20% of the montane ecoregion in the Banff–Bow Valley is directly occupied by human infrastructure (Pacas et al. 1996). When the amount of alienated habitat is taken into account, this proportion rises to 33% (Pacas 1996). This further constricts already narrow valleys for wildlife and dramatically alters their travel corridors.

Wary species, such as bear, are alienated from areas of high-quality habitat, preferring to utilize increasingly marginal habitat rather than come into contact with humans (Gibeau et al. 1996). Those species that become habituated to human presence and which are tolerated by residents, visitors, and park management—for example, elk—become decoupled from important interspecies relationships, such as predator/prey interactions (Woods et al. 1996). This decoupling has further implications for vegetation mosaics, which have been dramatically altered in the valley owing to concentrated areas of browse pressure (Achuff et al. 1996).

Some of the problems in the Bow Valley are the result of park management policies or land use management in surrounding areas. For example, the policy of fire suppression has dramatically altered the vegetation mosaic of the montane ecoregion since the late 1800s (Achuff et al. 1996). The damming of the Cascade and Spray Rivers and Lake Minnewanka for hydroelectric power has altered important wetland and riparian vegetation communities through flooding and reduction or cessation of flow (Achuff et al. 1996). Finally, logging, mining, hunting, and development adjacent to the park are causing increased pressure on the park's wildlife populations.

Although the amount of alienated habitat within the park's boundary has been considered extreme, Banff National Park is legislated as core refugia. Wilderness areas and the wildlife associated with them are highly valued, particularly in Canada. Canadians place their national parks in high esteem, perhaps higher than any other country. When asked to select factors defining their national identity, Canadians placed national parks second (Cameron 1997). They also indicated overwhelming support for the Canada National Parks Act's mandate to maintain ecological integrity (Parks Canada 1988), even if this meant restricting human use of parks (Cameron 1997). It was in this context that the Banff–Bow Valley Study (BBVS) was initiated.

The Banff–Bow Valley Study

Public involvement was a critical component of the BBVS with the understanding that "the future of the Bow Valley depends on the ability of . . . various interest groups to work together in an open and independent atmosphere" (BBVS 1996a). Indeed, the level of public participation on the study was unprecedented in the history of Canadian national parks (BBVS 1996a). The public was encouraged to attend monthly meetings, submit written or oral presentations, visit the study office to discuss concerns, review written materials or utilize the study's library. The task force reported progress on the study through newsletters, presentations throughout Canada, news releases, public television, workshops, and the Internet. Task force members also made themselves available to interest groups wishing to discuss issues of concern or progress on the study, in general. In short, the goal of the BBVS process was to be open, transparent, and accessible to the citizens of Canada.

The most comprehensive mechanism of participation was the Banff–Bow Valley Round Table, a broadly representative, highly participatory mediated negotiation process involving major stakeholders in the region. The Banff–Bow Valley Round Table was "the primary mechanism for public participation in the identification, analysis and resolution of issues for the Banff–Bow Valley study area [and was] empowered to select an appropriate mediator, develop rules of procedure, establish a vision and goals for the study area, identify and prioritize issues and develop recommendations to the Task Force on issue resolution" (BBVS 1996b). The task force utilized the round table's consensus recommendations as a basis for their report to the minister.

The round table was made up of interest sectors, each being a "constituency of like-minded persons that identified with certain values in priority to others that contributed a unique perspective to the issues being negotiated" (BBVS 1996b). Each constituency was represented by a committee, which in turn elected a chair to represent the interest sector at the table. Fourteen interest sectors were identified: Culture and Heritage; National Environment; Local Environment; Municipal Government; Federal Government; Park Users; BBVS Task Force; Infrastructure and Transportation; Social, Health, and Education; Commercial Outdoor Recreation; Commercial Visitor Services; Tourism and Marketing; First Nations—Siksika; and First Nations—Wesley. The First Nations sectors did not attend round table meetings. For purposes of the study, therefore, the round table working group consisted of twelve active interest sectors. The table met formally (with mediation and according to rules of procedure) for two days each month over a fourteen-month period. Interest sectors also held separate meetings throughout the month.

One of the primary objectives of the study was to utilize the best available scientific information to resolve key issues in the valley and provide recommendations for future management, including the collection of data. The task force initiated a research and consultation program, which consisted of an international group of scientists, consultants, and governmental agency employees. Areas of expertise included wildlife ecology, tourism, socioeconomic impact assessment, tourism impact assessment, parks management, business, engineering, and public policy. Technical experts were available to the task force and round table for consultation.

A number of studies were also completed as part of the research program. These included an exhaustive compendium of existing social, economic, and ecological data including the State of the Bow Valley Report; the Visitor Behavioral Research Project; the Social, Economics and Cultural Data Assessment; the Tourism Outlooks Project; the Review of the Governance Model; and the Ecological Outlooks Project.

The Ecological Outlooks Project

In addition to the round table and the group of technical experts, the Ecological Outlooks Project (EOP) included additional mechanisms for citizen participation and inclusion of scientific information. Round table sectors appointed members to both a Scientific Review Committee and a Technical Working Group. The Scientific Review Committee, a twelve-member group of international scientists and a tourism expert, provided peer review to assess the scientific merits of the EOP, including assumptions, methodology, statistical analyses, results, and conclusions. The Technical Working Group included a member from each of the twelve interest sectors and informed the round table and interest sector committees on a monthly basis of the approach and progress of the EOP. Specifically, the Technical Working Group was set up to facilitate active participation in the participatory modeling component, described in more detail below.

The Modeling Process

To assist the task force in making their recommendations, the Ecological Outlooks Project utilized a number of ecological, economic, and social indicators to (1) evaluate the cumulative environmental effects of land use, development, and human presence in the Banff–Bow Valley and (2) predict how current trends, behavior, and decisions would affect the future of the valley. Scientific and technical experts selected indicators during a two-day workshop by identifying key stressors on environmental and social systems in the valley. Selected indicators included humans, grizzly bear, wolf, elk, vegetation (habitat), cutthroat trout, bulltrout, quality of experience for visitors, quality of life for residents, and economic development.

The EOP was comprised of the Cumulative Effects Assessment (CEA) and the Futures Outlook Project (FOP) (Green 1996). The temporal scale of the CEA was 1950 to the present, while the FOP was intended to assess the long-term consequences of land use and management decisions fifty years into the future.

The objective of the Futures Outlook Project was to examine the interactions among environmental, economic, and sociocultural indicators in a range of potential future scenarios to assist with the formulation of park management. The FOP utilized modeling, with the participation of stakeholders and technical experts, as a tool to promote understanding of the system and to assess the potential effects of future land use and human presence and activities on natural and human systems in the Banff–Bow Valley region.

A participatory, dynamic simulation model-building exercise with the round table in July 1995 initiated the FOP. The objectives of this initial exercise were to acquaint round table participants with the basics of modeling, to inform them how to construct a conceptual model, and to begin developing a regional model of Banff National Park and the surrounding area to facilitate a better understanding of the interdependence between the socioeconomic and ecological systems in the park. Figure 7.1 illustrates the round table's initial attempts to identify important issues in the valley. The preliminary conceptual model included eleven sectors: Bioregions, Regional Ecosystems, Species, Community, Built Infrastructure, Economic Systems, National and Global Economy, Quality of Experience, Park Image, Park Management, and Culture.

After the preliminary conceptual model was developed, meetings with the task force and round table committee members resulted in several revisions. Additional sectors were added, while others were revised to more fully address the issues in the region and concerns of the round table. As a result, the Bioregions sector was divided into Montane and Subalpine/Alpine sectors, and the Species sector was divided into the main organism groups of interest, including ungulate and carnivore. Community was renamed Resident Population; Built Infrastructure was renamed Infrastructure; and Economic Systems was renamed Park Economics. Finally, a Visitor sector was added to the model. More detail and functional connections between variables were added at the request of the task force. Variable values were based on data already compiled by the study, expert opinion, or best estimates.

Once a preliminary version of the model was constructed, simulations were utilized to develop a better understanding of model dynamics and sensitivity, to compare model behavior to what was known about the system, and to help decide where to focus additional efforts. This initial step in the process of building participatory dynamic simulation models with stakeholders has been

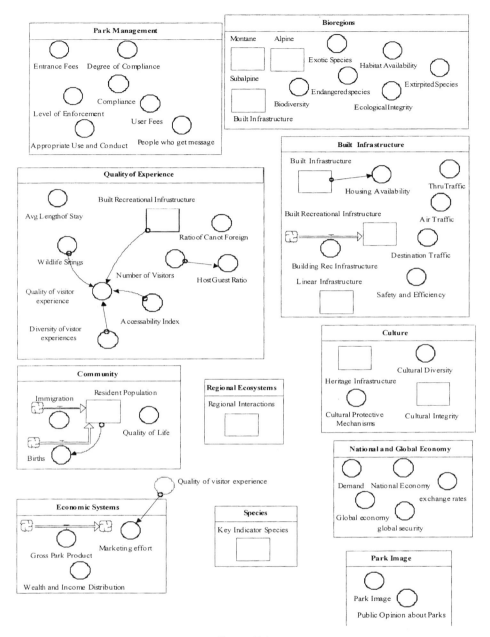

Figure 7.1.
Banff–Bow Valley Round Table initial model

termed *scoping* (van den Belt et al. 1998; Costanza and Ruth 1998). After the scoping phase, the table determined that more time was needed for model building and scenario development than the formal, monthly round table meetings allowed. The Technical Working Group was created as a result. The Technical Working Group determined early on that indicators selected by experts as a result of the EOP workshop, and which were also being utilized in the CEA, fit well into the framework of the round table's interests for the FOP and would also provide a more cohesive product. Indicators would then be examined for fifty years into the past, as well as for fifty years into the future. Additionally, model components could then receive input from the scientific experts working on indicator analyses for the CEA. It was determined, however, that the FOP should not include an aquatics component.

Monthly meetings with the Technical Working Group were used to continue the iterative process of participatory, dynamic simulation model development; to evaluate the process and assumptions; to reveal data gaps and limitations; and to ensure that the model, to the extent possible, contained the capabilities to address management questions of interest. Members of the Technical Working Group made monthly presentations to their sectors and provided them with written materials if they deemed it necessary, for sector members and table chairs to maintain an understanding of the process. Issues being discussed in monthly round table meetings often coincided with work in progress on the model.

For information learned in the modeling component to be most useful, it was important to keep public participants informed of the status of the project. At critical model development phases, presentations were made to the round table during formal monthly meetings, particularly if consensus was required for model assumptions. Individual sector meetings were also utilized to discuss aspects of the model, difficulties acquiring data, or any other concerns or interests sector members may have had.

Scientific and technical experts were available to provide data, expert opinion, professional judgment, and assistance with model design. As was mentioned previously, in some cases scientific and technical experts were provided with specific assumptions or future scenarios and utilized either geographic information systems (GIS) models or input-output models to generate data or examine questions of interest. Generally, Technical Working Group members tasked the project team to work with the scientific experts between monthly meetings and to report findings at subsequent meetings. In some cases, Technical Working Group members met with experts directly. Interest sectors were also invited to observe all EOP workshops—including those involving the task force, scientific experts, and the Scientific Review Committee—in which the scientific merits of the EOP were discussed, including the modeling project.

The Resulting Model

The dynamic simulation portion of the modeling component was termed the Banff–Bow Valley Futures Model (BVFM) and went through many iterations after the initial scoping phase. Several tools were used to inform the modeling process and develop algorithms. Five main methods were employed:

- Where possible, basic first principles, such as conservation of mass were applied.
- Some algorithms were dictated by limits in capacity (e.g., infrastructure, space).
- Past trends were used as predictive tools, with the assumption that well-defined trends will continue into the future.
- If trend data were stochastic or not available, or there was reason to believe that past trends would not continue, the modeling process relied on expert opinion/intuition.
- In some cases, output from other models (input-output and GIS) was used as input into the BVFM.

Assumptions for specific indicators are outlined in Appendix 8.

Social Indicators

Five categories of social indicators were examined:

- Visitors
- Built infrastructure
- Linear infrastructure
- Economic development
- Quality of life for park residents

The major driving variables in the BVFM are visitor numbers and use. Total overnight visitors and the number of residents in the town of Banff are capped by total capacity at infrastructure buildout. Buildout is defined as the maximum allowable infrastructure under current zoning regulations and is measured in terms of bed units. The number of bed units in a given facility (resident or commercial) is defined as the number of persons that can be accommodated by that facility. One bed unit is equal to one person. The remainder of visitors and residents are assumed to overnight or reside in nearby Canmore, a town just outside the park, and are considered to be day users. Visitors are also partitioned by their country of origin. Categories include Albertans, non-Albertan Canadians, visitors from the United States, and non-U.S. international visitors.

Amount of infrastructure in the two park towns is based on the growth management plans of the town of Banff and the hamlet of Lake Louise. Linear infrastructure is determined by the visitor growth rate assumption being considered and its relationship to traffic. The BVFM assumes no increase in trail or other park infrastructure (e.g., campgrounds and parking lots). However, twinning (increasing a two-lane highway to four lanes) of the Trans-Canada

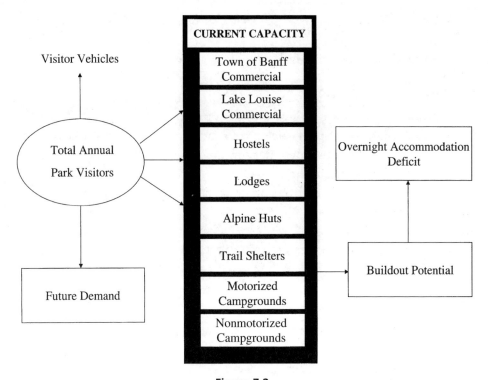

Figure 7.2.
Banff–Bow Valley Futures Model infrastructure components

Highway (TCH) is included in some scenarios as portions of the highway are already twinned and plans are underway for highway expansion. A conceptual depiction of the build and linear infrastructure components of the BVFM are presented in Figure 7.2.

Total visitor expenditures, expenditures by visitor origin and user type, expenditure by industry category, economic impact, tax revenues, and the employment effects of expenditures make up the components of economic development in the model.

Sales of goods and services (expenditures) in a particular region are measures of total economic activity. They are problematic measures of economic impact, however, because they (1) involve double counting and (2) do not take into account the economic activity generated outside the region of expenditure. A multiplier, therefore, is generally used to measure total economic impact.

A multiplier measures the level of economic change caused by an additional unit of spending. To examine the economic impact of visitor expenditures in the park, the demand economic impact model (DEIM) was utilized. As mentioned earlier, DEIM is an input-output model developed specifically for assessing the economic impacts of tourism and has the capability of examining a range of scenarios under various visitor growth rate assumptions. In the case of the DEIM, the multiplier used is the income multiplier, and visitors to the park generate additional units of spending.

The income multiplier measures value added rather than total sales. Value added can be thought of as the revenue gained from sales of a particular item minus the total cost of producing that item. Using value added rather than total sales adjusts for the problem of double counting.

The amount of spending by visitors to a particular area (in this case, BNP) generates economic activity outside of that area. For example, when visitors purchase steak dinners at restaurants in the park, this activity is economically beneficial for the beef industry in the province of Alberta. Total economic impact includes this additional economic activity. Important input variables into the DEIM include visitor numbers, origin, median expenditures per trip, allocation of expenditures, and ratio of day users to overnight users.

Quality of life for park residents is measured by examining the ratio of visitors to residents over time. Members of the Social, Health and Education sector of the round table specifically requested this indicator.

A ten-year time period was used for most social indicators because time horizons are generally shorter for these indicators than for ecological indicators, and the DEIM model, utilized for all economic impact analyses, is only valid to the year 2005. Two time periods were considered for the DEIM: 2000 and 2005. The year 2010 was also included in the analyses for quality of life. All model simulations report data on an annual basis.

Ecological Indicators

Two categories of ecological indicators were included in the dynamic simulation model: elk and wolves. Conceptual depictions of these model components are presented in Figures 7.3 and 7.4. Elk are indicators of impacts of human use on wildlife, management intervention in the valley, and large-mammal predator/prey systems. Wolves are utilized in the model as indicators of wildlife movement capability (habitat connectivity/wildlife corridor integrity), because of their dependence on ungulate densities and accessibility. Vegetation is included indirectly through changing habitat quality for elk but is not a specified parameter in the model.

Because of their dependence on the montane ecoregion, the spatial consideration for both elk and wolves in the Bow Valley corridor was partitioned into four zones of interest: the Canmore Golf Course to the East Gate (far east, or FE); the East Gate to the Lake Minnewanka Interchange (east, or E); the Lake Minnewanka Interchange to Five Mile Bridge (central, or C); and Five Mile Bridge to the Yoho boundary of the park (west, or W). Zones of interest were spatially delineated by wildlife experts working on the elk and wolf modules of the CEA (see Paquet et al. 1996; Woods et al. 1996).

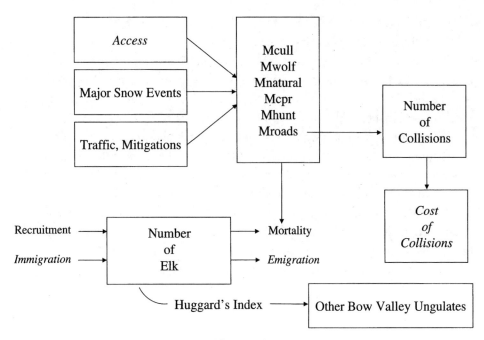

Figure 7.3.

Conceptual depiction of elk as an ecological indicator in the Banff–Bow Valley Futures Model

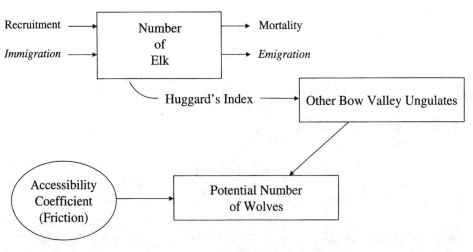

Figure 7.4.

Conceptual depiction of wolves as an ecological indicator in the Banff–Bow Valley Futures Model

These zones were used as the basic landscape subdivisions for all futures outlook analyses. Using the park's geographical information system, the altitudinal cut was based on 3,450 elk radiotelemetry points representing 68 individuals (BNP, unpublished data; Hurd, pers. comm.), with observations separated by at least five days for any given individual to adjust for autocorrelation. Elk winter range was chosen as the limiting factor (P. Paquet, pers. comm.; Woods, pers. comm.). Based on three years of data, 95% of all telemetry points were 1,576 meters in elevation or lower. The correlation between elk and wolf was determined to be 95% by overlaying telemetry points of wolf on the elk database. The elk/wolf corridor, therefore, extends from valley bottom to 1,576 meters.

Results

The BVFM allowed users to examine trends and trade-offs between ecological and social indicators on the basis of visitation growth rate and management scenarios. The model is most sensitive to human numbers and their use of the landscape. A conceptual schematic of the BVFM is presented in Figure 7.5. Mathematical formulas for all model components are reported in Appendix 8. The potential to examine different futures scenarios is practically limitless. Results presented here, therefore, are some of those requested by the round

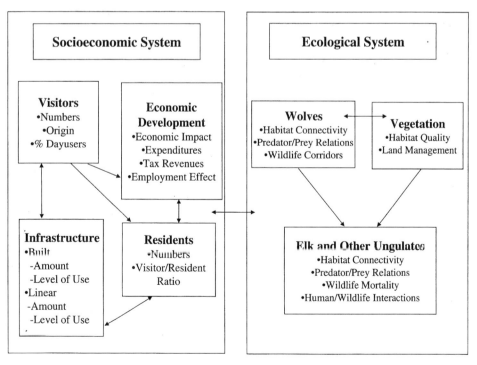

Figure 7.5.
Conceptual schematic of the Banff–Bow Valley Futures Model

table or task force to assist in the formulation of recommendations to the minister.

Social Indicators

Results from the four categories of social indicators—visitor number, infrastructure, economic development, and quality of life—were used by the round table and task force to assist with management and policy recommendations, and are discussed below.

VISITOR NUMBER

Visitation was projected to the year 2045 using five different growth rates: four chosen by the round table (–0.5%, 1.0%, 3.0%, and 6.0 %, compounded annually), plus a rate of 5.46% chosen by the task force as representing the average annual growth in visitation over the past 45 years.

Total visitors are partitioned into day users and overnight users. Overnight users are further categorized into Albertans, non-Albertan Canadians, U.S. visitors, and other foreign visitors. The translation of overnight visitors to total visitor nights (the number of overnight visitors multiplied by the number of nights they stay) is also reported on an annual basis.

INFRASTRUCTURE

The task force and round table were interested in examining two infrastructure categories:

- *Visitor accommodations:* What would be the effect of capping overnight accommodations in the park under various infrastructure and occupancy scenarios? When would a deficit be reached? The infrastructure capacity scenarios examined included current capacity, 25% of buildout potential, 50% of buildout potential, and total buildout; the occupancy scenarios included two, three, and four bed-units per room.
- *Residential accommodations:* At what point, given various growth scenarios for the town of Banff, would there be forced shifts in residential demand to Canmore, given a cap on residential infrastructure?

Because the town of Banff is situated in a national park, standard theories about housing markets are not applicable. The town regulates home ownership through a need-to-reside clause. Home ownership is for dwelling only and does not include the property on which the structure sits. The land is, instead, leased from the government for a specified length of time.

Currently, and over the past several years, the demand for housing has been much greater than the supply (D. Leighton, pers. comm.). The only affordable new housing is subsidized by the town and distributed via a lottery system, with preferential treatment given to prospective owners meeting certain demographic profiles. Additionally, employers are required to provide housing for a certain percentage of their employees (depending on business type).

Growth in residents, therefore, is in part, a function of growth in business. The National Parks Act mandates that business service centers in national parks are to be only those that represent "basic and essential services" for park visitors (Parks Canada 1994). Growth in business, therefore, is some function of growth in visitation. Data on these parameters are not adequate to determine what the functional relationship might be between growth in visitors, increase in numbers of businesses, and increase in residents. The task force, therefore, chose to examine growth rates based on historic trends.

The government, of course, owns all land in the park, and the amount leased to the town of Banff is legislated. Development of this land is determined through zoning, and space for additional residential housing units is limited and inventoried by the town. The infrastructure capacity scenarios examined were the same as those for commercial accommodations: current capacity, 25% of buildout potential, 50% of buildout potential, and total buildout.

Overnight Visitor Accommodation Deficit

Though demand has been rising steadily, overnight accommodation capacity in Banff National Park is limited (Katic 1996). The park's facilities are fully booked up to six months in advance for the months of June–September, despite the 117 rooms that were added in 1995 (*Calgary Herald* 1996). Though some areas and facilities have potential for additional capacity, current guidelines for the park and the town of Banff include a maximum level of infrastructure. To understand the implications of capping overnight accommodation infrastructure in Banff National Park, the BVFM was utilized to examine a number of future scenarios. The purpose of selected scenarios was to examine the visitor and economic impacts of limiting the number of overnight visitors that can be accommodated in the park.

Town of Banff Commercial Infrastructure

The BVFM was used to run thirty-six scenarios to examine the effects of capping overnight commercial infrastructure in the town of Banff. These runs include four infrastructure capacity scenarios (current capacity, 25% of potential buildout, 50% of potential buildout, and buildout). Each infrastructure scenario examined three bed-unit assumptions (two, three, and four bed-units per room) and three visitor growth rate assumptions (1%, 3%, and 6%, compounded annually).

Under the assumption of double occupancy, bed unit deficits were apparent in the base year for current capacity and 25% of buildout potential. Even at buildout, under the 6% growth rate assumption, the double occupancy deficit is reached in 3 years. Though the town of Banff utilizes double occupancy to estimate total commercial capacity in the town, the assumptions of the model and best available data suggest this estimate to be low. The 6% visitation growth scenario matches past trends, given that the average growth in visitation since 1950 is 5.46%, compounded annually. Under this growth assumption, capacity is exceeded relatively quickly, no matter which scenario is being considered. Even under the scenario allowing for maximum infrastructure capacity (buildout at four bed-units per room), a deficit is reached in less than 15 years.

Hamlet of Lake Louise Commercial Infrastructure

Twelve scenarios were run to examine the effects of capping overnight commercial infrastructure in the hamlet of Lake Louise. These runs include four infrastructure capacity scenarios (current capacity, 25% of potential buildout, 50% of potential buildout, and buildout) and three visitor growth rate assumptions (1%, 3%, and 6%, compounded annually). Under the 6% visitation growth rate scenario, deficits are realized in less than 5 years for all infrastructure scenarios. Even under the 3% growth rate scenarios, deficits are reached in 10 years or less.

Outlying Commercial Accommodations

Nine scenarios were run to examine the effects of capping overnight commercial infrastructure in outlying commercial accommodations (OCAs). These runs include three bed-unit assumptions (two, three, and four bed-units per room) and four visitor growth rate assumptions (1%, 3%, and 6%, compounded annually). Under the 6% visitation growth rate scenario at the maximum bed-unit assumption, capacity is exceeded in 7 years.

Other Motorized Accessible Overnight Facilities and Backcountry Facilities

Three scenarios were run to examine overnight infrastructure for all other facility types. Because infrastructure capacity remains constant under current guidelines, only visitation growth rates were considered. Clearly these facilities have the greatest capacity to accommodate additional visitors. Under the 6% visitation growth rate scenario, hostel capacity would be exceeded in 13 years, but deficits for all other facilities would not be realized until at least 25 years into the future. Other than hostels, growth rate scenarios of 1% and 3% do not produce deficits in these facilities within the 50-year time horizon considered.

Regardless of the scenario being considered, overnight accommodations in the park are a key challenge for decision makers. Facilities that currently have the greatest demand are hotels, motels, and OCAs. Over 90% of overnight visitors choose these facility types, though less costly facilities are available and generally have more vacancy. Camping facilities, particularly in the backcountry, can still accommodate great increases in visitor numbers under current assumptions. Trends in backcountry camping over the past couple of years, for example, have been declining (Pacas 1996; Pacas et al. 1996).

Forced Shifts in Residential Demand from Banff to Canmore

Limiting infrastructure in the park will have an effect on the greater region, in terms of both infrastructure and dollars. Current thinking is that the town of Canmore, which is currently developing its commercial capacity at rates approaching 7%, will accommodate most of this demand. When visitors stay in accommodations outside the park, they are more likely to purchase meals and shop outside the park as well. The magnitude of the financial effects on Canmore is impossible to predict with current data. Within the assumptions of the model, however, it is possible to estimate the magnitude of bed unit demand that will occur, when this demand can be expected, and what accommodation types will be of interest. Of course, behavior and clientele shifts can alter these predictions substantially. The model has the capability of being updated as additional data are gathered.

The Town of Banff Residential/Commercial Inventory for 1995 (Town of Banff council file 7622) indicates that the town contains "approximately 11,446 residential bed-units in single family, duplexes and multi-family dwellings." Whereas, "at buildout, 19,900 bed units of residential . . . could exist." The difference in bed units is 8,454, which represents an increase of 42% over current capacity.

Of the total number of additional bed units that are possible at buildout (8,454), 25% of that potential plus the existing housing would represent a total of 13,560 bed-units in the town of Banff; 50% of that potential would represent a total of 15,673 bed-units. The magnitude of that demand can be determined over a 50-year time horizon by examining the total resident population numbers for each year beyond which the infrastructure capacity is reached, to 2045, and subtracting the limit imposed by the infrastructure capacity. For example, at 25% buildout, the infrastructure capacity is 13,560. At a 2% growth scenario, the forced residential demand on Canmore would begin in 2021. The magnitude of that demand would be the total estimated population (13,794) minus the infrastructure capacity, for a total demand on Canmore of 234 bed-units. At 1% growth in population, infrastructure capacity is not reached at any of the buildout scenarios.

ECONOMIC DEVELOPMENT

Banff is Canada's most visited tourism destination. Banff National Park and the town of Banff generate significant benefits to Alberta and Canada through the economic activity they generate in the region. Benefits include direct expenditures, the additional economic activity generated by those direct expenditures, tax revenues, and employment.

Total Visitor Expenditures

The most recent expenditure data for the park are contained in the 1990/91 surveys conducted by Alberta Economic Development and Tourism (AEDT) (1991; 1994c). In 1991, direct visitor expenditures exceeded $505 million. In 1995, based on assumptions outlined for the BVFM, direct visitor expenditures are estimated to be over $870 million. In the BVFM, total expenditures vary between $1.2 and $2.1 billion by the year 2005, depending on the scenario considered by the task force.

Economic Impact

AEDT estimated the economic impact resulting from direct expenditure of visitors to the park (AEDT 1994a, 1994b). Analysis of AEDT's data using the demand economic impact model (DEIM) determined that visitor expenditures in the park generated a total economic impact of $614 million for the province of Alberta in 1991. In 1995, on the basis of assumptions outlined for the BVFM, total economic impact is estimated to be over $960 million.

Economic impact from visitor expenditures for the province of Alberta varies between $1.3 billion and $2.2 billion for the year 2005, depending on the scenario being considered. Economic impacts for the Banff region vary between $723 million and $1,235 million depending on the scenario being considered.

Tax Revenues

The DEIM was also used to estimate tax revenues generated from visitor expenditures. Tax revenues accrue to all levels of government and were estimated at $170 million in 1991. This included $107 to federal government, $45 million to provincial government, and $18 million to municipal government (AEDT 1994a). On the basis of assumptions for the BVFM, taxes generated in 1995 exceeded $282 million.

Employment Effects

Another key finding by AEDT for the year 1991 was that visitor spending in the park sustains approximately 16,090 person-years of employment for the entire province of Alberta, of which 10,556 person-years were generated for the Banff region. Over 70% of these jobs were in the service sector, including overnight accommodations and food and beverage (AEDT 1994a). In the year 1995, the BVFM estimates that 22,906 person-years of employment will be generated in the province, with 13,307 person-years in the Banff region.

Person-years of employment generated by visitor expenditures for the year 2005 vary between 18,509 and 31,622 for the Banff region, depending on the scenario being considered.

QUALITY OF LIFE

For illustration purposes, one visitor-to-resident ratio scenario was considered, which used the median percentage of 2% for the growth rate. The observed annual rate of visitation growth of 5.46%, gathered over the past 45 years, was utilized for visitation. The visitor-to-resident ratio was calculated for the year 1950 for comparative purposes. The years 2005 and 2010 are reported for this scenario.

The visitor-to-resident ratio at the four time periods were as follows: 1950 (1:8); 1995 (1:9); 2005 (2:7); and 2010 (3:2). Quantitative means of determining how visitor-to-resident ratios affect quality of life for residents in the town of Banff were not developed. Discussions with members of the Social, Health, and Education sector of the round table indicated that the current ratio (1:9) is already "stressful." Past trends in resident numbers and scenarios examined by the BVFM suggest this quality-of-life indicator is on the decline.

Ecological Indicators

Results from the two categories of ecological indicators, elk populations and wolf populations, were used by the round table and task force to assist with recommendations on human use and other management intervention, and are discussed below.

ELK POPULATIONS

The elk component of the BVFM was utilized extensively by the scientific experts conducting analyses for the elk module of the Ecological Outlooks Project (see Woods et al. 1996), and a brief summary is presented here. These results were in turn utilized by the round table and task force to formulate recommendations.

One futures parameter was examined for elk in the BVFM: population change. Utilizing the elk population component of the BVFM, seven scenarios were executed, examining the effects of road mortality, rail mortality, fire management, and predator access to prey. For comparative purposes, the first scenario assumes no change in the current situation. That is, the central and eastern zones of the TCH are fenced, but the FE and western zones are not. As is observed currently (Paquet, unpublished data), 100% of the population of elk in the western zone is available to wolves, while only 20% is available in the central and FE zones, and 50% is available in the eastern zone. Mitigation measures are not implemented on the Canadian Pacific Railroad (CPR), but train traffic is also not increasing over time. Finally, vegetation does not "age"—that is, habitat quality remains constant over time. Results of the scenario were reported in terms of population of elk in the different zones under consideration (W, C, E, FE). This scenario suggests that elk numbers could decline slowly in the central zone while increasing slightly in the eastern zone. Populations in the W and FE—where mortality pressures are high from roadkill, railkill, and wolves—collapse in approximately 30 years.

The second scenario assumes no change in trends of management and mitigation. That is, all parameters are the same as for scenario 1, but vegetation "ages" (that is, habitat quality declines owing to successional advancement), causing the amount of high and very high habitat for elk to decrease and thus affecting the carrying capacity over time of each zone. Traffic on the TCH also increases over time at the current estimated rate of 3% (Parks Canada 1995). This scenario suggests that elk populations could decrease in the central zone, remain relatively constant in the eastern zone, but once again collapse in the western and far eastern zones. The rate of this collapse is accelerated owing primarily to the increase in mortality pressure from traffic.

The third scenario adds the mitigation measure of fencing to the western zone; otherwise, assumptions are the same as those for scenario 2. Results indicated that the mortality in the western zone is slowed by fencing but owing to mortality pressure from wolves and the railway, the population still declines, steadily.

The fourth scenario considers the effects of mitigating the railway in all zones. This scenario suggests higher elk numbers throughout all zones, except the far eastern population, which is still subject to high levels of highway mortality. The slight decrease in the western population is due to predation pressure from wolves. The central and eastern zones are still not fully available to predators in this scenario, so the west receives a disproportionate level of predation stress.

Scenario 5 assumes that the railway is not mitigated but that the entire population of elk in the park is available to wolves. The model suggests that restoring the predator/prey system in the park without mitigating the railway could have a detrimental effect on elk populations.

Scenario 6 is the same as scenario 5 but includes a railway mitigation component. The model suggests a slowing in the decline of elk, but declining habitat quality and wolf predation (assuming the entire population in the park is fully available to wolves) still causes declines.

Scenario 7 was termed utopia by the wildlife experts working on the elk module. In this scenario, the TCH and the railway are mitigated throughout the park, but not in the far eastern section. Wolves have access to the entire population of park elk, and a program of prescribed burn is implemented to maintain habitat quality to levels observed in 1995. A fire management program would presumably increase quality habitat, given the park's current history of fire suppression. Scenario 7 suggests that elk populations in the park would stabilize after approximately 30 years. The number of individuals at equilibrium would most likely be higher than those suggested by the model, owing to the increase in habitat quality with a prescribed-burn program. The population in the far east still collapses, of course, owing to high mortality pressure from the highway.

The BVFM allows for an explicit examination of assumptions and potential outcomes of mitigation actions. Visitation was set at 3% for all ungulate scenario runs. Road mortality in unmitigated scenarios could increase under higher rates of visitation. The model is also sensitive to both the carrying capacity and the recruitment rate developed by the scientific experts. Continued research in the valley should be utilized to refine the model as a working tool.

WOLF POPULATIONS

Potential wolf numbers are generated as a proportion of elk numbers and the availability of overall ungulate biomass. Variation in wolf numbers under various elk scenarios were therefore observed during the running of elk population simulations.

Conclusion

Participatory modeling allowed stakeholders with particular interests to develop and use models that examined management alternatives. As model developers, participants deliberated over assumptions of the models and issues that affected their interests. In doing so, they discovered hidden values and assumptions within their working group, causing them to ask questions that they previously had not considered. They also learned that the system they were trying to simulate is complex and, in some cases, found themselves faced with making decisions based on little or no scientific information. As model users, participants could ask "what if" and examine trade-offs among a variety of scenarios and assumptions. The result was a better understanding of the potential problems facing the valley, and of how management can help resolve those problems. As a result of the participatory process, stakeholders were better prepared to make recommendations for park management.

The 2.5-year Banff–Bow Valley Study was an iterative learning process for all those involved. Sometimes understanding of the complex ecological, economic, and social factors at work in the valley was subtle; other discoveries were staggering. The Futures Outlook Project was an integral part of the Banff–Bow Valley Study process that provided opportunity for comprehension and learning. The minister summed up her impression of the contribution made by the futures component of the study by stating: "The Banff–Bow Valley Study will continue to be a source of inspiration for decades to come. Its

conclusions were reached by looking 50 years into the future and trying to picture what the Park should look like. This is how we should ensure the future of
the Park" (Parks Canada 1997).

Some recommendations put forward to the minister seem obvious to those
who have been conducting research in the park for decades and warning of the
consequences of past park management decisions. Certainly some of the recommendations remain contentious. But recommendations were formulated by
the public through a deliberative and consensus-seeking process, informed by
the best available science, and are a reflection of the values and beliefs that the
public, as a whole, hold for Banff National Park.

As a result of the Banff–Bow Valley Study process, scientists' warnings
have largely been accepted by the public, and vocal opponents to more responsible management have been marginalized. The minister stated that change in
Banff National Park will take courage and sacrifice. Fear of constituent reaction
and resulting political fallout have caused noncourageous politicians to follow
a course of status quo in the past, often yielding to private businesses operating in the park. The BBVS recommendations are a message from the con-
stituents to policymakers that they support the implementation of dramatic
changes in park management.

DISCUSSION QUESTIONS

1. The Task Force of the Banff–Bow Valley Study determined that a mediated modeling process was needed in order to meet the objectives of the
   study. Was this an effective approach? Why or why not?
2. What is the best way to incorporate complex technical information into
   the mediated modeling process? What was the method used by the
   BVFM modeling team? Was the method effective? Why or why not?
3. How should technical information for which there are no data be incorporated into the mediated modeling process? What was the method
   used by the BVFM modeling team? Was the method effective? Why or
   why not?
4. In the context of a national park setting, were the stakeholder groups
   participating in the Banff–Bow Valley Study the appropriate mix to
   meet the study's objectives?
5. Fourteen stakeholder groups (interest sectors) were identified though
   two did not participate in the process. What, if anything, should be done
   in a mediated modeling exercise when critical sectors do not participate?
   Can the interests of these sectors be represented in the modeling
   process? Can these interests be represented in other ways? How?

8

Sage Grouse Populations in Southeastern Idaho, U.S.A.: Effect of Sheep Grazing and Fire

Ellen K. Pedersen and

William E. Grant

The sage grouse (*Centrocercus urophasianus*) is a unique western North American gallinaceous species that inhabits the sagebrush (*Artemisia* spp.) community. The sage grouse has attracted popular attention because of its spectacular mating ritual. In spring, males congregate on leks—open areas surrounded by stands of sagebrush. The displaying males perform a wonderful mating dance that includes vocalizations, wing slapping, air sack inflation, and display of their magnificent plumage (see Figure 8.1). This display attracts the females to the leks, where mating occurs. The dominant male performs most of the mating. After mating, females start the nesting process. Nesting and brood rearing occur in the sagebrush, often in the vicinity of the lek.

Sage grouse depend on sagebrush for food, shelter, and nesting to different degrees throughout the year and the different stages of their life cycle (Patterson 1952; Klebenow 1969; Martin 1970; Pyrah 1970; Wallested 1971; Eng and Schladweiler 1972, Wallested and Pyrah 1974; Autenrieth 1981; Connelly et al. 1988). Herbaceous vegetation and adequate sagebrush coverage are fundamental for nesting and early brood rearing. In winter, sagebrush is the sage grouse's only food source.

The dependency of this bird on sagebrush makes it vulnerable to changes in this vegetation. Populations are declining rangewide, and several reasons

Model available at www.mediated-modeling.com

Figure 8.1.
Male sage grouse
Source: National Image Library.

have been cited for this decline, including increasing agriculture and urban development, highway construction, ranch development, power line placements,
reservoir construction, military activity, use of pesticides and herbicides, hunting, predation, fire (both wild and prescribed), drought, livestock overgrazing,
and overgrazing combined with drought (Patterson 1952; Klebenow 1969;
Wallestad and Pyrah 1974; Autenrieth 1981; Connelly et al. 1988; Gregg et al.
1994; Ritchie et al. 1994; DeLong et al. 1995).

    For over a century the dominant use of the sagebrush rangelands occupied
by sage grouse has been grazing of livestock, such as cattle, sheep, and horses.
Sheep graze the rangelands seasonally, consuming forbs and grass.
Management for livestock includes periodic removal of sagebrush, usually by

burning, to increase herbaceous production and reduce sagebrush cover. Sage grouse are hunted for sport. Hunting regulations for sage grouse vary depending on local conditions. Whereas predation, hunting, pesticides and herbicides, and sagebrush removal often were identified as the cause of local reductions in sage grouse populations, the regionwide decline was attributed to factors occurring throughout the sage grouse range, such as changes in fire regimes, grazing, and weather patterns (Connelly and Braun 1997; Connelly et al. 2000a; Connelly et al. 2000b).

Populations of sage grouse, once abundant in the sagebrush ecosystem of the western United States and southwestern Canada, are declining rangewide (Dalke et al. 1963; Crawford and Lutz 1985; Connelly and Braun 1997; Schroeder et al. 1999). This decline, interspersed with periods of increasing numbers, has been observed for about a century. However, the decline was accelerated during the 1930s, 1950s, and 1980s (Patterson 1952; Braun 1995; Connelly and Braun 1997).

The concern about sage grouse decline has caused the species to be considered for inclusion in the U.S. federal threatened and endangered species list. Listing will likely result in changes in the management of the sage grouse and its habitat, including the possible elimination of livestock grazing on public lands that harbor populations of sage grouse. Consequently, several groups, including state and federal agencies, conservationists, ranchers, citizens, sport hunters, falconers, and Native Americans, are taking an active role in the management of sagebrush rangelands to aid in the recovery of sage grouse populations and other wildlife species dependent on the sagebrush ecosystem.

The Idaho Department of Fish and Game recognizes the negative trend of the sage grouse populations but does not attribute full responsibility to any of the above-mentioned potential threats to sage grouse abundance, and no single activity carries the blame for it. In December 1998, the Idaho Department of Fish and Game organized a meeting with the intention of establishing a local working group that would be in charge of the development of a management plan for the sage grouse. Interested individuals or organizations were invited to the meeting. Currently, a core group continues to meet and is producing documents leading to a final management plan.

Sage grouse management is so complex because of the life history of the species; the numerous and diverse interest groups affected, and the variety of causes attributed to the decline of sage grouse populations. Concrete information about the effect of grazing on the sage grouse populations is lacking.

As part of our extracurricular activities at the Department of Wildlife and Fisheries, Texas A&M University, we have gained extensive experience organizing modeling workshops to address complex problems surrounding ecology and natural resources, especially in Latin America. During the workshops, the interest of the participants is kept high by working on topics related to their areas of expertise. Our workshops provide individuals or groups with an introduction to the theory of systems analysis and simulation and apply the theory to build simulation models. The positive experience with modeling workshops on a focused topic has served as the framework for this case study, involving actual stakeholders to study the problem of the effects of sheep grazing and fire on sage grouse populations in Idaho.

The specific goal of this case study was to gather existing information and link this information together in a coherent picture. Although livestock grazing is included among the list of possible causes for the decline in sage grouse populations, there are virtually no studies that address this problem experimentally. Several studies have addressed the effect of fire on sage grouse populations (Fisher et al. 1996; Pyle and Crawford 1996; Fisher et al. 1997; Connelly et al. 2000a, 2000b; Nelle et al. 2000). The results of these studies are controversial; sagebrush recovery after fire depends on a variety of factors, the most important being which sagebrush species is involved, and the extent and the intensity of fire.

Modeling Process

We organized two workshops with the support of the U.S. Sheep Experiment Station located in Dubois, Idaho. The first workshop had a three-day duration, while the second lasted one day. The sheep station provided the facilities where we conducted the meetings and a list of suggested participants. This list included specialists in sagebrush and sage grouse ecology, sheep and cattle production, wildlife management, and environmental policy. Additionally, the sheep station provided funding to support the development of a simulation model.

Representatives of groups interested in aspects of sage grouse management were invited to assist in the construction of a simulation model in an interactive setting. The main interest of the U.S. Sheep Experiment Station was to obtain a final product: a model that could be used to simulate different management strategies and to observe the effect on the sage grouse populations.

FIRST WORKSHOP

The first workshop took place at the U.S. Sheep Experiment Station in December 1998 and lasted three days, with an eight-hour session each day. Participants represented the Idaho Department of Fish and Game, U.S. Forest Service, Natural Resources Conservation Service, U.S. Department of Agriculture, U.S. Bureau of Land Management, U.S. Sheep Experiment Station, county commissioners, livestock producers, a conservation organization, and a consulting firm.

A roundtable discussion was conducted the first morning, during which each participant presented his or her view of the problem. This roundtable turned into a lively discussion, because of the variety in the participants' backgrounds and their divergent views of the problem, as well as a general lack of information about the sage grouse ecology (in a systems ecology sense). For example, in general, livestock producers tend to perceive predators as the major cause of the population decline of sage grouse. However, the reason for a potential increase in nest predation may be the reduction of grass that serves to visually protect the nests, owing to overgrazing. On the other hand, predator control has been greatly reduced in recent years, and ranchers observe much higher levels of predation in general, suggesting the possibility of increasing predator populations.

Participants advocating the use of fire to remove sagebrush maintained that after burning there is an increase in forbs, grass, and arthropods, which are beneficial to young sage grouse. On the other hand, sage grouse researchers argued that even though young birds depend on those food sources to develop, the sagebrush is vital for shelter.

A short introduction to the theory of systems analysis and simulation was presented during the afternoon of the first day (Grant et al. 1997). This introduction was as simple as possible, given the heterogeneity and diverse background of the group, but we considered that providing the basic ideas would help everyone to understand the modeling process. Although most of the participants did not have a formal education in systems analysis, after one session they were able to understand some basic concepts. Most importantly, the participants were able to think in terms of the interconnectedness of a system and to visualize that the components are not isolated.

Subsequently, we provided a short introduction to the software (STELLA 6.1, High Performance Systems, Inc.) that we used to build the model. To exemplify model development and model use, we presented a running version of a preliminary model constructed prior to the workshop. This model had been developed without the input of expert opinion, which led to some incongruent results. In general, the participants focused on the results and not the structure of the model. For example, the biomass of grass and forbs did not parallel the real world, but perhaps more importantly, the participants pointed out that the time at which forbs and grass production peaked was incorrect. This was a subtle situation that demonstrated the active involvement of participants. These inaccuracies in our preliminary model resulted in a distraction that was overcome once we were able to change the parameters that had led to results that were unacceptable to some participants.

That preliminary model was not used again, although some of the structure served as a prototype for the participants to start developing their own models. Some participants looked at the preliminary model but decided that they preferred to start from scratch. Starting with a blank page in the STELLA program was less confusing than trying to adapt to another person's thinking.

Participants were divided into four groups for the development of individual submodels according to their area of expertise: sagebrush (including other vegetation, such as grass and forbs); sage grouse population dynamics; livestock (sheep) grazing; and climate. Each participant decided which submodel they wanted to develop.

Each group of two to four participants worked on their submodels on separate computers. These submodels would eventually form the final model after they were connected. During the afternoon of the last day of the workshop, each group presented a running version of the submodel. Although these models were necessarily somewhat flawed because of the short time and the limited training in systems analysis and use of the software, the process of building the model and its public presentation provided very useful insights into the problem.

In addition, data were only available as "expert opinion" during this phase of model development. The participants had not brought "hard data" with them, but their knowledge in their area of expertise gave us confidence in the quality of preliminary data used in the model constructed during the workshop. Expert opinion was an integral part of model development and was carefully considered and included in the final version of the model. The organizing team took careful notes during the participants' model development and final presentation in an attempt to capture their ideas.

During the year following the first workshop, the organizing team built a new model using the knowledge acquired during the workshop and the literature relevant to the model. Some submodels were expanded to include more detail; other submodels, such as the climate submodel, were reduced to include only the most important processes. The general tendency of the participants was to include too much information in the model instead of producing a simpler model. For example, people working on the climate submodel insisted on the importance of the different types of snow (wet, dry, heavy, etc.). Although this is a valid distinction, inclusion of such details would have complicated the model without increasing its usefulness.

The number of participants declined during the workshop for a variety of reasons, including other commitments, bad weather, and distance to the workshop location. However, some participants who were not present during the initial days participated in the construction of the models or attended the final presentation. In the period between the workshops, some participants were consulted about information included in the model and the results; after running the model, we asked if the results were coherent with their knowledge of a particular part of the system.

Second Workshop

A second, one-day workshop was held one year later (January 2000) to present an updated version of the quantitative model. This version of the model was close to completion; however, some controversial factors required input from several participants. The model was evaluated according to expert opinion, by comparing observed and simulated sagebrush response to fire, growth of grass and forbs under historical environmental conditions, and simulated population dynamics of sage grouse. After this workshop, in which the model was run in the presence of the participants who performed the evaluation, the organizing team finalized the model, and several scenarios were run to obtain a final product.

A third workshop was planned to present the final results of the simulation exercises. Unfortunately, owing to funding limitations, we were unable to conduct this workshop.

The Resulting Model

The system of interest that emerged from the workshop was bounded spatially by an area encompassing the movement of sheep as they are herded annually from low-elevation to higher-elevation areas that also include the home range of a sage grouse population. The temporal scale was defined as the length of time sufficient to represent the ecological succession associated with the sagebrush community following a fire—roughly 60 years. The questions of primary interest to the group focused on the response of sage grouse populations to different sizes and frequencies of fire and different levels of sheep grazing intensity.

The level of detail at which important ecological processes needed to be represented to adequately address these questions was, not surprisingly, a topic of debate. However, the general consensus was that the model needed to capture the week-by-week dynamics of sage grouse nesting and chick development, the weekly movements of grazing sheep, and the long-term dynamics of sagebrush recovery after fire. Important ecological relationships included the influence of forb biomass (*food*) and sagebrush canopy cover (*cover*) on nesting success and chick survival; the influence of cover on chick, juvenile, and adult survival; the effect of sheep grazing on forb biomass; and the role of environmental conditions in determining growth of vegetation and availability of food for sage grouse. Details of all aspects of the model are presented in Pedersen (2001).

Important temporal relationships represented in the model included sagebrush community dynamics and sage grouse population dynamics (see Figure 8.2). The sage grouse population considered in this model migrates between winter habitat and breeding habitat, seasonally sharing the spring area with grazing sheep.

Sagebrush community dynamics represent changes in canopy cover and height of sagebrush (see Figure 8.3) and changes in the biomass of grass and forbs (see Figure 8.4a and 8.4b) in response to environmental conditions, sheep

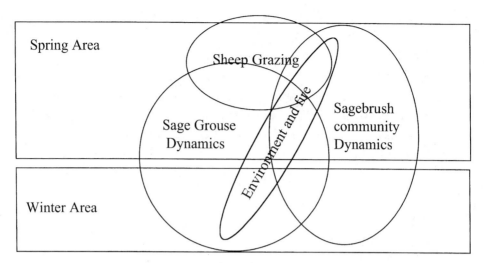

Figure 8.2.

Conceptual model representing the effect of sheep grazing and fire on sage grouse populations

grazing, and prescribed fire. Sage grouse population dynamics represent the female portion of an age-structured (weeks) population, with age-specific natural mortality (see Figure 8.5). Hunting mortality occurs during the fall. Environmental conditions affect vegetation growth and thus availability of forage and shelter for sage grouse and forage for sheep. Snow affects the availability of sagebrush for grouse during winter, and snowmelt initiates vegetation growth during spring. Fire reduces canopy cover, height of sagebrush, and biomass of herbaceous vegetation.

Spatially, the model represents spring and winter areas used by sage grouse and sheep. As sheep are herded toward their summer mountain ranges, they graze through the habitats used by sage grouse for spring breeding activities. During late summer and fall, sheep again graze through the sage grouse

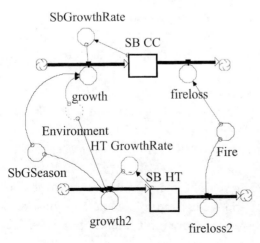

Figure 8.3.

Diagram of sagebrush module representing the dynamics of sagebrush canopy cover (SB CC) and height (SB HT). Symbols from Forrester (1961) as modified by High Performance Systems, Inc. (1996).

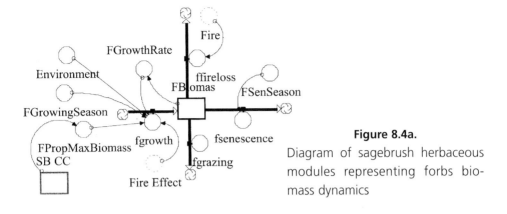

Figure 8.4a.
Diagram of sagebrush herbaceous modules representing forbs biomass dynamics

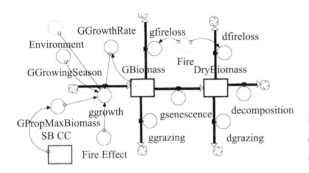

Figure 8.4b.
Diagram of sagebrush herbaceous modules representing grass biomass dynamics

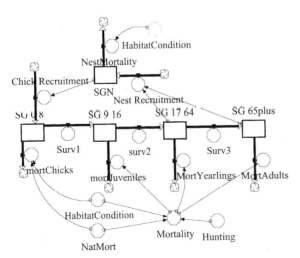

Figure 8.5.
Diagram of sage grouse module representing the dynamics of female chicks (0 to 8 weeks of age), juveniles (9 to 16 weeks of age), yearlings (17 to 64 weeks of age), and adults (>65 weeks of age).

breeding habitats (spring area) as they return to lower elevations. In the model, the spring area is divided into four sheep grazing zones, with each grazing zone potentially divided further into one unburned and two burned areas (see Figure 8.6a). The growing season is assumed to be different in the different grazing zones and can start with one to two weeks' difference, depending on snow accumulation and rate of snowmelt.

The winter area also is divided potentially into one unburned and two burned areas. It is assumed that fire removes all vegetation from a burned area;

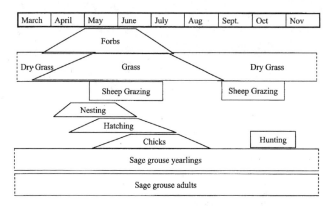

Figure 8.6a.

Overview of important temporal relationships in the sage grouse model, including movements of grouse and sheep among spring, summer, and fall ranges, life history events of grouse, plant phenology, and the hunting season.

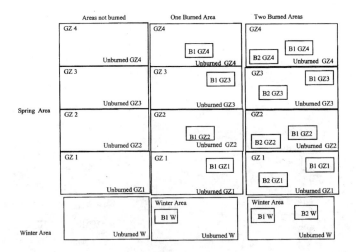

Figure 8.6b.

Overview of important spatial relationships in the sage grouse model, including the spring and winter (W) areas of sage grouse, sheep grazing zones (GZ1–GZ4), and unburned and burned areas (B1 and B2). B1 and B2 represent the areas burned first and second, respectively, in spring and winter areas.

therefore the model can create a complex habitat mosaic. The effect of different habitat conditions (sagebrush canopy cover and height, and biomass of grass and forbs) on sage grouse and forage available for sheep is calculated on the basis of the abundance and distribution of the salient habitat conditions of the unburned and burned areas in a grazing zone.

The size of the burned areas and frequency of burning can vary, producing a habitat mosaic of up to 15 patches in different stages of vegetation development: 12 patches in the spring area and 3 in the winter area. The size of the areas burned depends on the management strategy selected, and can vary during the simulation.

The annual seasons (spring, summer, fall, and winter) (see Figure 8.6b) are defined according to sage grouse use of the area and the potential vulnerability to habitat alteration. In winter, sage grouse migrate to low-elevation areas with less snow cover. During spring, summer, and fall, sage grouse are in the same area but are affected differently by habitat conditions. For example, in spring, during nesting, sagebrush canopy cover is relatively more important than in summer, when sage grouse use sagebrush mainly for roosting.

The level of detail was one of the main concerns of the organizing teams. The sheep submodel created by the participants became too complex and unwieldy, probably because one of the participants had prior experience with modeling. For example, participants considered details such as the sex, weight, and age of the animal grazing. Although this information might be important, we considered that the average consumption of an "eating machine" was sufficient for the model. Obviously, it was difficult to convince that group that we thought that less detail was better for the model. In fact, the final model does not even have a sheep submodel, but only information such as number of sheep, time spent grazing, and proportion of biomass consumed.

The sage grouse group also wanted to include as much detail as possible. For example, they considered the addition of males to be important. However, from the modeling standpoint, the fact that the hens produce the offspring was considered enough. Males were implicit in the model. Addition of more complexity does not necessarily increase the usefulness of the model.

Scenarios

To assess the effect of sheep grazing and fire on sage grouse population dynamics within a sagebrush community in southeastern Idaho, we ran twelve 60-year replicate stochastic simulations for each of the following situations:

- 3 levels of grazing intensity (none, light, heavy) without fire
- All 27 combinations of
  - 3 levels of grazing intensity

- 3 levels of fire size (small, medium, large)
- 3 levels of fire frequency (low, medium, high)

In all scenarios, hunting was represented as the annual harvest of 5% of the population distributed equally over four weeks during fall. In light- and heavy-grazing scenarios, 30% and 50%, respectively, of the annual forage produced was consumed by sheep during spring and fall, with forage removal distributed equally across the grazing period. In scenarios including fire, in each grazing zone pairs of fires two years apart burned either 1%, 5%, or 10% (small-, medium-, and large-sized fires, respectively) of the spring area at intervals of either 60, 25, or 17 years (low, medium, and high frequency, respectively).

Results of the Simulations

Simulation results suggest that grazing intensity, fire size, and fire frequency all have statistically significant effects on sage grouse breeding populations (Pedersen 2001; Pedersen et al.). The highest breeding populations were obtained with the baseline scenario (see Figure 8.7) and with scenarios with no

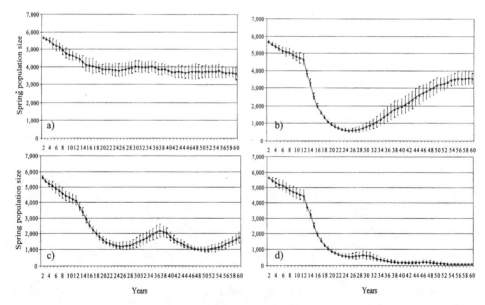

Figure 8.7.

Typical time-series curves of mean (±1 SD) sage grouse population size during spring (week 10 of the year) resulting from 12 replicate stochastic 60-year simulations. The 30 scenarios, which simulated different grazing intensity, fire size, and fire frequency, produced: a) stable populations (12 cases); b) decline and recovery (6 cases); fluctuations (2 cases); and d) collapse (10 cases).

grazing and small- to medium-sized, low-frequency fires. Under similar fire regimes, breeding populations decreased with increasing grazing intensity.

Size of burned areas, frequency of fire, and level of grazing all affected sage grouse population dynamics and the size of the breeding population during the final year of the simulation. The burning of small areas at low frequency had a slightly positive effect on sage grouse populations compared with unburned areas, whereas large fires burned at high frequency had the most negative effect on population size. Results from scenarios with the same fire regimes at different levels of grazing show that heavy grazing had a more pronounced effect than light grazing on sage grouse breeding populations (see Figures 8.8a, b, c; Figures 8.9a, b, c).

The results of the simulations were not unexpected; they are largely predictable with common sense. However, the main learning experience from this modeling process was the understanding of the interconnectedness of the system; no part of the system is isolated from other parts of the system.

Another important result of this effort was that of overcoming the antagonism present during the first round table discussion; once the participants collaborated in the construction of the model, they were working together toward a common purpose. We realized that modeling was the new common language spoken by the participants to solve their problem. None of the participants spoke this language correctly, but all communicated efficiently. Unfortunately,

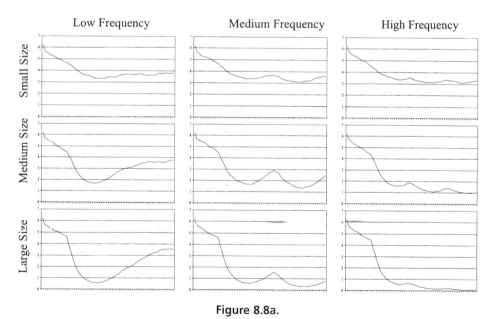

Figure 8.8a.

Time-series curves of mean sage grouse population size during spring (week 10 of the year) resulting from 12 replicate 60-year stochastic simulations under a no grazing scenario. (y axis are in thousands, x axis represent each of the 60 years).

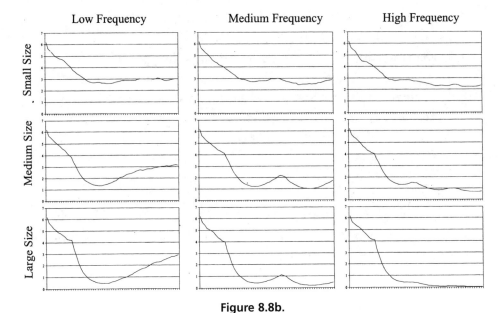

Figure 8.8b.

Time-series curves of mean sage grouse population size during spring (week 10 of the year) resulting from 12 replicate 60-year stochastic simulations (y axis are in thousands, x axis represent each of the 60 years) under low levels of grazing

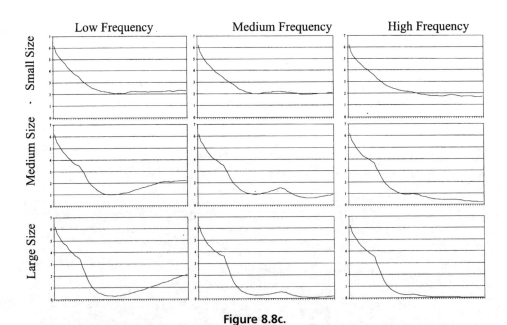

Figure 8.8c.

Time-series curves of mean sage grouse population size during spring (week 10 of the year) resulting from 12 replicate 60-year stochastic simulations (y axis are in thousands, x axis represent each of the 60 years) under high levels of grazing

No Burning

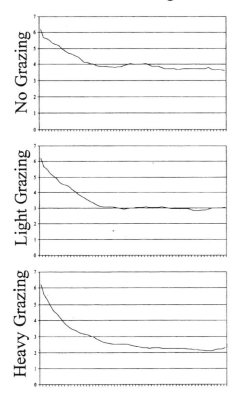

Figure 8.9a.

Time-series curves of mean sage grouse population size during spring (week 10 of the year) resulting from 12 replicate 60-year stochastic simulations under a no fire scenario. (y axis are in thousands). X axis represents each of the 60 years

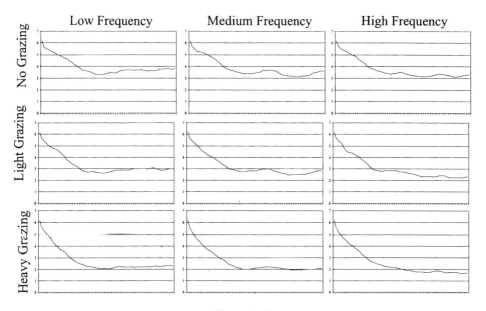

Figure 8.9b.

Time-series curves of mean sage grouse population size during spring (week 10 of the year) resulting from 12 replicate 60-year stochastic simulations. (y axis are in thousands). x axis represents each of the 60 years under a small-size fires scenario.

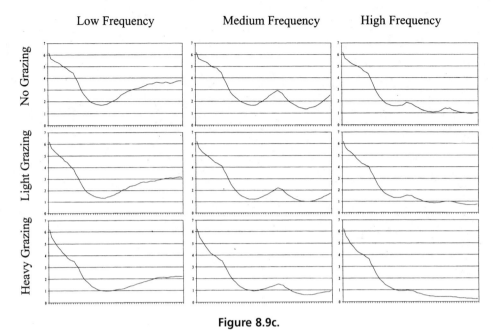

Figure 8.9c.

Time-series curves of mean sage grouse population size during spring (week 10 of the year) resulting from 12 replicate 60-year stochastic simulations. (y axis are in thousands). x axis represents each of the 60 years (c) medium-size fires.

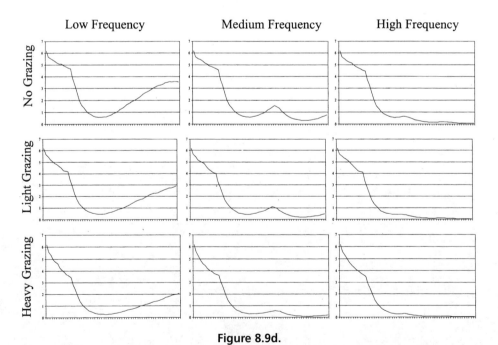

Figure 8.9d.

Time-series curves of mean sage grouse population size during spring (week 10 of the year) resulting from 12 replicate 60-year stochastic simulations. (y axis are in thousands). x axis represents each of the 60 years under a large-size fire scenario.

after the ending of this project, we have not been able to maintain contact because of a management change at the institution that hosted this project.

Conclusion

A simulation model built to assess the effect of sheep grazing and fire management on sage grouse populations illustrated the importance of habitat conditions (represented as sagebrush canopy cover, and biomass of grasses and forbs) for sage grouse abundance. In most scenarios, removal of grass and forbs through grazing and sagebrush through fire negatively affected sage grouse populations. Decline of sage grouse populations has been observed rangewide. Although livestock grazing has traditionally been considered one of the causes of decline, sufficient experimental data are not available to support this statement. This modeling process represents a first attempt to assess the lack of information surrounding this complex problem.

During data gathering for this model, we experienced a lack of basic information, especially in terms of the vegetation, such as growth rate of grass and forbs, and growth rate of sagebrush under local environmental conditions. Sage grouse parameters for southeastern Idaho were readily available. However, data on the effect of different sagebrush canopy cover on sage grouse survival were nonexistent.

A third workshop was planned to evaluate the model and resulting scenarios with the participants. However, this workshop did not materialize owing to a lack of funding and a shift of priorities after the leadership of the sheep station changed. Therefore, the modeling results mainly represent the learning within the organizing team. The participants did not evaluate the results of the "final" simulations, and we are not able to provide insights into how the group perceived these outcomes.

On the basis of simulation results, grazing by itself does not cause the extinction of sage grouse, although it may reduce population size. However, fires burning large-size areas (10% of the spring area) at high frequency (17 years between fires) will result in the extinction of sage grouse populations, as will fires burning medium-size areas (5% of the spring area) at medium frequency (25 years between fires) with heavy grazing (consumption of 50% of available forage).

Although results of this model support the idea of the negative effect of grazing on sage grouse populations, it must be taken into account that the model was used to compare strategies. Each strategy was applied during the entire simulation, rather than changing the management strategy according to an examination of the status of the sage grouse population. For example, in some of the strategies in which populations were declining, a change in sheep management might have reversed the overall negative effect.

However, the model clearly identified certain factors that are key for sage grouse abundance, such as herbaceous vegetation (both grass and forbs) and sagebrush canopy cover. These results are supported by limited field data.

The model can be used to simulate management scenarios that favor forbs, grass, and adequate sagebrush canopy cover that benefit the sage grouse during different phases of its life cycle.

DISCUSSION QUESTIONS

1. What are the characteristics of an "ideal" mix of stakeholders or representative technical persons (e.g., professional biologists, hydrologists, economists) in the mediated modeling group?
2. At what point in the mediated modeling process, and to what extent, should participants be presented with the technical aspects of systems modeling (e.g., how to program in a modeling language like STELLA)?
3. At what point in the mediated modeling process, and to what extent, should the participants be presented the theoretical basis for systems modeling?

9

Decision Support in Coastal Zone Management in the Ria Formosa, Portugal

Nuno Videira, Marjan van den Belt,

Paula Antunes, Rui Santos, and Sofia Gamito

The Ria Formosa is a coastal wetland of 18,400 hectares with sandy barrier islands, located in the south of Portugal in the Algarve region. It is a dynamic ecosystem subject to changes from physical forces. It is also a rich biological resource. The Ria Formosa is a haven for many bird species, including many migrating species. As a part of the International Conservation Network, it is an internationally important humid area considered in the 1971 Ramsar Convention on Wetlands and listed as a Special Bird Protection Area in the 1979 European Community Directive (79/409/EEC). It is also classified as a site of special interest for nature conservation (Site 13 of the Portuguese first list for the NATURA 2000 Network). The Ria Formosa is spread along 55 kilometers of low-lying coastline included in the municipalities of Faro, Loulé, Olhão, Tavira, and Vila Real de Santo António (see Figure 9.1).

The Ria Formosa was classified as a natural park in 1987. The aims of this designation included (1) promotion of the adequate use of the natural resources; (2) promotion of the cultural, social, and economic development of the resident population based on traditional activities; and (3) regulation of recreational activities in accordance with the natural and cultural resources (Decree-Law no. 373/87 of 9 December 1987).

The Ria Formosa model can be downloaded from www.mediated-modeling.com or http://gasa3.dcea.fct.unl.pt/ecoman/riaformosa/

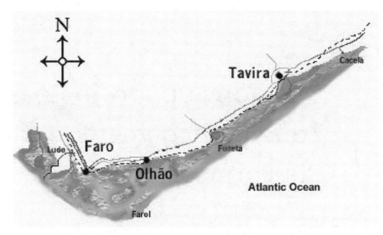

Figure 9.1.
Map of Ria Formosa

Ria Formosa and its surroundings constitute an attractive tourist destination area. The lagoon is used extensively for recreational purposes. Tourism in the area is primarily beach related. Golf courses, yachting, water sports, and game fishing also constitute important tourist activities. The intense influx of tourists during the summer creates impacts in sensitive areas, such as dune strips on barrier islands (see Figure 9.2). Other economic activities include agriculture and cultivation of bivalves and fish in the Ria Formosa complex system of channels and salt marshes (see Figure 9.3).

The growth of urban and tourist developments is localized in sensitive areas, such as the barrier islands. High urban growth pressure, the over-

Figure 9.2.
Construction on a barrier island of the Ria Formosa

Figure 9.3.
Complex system of salt marshes and channels of the Ria Formosa

exploitation of fish and shellfish stocks, the abandonment of salt pans and traditional activities more in harmony with conservation objectives, the inadequate treatment of domestic and industrial effluents, and the overexploitation of aquifers are just some of the problems affecting sustainable development of this area.

The Key Issues

The Ria Formosa is a multiple-use area where tourism, ecotourism, aquaculture, fishing, wildlife protection and nature conservation, effluent discharge, fishing, and navigation with recreational boats conflict with each other. Current stakeholders in the area include the Portuguese Institute of Nature Conservation through the Natural Park of Ria Formosa authority; the Regional Directorate for the Environment and Natural Resources; tourism authorities, trade associations, and industrial interests; fishermen and fishing authorities; other local/regional authorities, namely municipalities; nature conservationists; and the local population, including permanent and summer residents.

As in many Portuguese coastal areas, different authorities at the local, regional, and national level have jurisdiction in the Ria Formosa. For example, the natural park authority is responsible for environmental management of the area. However, the Regional Directorate for the Environment is responsible for the licensing of effluent discharges. In addition, municipalities have an important role in most decisions affecting land use, such as licensing of urban and industrial activities. National and regional tourism authorities are responsible for the licensing and operation of tourism infrastructures. Maritime authorities have jurisdiction over the coastal strip, including beaches. This set of institutions, with many different roles, and sometimes conflicting objectives, makes the implementation of integrated management approaches very challenging.

How the Mediated Modeling Process in the Ria Formosa Got Started

In June 1997 a group of scientists gathered in Lisbon at the Luso-American Foundation for Development (FLAD) to discuss the subject of "sustainable governance of the oceans." During the meetings, scientists developed six management principles (Costanza, Andrade, et al. 1998), one of which was the "participatory principle." This principle emphasized the necessity for local stakeholder involvement in decision support and decision making.

Marjan van den Belt proposed a mediated modeling project in the Ria Formosa to FLAD, and a team of researchers was established with contributors from the Ecological Economics and Management Center at the New University of Lisbon (ECOMAN/FCT-UNL) and from the University of Algarve. From a research perspective, this project functioned as a pilot project to scope out the possibilities of mediated modeling for involvement of local stakeholders in decision making. From a practical perspective, the project created an opportunity for stakeholders in the Algarve to develop a network addressing the complexities of environmental and interlinked economic challenges.

An initial list of potential participants was outlined from knowledge of the current decision makers and technicians with interests in the area. A first set of invitations was sent, providing as well additional information on the research project and its objectives. The invitations included a reply form that had a field designed for each stakeholder to suggest his or her own list of participants (other stakeholders that they thought should also be invited to the modeling workshops).

A total of 55 potential participants were invited for the meetings, including 21 decision makers and 34 technicians. In general, the response to the invitations was considered to be above initial expectations, given time and cultural constraints.

One of the major concerns with respect to the involvement of stakeholders in the Ria Formosa meetings had to do with the novelty of such an approach in Portugal, where there were as yet no references to the development of mediated modeling projects. To guarantee the success not only of the modeling workshop itself but also—and primarily—of the invitation process, we took the following cultural factors into consideration:

- The primary goal was to provide a useful integrative tool for stakeholders in the Ria Formosa. However, the secondary goal was to test this tool from a research perspective. Given the research nature of the study and the fact that the stakeholders initially were not the promoters of the project, we had to ensure that the mediated modeling process would add a beneficial component to the region without wasting the time of participants. Thus an effort was made during the invitation process to motivate individual participants to give this unusual form of collaboration a chance.
- Traditionally, stakeholders in this area have a competitive attitude and might have reservations with respect to collaborative approaches. Interviews with each potential participant revealed a relatively high level of skepticism toward collaboration. Most participants had not met each other before they were invited to participate in the mediated modeling process.
- Stakeholders are usually reluctant to share information and provide data. Very often institutions refuse to provide information as an attempt to mask environmental and socioeconomic problems.
- Many decision makers in Portugal have full agendas and short-term objectives. Their focus is strongly determined by political objectives, a fact that does not leave room for engaging in collaborative or research activities.
- The last problem cascades to the technicians. Unmotivated decision makers do not usually allow technicians to allocate full-time days for extra activities such as the collaborative approach we were about to propose.

Despite this potentially constraining environment, the response to the project proposal was positive. Table 9.1 presents the number of participants

Table 9.1.
Number of participants in the four Ria Formosa workshops

Workshop	Participants		
	Decision makers	Technicians	Total
1st	6	15	21
2nd	2	10	12
3rd	1	12	13
4th	2	13	15

Table 9.2.

Composition of the stakeholder group in the four Ria Formosa workshops

| | Workshop | | | |
Participants	1st	2nd	3rd	4th
Protected areas	3	2	2	3
Regional authorities	1	2	3	2
Local authorities	4	1	1	2
Academia	3	1	2	1
Nongovernmental organizations	10	6	5	7
Total	21	12	13	15

who attended each of the four workshops (partially or full-time); Table 9.2 shows their distribution across major institutional categories.

The original focus of the study was very broad to avoid getting locked in on one specific existing conflict. Instead, we wanted to provide a starting point that would allow for finding the connection and patterns between a host of pressing conflicts. The first problem statement had to be open enough to allow a free flow of ideas. The initial focus of the Ria Formosa modeling exercise was thus to collaboratively examine the linkages between ecology and economics in this area.

Why are the linkages between ecology and economics important? Often ecological and economic studies were undertaken separately. Although many studies addressing particular social, economic, and ecological aspects of the Ria Formosa have been published, there is a need for integrating the linkages between these subsystems. Furthermore, Geernaert et al. (1998) stress that in first-order coastal catchment areas such as the Ria Formosa, owing to their relevance in the ecological and economic context, integrated management instruments can help to balance trade-offs between the high conservation and recreational value of these areas and their sustainable development.

This chapter describes the experience of the mediated modeling process and the resulting model. Appendix 6 presents model details. The model may also be downloaded from http://gasa3.dcea.fct.unl.pt/ecoman/riaformosa/ or www.mediatedmodeling.com.

The Ria Formosa Modeling Process

Prior to the first meeting, we interviewed stakeholders who had expressed a commitment to participate, to get a feel for the problems as the participants perceived them. Also, since this was not a commissioned project, we had some explaining to do about why this could be a worthwhile endeavor. In early 1998, Marjan van den Belt and Nuno Videira visited potential participants at their workplaces and conducted preliminary interviews focusing on the following goals:

- Introducing the objectives and scope of the mediated modeling workshops
- Identifying potential outcomes and clarification of participants' role in the process
- Eliciting stakeholders' mental models of the cause-effect relationships driving the main problems in the Ria Formosa
- Establishing rapport with the participants.

At the end of this stage, after 15 participants had been interviewed, we started to get a clearer picture of the perceptions of our stakeholder group. The answers to the questionnaires used in the interviews were important, not only to further evaluate the results of this experience but also to come closer to the participants' own vision of the reference conditions in the Ria Formosa. On the other hand, the individual causal diagrams that were drawn for most of the interviewed participants warned us about the challenge ahead, as most of the stakeholders failed to identify, at this stage, the feedback relationships among the problem variables that they had identified.

Over a period of four months, the University of Algarve in Faro hosted four meetings.

First Meeting

On March 9 and 10, 1998, a group of participants met for the first time. The majority obviously attended to check out the situation and decide whether they were going to pursue the exercise. About 40% of the invitees showed up. Even though less than half of the invited participants attended, the distribution of representatives from different agencies was deemed satisfactory enough by the participants to pursue a mediated modeling process. The committed participants expressed confidence that the initial problem definition (linkage between ecology and economics) could be addressed from an integrative perspective.

However, some important and perhaps crucial representation was lacking. For example, participation by representatives from port authorities, tourism authorities, coastal defense, agriculture, and civil engineering might have given the group insightful information they could now only speculate about. In addition, not all of the five municipalities located within the national park were represented.

A few participants did not pursue the mediated modeling process after the first meeting. Even though the reasons for abandoning the process are not clear for all participants who did not continue, at least one cited difficulties in following the plenary discussions and the technical information being disclosed (although we provided simultaneous English-Portuguese translation and explanation of some of the technical concepts).

The mediated modeling process outlined in Chapter 3 is very representative for this case study. A brainstorming exercise generated a consensual and comprehensive definition of the problem to be addressed by the model. The group proposed the following list of problems (statements and questions):

- The Ria Formosa system is fragile.
- How to sustain the system from an ecological point of view?
- How to sustain the system in an artificial (managed by people) manner?
- Jurisdiction overlap is an issue not clearly tackled in Ria Formosa.
- How to address regional economic activities? How do regional economic activities influence the Ria Formosa?
- Urbanization in the barrier islands should be addressed.
- Areas of active salt production are decreasing.
- Which are the implications of fishing activities versus tourism activities in the Ria Formosa ecosystem?
- Ria Formosa provides valuable services to the society.
- How can humans preserve the resources on which they depend?
- How do economic activities interact with natural resources?
- How to balance economic activities with ecological sustainability?
- Should the model consider only the lagoon system or also the terrestrial system?

The facilitated brainstorming exercise about a host of problems freed up energy in the group. Participants appreciated the opportunity to share their points of view among people they usually didn't interact with. The next step was to integrate all the referred problems into one single problem statement. To this extent, the group produced in an iterative fashion a consensual problem statement that the model should address: "Development of a scoping model that aims at the balancing of the economic activities development with the conservation of the natural heritage of the Ria Formosa."

During the plenary discussion, the group also decided that the model boundaries should correspond with the physical boundaries of the Ria Formosa Natural Park. This choice allowed for considering the ecological and economic processes that take place in both the lagoon and the terrestrial systems. Especially, one environmental nongovernmental organization (NGO) felt very strongly about the model focusing on the park, while a representative from a municipality was concerned that such a focus would exclude regional economic influences, foreign tourists, or pollution from upstream agricultural areas.

This situation was resolved by focusing on the land use and how this is altered by certain activities within the Ria Formosa. Issues such as foreign tourists could then be integrated through the tourist sector and its effects on land use. In a similar manner, funds provided by the European Union are an important force from beyond the physical systems boundaries. Through management decisions (see Management Sector), these funds have an impact on land use issues such as the construction of infrastructure or the undertaking of dredging.

Nonspecific influences from outside the Ria Formosa, such as upstream pollution from agriculture, would be integrated in the model in relative terms. For example, What is the relative contribution to eutrophication from waste discharge due to tourism versus that from agricultural runoff? Unfortunately, no representative with a background in agriculture was present to contribute insights on this issue.

The time frame to be used in the model was also defined in the first meeting. It was decided that the period from 1980 to 1998 should be used to describe the behavior observed in the real world. Participants felt that adequate data would be available for this period to allow the model to run different scenarios for the period from 1998 to 2020. Even though the participants agreed that this time span was beyond the horizon the average decision maker would be interested in, they felt this simulation horizon was important for discovering patterns in the system.

Invited decision makers had declined participation; however, a few of the participants were technical staff and represented at least one decision maker. On several occasions during the series of workshops, several participants expressed frustration with the short time span and narrow-mindedness displayed by the decision makers, without attacking anyone in particular. Even though the participants believed that from a technical point of view, the medium-long time frame chosen for the model was necessary to address the challenge, they thought that political incentives limit decision makers to consider the proposed medium-long time frame.

On the second day of this meeting (March 10), the participants began the development of the model, starting with the definition of the model sectors. By the end of the day, four sectors had been outlined: Infrastructures, Natural System, Human Activities or Human System, and Management. The participants undertook this task quite confidently, and the early sector definition was essentially preserved throughout the continuous model improvements and iterations.

It was possible then to progress to the identification of the main variables that the participants thought should be included in each of the sectors. We challenged the group to start by thinking about the most important stocks—that is, variables that would represent the accumulations in each sector. It was expected that some of the identified variables, such as "cities" or "political decisions," would require improvements in the next stages, but the foundations of the mediated model had been set.

Second Meeting

The second and third workshops were primarily intended for the invited technicians, who provided their knowledge and insights as the modeling exercise progressed. A core group participated in all of the modeling workshops. This group included representatives from the Ria Formosa Natural Park, the Institute for Nature Conservation, local and regional authorities, universities, marine institutes, the Sea Foundation, and environmental associations.

On March 16–17, the participants resumed the definition of the qualitative model structure, conceptualizing many of the model's stocks, flows, auxiliaries, and connectors.

For the Ria Formosa model, participants worked in the first two meetings both in small-group sessions (each group focusing on the structure of each of the model sectors) and in plenary sessions (where the contributions from the small-group discussions were incorporated in the model and made transparent for the whole group to discuss).

The small-group sessions were particularly important in the second meeting, in which the four small groups (one for each of the sectors) engaged in lively discussions about the concepts underlying the model structure. Some participants would show up in the same small group, while others preferred to rotate and contribute to and learn from a variety of ongoing discussions. The members of the project team facilitated the small group sessions as much as possible. Following are some examples of the work done in small groups:

- The participants working on the Infrastructures sector conceptualized a web of relationships defining the accessibility of the Ria Formosa area. They started using the STELLA icons to draw the stocks and flows relating to the transformation of the land. Later on, this sector was to be renamed the Land Use sector.

- Similarly, the original Human Activities or Human System model sector underwent a transformation as the understanding about the specifics became more clear. This model sector was replaced with Socioeconomic Activities and defined a patchy structure representing the revenues of the main economic activities that take place in Ria Formosa: bivalve and fish aquaculture, salt-making industry, sand extraction, fisheries, shellfish gathering, and tourism.

- Meanwhile, another group was tackling the definition of water quality, the erosion processes, and the dredging activities, all of which were regarded as relevant issues to be depicted in the Natural System sector. At this point, the participants from the Ria Formosa Natural Park gave insightful information on the premises of the dredging plan that was being promoted in the park.

- The Management sector was being developed by another set of partici-

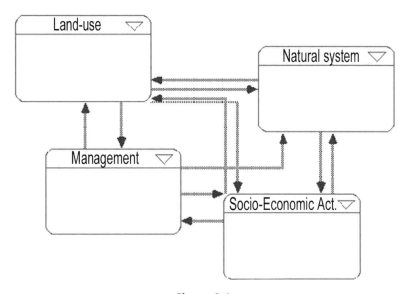

Figure 9.4.
Overview of the Ria Formosa model sectors

pants on the basis of knowledge of the existing types of funding and its allocation to the diverse areas of investment.

The four model sectors presented in Figure 9.4 had already been filled in with a set of interconnected variables by the end of the second meeting. The overview describes the land use in and accessibility of the Ria Formosa, the socioeconomic activities, some of the natural processes occurring in this ecosystem, and the managerial processes that fund most of the actions impacting the social, economic, and natural systems.

Third Meeting

The month separating the second and the third meetings was used by the project team, with the aid of the participants, for the collection of data and information needed for quantification of the variables. Personal meetings with participants, who offered data, took place. Appropriate stakeholders provided access to databases and official statistics. The same task was repeated in between the third and the final workshops. With the use of STELLA's simple dialogue boxes it was possible to convey the underlying assumptions and data used for some of the variables to the broad stakeholder group.

At the end of the third meeting, which took place on May 18–19, most of the linkages between the model sectors had been identified and a fair amount of variables had been quantified. Following are descriptions of the model sectors.

LAND USE SECTOR

In the Land Use sector, days spent by the population in Ria Formosa ("people _days") were defined by using a composite of days spent by residents and tourists. This composite number determines the amount of pollution, as measured by the biochemical oxygen demand (BOD). BOD in turn affects the model sector describing the natural system.

It was assumed that the resident population grows owing to a fixed birthrate (represented by the "natality" variable) and to immigration (which is a function of the quality-of-life and employment indices). The quality-of-life index expresses the idea that people deciding to immigrate to the Ria Formosa value accessibility, quality of water, and the existence of natural areas relatively unmanaged by human activities.

People may travel to Ria Formosa using four means of transportation: airplane, boat, train, or car. The existing capacity for each of these alternatives was defined (expressed in the relevant units for each case—e.g., length in kilometers for "roads") and then normalized in the same scale with a corresponding "access" variable—for example, "access_roads"—to yield a total "accessibility" value for the area.

Increasing the accessibility of the Ria Formosa is dependent on the investments made for each alternative mode of transportation. The investments are a function of the available funds and the unit price of capacity added. One general policy goal is to improve the accessibility of the Ria Formosa, which will increase the ease with which tourists can reach the area. The participants agreed that there should exist an optimum of accessibility, reflecting the idea that when too much investment is made in accessibility, the area may become full or congested, overshooting its optimum.

The Land Use sector also divides the Ria Formosa into Terrestrial and Humid areas. The terrestrial part consists of Natural Area, Urbanized Area, Area Tourist Resorts, and Natural and Constructed Area Barrier Islands. The humid part consists of Area Cultivated Bivalves (CB), Area Cultivated Fish (CF), Area Commercial Salt Marshes, and the Natural Area. All areas dominated by human activity were subtracted from the Natural Area available according to the rate of transformation that had occurred up until 1998. After 1998, the default scenario is to allow the trends to continue, assuming no changes in the parameters and relations defining the trends (e.g., the default scenario assumes no licensing of new fish, bivalve, or salt production areas).

In order to analyse and compare different management scenarios for the future of Ria Formosa several variables were defined as "input variables." For example, a slide bar representing "political will" can be placed on the value 0 (zero—no political will) or on 1 (existence of political will). In the model, the "political will" determines the occurrence of remediation actions in the Barrier Islands or lack thereof.

Land use changes impacting the natural humid area are a function of the natural accretion and erosion forces and the licensing of new areas for the economic activities (bivalve, fish, and salt production). On the other hand, activities requiring a license depend on the maximum areas that could conceivably be suitable for each of these economic activities, the demand for new areas, and the licensing policy of the management activity.

The quantification of the maximum suitable areas was not a straightforward task. The participants had contrasting opinions regarding the values to assign to these variables (e.g., Should the maximum area of bivalves be set equal to the total natural area of salt marshes?). We allocated a significant length of time for stakeholders to express their perceptions and their underlying reasoning. The values used in the model were finally assigned on the basis of the plenary discussions and further research conducted with some of the participants in between the third and the final workshop. Although the participants believed that the temporary estimation was based on reasonable assumptions, the issue was contentious enough to deserve further investigation.

Land use changes in the model that impact the natural terrestrial areas depend on the erosion/accretion forces, the urbanization rate, and the tourism development rate. The natural index indicates the relative amount of undisturbed natural space of the Ria. The attractiveness index was defined as a nonlinear relationship dependent on the relative natural area still existing and the quality of water. An information component was added to reflect the increase in attractiveness that is made possible when agencies invest in promoting and marketing of the Ria.

SOCIOECONOMIC SECTOR

Several economic activities generate income, and thereby profit, in the Ria Formosa. The stakeholders with expertise on fisheries felt that the model should portray the revenues of only those fisheries depending on the Ria Formosa—that is, revenues resulting from the catch (within and outside the Ria's limits) of fish species that have their nursery area inside the Ria. (In practice, since the statistics consider only the total fish catch, the participants estimated the percentage of this catch, which results from the juveniles coming from the Ria). Those revenues depend on the average fish price (an average for all commercial species was considered), on the average catch per boat, and on the capacity of the competent entities to avoid illegal catch (of juveniles).

Shellfish revenues depend on the wild bivalves that are caught both by tourists and by the local population (for commercial purposes). Salt-making revenues depend on the quantity of salt extracted and its average price and reflect the shrinking area of the commercial salt marshes (salt pans). Several tourism-related aspects, including the quality-of-life index, drive the tourist revenues. The profits in the tourism industry are (to a certain extent) driving the development of tourist resorts in the Land Use sector.

The revenues from cultivated bivalves and the cultivated fisheries are driven by their respective specific market aspects as well as by their area of occupation. The revenues from sand removal out of the Ria Formosa depend on the amount of sand extracted and the sand price per cubic meter.

A "benchmark value" for ecosystem services (disturbance regulation, waste treatment, raw material source, habitat, food production, and recreation) was also derived as an indicator, based on the "starting point" values for marshes proposed by Costanza, d'Arge, et al. (1997), which was multiplied by the natural area remaining in the Ria Formosa to yield a "total _value_tidal_marsh."

NATURAL SYSTEM SECTOR

The pollution generated by the population was measured in terms of an indicator of biochemical oxygen demand (BOD). Considering the average unit release of BOD per habitant, the size of the population, and the working conditions of the wastewater treatment plants (the efficiency and the percentage of served population), it was possible to estimate the released BOD, which affects the water quality index. The water quality is also affected by the organic pollution generated in aquaculture and other industries, but modestly compared with human waste. Given the fact that the model does not consider the spatial distribution of pollution, the water quality index reflects an average situation, although the impacts of pollution are significant only in specific areas. The quantity of wild bivalves was chosen to give some indication of the impacts that might be observed in situations of a bad water quality. Bivalves (both wild and cultivated) are also affected by the sediment grain of the substrate and therefore by sedimentation processes.

Natural processes and human activities on the barrier islands affect accretion processes. Erosion is also affected by natural and anthropogenic processes. Both accretion and erosion make up a need for dredging if the goal is to keep this dynamic system stable (from the human point of view). Depending on the available funds, a certain dredging effort is possible. The question remains whether the gap between the desired dredging and the possible dredging can be closed. Dredging is being undertaken for different purposes, one of which is the drainage of pollution out of the lagoon system. It remains to be seen whether this goal can be achieved with dredging.

The volume of water in the Ria influences the flushing processes of the pollutants. Dredging is the artificial solution to keep the flow in the Ria high and to prevent channels from closing. In other words, the sedimentation dumped owing to natural and anthropogenic causes can be remedied if the investments are available. The desired effects of dredging are of a short-term nature. Sedimentation and dredging are influencing the humid zones, which are very productive areas, from which several ecosystem services are derived.

MANAGEMENT SECTOR

The model sector labeled Management illustrates the allocation of monies from public funds, European Union (EU) funds, government funds, and local taxes. However, in the standard model settings, only the EU funds are active. These funds come in two major inputs associated with the financial aid to Portugal, provided by the EU Financial Frameworks I and II. The other funds were left open and remain nonactive in the model. The user can assume values as desired in order to explore potential incomes. The funds can be spent on policy enforcement, policymaking, technical projects, and information. The funds made available in the Management sector are the main promoters of activities in the other model sectors.

Fourth Meeting

For the final meeting of the Ria Formosa mediated modeling project, on May 25, decision makers were again invited, because their presence was important for evaluating policy development scenarios and for promoting commitment to the implementation of the main conclusions. However, a very low response rate from decision makers was observed, regardless of the fact that a few days prior to the final workshop a large number had expressed a commitment to participating. Apart from the stated time constraints, it is thought that decision makers had overly relied on their representatives by the end of the case study. Nevertheless, this lack of representation was balanced by the fact that the decision makers, who are part of the Ria Formosa Natural Park management council, agreed to organize in the future an additional meeting in which they would address the results of the research process (which represents an intention of commitment to project's results).

During the final meeting, a set of scenarios was run and discussed in a plenary session with the stakeholder group. The purpose was to conclude on the lessons learned from the process of building the model and from the model itself. Some of the issues discussed are presented in the following sections, including funding for the management of Ria Formosa, accessibility, licensing of new aquaculture areas, dredging of the Ria's channels, and restoring the barrier islands.

FUNDING

The first set of scenarios simulates the sources of funding (potential or available) and their allocation to different policy areas. In the base scenario, the only active sources are the EU funds, which are allocated to four types of funding targets: technical projects (85%), policy enforcement (5%), policy-making (5%), and information (5%). The participants deemed the technical projects to be the most significant portion of the funding targets in the base scenario.

With EU funds at zero, nothing will be achieved in terms of wastewater treatment or dredging. Considering what was known at the time about funding (from 1980 to 1999), one could observe two peaks in EU funds (corresponding to the first and second EU Financial Frameworks) impacting the development rate of several technical projects (see Figures 9.5a and 9.5b). According to historical data, the development of accessibility, dredging, urbanization, and wastewater treatment projects has been deeply dependent on the availability and distribution of EU funds.

Using the knob in the interface as an alternative to the slide bar, the settings can be changed. The effects of alternative sources for funding can be examined. In Figures 9.6a and 9.6b we present the results of what could happen in the period between 2000 and 2005 if government funds for the development of technical projects would be considered. Adding this funding source, three peaks of funding stimulate implementation of the desired projects.

ACCESSIBILITY

The accessibility to the Ria Formosa was identified as a major development objective at the beginning of the workshops. The reasoning was as follows: the higher the accessibility, the more tourists, the more money, and the more that can be invested in mitigating the adverse effects of tourism, such as the increase in waste production. Accessibility also influences the quality-of-life index. The data on accessibility are quite unsubstantiated, but the reasoning agreed on by the group was as follows: the more one invests in all forms of accessibility, the earlier the benefits will level off owing to overinvestment, which creates problems such as congestion and lower quality-of-life standards.

Figures 9.6a and 9.6b compare the effects of considering an investment rate of 50% in accessibility (in the base scenario) with an alternative strategy that consists of investing almost all (90%) of the available budget. The main difference is that the optimum investment level is achieved at an earlier date with a higher investment rate but levels off just the same. In addition, as later scenarios will show, too many tourists may reduce the quality of life through other pathways, such as a reduction of water quality. Since a tax on tourism is virtually nonexistent, the investment in end-of-pipe mitigation of the waste will have to come from other funding sources (the EU funds in this model).

LICENSING OF NEW AREAS

The enforcement of licensing of several activities (salt production, cultivation of bivalves, and cultivation of fish) in the Ria Formosa was discussed as a meas-

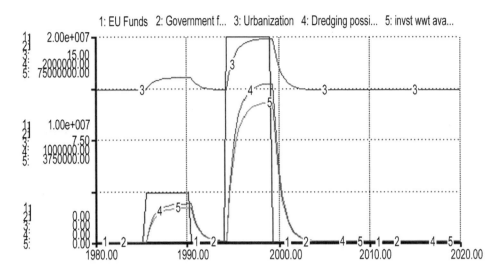

Figure 9.5a.
Ria Formosa base funding scenario

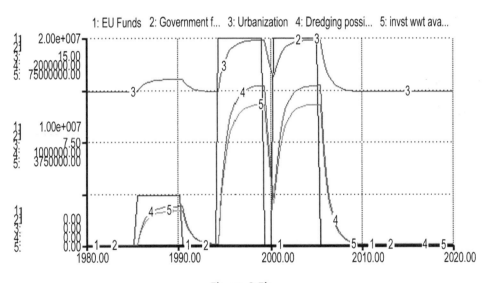

Figure 9.5b.
Ria Formosa funding scenario considering the allocation of government funds

ure to protect the integrity of the system. In 1998, licensing was often not enforced. In an attempt to gather data for the model, it became clear that the licensing of salt production was probably not making any difference since the salt production sector is decreasing for internal economic reasons. On the other hand, licensing of bivalve and fish cultivation is very relevant.

Figures 9.7a and 9.7b show the impact on the total value of the tidal marsh caused by two different licensing scenarios. In the base scenario, illustrated in Figure 9.7a, there is no licensing of new cultivated fish (CF) and cultivated

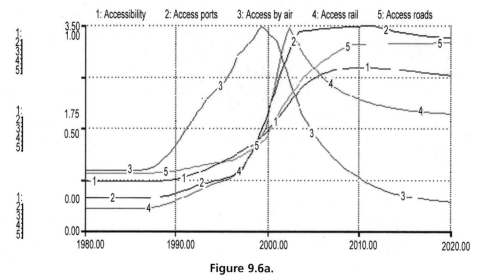

Figure 9.6a.

Ria Formosa base scenario for accessibility (investment rate of 50%)

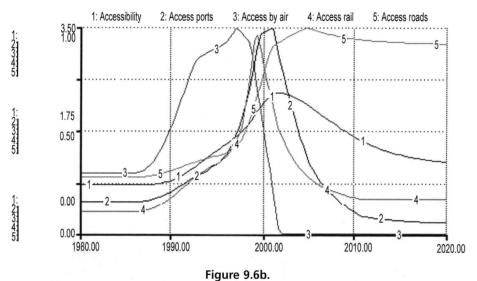

Figure 9.6b.

Ria Formosa alternative scenario for accessibility (investment rate of 90%)

bivalves (CB) areas. On the other hand, Figure 9.7b depicts a scenario in which new areas for fish and bivalve cultivation are allocated (after 1998), assuming that licensing rates allow for the CF and CB producers to fulfill their demand for new areas (which is as a function of their revenues). It may be observed that licensing new CB and CF areas causes a negative impact on the total value of the tidal marsh, since the development of those economic activities reduces the total natural area and thereby reduces the total value of ecosystem functions (such as disturbance regulation, waste treatment, and recreation, among others).

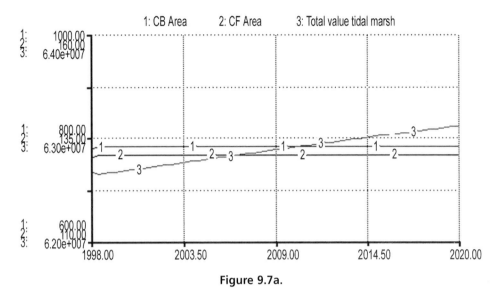

Figure 9.7a.

Ria Formosa base scenario for licensing of cultivated bivalves (CB) and cultivated fish (CF) areas, and its impact on the total value of the tidal marsh

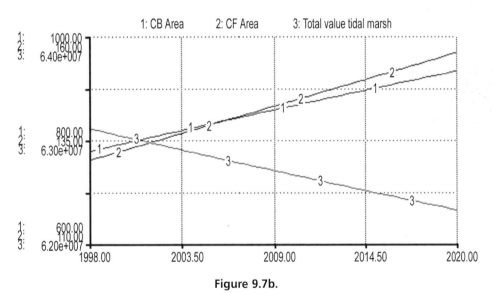

Figure 9.7b.

Ria Formosa scenario considering the licensing of cultivated bivalves (CB) and cultivated fish (CF) areas and its impact on the total value of the tidal marsh

DREDGING

Dredging of the channels in Ria Formosa is promoted to stabilize the system from a human point of view. The main goal is to increase water circulation inside the lagoon so that the effect of erosion and sedimentation processes is controlled. However, the contribution of dredging in solving BOD pollution problems may be very small, as simulated by the model.

Although additional data are needed to substantiate this conclusion, it is clear that dredging requires the continuous allocation of investments to fight against the complex and highly dynamic natural erosion/accretion processes. Figures 9.8a and 9.8b portray the effect of overinvesting in dredging. Compared with the base scenario, the alternative policy of investing in dredging 90% of the available budget from EU funds (destined for technical projects) solves only part of the problem for a limited period. Comparing Figures 9.8a and 9.8b (until the year 1998—when funds exist), it becomes clear that

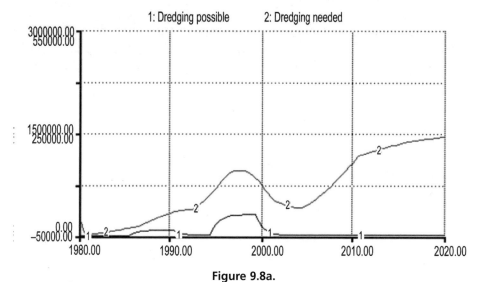

Figure 9.8a.

Ria Formosa base scenario for dredging (10% of the budget)

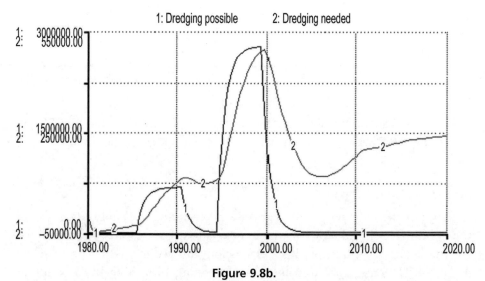

Figure 9.8b.

Ria Formosa alternative scenario for dredging (90% of the budget)

the more funds that are available to meet the dredging needs, the higher will be the amount that needs to be dredged to stabilize the system from the human perspective. On the other hand, when investments in dredging end, the "dredging needed" (see behavior after 2005) increases strongly, regardless of the investments previously made.

RESTORING THE BARRIER ISLANDS

First of all, "political will" was identified as a prerequisite for any action in the barrier islands. Without political will, there is no remediation of the islands, and the houses constructed illegally on these unstable sand strips will continue to produce negative impacts on the system.

On the other hand, if "political will" exists, the effectiveness of remediation is dependent on the costs and on the funds invested in policy enforcement. In the base scenario, the "political will" does not exist; therefore remediation of the barriers islands to the natural state (destruction of illegal construction) will not occur (see Figure 9.9a). An alternative scenario may be tested, considering that after 1999 there exists "political will" to allow for enforcement of a barrier island protection policy (see Figure 9.9b).

Figure 9.9b shows that with "political will" and budget for policy enforcement, the growth in the area of constructions in the barrier islands was stopped owing to remediation measures. However, this policy will not be sustained unless a continuous flow of investments is guaranteed and enforcement is made on a permanent basis.

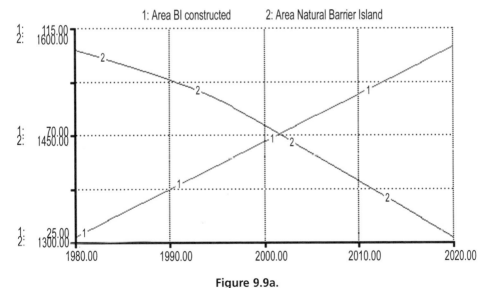

Figure 9.9a.
Ria Formosa base scenario for "no political will"

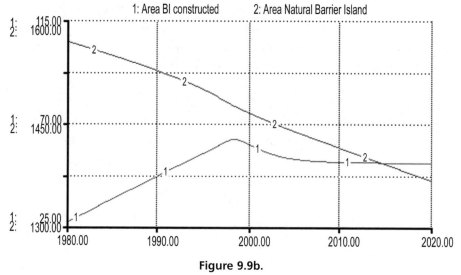

Figure 9.9b.
Ria Formosa scenario considering the existence of "political will"

Recommendations

The model represents a "starting point" discussion among the participants involved. Some consensual preliminary conclusions were drawn during the final workshop. These conclusions provide a list of useful indications for further investigation and additional discussion:

- Even though there is a realization that land use practices are important, there does not seem to be accessible information concerning land use practices over time or the effects of land use on water quality.
- The model has highlighted the need for a better exploitation of the existing infrastructures and a better understanding of the conditions under which an overshoot situation could occur.
- It is easiest to place a value on commercial activities, less easy to relate these activities to land use, and very hard to value other ecosystem services derived from nonused areas.
- The total value of salt marsh is very high compared with the current economic uses in the Ria. The estimation of the total value of the Ria Formosa marsh was based on a global general value for ecosystem services of a marsh (Costanza, d'Arge, et al. 1997).
- More effort should be put into the (e)valuation of ecosystem services.
- Salt making is a decreasing activity owing to the low profit margin. Licensing new areas to reduce salt marsh from being converted into salt pans will not have a large impact.
- Cultivation of bivalves and fish are increasing activities. If they are not restricted, they will steadily continue to grow, reducing the natural areas.

- Environmental management is extremely dependent on the existence of "political will" and external funds.
- The EU funds are crucial for the investments in wastewater treatment and dredging. The question remains whether the Ria Formosa can be economically and ecologically "self-sustaining" after the funds cease to exist.
- There is a need for economic instruments for environmental management to self-sustain the interdependent system of economic activities and ecological services on the local and regional level. An institutional setting (public and private) for redistribution of resources needs to be implemented.
- As the funds are limited and can only be spent once, cooperation between the Ria Formosa Natural Park and the other stakeholders needs to be deepened.
- Decision making should be based on integrated knowledge rather than beliefs.
- The model indicated that dredging provides only a small addition to the water volume. The model suggests that, owing to the strong dynamic effects of the system, dredging loses effect quickly. There is a need for a sustainable solution to work with the dynamic forces of the system, rather than fighting them.
- In relation to dredging, three questions have been identified for future investigation:

  - Do boating and bivalve aquaculture benefit from dredging?
  - Should sand and sediments from dredging stay in the system?
  - Does dredging make a significant impact during neap tide?

It should be noted that in order to demonstrate the model to others, the participants reported that additional calibration of some parameters was needed. In fact, the quantification of some of the model's variables and the estimation of parameters were considered to be critical tasks during the mediated modeling process in Ria Formosa. The project team therefore developed a rating system to assess the modelers' confidence in the data sources. A significant number of variables were rated as "unsubstantiated, however based on logical reasoning," which clearly points out the road for future research in this area.

Some of the most important pieces of the model structure that call for improvement are:

- Definition of the quality-of-life and quality-of-water indices
- Quantification of the investments in the Management sector

- Estimation of the functions and parameters related to the accretion, erosion, and dredging processes
- Quantification of some parameters related to the Socioeconomic sector (e.g., price of sediment, salt costs)
- Quantification of some variables related to the accessibility of the area (e.g., area tourist resorts, port capacity, area attractiveness index)

After the workshops, on May 26–31, we visited ten of the participants for a series of ex post facto interviews. For an in-depth analysis of the participants' responses to our questionnaires see van den Belt (2000) and van den Belt et al. (2000). It was especially interesting to observe that the answers proved our initial suspicions wrong regarding the potential cultural and institutional constraints that could have hindered the mediated modeling process. Participants indicated that:

- Although mediated modeling is a new tool in Portugal, it agrees with the Portuguese culture, which requires an emphasis on facilitated discussions, allowing all participants to contribute their points of view.
- The interactions and communication between stakeholders changed during the course of the meetings, leading to a relatively strong level of consensus, a respect for each other's perspectives, and an integrated discussion.
- Mediated modeling helped structure the thinking and the discussion.
- Exchange of ideas between stakeholders is a useful way to address complex problems.
- The participants indicated that balancing of economic activities with the conservation of natural heritage in the Ria Formosa had more sides to it than they originally thought, an indicator that paticipants learned something new during this experience.
- More linkages with other economic sectors and stakeholders were perceived by the group at the end of the workshops.
- The participants indicated that the model is a helpful tool for them to communicate some of the problems in the Ria Formosa.

To strengthen the momentum created by the Ria Formosa mediated modeling project we presented the model in the discussion forum "What Future for the Ria Formosa?" This meeting was organized by one representative (a participant in the mediated modeling project) of the local environmental association ALMARGEM in June 1998. It took place in the local municipality of Olhão and was open to the public and the local population (forty-three people attended). One of its main goals was to discuss the future of the Ria Formosa, taking as a point of departure the model and the preliminary conclusions that had been highlighted during the mediated modeling process.

The audience consisted of local population and local fishermen. Some participants were initially skeptical toward the use of computer modeling techniques. They argued that "computer models cannot be used to understand social problems and cannot substitute for people." As the discussion progressed, they agreed that the computer could be a tool used by people to expand their mental simulation ability—the computer depends on data and structure, which are given by people. In general, the dynamics of the discussion allowed for shifting the initial disbelief toward the acceptance of the potential benefits of mediated modeling. One of the more important aspects was the fact that this discussion was focused on the social impacts of management in the Ria Formosa area. This has indeed provided a new angle of analysis, which had not been fully explored during the modeling workshops (which were more focused on the environmental and economic impacts).

DISCUSSION QUESTIONS

During the mediated modeling project in Ria Formosa, some procedural questions were raised at certain times within the project team. Bringing such a broad stakeholder group into the modeling process uncovered a set of issues that should be carefully accounted for if we were to repeat this experience in a similar context:

1. What mechanisms could strengthen the representation of stakeholders in the modeling group?
2. What mechanisms, financial or other, could be used to guarantee the full engagement and participation of stakeholders throughout the process?
3. How much guidance should the facilitator/modeler provide in the definition of the model's structure?
4. How to optimize the process of data collection and quantification of the model variables during the mediated modeling process?
5. How to effectively introduce the model to local stakeholders who have not been involved in the mediated modeling process?

At the end of the journey, we felt that the learning experience of the stakeholder group that was involved in the construction of the model was an important, if not the most important outcome. The resulting model can be used by the participants to convey the insights gained during the model building workshops to broader groups as a basis for further discussion and decision making. This model is by no means a "final verdict" on the linkage between ecology and economics in the Ria Formosa. Rather, it provides a structure for in-depth discussion and a platform to advance research and consensus building among different stakeholder groups. More precise questions can be asked based on this model.

10

Lessons Learned

The case studies presented in Chapters 5–9 illustrate how process issues emerge in practical situations. In this chapter, we look at several aspects of the mediated modeling process, including group dynamics, consensus, and cultural issues. We compare the different ways in which these aspects were handled in different settings, with an eye toward identifying the key lessons to be learned from their relative success or failure in contributing to the process results. For example, the Upper Fox and Ria Formosa case studies applied participant surveys before and after the process and thus yielded quite a bit of specific information on how the process affected the stakeholders and how they perceived the usefulness of the process. The other case studies did not undertake a formal evaluation but relied only on observations from the organizing teams. The result was that those evaluations are weaker on depth, structure, and perspective.

Because there is no standardized format for a group modeling effort, it is even more important to pay attention to the differences in the settings and processes used during case studies in order to examine where improvements to the process can be made (Rouwette et al. 2002). For example, the level of active stakeholder involvement determines where a particular project is on the continuum between participatory and expert models. Similarly, cases can be placed on a continuum in regard to the period over which the meetings took place. The number of participants and the level of conflict among them also influence the decisions made during the process.

All of the models in this book are quantitative simulation models, as opposed to qualitative model structures. Not acknowledging this important distinction often leads to confusion in discussing participatory model building. Some use surveys before and after to evaluate the process, and some use preliminary models going into the series of meetings among stakeholders. These and other aspects of group modeling processes are summarized in Table 10.1.

Table 10.1.
Characteristics of the case studies in order of year of development

Characteristic	Banff National Park	Ria Formosa Coastal Wetland	Upper Fox River Basin	Sage Grouse	San Antonio Urban Watershed
Year of development	1995–1996	1998	1998	1999–2000	2000
Funding organizations	National government	Nonprofit	State government	State government	National government
Available on Web	No	Yes	Yes	Yes	No
Stakeholder involvement	Medium	High	High	Low	Medium
Number of participants	Medium	High	High	Low–medium	Medium–high
Conflict level	High	Medium	Medium	High	High
Model goal	Scoping	Scoping	Scoping	Scoping	Scoping
Quantification	Yes	Yes	Yes	Yes	Yes
Length of stakeholders in group meetings	2 days round table + 3 days technical work group Total = 40 hours	6 days (excluding tutorial) Total = 48 hours	9 evenings (5:00–9:30 P.M.) + tutorial Total = 45 hours	4 days Total = 32 hours	Collaborative learning = 56 hours / includes 8 hours modeling
Individual/small-group meetings in between	54 modeler days	2 modeler days	3 modeler days	0 modeler days	0 modeler days
modeling meetings	36 days per participant	0 days per participant	0.5 day per participant	3 days per participant	2 days per participant

(Continued)

Table 10.1. (Continued)

Characteristic	Banff National Park	Ria Formosa Coastal Wetland	Upper Fox River Basin	Sage Grouse	San Antonio Urban Watershed
Length of mediated modeler involvement	300 days	43 days	48 days	180 days	76 days
Period	13 months	4 months	4 months	1 year	1.5 years
Surveys	No	Yes	Yes	No	No
Preliminary model presented	No	Yes	Yes	Yes	Yes
Preliminary model accepted	n.a.	No	No	No	Yes
Focus	Geographical	Geographical	Geographical	Theme	Geographical toward theme
Time scale of model	100 years	40 years	50 years	60 years	48 hours
Times step	1 year	1 year	1 year	1 week	1 hour
Standing	Commissioned	Free-standing	Commissioned	Commissioned	Freestanding

Strengths and Weaknesses of the Mediated Modeling Processes

Each of the processes detailed in the case studies has its own strengths and weaknesses.

Strengths and Weaknesses of the Banff Case Study

The Banff project exemplifies the benefits of a very strong institutional basis. The mandate from the Canadian minister for the environment, abundant reliable funding sources, and the initiation of a broad program provided a firm platform for this process. The futures modeling component in the Banff case encouraged a formal network for stakeholder participation that kept stakeholders engaged in the process.

The formal process of mediated modeling within the round table process lasted two months, during which the formal modeling was addressed on two occasions. After the two months the round table decided that the mediated modeling process was useful enough to pursue with technical representatives, but that it was too time-consuming for the entire round table to be fully involved.

Twelve technical stakeholder representatives gathered in the same room to construct the model together in an informal working-group setting. The technical working group worked in an interactive process of model development for seven months. Stakeholders worked together for three hours during each session. This resulted in a relative emphasis on expert modeling and consultation with stakeholders, rather than fostering direct stakeholder interaction. However, the round table would periodically receive an update of the progress by the technical task force.

Strengths and Weaknesses of the San Antonio Case Study

The San Antonio case study exemplifies collaborative learning. The group model-building exercise was one component among a range of exercises geared toward collaborative learning. The group was brought together from scratch by means of an elaborate stakeholder selection process. In addition, the organizing team kept a good record of attendance rates and was able to quantify the degree of stakeholder participation.

Furthermore, the stakeholders had the opportunity to try two different modeling approaches. The first, an existing model (BASINS), was presented to the stakeholders, while the second, a flow model, was developed with the stakeholders. The latter earned a more favorable response from the stakeholders and was adopted as their own. In fact, the organizing team was relieved that the participants in the collaborative learning process were willing to take another crack at a quantitative modeling approach, one in which they would actively participate, after the first unpopular display of an already finished model.

Although the stakeholders completed a variety of interactive tasks over the course of the collaborative learning program, which spanned almost 1.5 years, the actual construction of the quantitative simulation model was completed in a relatively short amount of time. The model facilitated a constructive dialogue, but changes to the model structure were mainly implemented between meetings, rather than in the presence of the stakeholders. However, the eight meetings leading up to the construction of the flow model can in be regarded as an extended process of qualitative or conceptual model building. The quantitative model proved to be the vehicle that brought much of the learning together.

The main difference between the collaborative learning method used in the San Antonio case and the collaborative modeling process described in Chapter 4 is that the collaborative method used in the San Antonio case may or may not lead to the construction of a quantitative model. In the collaborative process described in Chapter 4, the participants commit to mediated modeling as the organizing method *before* they embark on a collaborative venture.

The overall legacy of the San Antonio project was a self-organizing nongovernmental organization equipped with tools to address future challenges in a collaborative way.

Sage Grouse

The Sage Grouse case study brought a variety of stakeholders together to explore the complex dynamics of sheep grazing and fire on the habitat of the sage grouse. In the face of relatively high conflict, stakeholders assessed what information was available and how crucial components were linked to each other in a dynamic manner.

The participants were trained in modeling during the process and constructed submodels in small groups. The modeler was instrumental in putting these submodels together. All subgroups presented their submodels at the end of the workshop. The interest among the subgroups for each submodel was high.

The advantage of encouraging stakeholders to take responsibility for submodels is that they develop modeling skills and will be more confident in showing the resulting model to others once it is finished. The downside of this approach is that the participants focus on a small segment of the problem, even though they are aware of the problems other groups are capturing in their submodels. The overall picture is mostly accessible to the modeler, who integrates the submodels.

Ria Formosa

The Ria Formosa case showed that mediated modeling as a participatory and collaborative approach can be useful in a country with a relatively strong hierarchical institutional structure, such as Portugal. The approach was novel to the participants, but that did not prove to be a problem. The participants were very content with the process and gained useful insights. However, they had trouble envisioning how these insights could find an audience in the existing rather hierarchical structure. The main weakness in this case study remained the lack of strong institutional buy-in.

An important seed was planted with this pilot project. Funding was made available to support the initial group and build more momentum. On the basis of the initial mediated modeling process, additional funding was made available to develop a more detailed model for management of the Ria Formosa Park.

Upper Fox

The Upper Fox case study exemplified an overall positive experience with a mediated modeling process, as described in Chapter 4, in which the actual model construction was performed in the presence of all the participants to the fullest extent. The process strengthened an existing group of geographic management unit partners (GMUP) in Wisconsin and provided a next step toward supporting Wisconsin's Department of Natural Resources (DNR) in ecosystem management in the Upper Fox.

The logical follow-up question for the Department of Natural Resources became, How can we transfer this experience to the other twenty-two GMUs in Wisconsin without having to commission twenty-two more projects to an outside mediated modeler? This question initiated a discussion concerning the transferability of knowledge and practical experience. The main point is that the design of a mediated modeling process could include this issue of transferability from the start—for example, by means of a local aspiring mediated modeler gaining hands-on experience or confidence with the process (as happened in the Ria Formosa case, Chapter 9).

As the mediated modeling process was unfolding in the Upper Fox, a course of three evenings was organized to entice DNR staff (not necessarily including GMUP participants) to explore the option of developing their own skills in mediated modeling. None of the students who attended the classes as part of an ecosystem management course pursued this option. However, one of the participants in the Upper Fox GMUP did pursue using and adjusting the model for his professional purposes, underlining the importance of actual hands-on experience in addition to, or instead of, a course.

How Does Mediated Modeling Help to Resolve Conflicts?

The mediated modeling process helps to resolve conflicts in two ways. The first involves *establishing a shared "big picture"* as a basis for discussing specific conflicts while getting beyond narrow interests and agendas. The second involves *quantifying relationships* as a way to force confrontation with the real issues.

Method 1: Establish a Shared Big Picture First

The participants in the case studies presented here all brought their own individual issues and agendas to the table. For example, in the Upper Fox case, a forester wanted to convince the other participants that cutting forests does not cause any harm. Likewise, the agenda of a developer was to convince participants that urban development does not cause unnecessary harm. Sport fisher associations and tourist-related organizations wanted to stop anyone else from disturbing their activities, and the farmers felt they had to defend their emissions. Each had an agenda, a set of interests to defend.

In the San Antonio case, an assistant to a city councilman repeatedly attempted to derail discussions of toxic materials seeping from a decommissioned military base into a shallow water table in his district. A planner consistently pushed his vision of a greenbelt, complete with jogging trails and bike paths. Another member hoped the council would assist her in expelling all-terrain vehicles from the segment of the creek that flowed through her neighborhood. A farmer simply wanted to restore flow so he could irrigate his vegetables. A neighborhood association officer continually tried to persuade the other participants that lining the creek bed with concrete was the only reasonable approach to management of the watershed. He frequently argued with a woman whose whole purpose in life revolved around restoring the rich riparian ecosystem of the creek.

During the mediated modeling process these kinds of issues were not addressed head-on. Instead, a higher conceptual level was sought to avoid fruitless arguments over who was right or wrong. Rephrasing the questions on a higher level allowed every participant to contribute to the bigger picture. For example, rather than starting off with "the overpopulation of deer" as a specific problem for the Upper Fox, the broader context of "land use" provided a framework from which specific issues such as the overpopulation of deer precipitated out into their rightful place.

Contentious issues can still enter into the discussion, but from a different angle, with a different weight, and in a broader context. Many of the concerns of the participants representing their agendas were vented during the mediated modeling process and received the appropriate attention. For example, in the Upper Fox case, the process gave foresters the chance to demonstrate that forested areas had actually increased over the period of interest. The developer had a chance to talk about "best management practices" applied in his industry, but the issue of clustering and zoning was considered of more importance, and the developer went along with this line of thinking. Tourism and sport fisheries had to admit that negative feedbacks are possible from these activities and learned more about the bigger picture. Deer populations popped up at the very last moment of the project and were not felt to be as pressing a problem in the bigger picture.

To summarize, the first level of conflict resolution is "Dodge the direct conflict and raise the conceptual level of the discussion before delving into the specifics." This often allows the initial conflicts to be approached in a more balanced manner.

Method 2: Quantification

The second means by which mediated modeling helps to resolve conflicts appears during the quantification stage, when the participants try to define the variables in the model or to share their perceptions about the relative magnitudes of the variables. If participants agree that, after quantification, something they perceived as a big problem turns out to be relatively minor, they are usually willing to drop their concern.

For example, the discussion about what to include under the terms *forest*, *wetland*, and *urban area* was quite extensive in the Upper Fox group. A consensus was ultimately reached on the definitions. The Ria Formosa group argued extensively about the area taken up by fish farms and the potential for this industry to expand into the areas of the Ria suitable for this activity. The defenders of the case did some homework, and a consensus was reached on the figure to be used. In addition, the slide bar option in the model showed that either alternative did not change the outcome of the overall model very much. This defused the argument considerably.

The Down Side of Mediated Modeling

As with any approach, there are limitations as to when to use the mediated modeling approach, reasons not to use this approach, and potential pitfalls with this approach. Potential users or practitioners are better off when they are aware of these problems.

Limitations of Mediated Modeling

Chapter 3 discusses a list of requirements that should be met for a mediated modeling process to be useful. In what situations should a mediated modeling process *not* be used?

- When stakeholders are not prepared to be present in a room and work together on a voluntary basis.
- When stakeholders are not willing to communicate with each other and be open to solutions to an identified problem.
- If the problem itself is not complex or dynamic, other methods may be more appropriate.

However, an unwilling attitude may be caused by the inability to see a pathway toward resolving a (anticipated) conflict. Revealing a potential pathway may alter an unwilling attitude into a cautiously optimistic one.

Arguments Against a Mediated Modeling Approach

There are good reasons to include stakeholders in the modeling process, including:

- To gain more or better data
- To build trust
- To create a mutual group learning process
- To foster the democratic process

However, there are also good reasons to exclude (or limit) stakeholders' input, including:

- Including stakeholder input is more costly and time-consuming.
- The stakeholder group may be biased or self-selected.
- Stakeholder input may result in a loss of credibility for the model and the model results among academic peers.
- A model built with stakeholder input, and the results of the model, may not be a good representation of the issue and may therefore not be better than a model excluding stakeholders in the first place.

Models built with stakeholder involvement face the challenge of maintaining stakeholder involvement from start to finish. So, one could ask, Why spend all the money and effort on something that has only a short life span and doesn't guarantee a solution to the problem? There are several answers to this question. Mediated modeling does not claim to solve all problems, but it does solve some very important and often neglected ones.

Optimally, a mediated modeling project should not stand on its own but should be embedded in an overall research and management program with the appropriate mandates in place. For example, for research purposes, it could be embedded in a "three-step modeling process" (Costanza and Ruth 1998) that makes the scoping model an input to more elaborate (and academically defensible) modeling efforts. In any case, the mediated modeling process contributes a valuable (and often missing) piece in a complex puzzle. The Ria Formosa model has progressed to the second and arguably third step. A management model for the Ria Formosa Park has now been built based on the initial scoping model described in Chapter 9.

Even if a scoping model does not progress toward a research or management model, a scoping model doesn't necessarily have a short life span when it evolves over the course of a larger program from a scoping model into a "summary" model that incorporates the output of more detailed academic models. The stakeholders can still understand this level of complexity and use the scoping or summary model in communications with individuals and groups that don't want to take the time and spend the effort to examine detailed academic models.

For example, an ongoing five-year program studying the "socioeconomic effects of ultraviolet radiation on aquatic ecosystems" started with the development of a scoping model including local stakeholders (professionals in education, medicine, tourism, fisheries, government) and scientists (experts in marine systems, freshwater systems, marsh systems, radiation, and ecological modeling). The scoping model assisted in a shared understanding among the local professionals about what the scientists were expecting to contribute to the bigger picture; likewise, the scientists learned about the questions and concerns of the local professional stakeholders. Over the course of five years the scoping model has evolved into a "summary" model, integrating the most significant research findings over the five-year period and making them understandable and useful to the professional stakeholders. Policy recommendations based on the summary model and endorsed by both the scientists and the professional stakeholders are expected.

Finally, the question of which stakeholders should participate remains an open-ended one. Stakeholder involvement is time-consuming by nature and therefore costly. It takes time to get a diverse group of stakeholders to a minimum required shared level of understanding to respect each other's positions, and to create a picture and goals for a future in which they can coexist. But the potential costs to society of *not* going this route may be even higher. Between the two extremes of inclusion of everybody and decision making by very few there is a wide spectrum of possibilities. An "adequate" level of inclusion should be the goal. While no one knows where this "adequate" level is, we should probably move toward more inclusion rather than less.

The degree to which a stakeholder group may be biased or self-selected is an issue that has received some research attention. On the one hand, it is important to assess the distribution of the participants thoroughly. On the other hand, to get anything done, one has to accept some of the practical complexities and the dynamics of the real world and make sure that steps in the right direction are taken within these constraints.

Pitfalls of a Mediated Modeling Approach

There are four potential drawbacks to the mediated modeling process.

- Mediated modeling is dependent on technical aids. If the projector or the computer doesn't function, there is a major problem.
- The mediated modeler plays a central role and may influence the outcome too greatly.
- The limitation on the number of people per mediated modeling project makes mediated modeling useful mainly for *parts* of a program. It can best function as an anchor in a broader institutional setting rather than

standing on its own. An institutional anchor helps the motivation of the participants to pursue the project.

- The transfer of knowledge to other areas with similar problems is not straightforward. With the appropriate inclination, aspiration, and commitment toward modeling and facilitation, individuals can develop the skills needed for a mediated model relatively quickly. However, often a starting group is initially dependent on an experienced mediated modeler before mediated modeling becomes an integrated part of an established group.

Improvements to the Mediated Modeling Process

Based on the experiences of the contributors to this book, the following general suggestions on how to improve the mediated modeling process can be made.

System Dynamics

Chapter 2 describes the assumption that the scoping models are based on system dynamics, and Chapter 3 illustrates the prominent role of system dynamics in a mediated modeling process. The models in the case studies presented here are somewhat dynamic but could be stronger in their dynamic nature.

For example, the Ria Formosa model has more time lags and feedback loops than the Upper Fox model. During the Ria Formosa modeling process, some time was available to specifically address feedback loops. During the Upper Fox modeling process, however, feedback loops and time lags were not specifically addressed owing to a lack of time.

In general, conscious attention should be paid to time lags and feedback structures in the system. Although feedback loops are, to a certain extent, naturally formed during the discussions—largely owing to leading questions from the facilitator/modeler—the resulting models are not extremely dynamic in their nature, and more insights could possibly follow from a focus on these issues. Addressing feedback loops and time lags should be a routine part of the process when the qualitative structure is being formed.

Recording

All the case studies relied on note taking to record the mediated modeling processes. However, the notes often proved to be taken from the perspective of the mediated modeler. Thus all the organizers of the case studies in this book had some trouble re-creating significant discussions among the stakeholders. Especially those discussions that in retrospect proved to be the basis for a turning point sometimes got lost.

However time-consuming, a designated person and/or video/audio tape to record the discussion may allow better retrospective analysis. Although such records may not necessarily improve any specific process, they would contribute to the research aspect of improving mediated modeling approaches, by making them more available to others.

Working in Small Groups

Working initially in small groups can help to reduce suspicion among participants when they see that the small groups have developed similar model sectors. Later in the process, small-group work speeds up the model construction process. However, when the participants are not used to working in small groups or when a high level of conflict is anticipated, the small groups deserve to be individually facilitated to allow the participants to concentrate on the issues rather than on the organizational chores.

Performance Measurements

Performance measurement of mediated modeling is a wide-open field. The surveying technique applied before and after a mediated modeling process proved to be very useful, but the topics included in the surveys could be improved. The challenge remains to design a before survey that actually provides a useful baseline to evaluate a process that can't be predicted by either the participants or the organizing team. Certain issues are especially difficult to assess. While individual perceptions and interpretations are manageable, baseline issues concerning group dynamics and where a group is with respect to the organizational platform and team learning deserve more attention. It is a challenge to design a survey that is shorter and more informative, while leaving less room for interpretation.

As more case studies that use a variation of mediated modeling become available, the impact of this approach can be better assessed, both as to the differences between mediated modeling cases and relative to other approaches. The meta-approach toward improved performance measurements has been initiated in the form of a database for group modeling interventions (Rouwette et al. 2002).

Contributions of Mediated Modeling

There are three major areas in which a process such as mediated modeling can make a contribution toward solving environmental problems: integration, participation, and intertemporal linking.

Integration

A mediated modeling process can help to integrate several important aspects of complex environmental problems, such as the economic, ecological, and socio-cultural issues involved.

Besides the evidence from the literature, the case studies presented here confirm that a mediated scoping model can help to integrate economics and ecology in a useful fashion for community development. The Banff case study, for example, covers a wide spread of economic, ecological, and social issues.

In the Ria Formosa and Upper Fox case studies, the ecological aspects are included to a more satisfactory degree from a quantitative point of view than are the economic aspects. The social and cultural aspects were not directly assessed in either of these models. Both models came closest to including these aspects by addressing management issues; also, the discussions among the stakeholders indirectly included cultural aspects.

The mix of stakeholders in the Ria Formosa and Upper Fox cases may have played a large role in their bias toward aspects of the "natural system" over the "economic system." In both cases, land use issues and the consequences for the natural system dominated the discussion. However, the questionnaires indicated that the mediated modeling process helped participants to think about the integration of ecology and economics.

The Sage Grouse case study had the potential for examining economic and social aspects and would have greatly benefited from doing so. However, owing to funding and organizational limitations, those aspects had to be obviated.

The flow model in the San Antonio case is a hydrological model and does not specifically address ecology, economics, and social issues. However, the discussion proceeding the modeling exercise covered a variety of issues.

Merely integrating different aspects of an environmental problem is not sufficient to solve environmental problems. A mediated modeling process helps to understand the dynamic behavior of a system. The relationships among these aspects are crucial in understanding the dynamic behavior of a system and in designing alternative solutions.

Participation

The mediated modeling process allows stakeholder participation in an effective way.

The success of stakeholder participation can be evaluated from two perspectives. First, was the range of stakeholder representation broad enough to ensure a balanced discussion and did the range of stakeholder representation expand or contract over the course of a mediated modeling process? Second, how did the level and manner of interaction among stakeholders change during this period? In the Ria Formosa and Upper Fox case studies, the participants were surveyed on the aforementioned perspectives of success. In general, the group members felt that the mediated modeling process allowed for effective stakeholder participation within the group. Again, stakeholder representation and their endorsement of the project are both crucial.

Within the groups, in both cases, more group coherency was formed in comparison to the initial situation. However, since a few participants discontinued participation in the process and were therefore not interviewed in follow-up, it cannot be confirmed with certainty that the process allows for effective participation in all cases. Those participants that stayed on were generally very positive about its potential.

The organizers of the San Antonio, Sage Grouse, and Banff case studies reported that the participants were very positive about the potential of model building and use. However, no formal surveys were performed to evaluate this statement.

Intertemporal Linking

A mediated modeling process helps to link understanding of past, present, and future. In the Ria Formosa and Upper Fox case studies, the linking of past and future was addressed through participants' insights, as indicated by the surveys. The majority of the participants reported that they had learned new aspects of the problem involved. Their views on the problems were originally rather linear and static and changed into more dynamic views with a longer-term perspective.

The organizers of the Banff and the Sage Grouse cases also reported a positive experience with the participants' ability to link past and future within a model. The flow model covers a relatively short time span (2 days) compared with the other models (40 to 100 years).

Mediated modeling fosters a shared, integrated understanding about the behavior of systems among existing or emerging communities. The following specific characteristics of mediated modeling contribute to making it work:

- The images are projected and always visible. The projected model structure helps structuring the discussion and the thinking about complex systems.
- Modeling forces the group to become specific and explicit. The participants have to define and quantify their assumptions and views each step of the way.

For example, the participants in Ria Formosa case study expressed great appreciation for the process, especially because it was not just another abstract discussion. Materializing the discussion is not only visually important; it credits and distinguishes the mediated modeling approach from other participatory nonmodeling techniques. The up-front commitment to developing a simulation model carried the majority of the participants in these processes to higher levels of shared understanding and consensus.

Conclusion

Modeling comes in many forms and shapes. The quantitative approach to group modeling has been used predominantly and successfully in industry for strategic decision support. However, this approach is now being used more and more to aid decision making about the extraordinarily complex environmental challenges we face at the community level. Communities in this context may be groups of stakeholders at the local, regional, or global level. These stakeholders are interconnected owing to their relationships to a particular problem or conflict.

Model building in a group setting provides a participatory path for existing or emerging communities to move toward a more sustainable future. By integrating the most critical aspects that define the behavior of a system, what were considered opposing interests (e.g., ecology and economics) can now be considered in an interdependent framework. The time frame in which crucial phenomena unfold can be examined from a "what if" perspective. Trade-offs among various alternatives become evident. Where the application of one management practice may not achieve the full desired effect, the application of two different management practices together may actually generate significantly better results owing to nonlinear behavior within and among systems.

So many initiatives fail to be implemented because a shared level of understanding is not present, despite good intentions and agreements on common goals. A mediated modeling process provides a space to represent special interests, and the opportunity to examine how interests are interdependent and how the system works at a more conceptual level, so that specific interests find their legitimate place within a larger framework and productive alternatives to resolving conflicts or addressing an anticipated problem can be developed.

Participating in modeling is no more demanding than using one's brain in general. It does not require modeling experience. However, it does require a willingness to think and specifically a willingness to think in systems terms. In our fast-paced day and age, thinking is even more essential. Independently thinking individuals who can create a shared understanding, and build consensus based on that shared understanding, can make a significant difference toward actually solving complex environmental problems. Mediated modeling creates the space for that kind of thinking.

Appendix 1

Comparison of the Case Studies

Following is a relatively detailed discussion and comparison of the case study models on such issues as confidence in the model, scale, and sensitivity. The information is useful for those interested in mediated modeling at a deeper level but can be skipped by those wanting only a broader overview.

Evaluation of the Models

The context in which the modeling processes were initiated varied widely. Logically, the resulting models vary widely as well. Following is an evaluation of several model-related issues.

Chapter 4 discussed the fact that the confidence in a model is an important benchmark for evaluation of a model. Confidence can be based on the "fit" of the model with observations and/or the transparency and acceptability of the structure of the model to the users. A model can be assessed from different perspectives to enhance confidence and foster learning. For example, counterintuitive behavior of a model and sensitivity analysis of individual parameters can contribute to the confidence model users have in a model. Finally, the characteristics of a model in terms of scale and in terms of the trade-offs it makes between realism, precision, and generality create a unique signature for each model.

Confidence Based on Data and Data Fit

Calibration of a model, as described in Chapter 4 and applied in Chapter 5, is one way to improve the confidence in dynamic models. The confidence due to calibration increases with the quality and coverage of data available and the degree of fit of the model with these data.

Complex dynamic simulation models of the type discussed in the case studies often suffer from incomplete data coverage and highly variable data quality. One simple way to address this issue is to have each of the users rate each individual model icon for data quality and coverage. For example, in the cases of the Upper Fox and the Ria Formosa, a number from 1 to 3 was assigned (by the organizing team) to all icons included in the models. The ratings roughly indicated a level of confidence in the data available for each of the individual items:

- A "1" was assigned when the issue was discussed in the group but no data sources were volunteered to substantiate the issue.
- A "2" was assigned when some source was identified to substantiate quantification. A source could be an expert participant or a previous study that was interpreted for the context of the modeling exercise.
- A "3" was assigned when a study or document was identified that provided quantitative information on a particular issue of interest.

Appendices 6 and 7 show a list of the model parameters used and rated in the Ria Formosa and Upper Fox models. A rating of 3 would come close to the criteria a researcher would like to see for the quality of the source data to which each icon would be calibrated. Therefore, if an average of 3.0 could be achieved, the researcher's confidence criteria would be fully met from the data quality point of view. Furthermore, a high degree of fit between the model and these high-quality data is necessary to achieve a high degree of confidence in models based on calibration.

However, the individual icons are linked to each other by means of equations. These links would have to be verified as well, by independent research. The problem with this approach is that such a synthesis model could only be constructed after the analytical data are produced. Precise questions would have to be asked to produce these answers. This is an unlikely and not necessarily desirable scenario. Instead, research can benefit by using the modeling process as a way to explore and set the research agenda.

The overall average stakeholder confidence in the data and structure for the Upper Fox model was 1.75; for the Ria Formosa it was 1.72. In both cases, the participants indicated that they felt relatively confident with the qualitative structure of the model.

Quantification of relations was weaker, and more effort was needed to draw firm conclusions (rather than preliminary conclusions) based on the Ria Formosa model. However, the lack of quantitative data was an eye-opener for most participants in both cases. This highlights the value of the modeling process in terms of its ability to draw out more specific questions about individual pieces of information as well as the linkages between components in the model.

The flow model developed in the San Antonio case study was a relatively small model, based on relatively well established knowledge about hydrology. The resulting model helped the stakeholders to interpret the hydrological data.

To a varying degree, the values incorporated in scoping models are "estimates," "guesstimates," or assumptions to further the discussion in terms of "what if" scenarios. It is very important that the documentation of the underlying assumptions be included as much as possible within the models themselves. More realistic or complete data and information can be incorporated when the discussion progresses or monitoring data of an implemented program becomes available, or when new data become available over time.

Confidence Based on Process Transparency

An often-heard concern voiced by people not participating in a mediated modeling process is that uncertain elements in the model are related to other uncertain elements, thereby compounding the uncertainty, making the model useless at best and dangerous at worst. This would be a justified criticism in the case of the typical "expert" (but obscure to the users) modeling process, in which the users don't understand the structure and assumptions in the model and have to accept (or reject) the results at face value. Mediated models are much more transparent to the users (who are also the constructors of the models) than most expert-based models and therefore allow the participants to better understand the uncertainty in the models and to use them more effectively in decision support.

Counterintuitive Results

As discussed in Chapter 4, unexpected model behavior means that either a modeling error has occurred or that an interesting, real "counterintuitive" behavior in the system has been discovered. Modeling errors can be traced relatively easily sector by sector. After all critical errors have been identified and addressed, the remaining unexpected behavior in the system represents an opportunity for learning.

The scenarios run by the Ria Formosa and the Upper Fox models largely behaved as expected and as desired by the groups. Surprising behavior in the Upper Fox model was the importance of sediment pollution over phosphorus pollution in the system. A surprise in the Ria Formosa model was the enormous amount of funding necessary to mitigate the pollution by dredging efforts and how little effect dredging efforts may actually have.

In the San Antonio group, members were surprised at how little change they were able to achieve by any single attempt to mitigate flooding. Given this limitation, they were further surprised that, by combining all available management approaches, they could achieve significant change. Some simply accepted these results as an opportunity for learning. Others were initially suspicious and spent considerable time searching for critical errors. Kenimer and Grant worked directly with any participants who desired to participate in this activity. Engaging in this search was valuable on at least two levels. First, once participants were satisfied that the unexpected behaviors were not artifacts of modeling errors, they were more confident in their own ability to determine how to devise management plans for their watershed. Second, they developed a much more systemic understanding of how flow related to other aspects of watershed management.

Sensitivity Issues

Sensitivity issues are strongly related to the confidence that can be placed in a model and a modeling process (as outlined in Chapter 4). Traditionally, the modeling community has discussed sensitivity of the model to changes in the parameters. However, the process of model building is emphasized in mediated modeling, which places importance on additional issues of sensitivity, such as the sensitivity of the model to stakeholder contributions, the level of contention, and the influence of the mediated modeler (as outlined in Chapter 3).

SENSITIVITY OF THE MODEL TO THE PARAMETERS

In general, parameters with high uncertainty are assigned slide bars in the user interface to allow users to investigate the sensitivity of the model to changes in these parameters themselves. Some values or relationships are calibrated to create a good fit to historical behavior. The process of building the models and the accompanying discussions are at least as important in relation to the final model.

The modeling process helps the participants in structuring their thinking and policy discussions. A major contribution of the modeling process is to expose the uncertainties in the data; the sensitivities to certain parameters; the data gaps; and the feedbacks, time lags, and complexity of the systems.

SENSITIVITY OF A MODEL TO THE STAKEHOLDER'S CONTRIBUTIONS

What would happen if the contribution of one person could be filtered out of the process? How differently does a model turn out when a stakeholder is not present? In theory it would be interesting to filter out the contributions of each individual. In practice this is impossible. Where does the contribution of a particular participant end? Do the reactions of other participants not also count? In any one project, the contribution of any one stakeholder is difficult to measure. At worst, the other participants can deem a part of the model redundant if one participant drops out. At best, the qualitative structure is maintained and filled out by other participants.

An example of the worst-case scenario was observed in the Ria Formosa case study, when a participant who was very concerned about salt making was present in the beginning, during the qualitative stages of model building, but dropped out later in the process. The salt-making part of the model was therefore weak after the quantification stage, because the salt-making representative was not present to discuss the quantification of this sector.

An example of the best-case scenario was observed in the San Antonio case. Although the San Antonio case could be considered inefficient in that it did not initiate quantitative model building until after several meetings, this approach helps address the issue of the sensitivity of the modeling process to individual participants. By the time the group decided to build a model, the group agenda had eclipsed the agenda of any single participant. In fact, the most vociferous proponent of a focus on flooding was not present at the two most crucial modeling sessions. Because the group had already accepted the necessity of this focus, the absence of this particular stakeholder was not critical.

To address this issue of the sensitivity of the process to individual participants in a statistically valid way would require a large-scale research project with parallel modeling projects and controls. In practice, a broad and balanced representation is the best inoculation against the undervaluation of a crucial aspect of the system under consideration. The loss of one participant will be felt more in smaller groups than in larger ones.

When stakeholders are physically present, their personal style influences contributions to a model. A mediated modeler must recognize the different shapes and forms of a contribution. For example, some participants are more confident in the small-group settings, and you may never hear them during the plenary sessions. Some are great synthesizers and say more in three words than others do in three minutes.

SENSITIVITY WITH REGARD TO DEGREE OF CONTENTION

A mediated modeling process should be able to withstand some level of conflict, the limits of which are addressed in Chapter 3. In fact, a major contribution of the mediated modeling approach is to deflect contention and conflict by focusing on a productive, shared activity—identifying interdependencies and finding strengths in the interdependencies among a group of stakeholders.

Most likely, the mediation skills of the facilitator are the main limiting factor with respect to the level of contention that can be handled. In addition, the initial willingness of participants to look at the complex problem at a more conceptual level to discover mutual grounds for a potential solution is a prerequisite. This willingness may increase during a mediated modeling process as the communication in a group improves.

All the case studies were performed in groups in which a medium to high level of conflict was present. All cases reported that the communication improved as the process developed. Using surveys of participants, the Ria Formosa and the Upper Fox cases measured that the perceived level of conflict was higher before the process than during and after the process.

Consider a situation in which a mining company wants pollution rights and a community wants to see the company closed. This direct conflict of interest can be addressed by having both the company representatives and the local stakeholders involved in looking at the dynamic interactions in the system. The conflict arises because the parties are pursuing their individual interests. The modeling process may allow them to discover shared interests and to produce novel ways to look at and address their special interests.

Alternatively, a mining company may not be interested in resolving this conflict in a collaborative manner. The stakeholders could still benefit from an inclusive and collaborative process to get all stakeholders to the point of a shared understanding and consequently a consensus on the next steps. Too often, opposing stakeholders cannot get organized, and polluters get away with more than they should.

Thus, a mediated modeling process can be appropriate for many groups, even ones with high levels of historical conflict, who are skeptical but willing to invest the time to come to meetings and to interact with diverse stakeholders.

SENSITIVITY TO THE MEDIATED MODELER

As discussed in Chapter 3, the role of the mediated modeler is a crucial one. The effectiveness of the mediated modeling process can't compensate for an ineffective modeler. The importance of the modeler became especially clear in the Upper Fox study participants' rating of their agreement with statement "The facilitation was effective" in their questionnaires. This statement was awarded the highest agreement (5.0). It should be noted that participants returning the questionnaire are a biased sample, since participants who dropped out or who did not return their questionnaires could hold a different opinion about the effectiveness of the facilitation. Although the same question was not posed to the Ria Formosa, San Antonio, and Sage Grouse groups, many informal comments to the same effect were received.

Comparing Models

A model can have strength in three areas (Levins 1966):

- Realism—the structure of the model mimics the real world relatively well and the output is realistic.
- Precision—the model predicts the outcomes somewhat accurately.
- Generality—the model applies to other systems.

There is always a trade-off between these three aspects of a model. A model cannot score high in all three areas (Levins 1966).

Table A1.1 shows the average ratings (from 1 to 5) of these three model aspects by the participants in the Upper Fox and the Ria Formosa case studies. The Ria Formosa model was rated higher on realism and precision, and the Upper Fox model was rated higher on

Table A1.1.

Comparison of participant ratings of the Ria Formosa and
Upper Fox Models for realism, precision, and generality

Model Aspects	Participant Rating	
	Ria Formosa	*Upper Fox*
Realism	4.0	3.4
Precision	3.3	2.7
Generality	2.3	4.1

Note: Participants rated model aspects on a scale of 1 to 5, with 5 being the highest rating.

realism and generality. One would expect a scoping model to be rated higher on generality and realism and lower on precision (or low in resolution), along the lines of the Upper Fox group rating. The unexpected low evaluation of generality for the Ria Formosa model would indicate participants' perception that the model would be difficult to apply to other areas.

The relative importance of these three aspects in the other three case studies was not quantified by the groups involved. However:

- The Sage Grouse model would be expected to score higher on realism and generality, since data were scarce, comparable to the situation in the Upper Fox case.
- The Banff mediated modeling team would describe this model as higher on realism and precision and lower on generality, because this model was more data driven.
- On the basis of relatively well known data and equations, and with a focus on hydrology, the organizing team of the San Antonio case study would rate the model that resulted from the collaborative learning process as higher on realism and precision, and lower on generality, similar to the Banff case.

Comparing Scale

A comparison may help a user or initiator of a mediated modeling process to assess what type of model is most appropriate for his or her situation. The three dimensions (time, space, and complexity) and two aspects (extent and resolution) of a model were introduced in Chapter 3. Table A1.2 evaluates how the models from the case studies compare on these issues.

The resolution of the complexity represented by state variables, auxiliary variables, and parameters does not necessarily mean that a model interconnects a web of complex interrelated issues. It may also mean that a choice was made to delve into one aspect of the question involved in great detail. The Sage Grouse model provides such an example. The extent of complexity is limited to ecology, while the resolution is represented by a relatively high number of state variables. The Sage Grouse age sequence takes up the majority of the state variables.

Table A1.2.

Comparison of scale issues in case study models

	Time	Space	Complexity
Upper Fox	Extent: 1970–2020 Resolution: 1 year	Extent: Watershed of 500,000 hectares	Extent: Economics, policy, ecology, biology
		Resolution: Spatially nonexplicit	Resolution: 10 state variables, 25 auxiliary variables, 52 constant parameters
Banff	Extent: 100 years Resolution: 1 year	Extent: National park of 6,641 km^2 Resolution: Somewhat spatially explicit (4 zones)	Extent: Socioeconomics, biology Resolution: 14 state variables, 162 auxiliary variables (including constant parameters)
San Antonio	Extent: 48 hours Resolution: 1 hour	Extent: Watershed of 4,180 mi^2 Resolution: 18 homogeneous subwatersheds within each watershed. Subwatershed sizes range from 33 to 6,600 hectares	Extent: Hydrology, stream hydraulics Resolution: For each watershed 18 state variables, 72 auxiliary variables, 90 constant parameters
Sage Grouse	Extent: 60 years Resolution: 1 week	Extent: Sagebrush community, approx. 100,000 hectares Resolution: Spatially nonexplicit	Extent: Ecology Resolution: 150 state variables 200 auxiliary variables 50 constant parameters
Ria Formosa	Extent: 1980–2020 Resolution: 1 year	Extent: Coastal wetland of 18,400 hectares Resolution: Spatially nonexplicit	Extent: Economics, ecology, biology, hydrology Resolution: 24 state variables, 71 auxiliary variables, 59 constant parameters

Evaluation of the Model-Building Process

A model resulting from a mediated modeling process is only one part of the evaluation. The process of model building provides an additional opportunity for performance measurement, specifically in the area of team learning. While a model can be evaluated on its robustness and soundness of thought, the evaluation of a model-building process requires a baseline from which changes can be assessed. Chapter 4 and the Upper Fox and Ria Formosa case studies provide some ideas of how an attempt toward a structured evaluation may be made. However, this field is wide open for innovative ideas.

Preliminary Model

The reasons for the construction of a preliminary model are described in Chapter 4. Four of the case studies (Sage Grouse, Ria Formosa, Upper Fox, and San Antonio) launched a preliminary model. Only in the San Antonio case was the preliminary model accepted. In the other three cases the preliminary model was rejected. The main difference between the San Antonio case and the other three cases was that in the San Antonio case, the formal quantitative model did not start until very late in the collaborative learning process. The process of a host of collaborative exercises leading up to the decision by the group to pursue a simulation model can be considered qualitative model building. The modeling exercise was requested by the participants in the San Antonio case to solidify the collaborative learning that had taken place over the course of nine meetings. The nine meetings provided the basis for Grant and Kenimer to construct a simulation model that was accepted as a final model by the participants after one iteration.

In the Sage Grouse case, the preliminary model was not based on stakeholder input and was rejected by the participants. Pedersen observed that the participants focused on the results, with which they did not agree for a variety of reasons, rather than on the structure of the model. The participants of the Ria Formosa and the Upper Fox case studies rejected the preliminary model as well, even though these preliminary models were based on interviews with individual stakeholders. In the Ria Formosa and the Upper Fox case studies, the participants immediately zoomed in on missing details in the preliminary model structure. This was interpreted by van den Belt as an indication of a lack of ownership of the model. These groups needed to build their own models from scratch to feel confident with them. Rather than defending the preliminary model, it was important to start over.

Many stakeholder groups reject a preliminary model and choose to start from scratch. Even though the final model produced by the group may not be significantly different in structure from the preliminary model, the difference is that the preliminary model is considered the "modeler's model" and the final model is the "participants' model." Since the purpose of the exercise is creating a commitment to the conclusions of the group, usually not much effort is made to convince the participants to accept a preliminary model. With the first signs of rejection, the preliminary model is deleted and a fresh start is made. In these cases, as in the Sage Grouse, Ria Formosa, and Upper Fox cases, the participants were not ready to accept a fixed frame and needed more open and exploratory discussion before committing to a shared frame of reference.

Even though rejected, the preliminary model still served a legitimate function, as outlined in Chapter 4. The purpose of a preliminary model is to give the participants an idea of how a potential model could look. Until then, most participants may never have seen a full-fledged scoping model. It is useful to prepare a preliminary model for the first meeting to show the participants a simple, workable model reflecting their problem. It serves as an example about a subject that they can recognize, rather than being an example about an unrelated issue. In addition, a rejection of a preliminary model clearly marks the beginning of the model-building exercise for the group. It increases the challenge and provides a motivating start of a mediated modeling process. A preliminary model shows the participants that the type of model they are about to construct is "feasible," and an achievable goal in the time allotted.

In the San Antonio case, the participants had not committed to a formal quantitative model as part of their collaborative learning project. This case study shows that a preliminary model is more readily accepted when the group is more advanced in its exploration and willing to solidify the shared understanding in a quantitative structure. The flow model also addressed a short time span (two days) and focused on one discipline (hydrology). Accepting a preliminary model somewhat locks in the direction of the thinking, as it induces and clarifies thinking within the outlined box of the model. Locking in the direction of thinking can be beneficial toward the end of a collaborative learning process. However, it may be inhibiting to creativity if it happens too early in a process.

A preliminary model was not chosen in the Banff case study because issues in the valley were very contentious. The mediated modeling team did not want to taint the process in any way, not even with a preliminary model.

Focus

The focus of a participant group is an interesting measure of tracking the progress of a participant group. The shift from a broad geographic toward a more specific theme is discussed, preferably without losing the elements required for a balanced focus.

GEOGRAPHIC AND THEME FOCUS

The case studies all refocused from a geographical framework to a theme. This progression can be interpreted as a higher level of shared understanding resulting in a more specific topic. In most cases, when discussing the conclusions, participants posed new questions. It was interesting to see that those questions were much better defined and less chaotic than those posed when the process started. Some participants seemed to be thinking out loud in developing their own future research agendas.

The theme-focus in the Sage Grouse case study seems to be linked to a higher level of conflict. The issues at stake, rather than the geographic area, provide the reference point for beginning the mediated modeling process. Better understanding among participants, better questions for future research, and an improved focus resulted from the modeling process in this case study as well.

BALANCING FOCUS

Complex issues, such as the integration of ecology and economics, require a balancing of focus. It is all too easy to focus on one side of the equation and neglect the other.

The Ria Formosa group was dominated by natural scientists, but they took economics and investments as a starting point. The group focused on "development" in terms of growth of the economy by means of increasing the infrastructure. Infrastructure was linearly equated with economic growth possibilities in the group's perception. Environmental protection initially seemed to equal "dredging." Dredging was presented as a general solution to the pollution problems in the Ria Formosa during the interviews before the mediated modeling process, albeit for different reasons. The group was not interested in looking at new policy instruments, such as establishing a local environmental tax on tourists. They choose to explore the enforcement of existing (mainly licensing) options.

On the other hand, professionals, mainly with a natural science background, dominated the Upper Fox group. This group emphasized the natural system rather than economics. The Upper Fox group was open to explore new policy alternatives, such as tradable development rights as a means to cluster development.

The Sage Grouse group balanced their focus by emphasizing submodels as chosen by the participants. The focus remained on ecological issues, in part because natural resource managers dominated the group. A ranger advocated broadening the scope of the model to include economic considerations. However, the consensus was that the resulting increase in complexity would not improve the discussion at the time the Sage Grouse model was developed.

The San Antonio group balanced their focus through a variety of collaborative exercises and used the simulation model to zoom in on hydrology. Recruitment efforts had produced a highly diverse group. Examples of the interests displayed by nontechnical members are offered earlier in the section on conflict. Technically oriented members exhibited the same diversity. Some were concerned primarily with restoring riparian habitat, others with drainage, and still others with the quality of recycled water.

All of these interests came together during small-group working sessions, in which members determined that concern with flooding would "be the driving force" behind any recommendations they would make. From their perspective, then, it made sense to model flow, because everything else had to answer to that central issue. They did not see their flow model as a conclusion—rather, as a foundation for ongoing work. Because portions of the watershed regularly experienced flood damage, the group members agreed that "protection of life and property would be in the forefront." The attempts to improve flood control, however, "should be done in such a way to protect the wildlife and also provide recreation opportunities and other economic opportunities." Thus, while the model focused specifically on hydrology, members viewed this focus as relating directly to other ecological, as well as socioeconomic dimensions of their watershed.

The Banff model considered the ecological, economic, and social aspects of natural resource management. The social elements—for example, quality of life for Banff town residents—were just as important as the ecological and economic factors.

Transition from Qualitative to Quantitative Model

The transition in focus from a qualitative model to a quantitative model was distinct in the Ria Formosa and Upper Fox case studies. It proved challenging to shift the focus from elaborating on the details of a qualitative model to finishing a quantitative simulation model. The transition marked a typical chaotic period, from which something new could emerge. It was worth the trouble of insisting on the transition. New possibilities for learning emerged when the icons were related in a quantitative manner to each other.

The participants in the San Antonio case study experienced an easy transition from qualitative to quantitative modeling. They spent more time on the development of different types of mental models, without the explicit goal of being involved in a quantitative modeling exercise. When the time was right, the process of quantitative model building was performed in a short amount of time and with trust in the model.

The Sage Grouse group was presented with the quantitative model one year after the qualitative model. The model had been refined and quantified during this interval and shown to the participants, who spent the time running scenarios and evaluating the model based on the results. The group members did not experience much of the transition from a qualitative to a quantitative model, because they constructed their own submodels. Trust in the overall integrated model was attained by the coherent results of the scenarios simulated.

The transition from qualitative to quantitative modeling in the Banff case was generally seamless to the stakeholders in the sense that stakeholders would interact in mediated modeling sessions about what important questions and trade-offs they thought were to be examined. The mediated modeler would then work on the quantitative aspects "behind the scenes" and in consultation with wildlife and other experts. Stakeholders would see the next iteration of the model in its more refined form during the next mediated session, and so forth. If value judgments were involved in portions of the quantitative process, the mediated modeler would bring this forward to the stakeholders and let them decide on values or the range of values or capabilities they were interested in for modeling scenarios. Sometimes this involved experts attending mediated modeling sessions to answers questions on, for example, the ecology of wolves.

The groups in the case studies that were most intimately involved in both the qualitative and quantitative model building experienced a more difficult transition than the groups that were less involved in the quantification of the actual model. The question remains to what extent and based on what characteristics of a group and a mediated modeling process the participants should be involved in the quantification of a model. The literature gives very little guidance in this respect. Evidently, this is a wide-open area for research and experimentation.

Data Gathering

In both the Upper Fox and the Ria Formosa case studies, the participants were relatively involved in the data-gathering process. They spent some amount of time discussing the data gathering in small teams in between meetings. In addition, the mediated modeler visited with some individuals or small groups to assist in data gathering. The participants did not always get the information they thought would be easy to attain. The requests for information were often posed in a novel way, for which easy answers didn't exist.

For example, in the Ria Formosa group, one person made the remark that nongovernmental and governmental organizations pay universities for many projects, but when you need data from scientists you can't get it. It was noticed that not many university people responded to the invitation to participate. When talking to a university staff person about university resources, a typical response was that university staff don't have time to participate in community efforts, unless you take them on a trip away from their university.

The following example illustrates some of the frustration during the data-gathering process in the Upper Fox case study. One person commented on the following situation re-garding the Department of Natural Resources:

> DNR has the mantra of ecology, socioeconomics, and institutions to be integrated, but in the search for data, two things happened: people didn't see why this type of information was needed (even higher-placed officials), and it turned out that the info was often not available, or if it was, it was available by county and not on drainage basin, which is supposed to be the new focus of the DNR.

The modelers in the San Antonio case gathered most of the data for the flow model. As requested by group members, the role of this simulation model was to run a limited set of scenarios in a hydrology context. Because the modeling group included members from several agencies that were active in collecting watershed data, the modelers relied on these members to assist in data gathering. For example, group members representing the San Antonio River Authority and the San Antonio Water System provided data that had been collected by their organizations and located data collected by other organizations. This participation increased the group members' trust when they were presented with the preliminary model. It also contributed to more interactivity during the tutorial.

As described in Chapter 6, members worked in small groups during this session. When one small group expressed a desire for more detailed information, one member stated that the river authority had the data they wanted. The group immediately dispatched him to get the requested information. When he returned, these data were integrated into the model. Although they did not make any discernable difference in the scenario results, their availability was important.

An exhaustive compendium of available data for Banff National Park was gathered prior to the futures modeling process. Data were also gathered during the modeling process when gaps in the required information were identified. Expert opinion was utilized in some cases. The emphasis of the mediated modeling process in Banff was on giving the available data a place in the dynamic structure to explore scenarios under existing and alternative conditions.

The evaluation of what data existed and what were needed was one of the primary goals in the Sage Grouse case. Data were obtained from publications and reports. In many cases, data were not available or were available in a form not useful for the model. In those cases, expert opinion was used. The results of the simulations were used to evaluate the accuracy of the information included.

When the information doesn't exist, there is a risk that the model is devalued. It is as if you are asking the wrong questions, for which no answers exist. Some realize that the questions are not wrong but that they haven't been asked or pursued in this way before. Decisions are being made, regardless of the information at hand.

Newcomers to a Modeling Process

Most of the case studies report issues concerning newcomers in the group. The Banff case study shows that a strong institutional basis and a well-organized network make a group more resilient to the disruption a newcomer can cause. Similarly, the San Antonio case study demonstrates that colleagues or representatives sharing a particular viewpoint can participate effectively as a subgroup.

The Upper Fox provides us with insights into what can happen when disruptive newcomers enter the group in the middle of a mediated modeling process. The new participants were not introduced by other participants or attending colleagues. They had originally committed to the mediated modeling process but had missed the first three meetings. They had received continuous (printed) updates after every meeting. The newcomers repeated much of the discussion on inclusion of the other forms of natural capital and more ecosystem services. This caused the rest of the group to start doubting their chosen route again. A circular reintroduction of ideas seemed to be necessary to get the newcomers to the same understanding as the rest of the group, but this took about half an hour of the group's time.

In the San Antonio, Upper Fox, and Ria Formosa cases, newcomers at the end of the process were very well taken care of by the group. Newcomers or stakeholders who had not previously participated had skeptical questions, and the participants filled them in on what had happened and defended the process themselves.

The capacity of a group to defend its work is crucial to the implementation of change. When a group can defend its work, it can be interpreted that it has reached a shared level of understanding and consensus on what needs to happen next. For example, the San Antonio group has since started a nongovernmental organization (NGO) to pursue the goals it established. In the Ria Formosa case, the most skeptical person at the final meeting was won over, and a few weeks after completion of the mediated modeling process the group was invited by him to present the model for a forum that he had organized.

Tutorial

The reasons for a tutorial are outlined in Chapter 4. The case studies demonstrate that there are different ways to achieve the goal of building confidence and preparing participants to present and defend the outcome of a mediated modeling process. The participants in the Sage Grouse case study had the opportunity to gain hands-on modeling skills from the very beginning since they constructed the submodels on the computer. However, an organizational problem prevented the participants from collectively exploring the overall model and plan for presentations by the group members.

The Upper Fox participants had the opportunity to attend a tutorial. Five computers and ten people were present. The participants clicked through the model, explored scenarios, and practiced explaining the model to nonparticipants. Some participants have successfully used the model in presentations. DNR personnel used the model in describing their approach to other geographic management units (GMUs). One participant revised the Upper Fox model to cover the county he works for and to justify his budget for environmental conservation.

The San Antonio participants used the flow model after the second iteration. Grant (justifiably includes the tutorial in the "model use" phase, since the goal of the tutorial is to use the model.

Unfortunately, the Ria Formosa group did not receive a tutorial, although funding was available for one. As time passed, it became harder to determine a date when all participants could attend a tutorial. Instead, the model produced in 1998 is used in a follow-up program funded by the Portuguese National Science Foundation for Park Management.

Group Issues

How cohesive a group is will determine much of its success in implementing consensus-based recommendations. All case studies reported an increase in openness and an improvement in communication as the mediated modeling process evolved. The participants in the Upper Fox and Ria Formosa case studies confirmed this improvement in the questionnaires.

Analysis of questionnaires shows that the level of group dynamics increased in both the Ria Formosa and the Upper Fox case studies. The level of "groupiness" was evaluated on the basis of the first four of the five group characteristics identified by Brown (1988):

- A group exists when the individual members perceive they are part of that group and outsiders perceive they are not part of the group.
- A group is oriented toward a common goal.
- Interaction between group members exists.
- A realization of interdependence is present.
- There is a structure of roles/status and norms.

The structure of roles/status and norms was not evaluated because of the short duration of the two respective case studies. Figures A1.1 and A1.2 show the four characteristics of the Upper Fox and Ria Formosa groups, respectively, and the changes that occurred from before to after the mediated modeling process. The Upper Fox GMU partner group expanded their level of groupiness on all four aspects. "Perception," "interdependence," and "common goal" were established through the interviews. "Interaction" was included on the basis of personal observations. For the Ria Formosa group, all data points were based on the questionnaires.

The case studies suggest how a new group identity can be created through a structured communication process such as mediated modeling or collaborative learning. The San Antonio Watershed case was based on collaborative learning and pursued a quantitative

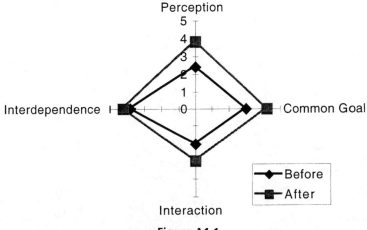

Figure A1.1.

Group characteristics before versus after the Upper Fox modeling workshops

Ria Formosa Group

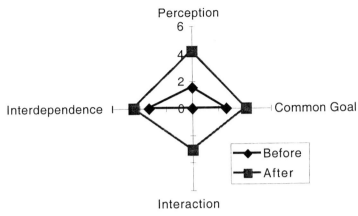

Figure A1.2.

Group characteristics before versus after the Ria Formosa modeling process

model at the end. One lesson from this particular case is that repeated communication opportunities between stakeholders allowed participants to develop a new, superordinate group identity that permitted the group to act.

As this case unfolded over time, individual identities became enmeshed in the group identity, which was mutually shaped by all participants. Responses of those who developed strong group identity through their participation indicate that, while this new identity did not minimize individual interests, it enabled members to position themselves in relationship with the identities of other members. This process encouraged all participants to identify more systemically with the entire watershed, without losing their original sense of personal identity.

Although the emergent group identity was not the only force guiding participants to choose to build the model, it was likely a significant contributing factor. The flow model would not have been developed without their newly forged group identity.

COMPARING ORGANIZATIONAL PLATFORMS

A prerequisite for the implementation of new ideas is that a group moves through a sequence of awareness, consensus, confidence, ownership, and commitment, referred to as the organizational platform. During the interviews, an attempt was made to establish where in the process the group was, and whether the mediated modeling process had helped the group to move higher on the organizational platform. It turned out that the interviews became too complicated and too long to pursue this objective to the fullest extent. Rouwette (2003) pursued the survey techniques in group settings in a dissertation.

Figure A1.3 shows a graphic based on the remaining questions in the "after" questionnaire. The Ria Formosa and Upper Fox case studies are compared on each item of the organizational platform. The numbers are not very significant, but the figure gives a broad indication that both groups scored higher than neutral on all accounts in the "after" questionnaire. Awareness was high in both cases from the beginning, and it can be argued that

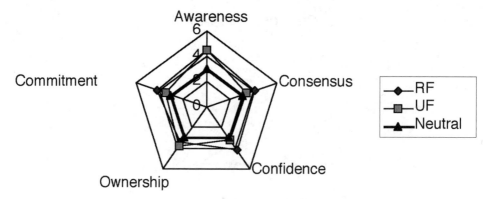

Figure A1.3.

Comparison of Upper Fox (UF) and Ria Formosa (RF) case study "after" questionnaires on items of the organizational platform

recognition of the challenges has increased owing to the learning that took place. A consensus on future goals and to a lesser extent on how the system currently works was achieved. Confidence in the conclusions was higher in the Ria Formosa case than in the Upper Fox case. Confidence in showing the model to other groups was neutral in the Upper Fox case. A sense of ownership seemed higher in the Upper Fox case than in the Ria Formosa case. Commitment to showing the model and pursuing the conclusions was higher in the Ria Formosa case than in the Upper Fox case, although the Upper Fox case was also rated well above neutral.

Consensus

TESTING THE THREE ASPECTS OF CONSENSUS

There are three aspects of consensus as a central part of the decision-making process—consensus on:

- How the world works in a certain domain, or worldview
- What would constitute a more desirable state of the world, or vision
- What policies will lead to that better state, given how the world works.

It is not necessary to achieve a formal consensus on "how the world works" in order to proceed toward "what would constitute a more desirable state of the world" and "what policies will lead to that better state." However, these three aspects of consensus are implicitly addressed at some point during a mediated modeling process, as discussed in Chapter 3. A serious attempt was made to address these differences in the questionnaires in the Upper Fox and Ria Formosa case studies. The result was often confusion on the part of the participants. These questions required too much explanation, and it was decided to abort this issue as an explicit item of the questionnaires. However, it can be argued that these three issues were implicitly addressed, as shown in Table A1.3.

All aspects of consensus were rated on the positive side of the scale. However, evaluation of the aspects of consensus suggests that it is easier to achieve consensus about the goals

Table A1.3

Consensus related questions

	Ria Formosa	Upper Fox
a)	The participants have a common view on how the linkages in the Ria Formosa system currently work. (3.2) work (3.5)	The participants have a common view on how the linkages between ecology and economics in the Upper Fox system currently
b)	A consensus on the goals for the future of the Ria Formosa exists in the group (4.1)	A consensus on the goal for the future of the Upper Fox exists in the group (3.4)
	The participants of the RF group are oriented toward a common goal (4.1)	The participants of the UF-GMU group are oriented toward a common goal (4.2)
c)	Viable alternatives were generated during the mediated modeling process (3.7)	Policy alternatives can evolve from the UF mediated modeling process (3.9)

than to achieve consensus about issues related to the current situation and about the specifics of how to achieve the common goals. This brings the discussion to an important difference between, on the one hand, a mediated modeling process and, on the other, a collaborative learning process that results in a quantitative model at the end of the process (as used in the San Antonio case study).

One explicit characteristic of the collaborative learning approach is that it does not require members to come to agreement regarding "how the world works." It is argued that participants may feel more comfortable if they are assured that they can agree to disagree about "how the world looks" and continue with "what would constitute a more desirable state of the world."

Collaborative learning also avoids addressing "visions." From a mediated modeling perspective, there is no formal requirement for an agreement on how the world works, or for a similar vision for the future (as described in Chapter 3). However, "how the world works" is acknowledged as one of the possible starting points for structuring a model and improve a challenging situation.

In practice, the collaborative learning approach and the mediated modeling approach don't differ much. As in the collaborative learning approach, in mediated modeling participants share different viewpoints on "how the world works" from their perspective, no matter what. In mediated modeling, sharing different viewpoints on "how the world works" is an integral part of constructing a model that partly covers the past and simulates the future. Even though participants are not required to come to consensus on "how the world works," the process of sharing perspectives on "how the world works" in a systematic way may lead to insights in the next levels of consensus. For some groups, this discussion may lead to the clarification of misconceptions and productive insights.

As an example of the clarification that can result from this process, in an African country, different stakeholders from government, academia, and agrobusiness could not agree on the use of a soil addition that would increase the level of iron in the locally grown crops. They all agreed on the need to solve the iron deficiency in the population. Some stakeholders claimed that soil additions did not work, while others claimed that soil additions worked wonders. After lengthy discussions, it was finally discovered that there were different products available, some of which worked for this particular locality and some of which did not. This situation illustrates the value of comparing existing notes.

In the context of the case studies in this book, the discussion of the Ria Formosa group also focused more on "how the world works in a certain domain, or worldview." The members of this group had much ground to cover in terms of reaching a common understanding of what they were actually talking about. "What would constitute a more desirable state of the world, or vision" was addressed explicitly in terms of the problem definition and implicitly during the entire process on several occasions. "What policies will lead to that better state, given how the world works" was not addressed in a novel way. The Ria Formosa group chose to focus on the existing policy alternatives and to evaluate the consequences of enforcing or not enforcing them.

On the other end of the spectrum is the San Antonio case. With its roots in collaborative learning, this case study focused on "what would constitute a more desirable state of the world" and "what policies will lead to that better state, given how the world works." The San Antonio group members decided that, although their worldviews remained divergent, they could agree on what would constitute an improvement of the current situation. For example, they all agreed that better flood control, removal of trash from the creek bed, and more consistent enforcement of existing regulations would improve the situation. Group members also began moving toward an agreement about how to effect this improvement. Getting to agreement was facilitated by their participation in the quantitative modeling exercise. For example, after running several simulations, they agreed on the combination of management strategies they would present to state and local entities responsible for various aspects of the watershed.

Similarly, the Upper Fox group had its focus on the last step, "what policies will lead to that better state," preferably regardless of the first step, "how the world currently works in a certain domain." Also, "what would constitute a more desirable state of the world, or vision" was addressed very smoothly during the problem definition.

DEGREE OF CONSENSUS

The degree of consensus can vary from strong to weak, as discussed in Chapter 2. From the perception of the organizing teams and contributors of the case studies, the consensus resulting from the modeling processes mostly falls between strong and weak.

In an ideal world, strong consensus would persist. Evidently, this is seldom the reality. The collaborative learning approach, applied in the San Antonio case study, suggests that any improvement of the situation is enough of a step in the right direction. In practice, that argument holds. However, from a research perspective of improving quantitative model building, it may be important to explore the differences in the kinds of consensus presented in Table A1.4. For example, it may be more important than ever to survey or interview the stakeholders who did not pursue the process until the end. Silence can have a powerful voice. Alternatively, what are the key elements that determine whether a group of stakeholders "can live with conclusions" or have reached "empowering conclusions"?

Table A1.4

Degree of consensus

	All participants stay involved	A critical mass of participants stayed involved
Empowering conclusions	Strong consensus:	Consensus with clues for follow up: Upper Fox San Antonio Ria Formosa
Can live with conclusions	Consensus with clues for follow up:	Weak consensus: Sage Grouse BanfF

Cultural Issues

The case studies in this book span experiences in three countries. Without attempting to be comprehensive, there are some cultural issues that jumped out in these experiences. Noteworthy are the differences in the way participant groups worked in small groups, their attitude toward hierarchy, worldview, and result fixation.

SMALL-GROUP WORK

Working in small groups caused an initial cultural clash in the Ria Formosa group. At first, the Ria Formosa participants refused to work in small groups, either because they were not used to this way of working or because they did not trust that the small groups were going to do an acceptable job. The Ria Formosa group needed a bit more time to get acquainted with each other and to trust the group dynamics. The problem definition was developed entirely in a plenary session, which took more time than anticipated. After lunch, the group was asked to establish model sectors in small-group sessions. The findings were discussed in a plenary session. The small groups had come up with very similar sectors, which reduced suspicion among the group members. During the second meeting, the participants were more adapted to this procedure and confidently worked in the small groups toward the definition of the qualitative model structure.

The Upper Fox group was less resistant to small-group work, but the same effect of confidence building in the group could be observed when the small groups reinforced each other's sector definitions.

HIERARCHY

The acceptable Portuguese way of interaction during meetings seems to be that people all talk at the same time. The participants assured me that this was nothing to worry about and that the meetings were well structured and productive. In the middle of a hot discussion (usually among the more dominant participants), I would invite the opinion of someone who had not contributed to the discussion yet. This would lower the frustration level of the discussion, and often a more quiet person would contribute a useful analysis of the situation and settle the matter. As one citizen observed, "This is a lesson in democracy."

The discussions in the Upper Fox group were quieter. The tools of voting in order to find out how the group was arrayed on certain issues or asking the quiet participants for their opinion were used less extensively in the Upper Fox group than in the Ria Formosa group. My personal explanation is that there was less of a sense of hierarchy in the Upper Fox group compared with the Ria Formosa group.

The survey question "The problem is not my responsibility" was much less of a problem for the Upper Fox group than in the Ria Formosa case. Personal responsibility seems an acceptable concept in Wisconsin as long as you are totally free to decide how to exercise that personal responsibility. In Portugal, there seems to be more reliance on governmental structures.

WORLDVIEW

The survey question about the current worldview, "The participants have a common view on how the linkages in the Ria Formosa/Upper Fox systems currently work," caused difficulty among the Upper Fox participants. Discussions about worldview took place with the first couple of interviewed participants of the Upper Fox group. Then the question was eliminated to save time for more informative questions. Individual personal territory seemed to be threatened or invaded when shared worldviews were proposed in the survey. "Individuals can never have the same worldview," many said. "It wouldn't be healthy or desirable." This was their first reaction. Sharing of a worldview, with the goal of better understanding where others come from, seemed an acceptable interpretation of "shared worldview." Common goals were acceptable, but it was as if it should be up to each individual how to personally reach those goals. Among the Ria Formosa interviewees, the worldview question did not pose a problem, either because the scope of the question wasn't really understood owing to translation issues or because the idea of sharing worldviews was acceptable among these participants.

RESULT ORIENTATION VERSUS FREE EXPLORATION

The Upper Fox group was very eager to get results out of the process, preferably at the second meeting. They seemed to only want to take a certain step if it was clear beforehand why they should take the step and what they would achieve by doing so. For example, they refused to think about stocks and flows before they knew how the stocks and flows would look and what they would gain from defining stock and flows. This attitude can obstruct explorative thinking, but it is very result oriented. One may gain results but may lose some insights along the way. One person would have preferred that some models be shown to him so he could pick the one he liked best and go with that. The same person indicated afterward, however, that he had learned a lot from going through the process of model building himself.

The Ria Formosa group seemed freer of result orientation and easier to guide through the steps of the mediated modeling process. This group didn't ask "Why?" so much—rather, they enthusiastically continued exploring the next phase of the process.

Both groups had a hard time making the transition from qualitative model building to quantification of the relations, however. The participants seemed comfortable with the discussions and the building of the qualitative model structure, and they seemed to enjoy dwelling on the qualitative model without committing to specifics. Gathering facts and confronting beliefs in a quantitative manner is the more difficult part of the process, but it provides essential learning possibilities.

As a way to make the participants think about specific linkages, they were asked "what if" questions. Some participants seemed to interpret some of these questions as "test questions" that should have a "correct" answer. If they didn't know the correct answer, they bailed out rather than thinking through the goal of the question, modifying the question, or massaging the data so that they fit the purpose. Mindful learning (Langer 1997) addresses this problem and emphasizes the importance of free exploration as a prerequisite for learning.

Comparing the Questionnaires

The goal of using surveys before and after the process in the Ria Formosa and Upper Fox case studies was to compare the learning of the individual participants as well as the groups. This goal was realized only to a certain extent.

Comparison of the groups succeeded partly, but comparison on an individual level was not possible. In the Ria Formosa case, the "before" and "after" questionnaires were to a great extent conducted with different people and were therefore not comparable on an individual level. All of the potential participants in the Upper Fox group were interviewed before the modeling exercise, but the "after" questionnaire was filled out only by a subset (60%) of the "before" group. And, unlike the "before" questionnaire, the "after" questionnaire in the Upper Fox study was not filled out during a personal interview but mailed in. A few of the Upper Fox participants chose to remain anonymous when the surveys were mailed in, which made individual before and after comparison impossible in the Upper Fox case as well.

Because the same individuals made up the "before" and "after" group in the Upper Fox case, comparison between the "before" and "after" questionnaires as a group is more significant in the Upper Fox case than in the Ria Formosa case. Most telling for evaluation purposes were the "after" questionnaires in both cases. The "before" questionnaires continue to be valuable for preparation purposes.

Apart from the questions aiming to define the level of groupiness, some questions were asked in an identical manner in both cases. For example:

- "The model is interesting enough to show to others" was rated 4.8 (out of 5) in the Ria Formosa case and 4.1 in the Upper Fox case.
- "The model is a helpful tool for me to communicate some problems in the area" was rated 4.7 in the Ria Formosa case and 4.0 in the Upper Fox case.
- "I realize more linkages with other sectors and stakeholders than before the project" was rated 4.4 in the Ria Formosa case and 4.2 in the Upper Fox case.

In general, the rating of the identical questions in both cases was relatively close. The questions about the usefulness of different aspects of the mediated modeling process were asked in rating form in the Upper Fox case and in yes/no format in the Ria Formosa case. Even though the answers cannot be compared directly in terms of a rating, the participants in both cases showed great enthusiasm for the mediated modeling technique. It is obvious that the participants agreed that mediated modeling helped to structure the discussion and the thinking. In both cases it was clear that learning in some form occurred.

This appendix evaluates the case studies in a level of detail that may be of interest to group modeling professionals. Comparisons are made on multiple facets of the models and the modeling process, especially for the Upper Fox and Ria Formosa case studies owing to the availability of surveys.

Appendix 2

Contact Information; System Dynamics Modeling Software

Powersim
ModellData AS
P.O. Box 642, N-5001
Bergen, Norway
www.powersim.com

STELLA
High Performance Systems, Inc.
45 Lyme Road, Suite 300
Hanover, NH 03755
USA
www.hps-inc.com

Vensim
Ventana Systems
149 Waverly Street
Belmont, MA 02178
USA
www.vensim.com

Appendix 3

Ranked Participant Statements from the Upper Fox "After" Questionnaire

Statements are ordered according to score, from most agreement to most disagreement: 5 = strongly agree; 4 = agree somewhat; 3 = neutral; 2 = disagree somewhat; 1 = strongly disagree.

Statement	Rating
The facilitation was effective.	5.0
The meetings were well organized.	4.9
Mediated modeling helped in structuring the discussions.	4.8
The problem was discussed in an open fashion.	4.7
Mediated modeling helped in structuring the thinking.	4.5
The human interactions (communication) were pleasant.	4.5
Team learning did occur.	4.5
The problem addressed by the model needs to be discussed on a regular basis across stakeholder groups.	4.5
The discussions were constructive during the meetings.	4.3
The participants of the UF-GMU group are oriented toward a common goal.	4.2
I realize more linkages with other sectors and stakeholders than before the project.	4.2
The meetings were well worth my time.	4.2
The model is of enough interest to show to others.	4.1
The mediated modeling procedure agrees with Wisconsin culture.	4.1
Generality: The model could apply to other systems.	4.1
Useful answers to the original questions were generated.	4.0
The model is a helpful tool for me in communicating some problems in the Upper Fox.	4.0
The link between ecology and economics is addressed appropriately by the model.	3.9
Policy alternatives can evolve from the mediated modeling process.	3.9
The UF-GMU modeling group operated as a real group.	3.8
The problem the group decided to focus on was addressed satisfactorily.	3.8
The model represents well the problem the group set out to investigate.	3.8
I feel that I contributed to the design of the model.	3.8
I support the conclusions drawn from the model.	3.7
Indicators for sustainable development were developed.	3.6
The participants have a common view on how the linkages between ecology and economics in the Upper Fox system currently work.	3.5

I am planning to use the model in communications with others.	3.5
A consensus on the goal for the future of the Upper Fox exists within the group.	3.4
Workable alternatives were generated during the mediated modeling process.	3.4
Realism: The structure mimics the real world, and the output is realistic.	3.3
I am confident that the conclusions will have an impact.	3.2
A consensus on the goals for the future of the Upper Fox exists among broader stakeholder groups.	2.7
Precision: The model predicts the outcomes accurately.	2.7
The participants of the UF-GMU group have goals that clearly conflict.	2.3
The model is lacking in precision to the point it should not be shown to others.	2.2

Appendix 4

Full Answers to the Upper Fox "After" Survey

1. How would you characterize the composition of the modeling group in terms of the type of stakeholders that participated?
   - Knowledge gained by experience, questions, and discussion.
   - Good: department staff and county employees who will be needed to help shape the future.
   - The group probably caught 75% of total stakeholder interests in the GMU.
   - A broad spectrum that soon narrowed down to those that were truly interested.
   - The ones that were able to make the most of the modeling were the agency people. "Citizens-at-large" reps were probably a bit overwhelmed by the modeling.
   - Great for first run. Slated too heavily to the converted for true comprehensive involvement.
   - I believe the stakeholders provided valuable input both from a lay and professional perspective on the issues and components required at the project.
   - Most participation by governmental representatives; good diversity of backgrounds and expertise.
   - Mostly agency people and people with strong backgrounds in environmental science, but some citizens.
   - Heavily represented by management agencies.

2. How would you characterize the interactions/communication during the modeling meetings?
   - Good opportunity for discussion, dialogue, and exploration of key issues.
   - Mediator did an excellent job. Discussion sometimes dominated by "experts" sharing irrelevant information.
   - Friendly, constructive, relatively effective.
   - The composition of the group enhanced productive discussions of the complex issues. Participants were able to challenge information, certain perspectives, etc.
   - Nonagency folks and people with lesser political influence tended to drop out or speak less.
   - This part of the experience was quite good. We all learned from each other about basin issues through this process.
   - Improved as the process unfolded and people began to think alike.
   - Open, honest, frank, polite.
   - It naturally took some time to get a feel for objectives, goals, and personal comfort. Just try + participate + answer = quite normal!
   - Very good and interesting.

3. Did the interactions/communications change during the course of the meetings?
   - Improved after the halfway point. Felt more at ease to speak.
   - They continually increased and became better, in fact very good.
   - Better openness at end of process.
   - We all became more comfortable about expressing our views and questioning what we didn't understand.
   - Respect toward each other developed as people interacted and were able to appreciate knowledge of other partners.
   - Seemed to be clearer understanding of the demands/needs of the model toward the last three sessions.
   - More participation by other members as time went on.
   - Folks got tired (and quiet) later in the evening.

4. What did you learn during the mediated modeling process?
   - The model helped visualize—together—all the factors. I can only think about its pieces.
   - The data available at a basin scale. Learned more about ecosystem services.
   - Citizens within the watershed must be educated about land use trends that will cause increased negative consequences to the natural environment. Local and state units must do more!
   - That I was not alone with my concerns. Other relationships and considerations I had forgotten. What a computer dummy I am!
   - Details and specific facts/data sources.
   - The wealth of expertise of the participants. How critical development patterns are to biodiversity.
   - That it was possible to formulate an effective team.
   - A new method, approach, or tool to use for problem solving.
   - Learned more fully about the linkages between ecological patterns in the basin and how they are tied into social and economic issues. Also about what each of the team members feel is a problem in the basin.
   - Biodiversity: we must learn to live together.

5. What is the worst that can happen during the coming workshops?
   - Screaming, angry, uncooperative.
   - Failing to focus on the big picture and instead focusing on narrow agendas.
   - Nothing gets accomplished, waste of time.
   - Investing time that doesn't result in anything.
   - Hurt feelings, putting up walls, people get alienated.
   - Too fast, too large an area, and too diverse a group.
   - Not keeping people engaged.
   - Fundamental disagreements among partners, agenda focusing.
   - Overly burdened by time commitment and disassociation.
   - Apathy and boredom, dropping out, views not addressed, dominant players.
   - Frustration about not being able to make a difference, disintegration.
   - No participation.
   - Conflicts.

- Partners don't support DNR's goals and obstruct DNR's goals.
- No respect of views.
- Critical participants refuse to continue, no consensus.
- Personal nervous breakdown and a waste of time.
- Apathy.
- No agreement.
- Don't accomplish anything.
- Enemies are created and a waste of time.
- Lack of understanding of the role of the public and no follow-through.
- Personally lost, losing members.

6. What is the best that can happen during the coming workshops?
   - Cooperation, knowing how to work together to accomplish something.
   - Learn about and understand the basin, well-informed decisions, and to feel good about it.
   - Well-oiled machine, identifying a mutual problem, and consensus on how to achieve goals; a usable document.
   - Get a broad-based group to understand the links and create an awareness.
   - To establish bonds and relationships to produce support for creative ideas.
   - Establish common goals.
   - Focus on causes.
   - A clear picture of the linkages between ecology and economics.
   - Clear consensus that they see how to use information to create strategies for wise management and commitment to rescue the basin.
   - Consensus about primary stressors in the system and how to attack them.
   - Understanding by a large majority beyond the group, implementation.
   - Define the problems and some solutions; find ways to implement some at least locally.
   - Long-range plan for quality of the Upper Fox.
   - Empowerment of the Department of Natural Resources.
   - Open dialogue and the desire to learn.
   - Public awareness and perception of the problem.
   - Identifying solutions.
   - Find common goals and objectives and a vision on implementation.
   - Set goals and implement.
   - A balanced picture of ecology and economics.
   - An acceptable course of actions that is implemented the next two years.
   - Overview of direction of the Upper Fox.

7. What was the worst about the overall mediated modeling process/experience?
   - Never enough time for thorough discussion, lack of complete information/expertise, not enough time for social interaction.
   - Too many meetings in a short time frame that lasted too long each night; for me anyway, it was difficult to commit that kind of time at night.
   - The number of meetings spread out over time.
   - Lack of current information. Relying too much on student project.

- I need to reduce my workload in order to participate at a more meaningful level. I'd prefer it was spread out over more time.
- It's hard to get started without information. It is tough to work into DNR's schedules.
- Lack of good data made some conclusions difficult to make.
- It came at an ultrabusy workload time and I couldn't follow through as I would have liked.

8. What was the best about the overall mediated modeling process/experience?
   - Learning the complex interactions and common goals. Recognizing the values of agricultural lands.
   - The group process and discussion were a great way to draw out individual opinions on ecological issues in the basin. We had thorough discussions about how resources and problems in the basin are connected.
   - The discussion, the process, and the dialogue helped establish new relationships and understanding.
   - The knowledge gained from the discussions.
   - Reaching a final product, which will hopefully produce positive benefits in the basin. The process was a tremendous learning experience for me.
   - Systems approach.
   - Networking, accessing new information.
   - The presenter—our facilitator.
   - Having a structure for various and conflicting stakeholders to communicate about tough issues.
   - Contacts with other agencies and ideas.

Appendix 5

Participant Rating of Upper Fox Model Parameters

1 = Unsubstantiated, however based on logical reasoning
2 = Somewhat substantiated
3 = Substantiated

The overall confidence in the data based on the average assigned value by the mediated modeling team of the parameters was 1.75.

The model sectors (Economics, External Forces, Land Use and Natural Capital, and Ecosystem Service) appear in alphabetical order. The parameters are presented in alphabetical order within each model sector. The cryptic format of the parameters is the way they appear as names of the model icons. Owing to limited space on the computer screen, the icon names are often abbreviated. At the first level or equation level in STELLA, the software replaces a space in a name of an icon with an underscore.

Economics

Agri_market_land_value	1	Spending_per_fishing_license	2
Angler_hours	2	Annual_hunting_value	1
Boating_days	2	Revenue_per_agri_acre	1
Spending_boat_per_day	1	Soil_value	2
Number_fish_permits	3		

External Forces

Population	3	New_homes	2
Economic_trends	2	Homes	2

Land Use

Urban_area	2	Agri_run_off_P	3
Agriculture_area	3	BMP_agriculture_P	2
Wetland_area	1	Agri_run_off_sediment	3
Forest_area	3	BMP_agriculture_S	2
Grassland_area	3	CRP_land	3
Lake_and_stream_area	3	Farm_animals_per_acre	1
Acres_per_new_resident_without_ clustering	2	Average_parcel_size_wildlife_habitat	1
		Edge_length_wildlife_habitat	1
Acres_per_new_resident_with_ clustering	2	Length_roads	2
		Urban_run_off_P	3

BMP_urban_P	2	Lawn_management	1
Urban_run_off_S	3	Price_per_acre_grassland	2
Erosion_control	1	Quality_of_life	1
Human_waste_processing	1		

Natural Capital and Ecosystem Services

Effective_habitat	1	Habitat_quality_&_IBI	2
Forest_P_filtering	2	Sediment_retention_service	2
Grassland_P_filtering	2	Water_quality_index	1
Wetland_P_filtering	2	Clarity_index	2
Forest_S_retention	2	Eutrophication_index	2
Grass_S_retention	2	Temperature_index	2
Wetland_S_retention	2	Dissolved_oxygen_index	1

Appendix 6

The Ria Formosa Model: Structure and Equations

The resulting "scoping" model for the Ria Formosa includes four main sectors as defined by the stakeholder group: Land-Use, Natural System, Socioeconomic Activities, and Management. The following sections "break down" the structure analysis sector-by-sector. Each piece of the model's sectors is depicted in Figures A6.1 to A6.7, and is followed by a summary description of the structure rationale and main assumptions.

Land-use sector

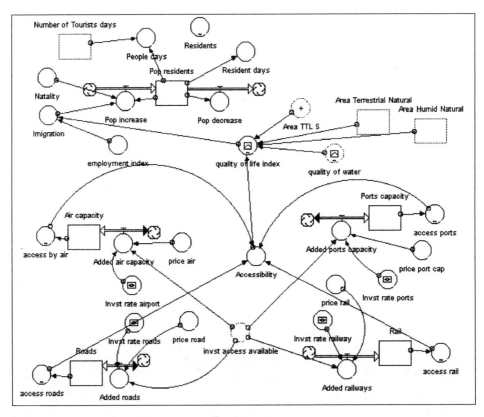

Figure A6.1.

Land Use sector (Population and Accessibility)

Population and Accessibility

▢	$Pop\_residents(t)$ = Pop_residents(t - dt) + (Pop_increase - Pop_decrease) * dt
⧖	$Pop\_increase$ = Pop_residents * (Natality + Immigration)
⧖	$Pop\_decrease$ = Pop_residents*0.0133
○	$Natality$ = 0.02
○	$Immigration$ = quality_of_life_index *employment_index
○	employment_index = 1 * 0.01
⊘	quality_of_life_index = GRAPH (Accessibility * quality_of_water * ((Area_Humid_Natural +Area_Terrestrial_Natural)/Area_TTL_S))(0.00, 0.00), (0.1, 0.00), (0.2, 0.01), (0.3, 0.035), (0.4, 0.13), (0.5, 0.405), (0.6, 0.76), (0.7, 0.905), (0.8, 0.955), (0.9, 0.985), (1, 1.00)
▢	$Air\_capacity(t)$ = Air_capacity(t - dt) + (Added_air_capacity) * dt
⧖	$Added\_air\_capacity$ = (invst_access_available*Invst_rate_airport)/price_air
○	$Invst\_rate\_airport$ = 0.2
○	$price\_air$ = 150
⊘	$access\_by\_air$ = GRAPH(SMTH1(Air_capacity,5)) (0.00, 0.015), (2500, 0.075), (5000, 0.135), (7500, 0.215), (10000, 0.295), (12500, 0.85), (15000, 1.00), (17500, 0.925), (20000, 0.6), (22500, 0.32), (25000, 0.00)
▢	$Ports\_capacity(t)$ = Ports_capacity(t - dt) + (Added_ports_capacity) * dt
⧖	$Added\_ports\_capacity$ = (Invst_rate_ports*invst_access_available)/price_port_cap
○	$Invst\_rate\_ports$ = 0.2
○	$price\_port\_cap$ = 370
⊘	$access\_ports$ = GRAPH(SMTH1(Ports_capacity,5)) (0.00, 0.00), (1400, 0.08), (2800, 0.13), (4200, 0.3), (5600, 0.605), (7000, 0.97), (8400, 1.00), (9800, 0.675), (11200, 0.32), (12600, 0.085), (14000, 0.00)
▢	$Rail(t)$ = Rail(t - dt) + (Added_railways) * dt
⧖	$Added\_railways$ = (invst_access_available*Invst_rate_railway)/price_rail

○	*Invst_rate_railway* = 0.1
○	*price_rail* = 7400
⊘	*access_rail* = GRAPH(SMTH1(Rail,5)) (0.00, 0.01), (30.0, 0.035), (60.0, 0.105), (90.0, 0.31), (120, 0.515), (150, 1.00), (180, 0.73), (210, 0.505), (240, 0.355), (270, 0.245), (300, 0.17)
▢	*Roads(t)* = Roads(t - dt) + (Added_roads) * dt
⊰	*Added_roads* = (invst_access_available*Invst_rate_roads)/price_road
○	*Invst_rate_roads* = 0.5
○	*price_road* = 37000
⊘	*access_roads* = GRAPH(SMTH1(Roads,5)) (0.00, 0.01), (70.0, 0.05), (140, 0.125), (210, 0.245), (280, 0.455), (350, 0.905), (420, 1.00), (490, 0.9), (560, 0.395), (630, 0.11), (700, 0.04)
○	Accessibility = *SMTH1(access_by_air+access_ports+access_rail+access_roads,5)*

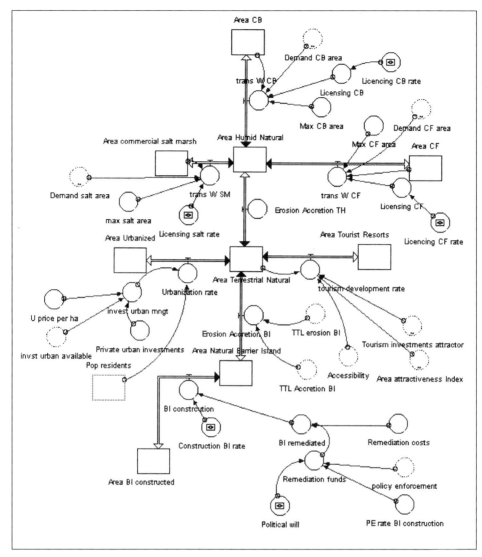

Figure A6.2.

Ria Formosa Land Use model sector (areas and land use changes)

		Areas and land use changes
□		$Area\_Humid\_Natural(t)$ = $Area\_Humid\_Natural(t - dt)$ + $(Erosion\_Accretion\_TH - trans\_W\_SM - trans\_W\_CB - trans\_W\_CF) * dt$
⇌		$Erosion\_Accretion\_TH = -0.1$
⇌		$trans\_W\_SM$ = IF Demand_salt_area<0 THEN Area_commercial_salt_marsh * Demand_salt_area ELSE (max_salt_area - Area_commercial_salt_marsh) * Licensing_salt_rate * Demand_salt_area
⇌		$trans\_W\_CB$ = (Max_CB_area-Area_CB)*Licensing_CB*(Demand_CB_area/10)
⇌		$trans\_W\_CF$ = (Max_CF_area-Area_CF)*Licensing_CF*(Demand_CF_area/10)
□		$Area\_Natural\_Barrier\_Island(t)$ = $Area\_Natural\_Barrier\_Island(t - dt)$ + $(Erosion\_Accretion\_BI - BI\_constrcution) * dt$
□		$Area\_Terrestrial\_Natural(t)$=Area_Terrestrial_Natural(t- dt) + (- tourism_development_rate-Urbanization_rate- Erosion_Accretion_BI - Erosion_Accretion_TH) * dt
□		Area_Tourist_Resorts(t) = Area_Tourist_Resorts(t - dt) + (tourism_development_rate) * dt
⇌		$tourism\_development\_rate$ = Tourism_investments_attractor * ((Accessibility + Area_attractiveness_Index)) * (.001*Area_Terrestrial_Natural)
⇌		$Urbanization\_rate$ = IF (Pop_residents-DELAY(Pop_residents,1))>0 THEN invest_urban_mngt ELSE invest_urban_mngt
⇌		$Erosion\_Accretion\_BI$ = (TTL_Accretion_BI-TTL_erosion_BI)/50000
⇌		$Erosion\_Accretion\_TH = -0.1$
□		$Area\_Urbanized(t)$ = $Area\_Urbanized(t - dt)$ + $(Urbanization\_rate) * dt$
○		$invest\_urban\_mngt$ = (invst_urban_available+Private_urban_investments)/U_price_per_ha
○		$Private\_urban\_investments$ = 1000000

○	*U_price_per_ha* = 90000
▢	*Area_CB(t)* = Area_CB(t - dt) + (trans_W_CB) * dt
⚯	*trans_W_CB* = (Max_CB_area-Area_CB)*Licensing_CB*(Demand_CB_area/10)
○	*Max_CB_area* = 2000
○	*Licensing_CB* = IF TIME<1998 THEN 1 ELSE Licencing_CB_rate
○	*Licencing_CB_rate* = 0
▢	*Area_CF(t)* = Area_CF(t - dt) + (trans_W_CF) * dt
⚯	*trans_W_CF* = (Max_CF_area-Area_CF)*Licensing_CF*(Demand_CF_area/10)
○	*Max_CF_area* = 2500
○	*Licensing_CF* = IF TIME<1998 THEN 1 ELSE Licencing_CF_rate
○	*Licencing_CF_rate* = 0
▢	*Area_commercial_salt_marsh(t)* = Area_commercial_salt_marsh(t - dt) + (trans_W_SM) * dt
○	*max_salt_area* = 1300
○	*Licensing_salt_rate* = 0
▢	*Area_BI_constructed(t)* = Area_BI_constructed(t - dt) + (BI_construction) * dt
⚯	*BI_construction* = IF Political_will=0 THEN Construction_BI_rate ELSE Construction_BI_rate- BI_remediated
○	*Construction_BI_rate* = 2
○	*BI_remediated* = SMTH1(Remediation_funds/Remediation_costs,3)
○	*Remediation_costs* = 12000
○	*Remediation_funds* = IF Political_will>0 THEN policy_enforcement*PE_rate_BI_construction ELSE 0
○	*PE_rate_BI_construction* = 0.3
○	*Political_will* = 0

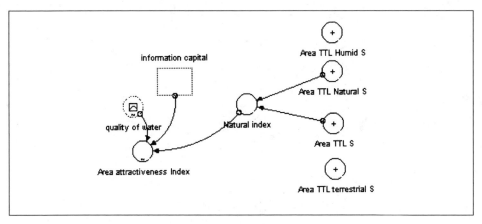

Figure A6.3.

Ria Formosa Land Use model sector (area attractiveness and natural index)

Area attractiveness and Natural Index	
○	*Area_TTL_Humid_S* = Area_CB + Area_CF + Area_commercial_salt_marsh + Area_Humid_Natural
○	*Area_TTL_Natural_S* = Area_Humid_Natural + Area_Natural_Barrier_Island + Area_Terrestrial_Natural
○	*Area_TTL_S* = Area_BI_constructed + Area_CB + Area_CF + Area_commercial_salt_marsh + Area_Humid_Natural + Area_Natural_Barrier_Island + Area_Terrestrial_Natural + Area_Tourist_Resorts + Area_Urbanized
○	*Area_TTL_terrestrial_S* = Area_BI_constructed + Area_Terrestrial_Natural + Area_Tourist_Resorts + Area_Natural_Barrier_Island + Area_Urbanized
○	*Natural_index* = Area_TTL_Natural_S/Area_TTL_S
⊘	*Area_attractiveness_Index* = GRAPH(Natural_index*quality_of_water*information_capital) (0.00, 0.03), (0.1, 0.15), (0.2, 0.38), (0.3, 0.63), (0.4, 1.13), (0.5, 1.54), (0.6, 1.81), (0.7, 1.94), (0.8, 2.00), (0.9, 2.00), (1, 5.00)

Socioeconomic Activities Sector

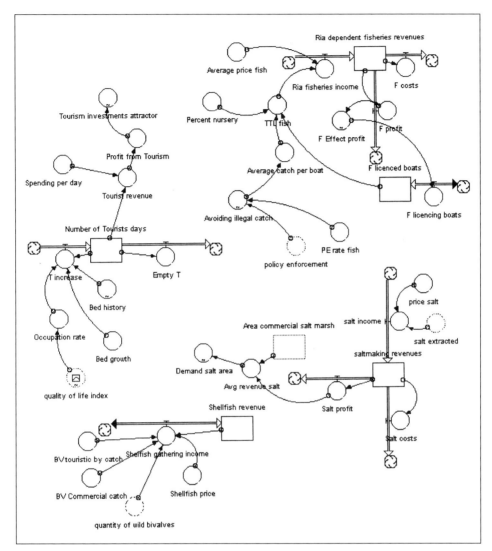

Figure A6.4.

Ria Formosa Socioeconomics model sector (tourism, fisheries, shellfish gathering, salt industry)

	Socioeconomic activities (Tourism, fisheries, shellfish gathering, salt-making industry)
☐	*F_licenced_boats(t)* = F_licenced_boats(t - dt) + (F_licencing_boats) * dt
⏚	*F_licencing_boats* = SMTH1(F_Effect_profit,5)
⊘	*F_Effect_profit* = GRAPH(F_profit) (0.00, -47.0), (30000, -44.0), (60000, -43.5), (90000, -42.5), (120000, -41.0), (150000, -40.5), (180000, -38.5), (210000, -29.5), (240000, -13.5), (270000, -1.00), (300000, 50.0)
☐	*Ria_dependent_fisheries_revenues(t)* = Ria_dependent_fisheries_revenues(t - dt) + (Ria_fisheries_income - F_profit - F_costs) * dt
⏚	*Ria_fisheries_income* = Average_price_fish*TTL_fish
◯	*Average_price_fish* = 200
◯	*TTL_fish* = F_licenced_boats*Average_catch_per_boat*Percent_nursery
◯	*Percent_nursery* = 0.07
◯	*Average_catch_per_boat* = 4*Avoiding_illegal_catch
⊘	*Avoiding_illegal_catch* = GRAPH(PE_rate_fish*policy_enforcement) (0.00, 1.00), (700000, 1.03), (1.4e+006, 1.06), (2.1e+006, 1.11), (2.8e+006, 1.15), (3.5e+006, 1.19), (4.2e+006, 1.23), (4.9e+006, 1.28), (5.6e+006, 1.35), (6.3e+006, 1.39), (7e+006, 1.40)
◯	*PE_rate_fish* = 0.7
⊘	*Avoiding_illegal_catch* = GRAPH(PE_rate_fish*policy_enforcement) (0.00, 1.00), (700000, 1.03), (1.4e+006, 1.06), (2.1e+006, 1.11), (2.8e+006, 1.15), (3.5e+006, 1.19), (4.2e+006, 1.23), (4.9e+006, 1.28), (5.6e+006, 1.35), (6.3e+006, 1.39), (7e+006, 1.40)
⏚	*F_profit* = Ria_dependent_fisheries_revenues*0.1
⏚	*F_costs* = Ria_dependent_fisheries_revenues*0.9

☐	*saltmaking_revenues(t)* = saltmaking_revenues(t - dt) + (salt_income - Salt_costs - Salt_profit) * dt
⇴	*salt_income* = salt_extracted*price_salt
○	*price_salt* = 1.72
⇴	*Salt_costs* = saltmaking_revenues*0.6
⇴	*Salt_profit* = IF TIME< 1981 THEN 41000 ELSE .4*saltmaking_revenues
○	*Avg_revenue_salt* = Salt_profit/Area_commercial_salt_marsh
⊘	*Demand_salt_area* = GRAPH(Avg_revenue_salt) (0.00, -0.0094), (10.0, -0.0076), (20.0, -0.0055), (30.0, -0.0031), (40.0, -0.0011), (50.0, 0.0003), (60.0, 0.0027), (70.0, 0.005), (80.0, 0.0068), (90.0, 0.0084), (100, 0.01)
☐	*Shellfish_revenue(t)* = Shellfish_revenue(t - dt) + (Shellfish_gathering_income) * dt
⇴	*Shelfish_gathering_income* = BV_Commercial_catch * BV_touristic_by_catch * quantity_of_wild_bivalves *Shellfish_price -Shellfish_revenue
○	*BV_Commercial_catch* = 0.1
○	*BV_touristic_by_catch* = 0.15
○	*Shellfish_price* = 1000+RAMP(100,1981)+RAMP(50,1984)-RAMP(200,1994)+RAMP (50, 1998)
☐	*Number_of_Tourists_days(t)* = Number_of_Tourists_days(t - dt) + (T_increase- Empty_T) * dt
⇴	*T_increase* = IF TIME < 1995 THEN (Bed_history*Occupation_rate*365) ELSE (Bed_growth*Number_of_Tourists_days)
○	*Occupation_rate* = 1.4*quality_of_life_index
⊘	*Bed_history* = GRAPH(TIME) (1980, 17466), (1981, 17466), (1982, 18732), (1984, 18732), (1985, 18478), (1986, 18478), (1987, 18908), (1988, 18908), (1989, 18478), (1991, 20168), (1992, 20168), (1993, 23897), (1994, 22586)
⇴	*Empty_T* = Number_of_Tourists_days
○	*Tourist_revenue* = Number_of_Tourists_days*Spending_per_day
○	*Spending_per_day* = 4
○	*Profit_from_Tourism* = 0.15 * Tourist_revenue
⊘	*Tourism_investments_attractor* = GRAPH(Profit_from_Tourism) (0.00, 0.215), (1e+006, 0.225), (2e+006, 0.235), (3e+006, 0.265), (4e+006, 0.33), (5e+006, 0.425), (6e+006, 0.68), (7e+006, 0.805), (8e+006, 0.885), (9e+006, 0.95), (1e+007, 1.00)

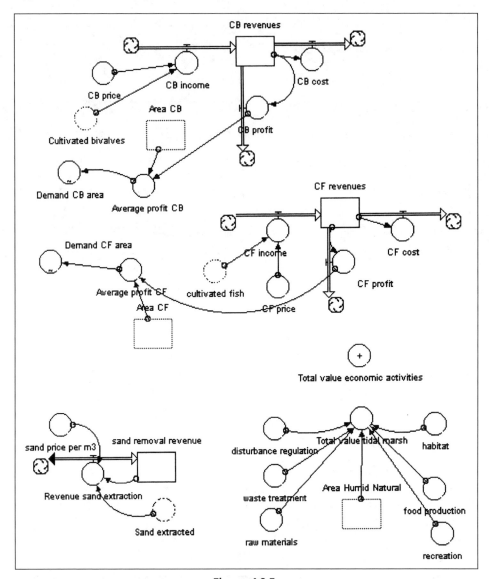

Figure A6.5.

Ria Formosa Socioeconomics model sector (bivalve and fish aquaculture, sand extraction, total value of economic activities)

Socioeconomic activities (Bivalve and fish aquaculture, sand extraction and total values of economic activities,

▢	$CB\_revenues(t) = CB\_revenues(t - dt) + (CB\_income - CB\_cost - CB\_profit) * dt$
⚙	$CB\_income = CB\_price*Cultivated\_bivalves$
○	$CB\_price = 100+RAMP(100,1981)+RAMP(50,1984)-RAMP(200,1994)+RAMP (50, 1998)$
⚙	$CB\_cost = 0.7*CB\_revenues$
⚙	$CB\_profit = 0.3*CB\_revenues$
○	$Average\_profit\_CB = CB\_profit/Area\_CB$
⊘	$Demand\_CB\_area = GRAPH(Average\_profit\_CB)$ (0.00, 0.005), (400, 0.02), (800, 0.04), (1200, 0.06), (1600, 0.095), (2000, 0.135), (2400, 0.19), (2800, 0.27), (3200, 0.38), (3600, 0.525), (4000, 1.00)
▢	$CF\_revenues(t) = CF\_revenues(t - dt) + (CF\_income - CF\_profit - CF\_cost) * dt$
⚙	$CF\_income = cultivated\_fish*CF\_price$
⚙	$CF\_profit = 0.3*CF\_revenues$
⚙	$CF\_cost = 0.7*CF\_revenues$
○	$Average\_profit\_CF = CF\_profit/Area\_CF$
○	$CF\_price = 1400$
⊘	$Demand\_CF\_area = GRAPH(Average\_profit\_CF)$ (0.00, 0.00), (2500, 0.02), (5000, 0.04), (7500, 0.09), (10000, 0.155), (12500, 0.25), (15000, 0.33), (17500, 0.415), (20000, 0.505), (22500, 0.64), (25000, 1.00)
▢	$sand\_removal\_revenue(t) = sand\_removal\_revenue(t - dt) + (Revenue\_sand\_extraction) * dt$

⚙	$Revenue\_sand\_extraction = (Sand\_extracted*sand\_price\_per\_m3)-sand\_removal\_revenue$
○	$sand\_price\_per\_m3 = 1.2$
○	$Total\_value\_economic\_activities = CB\_revenues + CF\_revenues + Ria\_dependent\_fisheries\_revenues + saltmaking\_revenues + sand\_removal\_revenue + Shellfish\_revenue + Tourist\_revenue$
○	$Total\_value\_tidal\_marsh = Area\_Humid\_Natural *(disturbance\_regulation + food production +habitat+raw\_materials+recreation+waste\_treatment)$
○	$disturbance\_regulation = 340215$
○	$waste\_treatment = 1238760$
○	$raw\_materials = 29970$
○	$habitat = 31265$
○	$food\_production = 86210$
○	$recreation = 121730$

Natural System Sector

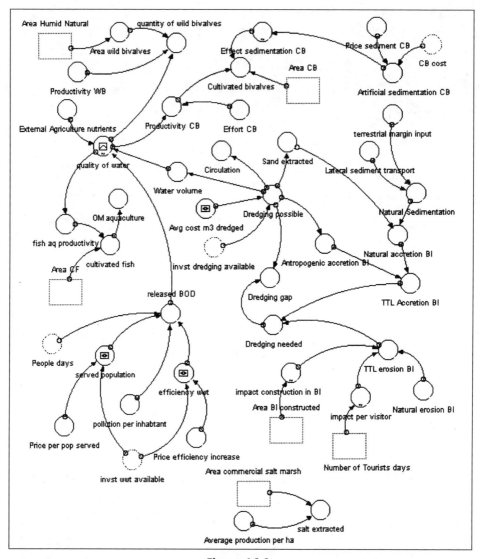

Figure A6.6.

Ria Formosa Natural System model sector (water pollution and quality, dredging, erosion, accretion)

Natural system (water pollution and quality, dredging, erosion and accretion processes)

○	*Antropogenic_accretion_BI* = SMTH1(Dredging_possible*0.4,3)
○	*Area_wild_bivalves* = (Area_Humid_Natural*0.4)*0.4
○	*Artificial_sedimentation_CB* = CB_cost/Price_sediment_CB
○	*Average_production_per_ha* = 50
○	*Avg_cost_m3_dredged* = 1.1
○	*Circulation* = 1.45*Dredging_possible
○	*Cultivated_bivalves* = Area_CB*Productivity_CB*Effect_sedimentation_CB
○	*cultivated_fish* = Area_CF*fish_aq_productivity
○	*Dredging_gap* = Dredging_needed-Dredging_possible
○	*Dredging_needed* = TTL_erosion_BI-TTL_Accretion_BI
○	*Dredging_possible* = invst_dredging_available/Avg_cost_m3_dredged
○	*efficiency_wwt* = .6+((invst_wwt_available/Price_efficiency_increase)*0)
○	*Effort_CB* = 1
○	*External_Agriculture_nutrients* = 0
○	*fish_aq_productivity* = 10*quality_of_water
○	*Lateral_sediment_transport* = 100000
○	*Natural_accretion_BI* = 259000+Natural_Sedimentation - Sand_extracted
○	*Natural_erosion_BI* = 316000
○	*Natural_Sedimentation* = terrestrial_margin_input+Lateral_sediment_transport
○	*OM_aquaculture* = cultivated_fish*1

○	*pollution_per_inhabtant* = 55/1000000
○	*Price_efficiency_increase* = 1
○	*Price_per_pop_served* = 1
○	*Price_sediment_CB* = 4.5
○	*Productivity_CB* = 4*(Effort_CB*quality_of_water)
○	*Productivity_WB* = 5
○	*quantity_of_wild_bivalves* = area_wild_bivalves*Productivity_WB*quality_of_water
○	*released_BOD* = (1.5-served_population)*(1.5-pollution_per_inhabtant)*(1-efficiency_wwt) *People_days
○	*salt_extracted* = Average_production_per_ha*Area_commercial_salt_marsh
○	*Sand_extracted* = SMTH1(0.6*Dredging_possible,3)
○	*served_population* = 0.33 + ((invst_wwt_available/Price_per_pop_served)*0)
○	*terrestrial_margin_input* = 96000
○	*TTL_Accretion_BI* = Antropogenic_accretion_BI+Natural_accretion_BI
○	*TTL_erosion_BI* = Natural_erosion_BI*impact_per_visitor*impact_construction_in_BI
○	*Water_volume* = 78 + SMTH1((Dredging_possible/1000000),4)
⊘	*Effect_sedimentation_CB* = GRAPH(Artificial_sedimentation_CB) (0.00, 0.21), (175, 0.235), (350, 0.275), (525, 0.385), (700, 0.505), (875, 0.65), (1050, 0.775), (1225, 0.885), (1400, 0.955), (1575, 0.98), (1750, 1.00)
⊘	*impact_construction_in_BI* = GRAPH(Area_BI_constructed) (0.00, 1.02), (10.0, 1.05), (20.0, 1.10), (30.0, 1.17), (40.0, 1.23), (50.0, 1.35), (60.0, 1.83), (70.0, 1.94), (80.0, 1.99), (90.0, 2.00), (100, 2.00)
⊘	*impact_per_visitor* = GRAPH(Number_of_Tourists_days) (1e+006, 1.11), (1.5e+006, 1.13), (2e+006, 1.17), (2.5e+006, 1.23), (3e+006, 1.37), (3.5e+006, 1.54), (4e+006, 1.71), (4.5e+006, 1.86), (5e+006, 1.93), (5.5e+006, 1.96), (6e+006, 1.98)
⊘	*quality_of_water*=GRAPH ((released_BOD+External_Agriculture_nutrients)/(Water_volume)) (0.00, 2.00), (2.00, 1.98), (4.00, 1.96), (6.00, 1.87), (8.00, 1.62), (10.0, 1.36), (12.0, 0.395), (14.0, 0.22), (16.0, 0.06), (18.0, 0.015), (20.0, 0.015)

Management Sector

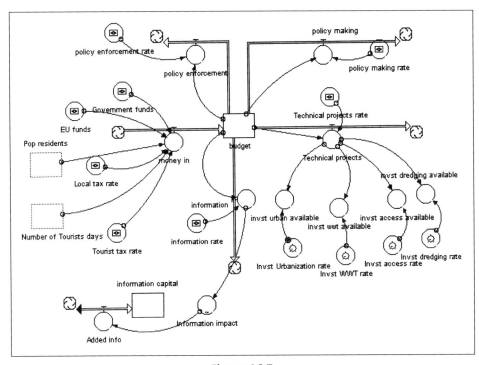

Figure A6.7.

Ria Formosa Management model sector (funds and investments)

Management sectors (Funds and Investments)	
▢	$budget(t)$ = budget(t - dt) + (money_in - Technical_projects - policy_enforcement - information - policy_making) * dt
⏦	$money\_in$= EU_funds + Government_funds + (Local_tax_rate *Pop_residents) +(Tourist_tax_rate *Number_of_Tourists_days)
⏦	$Technical\_projects$ = budget*Technical_projects_rate
⏦	$policy\_enforcement$ = budget*policy_enforcement_rate
⏦	$information$ = budget*information_rate
⏦	$policy\_making$ = budget*policy_making_rate
▢	$information\_capital(t)$ = information_capital(t - dt) + (Added_info) * dt

⌷	*Added_info* = Information_impact/7
◯	*EU_funds* = STEP(4800000/5,1985)-STEP(4800000/5,1990)+STEP(20000000/5,1994)-STEP(20000000/5,1999)
◯	*Government_funds* = 0+STEP(20000000/5,2000)-STEP(20000000/5,2005)
◯	*information_rate* = 0.05
◯	*invst_access_available* = Technical_projects*Invst_access_rate
◯	*Invst_access_rate* = 0.5
◯	*invst_dredging_available* = Technical_projects*Invst_dredging_rate
◯	*Invst_dredging_rate* = 0.1
◯	*Invst_Urbanization_rate* = 0.1
◯	*invst_urban_available* = Technical_projects*Invst_Urbanization_rate
◯	*invst_wwt_available* = Technical_projects*Invst_WWT_rate
◯	*Invst_WWT_rate* = 0.3
◯	*Local_tax_rate* = 0
◯	*policy_enforcement_rate* = 0.05
◯	*policy_making_rate* = 0.05
◯	*Technical_projects_rate* = 0.85
◯	*Tourist_tax_rate* = 0
⊘	*Information_impact* = GRAPH(information) (0.00, 0.005), (8500, 0.035), (17000, 0.045), (25500, 0.06), (34000, 0.08), (42500, 0.145), (51000, 0.28), (59500, 0.74), (68000, 0.885), (76500, 0.945), (85000, 0.99)

Appendix 7

Participant Rating of Ria Formosa Model Parameters

All the parameters in the Ria Formosa model are rated with values corresponding to:
   1 = Unsubstantiated, however based on logical reasoning
   2 = Somewhat substantiated
   3 = Substantiated

The overall confidence in the data based on an average assigned value by the mediated modeling team of the parameters was 1.72.

The model sectors are condensed to Land Use and Natural System. The cryptic format of the parameters is the way they appear as names of the model icons. Owing to limited space on the computer screen, the icon names are often abbreviated. At the first level or equation level in STELLA, the software replaces a space in a name of an icon with an underscore.

Land Use

Air_capacity	1	Area_tourist_resorts	1
Invst_rate_airport	1	Tourism_development_rate	2
Price_air	1	Tourism_investments_attractor	2
Invst_access_available	1	Accessibility	1
Area_BI_constructed	2	Area_attractiveness_index	1
BI_remediated	2	Number_of_tourists_days	3
Remediation_costs	2	Area_urbanized	1
Area_natural_barrier_island	2	Urbanization_rate	1
Erosion_accretion_BI	2	Pop_residents	3
TTL_accretion_BI	2	Natality	2
TTL_erosion_BI	2	Immigration	2
Area_CB	2	Ports_capacity	1
Licensing_CB	3	Rail	1
Demand_CB_area	2	Roads	2
Area_CF	2	Invst_rate_roads	1
Licensing_CF	3	Price_road	1
Demand_CF_area	2	Employment_index	1
Area_commercial_salt_marsh	3	Quality_of_life_index	1
Licensing_salt_rate	3	Quality_of_water	1
Demand_salt_area	2	Information_capital	1
Area_humid_natural	2	Invest_urban_mngt	1
Erosion_accretion_TH	2	Political_will	1
Area_terrestrial_natural	2	Budget	2

Technical_projects	1	Local_tax_rate	1
Policy_enforcement	1	Tourist_tax_rate	1
Information	1	Invst_dredging_available	1
Policy_making	1	Invst_urban_available	1
EU_funds	3	Invst_wwt_available	1
Government_funds	1		

Natural System

Anthropogenic_accretion_BI	2	Natural_erosion_BI	2
Dredging_possible	1	Natural_sedimentation	2
Area_wild_bivalves	2	Terrestrial_margin_input	2
Artificial_sedimentation_CB	2	Lateral_sediment_transport	2
CB_cost	1	OM_aquaculture	1
Price_sediment_CB	1	Pollution_per_inhabitant	2
Average_production_per_ha	3	Quantity_of_wild_bivalves	2
Avg_cost_m^3_dredged	2	Area_wild_bivalves	2
Productivity_CB	2	Productivity_WB	2
Effect_sedimentation_CB	2	Salt_extracted	2
Area_CF	2	Impact_per_visitor	2
Fish_aq_productivity	2	Impact_construction_in_BI	2
Dredging_gap	1	Water_volume	2
Dredging_needed	1	CB_revenues	2
Dredging_possible	1	CF_revenues	2
Avg_cost_m<^{3}_dredged	2	Ria_dependent_fisheries_revenues	2
Efficiency_wwt	3	Saltmaking_revenues	2
Invst_wwt_available	1	Sand_removal_revenue	2
Lateral_sediment_transport	2	Shellfish_revenue	2
Natural_accretion_BI	2	Tourist_revenue	2
Natural_sedimentation	2	Total_value_economic_activities	2
Sand_extracted	2	Total_value_ecosystem_services	2

Appendix 8

Assumptions for Banff–Bow Valley Futures Model Indicators

Social Indicators

As with all modeling efforts, the Banff-Bow Valley Futures Model included a set of assumptions. Appendix B describes these assumptions in detail.

Visitor Numbers, Origins, and Distribution

Scenarios for growth in park visitation were considered to be one of the most important assumptions for the Banff–Bow Valley Futures Model (BVFM). Scenarios were therefore selected during the formal November round table meetings and agreed to by consensus. The table chose annual compounded rates of –0.5%, 1.0%, 3.0%, and 6.0%. Using the estimated visitation number from 1994 (as reported in the AEDT, *Alberta Tourism Pulse* 1995) for the base year was also agreed on. The number of overall visitors was translated into the number of visitor nights by utilizing data from the 1990/91 Alberta Economic Development and Tourism (AEDT) surveys (1991, 1994c). A visitor night is defined as the number of nights a given individual overnights in the park. Two people staying two nights would therefore make up four visitor nights. The proportion of visitors desiring to spend the night in the park and the number of nights they stay are held constant throughout all scenarios.

The *Alberta Tourism Pulse,* published by AEDT, reported key tourism indicators for Banff National Park (BNP) on a monthly basis, including total visitors to the park. The publication was stopped in September 1995, and this information is no longer readily available. Total visitor scenarios for 1995 were developed from visitation figures provided by Parks Canada and are based on monthly vehicle counts (the same data that were used by the *Alberta Pulse*). Some data were missing from the 1995 database—specifically, data from eastbound Trans-Canada Highway (TCH) for the months of September and October, and from southbound Highway 93 for the months of November and December. Corresponding vehicle counts for 1994 were utilized in these cases. Therefore, based on trends in 1995 visitation to the park, the total visitor estimation for 1995 is conservative.

For 1995, visitor origins were based on AEDT surveys (AEDT 1991, 1994c). According to the surveys, Albertans make up 74% of visitors. Of the remaining 26%, 35% are non-Albertan Canadians, 40% are from the United States, and 25% are from other international destinations.

For future scenarios, proportions of provincial and nonprovincial visitors were adjusted with the assistance of the Banff–Lake Louise Tourism Bureau (BLLTB). For the years 2000 and 2005, the proportion of Albertan visitors decreases by 4%, on the basis trends in the tourism market suggesting that (1) the status of the Canadian dollar will continue to attract international visitors to Canadian destinations; (2) the recent open-skies policy will continue to increase the proportion of visitors from the United States; and (3) as demand continues to increase (and the cap on supply is approached), prices will continue to rise. Banff will become less affordable as a destination for Albertans, particularly since they can get comparable experiences elsewhere in the province, where price trends will not be as steep (nearby provincial parks, for example). As a result, the tourism industry in Banff felt that (1) the U.S. market offers the greatest potential for growth; (2) the non-U.S. international market would be constrained by airline flights coming into Canada and the United States; and (3) the proportion of Canadian visitors would decrease.

With these factors in mind, proportions of non-Albertan visitors were also adjusted with the assistance of BLLTB. For the year 2000, non-Albertan Canadians represent 30% of non-Albertan visitors to the park, and the U.S. market represents 45%. Other international visitors remain at 25%. For the year 2005, non-Albertan Canadians represent 30% of the market, while U.S. visitors make up 48% and international visitors represent 22%.

The proportion of day users to overnight users for both Albertans and non-Albertans is based on the 1990/91 AEDT surveys (AEDT 1991, 1994c). This proportion is held constant in the scenarios until the cap on overnight accommodations is reached. At an occupancy rate of 80%, this takes place in the year 2005 in the 6% visitation growth scenario.

Occupancy, or "actual use," data were utilized to determine how overnight visitors are distributing themselves among different accommodation types. Overnight accommodation scenarios assume that as visitation increases, the proportion of visitors opting to overnight in a given accommodation type remains constant. The effects of capping infrastructure under different growth rate scenarios are therefore reported in terms of room deficits per year for each overnight accommodation type. A room deficit for any given scenario is the difference between the number of visitors that desire to stay in a particular accommodation type in the park and the maximum number of bed units available in that type. Facility types were grouped into the following categories: town of Banff commercial; hamlet of Lake Louise commercial; outlying commercial accommodations (see below); other motorized accessible facilities, including Tunnel Mountain Campground, other campgrounds, and hostels; and backcountry facilities, including lodges, huts and shelters, and campgrounds.

Because the demand for accommodation type differs (hotels and motels in the town of Banff have a higher occupancy rate than backcountry campgrounds, for example), facility deficits are realized at different times in the future. Redistributing deficits from one facility type to other facility types in the park with remaining capacity was not attempted. It was assumed that if a visitor wished to stay in a hotel in the park, they would seek alternatives of the same type in the region rather than tent-camp in the backcountry, for example.

Built and Linear Infrastructure

To examine the capacity of built infrastructure in Banff National Park, overnight accommodations were utilized as the indicator. An extensive database of overnight facilities was developed to determine capacity and use in 1995, as well as potential future capacity. These data quantify the potential and existing overnight opportunities for park visitors and residents and were utilized to evaluate overnight use distribution patterns, identify areas that can accommodate additional use, and help identify areas in need of near-term management action. Having a complete understanding of the overnight accommodations in the park is critical since it is the only factor currently limiting the number of overnight visitors to the park.

Commercial capacity in Banff National Park can vary among scenarios, both in terms of number of rooms and in terms of the number of bed units per room. Under current zoning, the town of Banff and hamlet of Lake Louise can accommodate additional overnight infrastructure. Some of this potential is in terms of new facilities, and some is in expansion of existing facilities. In these locations, four infrastructure scenarios were considered: current capacity; 25% of buildout potential; 50% of buildout potential; and total capacity at buildout.

In the hamlet of Lake Louise, current capacity for hotels and motels is reported in terms of bed units. In the town of Banff, current capacity for hotels and motels and the Banff Centre, a residential conference and arts facility, are reported in terms of number of rooms. It was therefore necessary to determine number of bed units per room before maximum capacity could be calculated. Two, three, and four bed-units per room were utilized to understand the magnitude of change over a range of potential scenarios. The two bed-units per room scenario is intended to represent the standard in the industry of double occupancy. The four bed-units per room scenario is intended to represent an average family of two adults and two children staying in one room. Maximum capacity for all scenarios is determined by multiplying number of bed units per room by the total number of rooms.

Though 100% year-round occupancy is considered unrealistic in the industry, owing to factors such as drop in demand during "nonholiday" periods, inclement weather, and last-minute reservation cancellations, information on the maximum potential occupancy rate is not available. Experts at Banff–Lake Louise Tourism Bureau determined a yearly average occupancy rate of 80% to be a reasonable estimate for the town of Banff. All scenarios in the town of Banff, therefore, reflect this adjustment. A study conducted in the park in 1995 determined the average annual occupancy rate in Banff to be 76.7% (Price Waterhouse 1995). This adjustment is therefore conservative.

Outlying commercial accommodations (OCAs) are defined as "sheltered overnight accommodation for Park visitors such as bungalow camps, lodges, chalets, hotels or motels, which are located outside the boundaries of a town or visitor center and which are operated by an individual or agency other than charitable or non-profit organizations" (Pacas et al. 1996). These facilities are accessible by private vehicle.

According to the Four Mountain Parks Outlying Commercial Accommodation Redevelopment Guidelines (Parks Canada 1988), and In Trust for Tomorrow, "No additional OCAs will be permitted." Additional capacity for OCAs is therefore limited to allowable expansion of existing facilities. A limit to the density of development for each OCA is determined by a floor to-area ratio (FAR) (Parks Canada 1988).

Because the majority of OCAs are at or near their maximum FAR, or in some cases exceed it, and because it is not possible to translate the FAR into number of rooms, current room numbers were utilized for all scenarios. The number of bed units for OCAs is therefore conservative. Most OCAs report capacity in terms of bed units. For those that report number of rooms only, the two, three, and four bed-unit scenarios were applied.

Capacity for international hostels and backcountry lodges, huts, and outfitters is measured in terms of number of persons per night or bed units. Under current guidelines, hostels, lodges, huts, and group camps cannot accommodate additional capacity. Current capacity is therefore utilized for all scenarios. The International Hostel in Banff Townsite began expansion after the completion of the Banff–Bow Valley Study (BBVS).The estimate for total capacity of hostel bed units is therefore conservative.

All park-operated facilities, including both frontcountry and backcountry campgrounds and shelters, cannot accommodate additional capacity under current guidelines. Therefore, current capacity is utilized in all scenarios.

Current resident infrastructure capacity in the town of Banff is based on the 1995 residential inventory conducted by the town. Under current zoning, residential infrastructure can increase. Maximum capacity is based on maximum allowable buildout under current zoning regulations. Current residential infrastructure capacity for the hamlet of Lake Louise is based on a 1993 Parks Canada inventory. The maximum capacity is difficult to predict for Lake Louise. Though the 1979 Low Growth Action Plan for Lake Louise sets out guidelines for visitor accommodations, guidelines are not indicated for residential infrastructure.

Linear infrastructure remains constant over time except the Trans-Canada Highway, which includes the final phase of twinning to the Yoho boundary in some scenarios.

Economic Development

Expenditures for overnight visitors in 1995 of Albertans, non-Albertan Canadians, and U.S. visitors were developed with the assistance of Banff–Lake Louise Tourism Bureau. Expenditures are based on a 20% increase over those reported by AEDT surveys (1991, 1994c). Because 1990/91 were recession years, and on the basis of observations in the Banff tourism industry and results from Stats Canada's international travel survey (Statistics Canada 1995), a 20% increase in expenditures was deemed a reasonable estimate for these visitor groups. Observations in the Banff tourism industry suggest that non-U.S. international visitor expenditures grew faster than for other visitor groups. Observations varied between 25% and 45% between the years 1990 and 1995. Therefore, non-U.S. international visitor expenditures for 1995 were subjected to a 35% increase over those reported in the 1990 AEDT exit survey. Expenditures for overnight visitors are reported on a per trip basis.

Expenditures for overnight visitors for the years 2000 and 2005 are based on two rates of expenditure growth: low (2.09% per year, compounded) and high (3.72% per year, compounded). The low rate is based on the trends of expenditure increases from the years 1976 to 1990/91, as reported by AEDT (AEDT 1991, 1994; ABDT 1976; ATSB 1982). The high rate is based on observations by the Banff tourism industry between the period 1990 and 1995 and Stats Canada's international travel survey (Statistics Canada 1995).

Expenditures for Albertan day users for 1995 represent a 20% increase (as discussed with BLLTB and reported above) over those reported by AEDT (AEDT 1994c). Values represent median expenditures per visitors. For the years 2000 and 2005, low and high rates of expenditure growth were utilized to calculate day user expenditures per trip.

Expenditures for non-Albertan day users were calculated using a weighted average across median expenditures for all visitor types, as reported in the 1990 AEDT exit survey (1991). This average median expenditure was subject to the 20% increase reported above for 1995. For the years 2000 and 2005, low and high rates of expenditure growth were utilized to calculate day user expenditures per trip.

All dollars are standardized for the year 1995, using the consumer price index as reported by Statistics Canada. All currencies are reported in Canadian dollars. Expenditure distribution by industry category is held constant, as reported by AEDT (1991, 1994c) throughout all scenarios.

AEDT executed a total of 15 scenarios with the demand economic impact model (DEIM) for the BBVS, including 9 baseline scenarios: 1 for the year 1995; 4 for the year 2000 (–0.5%, 1%, 3%, and 6%); and 4 for the year 2005 (–0.5%, 1%, 3%, and 6%). In addition to these 9 baseline scenarios, 6 scenarios were executed for the year 2005 (a low annual percentage expenditure increase at 1%, 3%, and 6% and a high annual percentage expenditure increase at 1%, 3%, and 6%).

Visitor demographics and expenditures for baseline scenarios are based on those reported by AEDT surveys (AEDT 1991, 1994c) and remain constant throughout all baseline scenarios. Expenditures are adjusted to 1995 dollars using the consumer price index. All currencies are reported in Canadian dollars. Baseline scenarios are used to examine visitation effects only—that is, visitor number is the only parameter that is changing. Demographics and expenditures per visitor type remain constant.

Reported tax revenues are based on visitor expenditures and are generated by the DEIM. All reporting of employment effects resulting from visitor expenditures in the park are generated by the DEIM. These values were then included in the BVFM.

Park Residents

The town of Banff does not report a growth rate for its resident population and does not conduct an annual census. The most current population numbers reported by the town at the time of the study were from the 1991 *Dominion Census* (Statistics Canada 1991), which indicates a permanent population of 5,688 and an estimated transient population of 1,927, for a total estimated population of 7,615. The town reports that residential infrastructure is growing at a rate of 1.2% per annum. The *Dominion Census* indicates a compounded annual increase in population of 1.82% between the years 1986 and 1991, and 3.06% between the years 1981 and 1991. The town of Banff does project a permanent population of approximately 10,000 residents by the year 2005. This represents a compounded growth rate of 4.1% per annum. For the purposes of the model, compounded annual increases of 1%, 2%, and 3% were considered.

To determine quality of life for park residents, visitor-to-resident ratios are calculated for an *average* day in the summer for the town of Banff. AEDT reports that 34.4% of visitation occurs during the 87 days of summer (June 15–September 9) and that 80% of these visitors spend time in the town of Banff (AEDT 1991,1994a). Of those visitors spending the night in the park, approximately 80% overnight in the town of Banff. Therefore, total annual visitation was adjusted to average visitors per day in the summer, with the assumption that 80% were utilizing facilities in the town of Banff on any given day.

Ecological Indicators

Two ecological indicators were examined in the BVFM; elk populations and wolf populations.

Elk Populations

The elk component of the BVFM includes population models for each of the spatial regions of interest. The model structure is the same for all subpopulations and is based on the following general equation:

$$Nt+1 = Nt + Rt - Mt + It - Et$$

Where:

N is the adult population size

R is recruitment, expressed as a rate: i.e., Elk(t) = Elk(t – dt)+ (recruitment) * dt

M is mortality, expressed as a rate: i.e., Elk(t) = Elk(t – dt)+ (recruitment – deaths) * dt

I is immigration expressed as a rate: i.e., Elk(t) = Elk(t – dt) + (births + immigration – deaths) * dt

E is emigration expressed as a rate: i.e., Elk(t) = Elk(t – dt) + (births + immigration – deaths – emigration) * dt

The conceptual model upon which the elk subpopulations are based is shown in Figure 7.3. Initial conditions for the population of elk are based on spring 1995 aerial counts (BNP, unpublished data; T. Hurd, pers. comm.), adjusted for sightability (by 1.09) after Woods (1991).

Recruitment is based on empirical data (Woods 1991) and is being expressed as calves per 100 animals. An inverse relationship between recruitment and population is assumed, with a linear regression for carrying capacity based on Houston (1982). Experts in the elk module assumed a total carrying capacity of 2,000 animals for the Bow Valley based on historical record and habitat carrying capacity determined through rankings of elk habitat (Holroyd and VanTighem 1983). Using the amount of high and very high habitat for elk (based on Achuff et al. 1996) in each zone, the total assumed carrying capacity (K) was partitioned among the three zones in the valley. Regression equations describing recruitment were adjusted for the K in each zone. The value of K, therefore, varies among years with changes in vegetation. For example, under a status quo vegetation management scenario (i.e., fire suppression), as the amount of high- and very high-quality habitat decreases, the model assumes a proportional decrease in K.

Elk mortality is based on six parameters: culling, predators, natural death, road and rail kills, and hunting. Parameter values are based on empirical data (Woods 1990). In the model, the proportion of elk killed by trains doubles during severe snow events (accumulation greater than 40 cm) because elk tend to use the railroad track as a travel route. Severe snow events are determined stochastically in the model with a probability of 6% after Woods (1987). The model utilizes a random number generator to facilitate stochastic snow events. Proportion of elk killed on mitigated versus nonmitigated sections of the highway are based on Woods (1990). In the model, this rate is assumed to remain constant, regardless of which section of the highway is mitigated. In other words, in future scenarios in which mitigation measures are "implemented" in currently unmitigated sections of the highway, the model assumes those measures will have the same success rate as current measures. Accessibility adjusts for the difference between elk and wolves in their habituation to humans and facilities. The percentage of the elk population accessible by wolves is based on P. Paquet (pers. comm.).

Empirical data for elk killed on the highway are translated into car collisions. One elk death translates into one car collision. The cost of damage per collision is assumed to be $2,000.

Data on immigration and emigration, both between and within the Bow Valley elk population, are lacking. For the BVFM, therefore, they are assumed to be equal.

Numbers of other ungulates are calculated as a proportion of elk using Huggard's index (Huggard 1991). Indices for ungulate in the valley are as follows: moose, 0.068; deer, 0.364; caribou, 0.02; goat, 0.223; and sheep, 0.573. Other ungulate numbers calculated are those that reside in the Bow Valley and make up a component of the diet of Bow Valley wolves. These include moose, deer (both mule and whitetail), goat, sheep, and caribou.

Wolf Populations

Total ungulate biomass is utilized to calculate number of wolves in the valley. The relationship between ungulate biomass and number of wolves is based on empirical data from P. Paquet (unpublished data). This number is then adjusted, on the basis of the availability of the ungulate population, to wolves—termed "potential wolves."

Appendix 9

Symbol Definition and Mathematical Algorithms for All Model Components in the Banff–Bow Valley Study Futures Model

Appendix 9 includes symbol definitions and mathematical algorithms for all model components in the Banff-Bow Valley Futures Model. Symbol definition and algorithms are displayed in the format generated by STELLA software.

Symbol	Definition
State Variables	
Annual_Visitors(t)	Annual_Visitors(t) =Annual_Visitors(t – dt) + (Annual_increase_visitors) * dt INIT Annual_Visitors = 4794299
Expend_day_Albertan(t)	Expend_day_Albertan(t) = Expend_day_Albertan (t – dt) + (day_Albertan_expend_increase) * dt INIT Expend_day_Albertan = 49.67
Expend_day_Other(t)	Expend_day_Other(t) = Expend_day_Other(t – dt) + (day_Other_expend_increase) * dt INIT Expend_day_Other = 117.34
Expend_Other_CN_overn(t)	Expend_Other_CN_overn(t) = Expend_Other_CN_overn(t – dt) + (Other_CN_overn_expend_increase) * dt INIT Expend_Other_CN_overn = 277.24
Expend_Other_foreign _overn(t)	Expend_Other_foreign_overn(t) = Expend_Other foreign_overn (t – dt) + (Other_foreign_overn_ expend_ increase) * dt INIT Expend_Other_foreign_overn = 643.68
Expend_overn_Albertan(t)	Expend_overn_Albertan(t) = Expend_overn_Albertan(t – dt) + (overn_Albertan_ expend_increase) * dt INIT Expend_overn_Albertan = 216.32
Expend_US_overn(t)	Expend_US_overn(t) = Expend_US_overn(t – dt) + (US_overn_expend_increase) * dt INIT Expend_US_overn = 377.38
summer_TCH_west_bound _thru_traffic(t)	summer_TCH_west_bound_thru_traffic(t) = summer_TCH_west_bound_thru_traffic(t – dt) + (annual_thru_traffic_increase) * dt INIT summer_TCH_west_bound _thru_traffic = 5452

TOTAL_ELK_C(t)	TOTAL_ELK_C(t) = TOTAL_ELK_C(t – dt) + (ELK_YOY_C + ELK_IN_MOVEMENT_C – ELK_DEATHS_C – ELK_OUT_MOVEMENT_C) * dt INIT TOTAL_ELK_C = 567
TOTAL_ELK_E(t)	TOTAL_ELK_E(t) = TOTAL_ELK_E(t – dt) + (ELK_YOY_E + ELK_IN_MOVEMENT_E – ELK_DEATHS_E – ELK_OUT_MOVEMENT_E) * dt INIT TOTAL_ELK_E = 150
TOTAL_ELK_FE(t)	TOTAL_ELK_FE(t) = TOTAL_ELK_FE(t – dt) + (ELK_YOY_FE + ELK_IN_MOVEMENT_FE – ELK_DEATHS_FE – ELK_OUT_MOVEMENT_FE) * dt INIT TOTAL_ELK_FE = 300
TOTAL_ELK_W(t)	TOTAL_ELK_W(t) = TOTAL_ELK_W(t – dt) + (ELK_YOY_W + ELK_IN_MOVEMENT_W – ELK_DEATHS_W – ELK_OUT_MOVEMENT_W) * dt INIT TOTAL_ELK_W = 108
Total_LLResidents(t)	Total_LLResidents(t) = Total_LLResidents(t – dt) + (annual_LL_res_in) * dt INIT Total_LLResidents = 1461
Total_ToBResidents(t)	Total_ToBResidents(t) = Total_ToBResidents(t – dt) + (annual_ToB_res_in) * dt INIT Total_ToBResidents = 7615

Inputs

Annual_increase_visitors	Annual_increase_visitors = Annual_Visitors *visitation_growth_rate
day_Albertan_expend _increase	day_Albertan_expend_increase = Expend_day_Albertan*Annual_expend_rate
day_Other_expend_increase	day_Other_expend_increase = Expend_day_Other*Annual_expend_rate
Other_CN_overn_expend _increase	Other_CN_overn_expend_increase = Expend_Other_CN_overn*Annual_expend_rate
Other_foreign_overn_expend _increase	Other_foreign_overn_expend_increase = Expend_Other_foreign_overn*Annual_expend_rate
overn_Albertan_expend _increase	overn_Albertan_expend_increase = Expend_overn_Albertan*Annual_expend_rate
US_overn_expend_increase	US_overn_expend_increase = Expend_US_overn*Annual_expend_rate
annual_thru_traffic_increase	annual_thru_traffic_increase = summer_TCH_west_bound_thru_traffic* percent_increase_in_thru_traffic

ELK_YOY_C	ELK_YOY_C = TOTAL_ELK_C*YOY_rate_ratio
ELK_IN_MOVEMENT_C	ELK_IN_MOVEMENT_C = TOTAL_ELK_C*0
ELK_YOY_E	ELK_YOY_E = TOTAL_ELK_E*YOY_Rate_E
ELK_IN_MOVEMENT_E	ELK_IN_MOVEMENT_E = TOTAL_ELK_E*0
ELK_YOY_FE	ELK_YOY_FE = TOTAL_ELK_FE*YOY_Rate_FE
ELK_IN_MOVEMENT_FE	ELK_IN_MOVEMENT_FE = TOTAL_ELK_FE*0
ELK_YOY_W	ELK_YOY_W = TOTAL_ELK_W*YOY_Rate_W
ELK_IN_MOVEMENT_W	ELK_IN_MOVEMENT_W = TOTAL_ELK_W*0
annual_LL_res_in	annual_LL_res_in = Total_LLResidents * annual_LL _res_increase
annual_ToB_res_in	annual_ToB_res_in = Total_ToBResidents * annual_ToB_res_increase

Outputs

ELK_DEATHS_C	ELK_DEATHS_C = TOTAL_ELK_C*Mortality_Rate_C
ELK_OUT_MOVEMENT_C	ELK_OUT_MOVEMENT_C = TOTAL_ELK_C*0
ELK_DEATHS_E	ELK_DEATHS_E = TOTAL_ELK_E*Mortality_Rate_E
ELK_OUT_MOVEMENT_E	ELK_OUT_MOVEMENT_E = TOTAL_ELK_E*0
ELK_DEATHS_FE	ELK_DEATHS_FE = TOTAL_ELK_FE * Mortality _Rate_FE
ELK_OUT_MOVEMENT_FE	ELK_OUT_MOVEMENT_FE = TOTAL_ELK_FE*0
ELK_DEATHS_W	ELK_DEATHS_W = TOTAL_ELK_W*Mortality_ Rate_W
ELK_OUT_MOVEMENT_W	ELK_OUT_MOVEMENT_W = TOTAL_ELK_W*0

External Variables

Albertan_average_nights	Albertan_average_nights = 2
Albertan_visitor_nights	Albertan_visitor_nights = Albertan_average _nights*overnight_Albertans
Annual_expend_rate	Annual_expend_rate = .0209
annual_LL_res_increase	annual_LL_res_increase = .14
annual_occup_rate	annual_occup_rate = INT(1)
annual_ToB_res_increase	annual_ToB_res_increase = .02
annual_visitor_cars	annual_visitor_cars = Annual_Visitors/2.5
available_elk_C	available_elk_C = TOTAL_ELK_C*.2
available_elk_E	available_elk_E = TOTAL_ELK_E*.5
avail_ungulate_bio_index	avail_ungulate_bio_index = caribou_avail_bio_index + deer_avail_bio_index + goat_avail_bio_index + moose_avail_bio index + sheep_avail_bio_index
BC_huts&shelters	BC_huts&shelters = BC_huts & shelters % * Total_visitor_nights

BC_huts&shelters%	BC_huts&shelters% = IF((annual_occup_rate=1) AND (rm_occup_rate=2)) THEN .0012 ELSE IF((annual_occup_rate=1) AND (rm_occup_rate=3)) THEN .0009 ELSE IF((annual_occup_rate=1) AND (rm_occup_rate=4)) THEN .0007 ELSE IF((annual_occup_rate=2) AND (rm_occup_rate=2)) THEN .0013 ELSE IF((annual_occup_rate=2) AND (rm_occup_rate=3)) THEN .0010 ELSE IF((annual_occup_rate=2) AND (rm_occup_rate=4)) THEN .0008 ELSE IF((annual_occup_rate=3) AND (rm_occup_rate=2)) THEN .0014 ELSE IF((annual_occup_rate=3) AND (rm_occup_rate=3)) THEN .0010 ELSE IF((annual_occup_rate=3) AND (rm_occup_rate=4)) THEN .0008 ELSE 0
BC_lodges	BC_lodges = BC_lodges%*Total_visitor_nights
BC_lodges%	BC_lodges% = IF((annual_occup_rate=1) AND (rm_occup_rate=2)) THEN .0012 ELSE IF((annual_occup_rate=1) AND (rm_occup_rate=3)) THEN .0009 ELSE IF((annual_occup_rate=1) AND (rm_occup_rate=4)) THEN .0007 ELSE IF((annual_occup_rate=2) AND (rm_occup_rate=2)) THEN .0013 ELSE IF((annual_occup_rate=2) AND (rm_occup_rate=3)) THEN .0009 ELSE IF((annual_occup_rate=2) AND (rm_occup_rate=4)) THEN .0007 ELSE IF((annual_occup_rate=3) AND (rm_occup_rate=2)) THEN .0013 ELSE IF((annual_occup_rate=3) AND (rm_occup_rate=3)) THEN .0010 ELSE IF((annual_occup_rate=3) AND (rm_occup_rate=4)) THEN .0008 ELSE 0
BC_nonroofed	BC_nonroofed = BC_nonroofed%*Total_visitor_nights
BC_nonroofed%	BC_nonroofed% = IF((annual_occup_rate=1) AND (rm_occup_rate=2)) THEN .0041 ELSE IF((annual_occup_rate=1) AND (rm_occup_rate=3)) THEN .0030 ELSE IF((annual_occup_rate=1) AND (rm_occup rate=4)) THEN .0024 ELSE IF((annual_occup_rate=2) AND (rm_occup_rate=2)) THEN .0043 ELSE IF((annual_occup_rate=2) AND (rm_occup_rate=3)) THEN .0032 ELSE IF((annual_occup_rate=2) AND (rm_occup_rate=4)) THEN .0025 ELSE IF((annual_occup_rate=3) AND (rm_occup_rate=2)) THEN .0046 ELSE IF((annual_occup_rate=3) AND (rm_occup_rate=3)) THEN .0034 ELSE IF((annual_occup_rate=3) AND (rm_occup_rate=4)) THEN .0027 ELSE 0

BNPCamping	BNPCamping = BNPCamping%*Total_visitor_nights
BNPCamping%	BNPCamping% = IF((annual_occup_rate=1) AND (rm_occup_rate=2)) THEN .0236 ELSE IF((annual_occup_rate=1) AND (rm_occup_rate=3)) THEN .0174 ELSE IF((annual_occup_rate=1) AND (rm_occup_rate=4)) THEN .0138 ELSE IF((annual_occup_rate=2) AND (rm_occup_rate=2)) THEN .0249 ELSE IF((annual_occup_rate=2) AND (rm_occup_rate=3)) THEN .0184 ELSE IF((annual_occup_rate=2) AND (rm_occup_rate=4)) THEN .0146 ELSE IF((annual_occup_rate=3) AND (rm_occup_rate=2)) THEN .0262 ELSE IF((annual_occup_rate=3) AND (rm_occup_rate=3)) THEN .0194 ELSE IF((annual_occup_rate=3) AND (rm_occup_rate=4)) THEN .0154 ELSE 0
BNPComm	BNPComm = IF(Total_visitor_nights * BNPComm % < Capacity_BNPComm) THEN (Total_visitor_nights*BNPComm%) ELSE Capacity_BNPComm
BNPComm%	BNPComm% = IF((annual_occup_rate=1) AND (rm_occup_rate=2)) THEN .0290 ELSE IF((annual_occup_rate=1) AND (rm_occup_rate=3)) THEN .0234 ELSE IF((annual_occup_rate=1) AND (rm_occup_rate=4)) THEN .0202 ELSE IF((annual_occup_rate=2) AND (rm_occup_rate=2)) THEN .0238 ELSE IF((annual_occup_rate=2) AND (rm_occup_rate=3)) THEN .0177 ELSE IF((annual_occup_rate=2) AND (rm_occup_rate=4)) THEN .0142 ELSE IF((annual_occup_rate=3) AND (rm_occup_rate=2)) THEN .0287 ELSE IF((annual_occup_rate=3) AND (rm_occup_rate=3)) THEN .0233 ELSE IF((annual_occup_rate=3) AND (rm_occup_rate=4)) THEN .0201 ELSE 0
BNPComm_deficit	BNPComm_deficit = IF (Total_visitor_nights * BNPComm%) <Capacity_BNPComm THEN 0 ELSE (Total_visitor_nights*BNPComm%) – Capacity_BNPComm
BNPHostels	BNPHostels = IF (Total_visitor_nights * BNPHostels% <Capacity_BNPHostels) THEN (Total_visitor_nights*BNPHostels%) ELSE Capacity_BNPHostels
BNPHostels%	BNPHostels% = IF((annual_occup_rate=1) AND (rm_occup_rate=2)) THEN .0108 ELSE

IF((annual_occup_rate=1) AND (rm_occup_rate=3)) THEN .0079 ELSE IF((annual_occup_rate=1) AND (rm_occup_rate=4)) THEN .0063 ELSE IF((annual_occup_rate=2) AND (rm_occup_rate=2)) THEN .0113 ELSE IF((annual_occup_rate=2) AND (rm_occup_rate=3)) THEN .0084 ELSE IF((annual_occup_rate=2) AND (rm_occup_rate=4)) THEN .0067 ELSE IF((annual_occup_rate=3) AND (rm_occup_rate=2)) THEN .0120 ELSE IF((annual_occup_rate=3) AND (rm_occup_rate=3)) THEN .0089 ELSE IF((annual_occup_rate=3) AND (rm_occup_rate=4)) THEN .0070 ELSE 0

BNPHostels_deficit	BNPHostels_deficit = IF (Total_visitor_nights * BNPHostels%)<Capacity_BNPHostels THEN 0 ELSE (Total_visitor_nights*BNPHostels%) – Capacity_BNPHostels
Capacity_BNPComm	Capacity_BNPComm = IF(rm_occup_rate=2) THEN 170513 ELSE IF(rm_occup_rate=3) THEN 186833 ELSE IF(rm_occup_rate=4) THEN 203153 ELSE 0
Capacity_BNPHostels	Capacity_BNPHostels = IF(rm_occup_rate=2) THEN 100375 ELSE IF(rm_occup_rate=3) THEN 100375 ELSE IF(rm_occup_rate=4) THEN 100375 ELSE 0
Capacity_LLComm	Capacity_LLComm = IF(rm_occup_rate=2) THEN 1090255 ELSE IF(rm_occup_rate=3) THEN 1090255 ELSE IF(rm_occup_rate=4) THEN 1090255 ELSE 0
capacity_ToBComm	capacity_ToBComm = IF(rm_occup_rate=2) THEN 4244950 ELSE IF(rm_occup_rate=3) THEN 6312675 ELSE IF(rm_occup_rate=4) THEN 8380400 ELSE 0
caribou	caribou = total_elk*.045
caribou_avail_bio_index	caribou_avail_bio_index = caribou*.63*2
costs_of_collisions_W	costs_of_collisions_W = road_collisions_W*2000
cost_of_collisions	cost_of_collisions = road_collisions_FE*2000
cost_of_collisions_C	cost_of_collisions_C = road_collisions_C*2000
cost_of_collisions_E	cost_of_collisions_E = road_collisions_E*2000
day_Albertans	day_Albertans = Total_Albertans*.70
day_Other	day_Other = Total_Other – overnight_Other
deer	deer = total_elk*.364
deer_avail_bio_index	deer_avail_bio_index = deer*.75*1
elk_density_C_zone	elk_density_C_zone = TOTAL_ELK_C/ Sq_Km_in_C_zone
extreme_snow_event	extreme_snow_event = IF (Random_snow < 0.06) THEN(1)ELSE(0)
Females_C	Females_C = TOTAL_ELK_C*RANDOM(.63,.71)
Females_E	Females_E = TOTAL_ELK_E*RANDOM(.58,.69)

Females_FE	Females_FE = TOTAL_ELK_FE*RANDOM(.58,.69)
Females_W	Females_W = TOTAL_ELK_W*RANDOM(.45,.89) {example for W zone}
Female_Biomass_C	Female_Biomass_C = Females_C*226
Female_Biomass_E	Female_Biomass_E = Females_E*226
Female_Biomass_FE	Female_Biomass_FE = Females_FE*226
Female_Biomass_W	Female_Biomass_W = Females_W*226
goat	goat = total_elk*.223
goat_avail_bio_index	goat_avail_bio_index = goat*.5*1
highway_mitigation_C	highway_mitigation_C = 1
highway_mitigation_E	highway_mitigation_E = 1
highway_mitigation_FE	highway_mitigation_FE = 0
highway_mitigation_W	highway_mitigation_W = 0
LLComm	LLComm = IF(Total_visitor_nights * LLComm % < Capacity_LLComm) THEN (Total_visitor_nights*LLComm%) ELSE Capacity_LLComm
LLComm%	LLComm% = IF((annual_occup_rate=1) AND (rm_occup_rate=2)) THEN .1851 ELSE IF((annual_occup_rate=1) AND (rm_occup_rate=3)) THEN .1367 ELSE IF((annual_occup_rate=1) AND (rm_occup_rate=4)) THEN .1084 ELSE IF((annual_occup_rate=2) AND (rm_occup_rate=2)) THEN .1855 ELSE IF((annual_occup_rate=2) AND (rm_occup_rate=3)) THEN .1372 ELSE IF((annual_occup_rate=2) AND (rm_occup_rate=4)) THEN .1089 ELSE IF((annual_occup_rate=3) AND (rm_occup_rate=2)) THEN .1837 ELSE IF((annual_occup_rate=3) AND (rm_occup_rate=3)) THEN .1360 ELSE IF((annual_occup_rate=3) AND (rm_occup_rate=4)) THEN .1079 ELSE 0
LLComm_deficit	LLComm_deficit = IF (Total_visitor_nights * LLComm%) < Capacity_LLComm THEN 0 ELSE (Total_visitor_nights*LLComm%) – Capacity_LLComm
LL_Resident_Infra	LL_Resident_Infra = IF(Total_LLResidents)<1700 THEN (Total_LLResidents) ELSE 1700
LL_Resident_Infra_deficit	LL_Resident_Infra_deficit = IF(Total_LLResidents)<1700 THEN 0 ELSE (Total_LLResidents – LL_Resident_Infra)
Males_C	Males_C = TOTAL_ELK_C*RANDOM(.07,.13)
Males_E	Males_E = TOTAL_ELK_E*RANDOM(.19,.4)
Males_FE	Males_FE = TOTAL_ELK_FE*RANDOM(.19,.4)

Males_W	Males_W = TOTAL_ELK_W*RANDOM(.13,.3) {example for W zone}
Male_Biomass_C	Male_Biomass_C = Males_C*315
Male_Biomass_E	Male_Biomass_E = Males_E*315
Male_Biomass_FE	Male_Biomass_FE = Males_FE*315
Male_Biomass_W	Male_Biomass_W = Males_W*315
Mcpr_C	Mcpr_C = IF (extreme_snow_event =1) THEN(.15)ELSE.015
Mcpr_E	Mcpr_E = IF(extreme_snow_event=1) THEN (.15)ELSE.015
Mcpr_FE	Mcpr_FE = IF(extreme_snow_event=1) THEN (.15)ELSE.015
Mcpr_W	Mcpr_W = IF(extreme_snow_event=1) THEN (.15)ELSE.015
Mcull_C	Mcull_C = 0
Mcull_E	Mcull_E = 0
Mcull_FE	Mcull_FE = 0
Mcull_W	Mcull_W = 0
Mhunt_C	Mhunt_C = 0.0
Mhunt_E	Mhunt_E = 0.0
Mhunt_FE	Mhunt_FE = .067
Mhunt_W	Mhunt_W = 0
Mnat	Mnat = .023
moose	moose = total_elk*.068
moose_avail_bio_index	moose_avail_bio_index = moose*.88*6
Mortality_Rate_C	Mortality_Rate_C = Mcpr_C + Mhunt_C+ Mnat+ Mroads_C + Mwolf_C+Mcull_C
Mortality_Rate_E	Mortality_Rate_E = Mcpr_E + Mhunt_E + Mroad_E + Mwolf_E+Mnat+Mcull_E
Mortality_Rate_FE	Mortality_Rate_FE = Mcpr_FE + Mhunt_FE + Mroad_FE + Mwolf_FE+Mnat+Mcull_FE
Mortality_Rate_W	Mortality_Rate_W = Mcpr_W + Mhunt_W + Mnat + Mroads_W+Mwolf_W+Mcull_W
Mroads_C	Mroads_C = IF((Number_of_TCH_lanes_required=2) AND (highway_mitigation_C=0)) THEN .05 ELSE IF((Number_of_TCH_lanes_required=3) AND (highway_mitigation_C=0)) THEN .075 ELSE IF((Number_of_TCH_lanes_required=4) AND (highway_mitigation_C=0)) THEN .10 ELSE IF((Number_of_TCH_lanes_required=5) AND (highway_mitigation_C=0)) THEN .125 ELSE IF((Number_of_TCH_lanes_required=6) AND (highway_mitigation_C=0)) THEN .15 ELSE IF((Number_of_TCH_lanes_required=7) AND (highway_mitigation_C=0)) THEN .175 ELSE IF((Number_of_TCH_lanes_required=8) AND

(highway_mitigation_C=0)) THEN .20 ELSE
IF(highway_mitigation_C=1) THEN .01 ELSE .05

Mroads_W   Mroads_W = IF((western_TCH_lanes=2) AND
(highway_mitigation_W=0)) THEN .05 ELSE
IF((western_TCH_lanes=3) AND
(highway_mitigation_W=0)) THEN .075 ELSE
IF((western_TCH_lanes=4) AND
(highway_mitigation_W=0)) THEN .10 ELSE
IF((western_TCH_lanes=5) AND
(highway_mitigation_W=0)) THEN .125 ELSE
IF((western_TCH_lanes=6) AND
(highway_mitigation_W=0)) THEN .15 ELSE
IF((western_TCH_lanes=7) AND
(highway_mitigation_W=0)) THEN .175 ELSE
IF((western_TCH_lanes=8) AND
(highway_mitigation_W=0)) THEN .20 ELSE
IF(highway_mitigation_W=1) THEN .01 ELSE .025

Mroad_E   Mroad_E = IF((Number_of_TCH_lanes_required=2)
AND (highway_mitigation_E=0)) THEN .05 ELSE
IF((Number_of_TCH_lanes_required=3) AND
(highway_mitigation_E=0)) THEN .075 ELSE
IF((Number_of_TCH_lanes_required=4) AND
(highway_mitigation_E=0)) THEN .10 ELSE
IF((Number_of_TCH_lanes_required=5) AND
(highway_mitigation_E=0)) THEN .125 ELSE
IF((Number_of_TCH_lanes_required=6) AND
(highway_mitigation_E=0)) THEN .15 ELSE
IF((Number_of_TCH_lanes_required=7) AND
(highway_mitigation_E=0)) THEN .175 ELSE
IF((Number_of_TCH_lanes_required=8) AND
(highway_mitigation_E=0)) THEN .20 ELSE
IF(highway_mitigation_E=1) THEN .01 ELSE .05

Mroad_FE   Mroad_FE = IF((Number_of_TCH_lanes_required=2)
AND (highway_mitigation_FE=0)) THEN .05 ELSE
IF((Number_of_TCH_lanes_required=3) AND
(highway_mitigation_FE=0)) THEN .075 ELSE
IF((Number_of_TCH_lanes_required=4) AND
(highway_mitigation_FE=0)) THEN .10 ELSE
IF((Number_of_TCH_lanes_required=5) AND
(highway_mitigation_FE=0)) THEN .125 ELSE
IF((Number_of_TCH_lanes_required=6) AND
(highway_mitigation_FE=0)) THEN .15 ELSE
IF((Number_of_TCH_lanes_required=7) AND
(highway_mitigation_FE=0)) THEN .175 ELSE
IF((Number_of_TCH_lanes_required=8) AND
(highway_mitigation_FE=0)) THEN .20 ELSE
IF(highway_mitigation_FE=1) THEN .01 ELSE .05

Mwolf_C	Mwolf_C = .014
Mwolf_E	Mwolf_E = .035
Mwolf_FE	Mwolf_FE = .00
Mwolf_W	Mwolf_W = .07
Number_of_TCH_lanes _required	Number_of_TCH_lanes_required = IF total_ west_bound_TCH_traffic_in_ summer_per_day< 7500) THEN 1 ELSE IF((total_ west_bound _TCH_traffic_in_summer_per_day > 7500) AND (total_ west_ bound_TCH _traffic_in_summer_per _day < 15000)) THEN 2 ELSE IF ((total_west_bound_TCH _traffic_ in_summer _ per_day > 15000) AND (total_ west_bound_TCH_ traffic_in _summer_per_ day<22500)) THEN 3 ELSE IF((total_west_bound_ TCH_traffic_ in_ summer_per_day > 22500) AND (total_west_ bound_TCH_traffic_in_summer_ per_day < 30000)) THEN 4 ELSE IF((total_west_ bound_TCH_traffic_in_summer_per_day > 30000) AND (total_west_bound_ TCH_traffic _in_summer_ per_day<37500)) THEN 5 ELSE IF((total_west_bound_TCH_traffic_in_ summer_ per_day > 37500) AND (total_west_bound _TCH_traffic_in_ summer_per_day<45000)) THEN 6 ELSE IF ((total_west_ bound_TCH_traffic _in_ summer_per_day > 45000) AND (total_ west_bound_TCH_traffic_in _summer_per_day < 52500)) THEN 7 ELSE 8
Other_average_nights	Other_average_nights = 3
Other_CN_overnight	Other_CN_overnight = IF(TIME=0) THEN(overnight_Other*.35) ELSE IF(TIME=1) THEN(overnight_Other*.35) ELSE IF(TIME=2) THEN(overnight_Other*.34) ELSE IF(TIME=3) THEN (overnight_Other*.33) ELSE IF(TIME=4) THEN(overnight_Other*.32) ELSE IF(TIME=5) THEN(overnight_Other*.31) ELSE overnight_Other*.30
Other_foreign_overnight	Other_foreign_overnight = IF(TIME<9) THEN(overnight_Other* 25) ELSE IF(TIME=9) THEN(overnight_Other*.24) ELSE IF(TIME=10) THEN(overnight_Other*.23) ELSE(overnight_Other*.22)
Other_visitor_nights	Other_visitor_nights = Other_average_nights * Total_other_overnight
overnight_Albertans	overnight_Albertans = Total_Albertans*.3
overnight_Other	overnight_Other = Total_Other*.92
percent_increase_in_thru _traffic	percent_increase_in_thru_traffic = .015

probability_of_human&elk_encounter	probability_of_human&elk_encounter = (elk_density _C_zone*visitor_density_C_zone)/10000
Random_snow	Random_snow = RANDOM(0.00,1.00)
	rm_occup_rate = INT(2)
road_collisions_C	road_collisions_C = TOTAL_ELK_C*Mroads_C
road_collisions_E	road_collisions_E = TOTAL_ELK_E*Mroad_E
road_collisions_FE	road_collisions_FE = TOTAL_ELK_FE*Mroad_FE
road_collisions_W	road_collisions_W = TOTAL_ELK_W*Mroads_W
sheep	sheep = total_elk*.573
sheep_avail_bio_index	sheep_avail_bio_index = sheep*.38*1
Sq_Km_in_C_zone	Sq_Km_in_C_zone = 70.1
summer_visitor_cars_entering_Egate_per_day	summer_visitor_cars_entering_Egate_per_day = summer_visitor_cars_per_day*.5379
summer_visitor_cars_per_day	summer_visitor_cars_per_day = (annual_visitor _cars * .344)/86
ToBCamping	ToBCamping = ToBCamping%*Total_visitor_nights
ToBCamping%	ToBCamping% = IF((annual_occup_rate=1) AND (rm_occup_rate=2)) THEN .0242 ELSE IF((annual_occup_rate=1) AND (rm_occup_rate=3)) THEN .0179 ELSE IF((annual_occup_rate=1) AND (rm_occup_rate=4)) THEN .0142 ELSE IF((annual_occup_rate=2) AND (rm_occup_rate=2)) THEN .0255 ELSE IF((annual_occup_rate=2) AND (rm_occup_rate=3)) THEN .0189 ELSE IF((annual_occup_rate=2) AND (rm_occup_rate=4)) THEN .0150 ELSE IF((annual_occup_rate=3) AND (rm_occup_rate=2)) THEN .0269 ELSE IF((annual_occup_rate=3) AND (rm_occup_rate=3)) THEN .0199 ELSE IF((annual_occup_rate=3) AND (rm_occup_rate=4)) THEN .0158 ELSE 0
ToBComm	ToBComm = IF(Total_visitor_nights * ToBComm% < capacity_ToBComm) THEN (Total_visitor_nights * ToBComm%) ELSE capacity_ToBComm
ToBComm%	ToBComm% = IF((annual_occup_rate=1) AND (rm_occup_rate=2)) THEN .7208 ELSE IF((annual_occup_rate=1) AND (rm_occup_rate=3)) THEN .7918 ELSE IF((annual_occup_rate=1) AND (rm_occup_rate=4)) THEN .8333 ELSE IF((annual_occup_rate=2) AND (rm_occup_rate=2)) THEN .7221 ELSE IF((annual_occup_rate=2) AND (rm_occup_rate=3)) THEN .7943 ELSE IF((annual_occup_rate=2) AND (rm_occup_rate=4)) THEN .8367 ELSE IF((annual_occup_rate=3) AND (rm_occup_rate=2)) THEN .7152 ELSE IF((annual_occup_rate=3) AND (rm_occup_rate=3))

	THEN .7872 ELSE IF((annual_occup_rate=3) AND (rm_occup_rate=4)) THEN .8295 ELSE 0
ToBComm_deficit	ToBComm_deficit = IF(Total_visitor_nights * ToBComm%) <capacity_ToBComm THEN 0 ELSE (Total_visitor_nights*ToBComm%) – capacity_ToBComm
ToB_Resident_BOInfra	ToB_Resident_BOInfra = IF(Total_ToBResidents)<19900 THEN (Total_ToBResidents) ELSE 19900
ToB_Resident_BOInfra_deficit	ToB_Resident_BOInfra_deficit = IF (Total_ToBResidents) <19900 THEN 0 ELSE (Total_ToBResidents – ToB_Resident_BOInfra)
ToB_Resident_Infra	ToB_Resident_Infra = IF(Total_ToBResidents)<11446 THEN (Total_ToBResidents) ELSE 11446
ToB_Resident_Infra_deficit	ToB_Resident_Infra_deficit = IF (Total_ToBResidents) < 11446 THEN 0 ELSE (Total_ToBResidents – ToB_ Resident _Infra)
Total_Albertans	Total_Albertans = IF(TIME=1) THEN (Annual_Visitors * .74) ELSE IF(TIME=2) THEN (Annual_Visitors * .73) ELSE IF (TIME=3) THEN (Annual_Visitors*.72) ELSE IF (TIME=4) THEN (Annual_Visitors*.71) ELSE (Annual_Visitors*.70)
Total_Annual_Expenditures	Total_Annual_Expenditures = Total_expend_dayu + Total_expend_overn
total_collisions road_collisions_C +	total_collisions = road_collisions_W + road_collisions_E + road_collisions_FE
total_cost_of_collisions	total_cost_of_collisions = total_collisions*2000
Total_day_users	Total_day_users = day_Albertans+day_Other total_elk = available_elk_C + available_elk_E + TOTAL_ELK_W
Total_expend_dayu	Total_expend_dayu = Total_expend_day_Albertan + Total_expend_day_Other
Total_expend_day_Albertan	Total_expend_day_Albertan = Expend_day_Albertan * day_Albertans
Total_expend_day_Other	Total_expend_day_Other = Expend_day_Other * day_Other
Total_expend_foreign_overn	Total_expend_foreign_overn = Expend_Other_foreign_overn* Other_foreign_overnight
Total_expend_Other_CN _overn	Total_expend_Other_CN_overn = Expend_Other_ CN_overn*Other_CN_overnight
Total_expend_overn	Total_expend_overn = Total_expend_foreign_overn + Total_expend_Other_CN_overn +

	Total_expend_overn_Albertan + Total_expend_US_overn
Total_expend_overn	Total_expend_overn_Albertan = Expend_overn_Albertan
_Albertan	* overnight_Albertans
Total_expend_US_overn	Total_expend_US_overn = Expend_US _overn * US_overnight
Total_Other	Total_Other = Annual_Visitors – Total_Albertans
Total_other_overnight	Total_other_overnight = Other_CN_overnight + Other_foreign_overnight+US_overnight
total_pred	total_pred = total_pred_C+total_pred_E+total_pred_W
total_pred_C	total_pred_C = TOTAL_ELK_C*Mwolf_C
total_pred_E	total_pred_E = TOTAL_ELK_E*Mwolf_E
total_pred_W	total_pred_W = TOTAL_ELK_W*Mwolf_W
Total_visitor_days	Total_visitor_days = Total_day_users+Total_visitor_nights
Total_visitor_nights	Total_visitor_nights = Albertan_visitor_nights + Other_visitor_nights
total_west_bound_TCH_	total_west_bound_TCH_traffic _in_summer_per_day =
traffic_in_summer_per_day	summer_TCH_west_bound_thru_traffic + summer_visitor_ cars_entering_Egate_per_day
US_overnight	US_overnight = IF(TIME=0) THEN(overnight_Other*.4) ELSE IF(TIME=1) THEN(overnight_Other*.4) ELSE IF(TIME=2) THEN(overnight_Other*.41) ELSE IF(TIME=3) THEN (overnight_Other*.42) ELSE IF(TIME=4) THEN(overnight_Other*.43) ELSE IF(TIME=5) THEN(overnight_Other*.44) ELSE IF(TIME=6) THEN(overnight_Other*.45) ELSE IF(TIME=7) THEN(overnight_Other*.45) ELSE IF(TIME=8) THEN(overnight_Other*.45) ELSE IF(TIME=9) THEN(overnight_Other*.46) ELSE IF(TIME=10) THEN(overnight_Other*.47) ELSE (overnight_Other*.48)
visitation_growth_rate	visitation_growth_rate = .06
VisitorResident_Ratio	VisitorResident_Ratio = Annual_Visitors/Total_ToBResidents
visitors_in_ToB	visitors_in_ToB = Total_day_users + Total_visitor_nights * .8*.5
visitors_per_day_ ToB_in_Summer	visitors_per_day_ToB_in_Summer = (visitors_in_ToB * .3440)/86
visitor_density_C_zone	visitor_density_C_zone = visitors_per_day_ToB_in_ Summer/Sq_Km_in_C_zone

Western_TCH_lanes	Western_TCH_lanes = Number_of_TCH_lanes_required–1
Wolves	Wolves = .041*avail_ungulate_bio_index+4.246
YOY_biomass_C	YOY_biomass_C = ELK_YOY_C*100
YOY_biomass_E	YOY_biomass_E = ELK_YOY_E*100
YOY_biomass_FE	YOY_biomass_FE = ELK_YOY_FE*100
YOY_biomass_W	YOY_biomass_W = ELK_YOY_W*100
YOY_Rate_E	YOY_Rate_E = .1226 – .00015*TOTAL_ELK_E
YOY_Rate_FE	YOY_Rate_FE = .075 – .00015*TOTAL_ELK_FE
YOY_rate_ratio	YOY_rate_ratio = .1250 – .00015*TOTAL_ELK_C
YOY_Rate_W	YOY_Rate_W = .0927 – .00015*TOTAL_ELK_W

Appendix 10

An Example to Illustrate the Software

This appendix is an exercise to demonstrate the STELLA software as an example of one of several system dynamic software packages (see Appendix 2) that could be used in the context of a mediated modeling process.

STELLA software is best explained with a simple modeling example, such as keeping track of the capital in a bank account as part of a financial component of a possibly more elaborate model. A "model sector" can be drawn on the screen and in this example it is labeled "Finances" (see Figure A10.1). Sectors are used to maintain an overview of the model. In this example, everything related to finances is placed in the "Finances" sector, as opposed to other relevant aspects to be modeled.

The bank account is presented as a "stock" because it is the variable we are trying to explain. Stocks (see Figure 4.1) are items or entities that are of primary interest to a group. Of particular importance is tracking the way in which these items or entities change over time. Many of us are interested in keeping track of a bank account and understanding why and how it fluctuates.

There may be periodic "flows" (see Figure A10.2) into and out of a bank account. An inflow shows income, and an outflow represents withdrawals. The clouds at the beginning and end of the flow valves in the figure signify that it is not necessarily of interest where the income comes from or where money withdrawn is spent.

The interest rate is an exogenous (not to be influenced by what goes on inside the model) variable and in STELLA terminology is represented as an auxiliary variable. Auxiliary variables (see Figure 4.1), which help to define the flows, are used to calculate or convert variables of interest that do not directly influence the flows.

The final model icon is the "information connector" arrow (see Figure 4.1). First, an

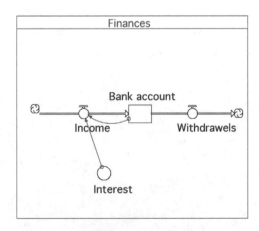

Figure A10.1.

Example of a bank account

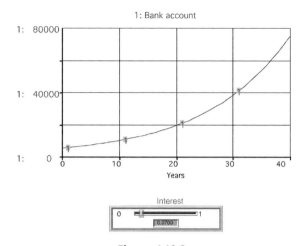

Figure A10.2.

Example of a user interface with a slide bar

arrow connects the bank account to the income, because whatever is in the bank account will earn interest. Then another arrow connects the interest to income, because whatever is earned in interest is added to income and reinvested in the bank account. This simple system uses the four model icons, the building blocks with which one can describe any dynamic system to a varying degree of detail. Building the model structure happens at the middle layer in STELLA software as presented in Figure 4.2.

The next step is to quantify the relationships in the system. One unlocks the qualitative structure in STELLA by clicking on the "globe" on the left hand of the screen. Question marks appear on the icons. A double click on an icon will open the icon for quantification and determination of relationships among icons. When an icon is quantified and related to the appropriate icons, the question mark on that icon will disappear. When all questions marks are dissolved, the model can be run and simulate what happens to the bank account under different scenarios. This happens at the user-interface on the fist level (Figure 4.2). Set the time step (e.g., years) and the range of the time period (e.g., 40 years) over which the behavior of the bank account is of interest. "Run" the model by choosing the appropriate item form the menu bar. The output graph on the user interface (Figure A10.2) can be considered as a stack of pages on top of each other. This example of a bank account demonstrates how icons can be linked to each other to form a simple model. Even participants unsophisticated in modeling can easily follow this process and can be active contributors in the construction of more complex models.

As discussed in Chapter 4, the demonstration of system dynamic software can also be related to an introduction to systems thinking. This simple demonstration of the software is meant to open the possibility for dynamic thinking and explore sensitivity of parameters in the system. Therefore, some of the frequently used tools to facilitate that type of discussion may be shown in the context of the bank account example. First, the ease with which the slide bar in the user interface can be manipulated can be demonstrated. Grabbing the handle with the mouse and moving it to a desired value can alter the slide bars. A slide bar can be used to facilitate a discussion about a parameter whose value is uncertain. It lets users easily explore the sensitivity of the model's behavior to a given parameter.

The ease with which parts of a model can be erased is demonstrated with the "dynamite stick." An icon will disappear when the dynamite stick is clicked on it. The demonstration of the dynamite stick can be used to reassure the participants that the model building process is a flexible and interactive process. Once an icon is posted on the screen, its validity and place within the system remain up for discussion.

The "ghost" option enables a user to move parameters defined in one part of the model to other parts of the model without having to connect them with an information connector arrow. The use of the ghost helps those constructing the model to keep an overview of the model.

Equally helpful is the option for inserting a relationship between variables based on a discussion about general nonlinear behavior and the extremes on the axes. Thresholds and overshoot situations can be made visible, and their impact can be traced throughout the system. For example, in the Upper Fox case study the participants integrated a piece of information about the impact of different kinds of land use on streams and lakes. A study (Lyons 1996) showed that when more than 10% of an area is urbanized, the impacts on the integrity of the lakes and streams are reduced dramatically (see Chapter 5, for example). The possibility of drawing graphical relationships between parameters greatly enhances the discussion.

Andrew Ford (1999), Hannon and Ruth (1994), and Deaton and Winebrake (1999) provide excellent textbooks on the use of STELLA in environmental modeling.

Appendix 11

R-squared Template

R-squared is a statistical procedure that can be used to determine the overlap between two curves. This method is often used to determine how well a model output mimics an actual data set. Below is an R-squared template that can be introduced within a STELLA model structure and linked to the appropriate icons. This will provide a more accurate measure of fit between model and data than "eye-balling."

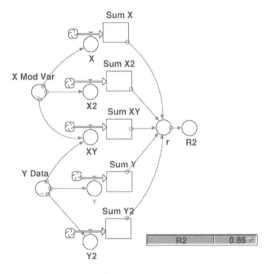

Figure A11.1.
R-squared template in STELLA icons

References

Achuff, P. L., I. Pengelly, and J. Wierchowski. 1996. Vegetation: Cumulative effects and futures outlook. Chapter 4 in *Ecological Outlooks Project: A cumulative effects assessment and futures outlook of the Banff Bow Valley*, ed. J. Green, C. Pacas, L. Cornwell, and S. Bayley. Prepared for the Banff Bow Valley Study. Ottawa: Department of Canadian Heritage.

Achuff, P. L., I. Pengelly, and C. White. 1986. *Special Resources of Banff National Park*. Environment Canada. Banff National Park.

Addis, J. 1994. Ecosystems management. Memorandum to WI DNR resource management personnel. Madison, WI, October 25, 1994.

Akkermans, H. A. 1995. Modeling with managers: Participative business modeling for effective strategy decision-making. PhD diss., Technical University, Eindhoven, Netherlands.

Alberta Business Development and Tourism (ABDT). 1976. *1976 Alberta travel survey*. Edmonton, AB: Stevenson & Kellogg, Ltd., for Alberta Business Development and Tourism.

Alberta Economic Development and Tourism (AEDT). 1991. *1990 Alberta non-resident travel exit survey*. Edmonton, AB: Alberta Economic Development and Tourism.

——. 1994a. *Economic impact analysis of visitors to Banff National Park in 1991*. Edmonton, AB: Alberta Economic Development and Tourism.

——. 1994b. *Economic impact analysis of visitors to the Town of Banff in 1991*. Edmonton, AB: Alberta Economic Development and Tourism.

——. 1994c. *1991 Alberta resident travel survey*. Edmonton, AB: Alberta Economic Development and Tourism.

——. 1995. *Tourism pulse summary for 1994*. Edmonton, AB: Alberta Economic Development and Tourism.

Alberta Tourism and Small Business (ATSB). 1982. *1982 Alberta travel survey*. Edmonton, AB: Alberta Tourism and Small Business.

Allen, W. J. 2001. Working together for environmental management: the role of information sharing and collaborative learning. PhD diss., Massey University. http://nrm.massey.ac.nz/changelinks/thesis_contents.html (accessed November 24, 2002).

Andersen, D. F., and G. P. Richardson. 1997. Scripts for group model building, *Systems Dynamics Review* 13 (2):107–30.

Andersen, D. F., G. P. Richardson, and J. A. M. Vennix. 1997. Group model building; adding more science to the craft. *Systems Dynamics Review* 13(2): 187–203.

Autenrieth, R. E. 1981. Sage grouse management in Idaho. Idaho Department of Fish & Game *Wildlife Bulletin* 9:1–38.

Bakken, B., J. Gould, and D. Kim. 1994. Experimentation in learning organizations: A management flight simulator approach. In *Modeling for Learning Organizations*, ed. J. D. W. Morecroft and J. D. Sterman, 243–66. Portland, OR: Productivity Press.

Bazerman, M. H., and M. A. Neale. 1992. *Negotiating rationally*. New York: Free Press.

BBVS. 1996a. *Banff-Bow Valley: At the Crossroads*. Technical report of the Banff-Bow Valley Task Force. Prepared for the Honorable Sheila Copps, Minister of Canadian Heritage, Ottawa, Canada.

BBVS. 1996b. *Banff-Bow Valley Round Table Summary Report*. Submitted to the Banff-Bow Valley Task Force, Banff, Alberta.

Bennis, W. 1999. *Managing people is like herding cats*. Provo: Executive Excellence Publishing.

Berger, P., and T. Luckmann. 1966. *The social construction of reality*. New York: Penguin Books.

Berkes, F., J. Colding, and C. Folke, eds. 2003. *Navigating social-ecological systems: Building resilience for complexity and change*. Cambridge, UK: Cambridge University Press.

Bingham, G. 1986. *Resolving Environmental Disputes*. Washington, DC: Conservation Foundation.

Bingham, G. 1987. Resolving environmental disputes: A decade of experience. In *Resolving Locational Conflict*, ed. R. W. Lake, 314–23. Center for Urban Policy Research—The State University of New Jersey.

Blumenthal, D., and J. L. Jannik. 2000. A classification of collaborative management methods, *Conservation ecology* 4(2):13.

Bramson, R. M. 1981. *Coping with difficult people*. Garden City, NY: Anchor Press.

Braun, C. E. 1995. Distribution and status of sage grouse in Colorado. *Prairie Nat.* 27:1–9.

Brehmer, B. 1989. Feedback delays and control in complex dynamic systems. In *Computer-based management of complex dynamic systems*, ed. P. Milling and E. Zahn, 189–96. Berlin: Springer-Verlag.

Brown, R. 1988. *Group processes: Dynamics within and between groups*. Oxford, UK: Blackwell.

Bunning, C. 1995. *Professional development using action research*. Action Learning, Action Research and Process Management Internet Conference. Bradford, UK: MCB University Press.

Calgary Herald. 1996. "Staying in Banff? Not this summer you're not." February 24.

Cameron, B. 1997. An exploration of the link between public opinion and public policy decision making on environmental issues. Keynote speaker, 3rd International Conference of Science and Management of Protected Areas: Linking Protected Areas with Working Landscapes Conserving Biodiversity, May 16, Calgary, Alberta.

Chambers, R. 1997. *Whose reality counts? Putting the 4* London: Intermediate Technology.

Chawla, S., and J. Renesch. 1995. *Learning organizations: Developing cultures for tomorrow's workplace*. Portland, OR: Productivity Press.

Checkland, P. 1981. *Systems thinking, systems practice*. New York: Wiley.

Checkland, P., and J. Scholes. 1990. *Soft systems methodology in action* New York: Wiley.

Connelly, J. W., H. W. Browers, R. J. Gates. 1998. Seasonal movements of sage grouse in southeastern Idaho. *Journal of wildlife management*. 52, 116–22.

Connelly, J. W., and C. E. Braun. 1997. Long term changes in sage grouse *Centrocercus urophasianus* populations in western North America, *Wildlife Biology* 3, 229–34.

Connelly, J. W., K. P. Reese, R. A. Fisher, and W. L. Wakkinen. 2000a. Response of sage grouse breeding populations to fire in southeastern Idaho. *Wildl. Soc. Bull.* 28, 90–96.

Connelly, J. W., M. H. Schroeder, A. R. Sands, and C. E. Braun. 2000b. Guidelines to manage sage grouse populations and their habitats. *Wildl. Soc. Bull.* 28:90.

Costanza, R., ed. 1991. *Ecological economics: The science and management of sustainability.* New York: Columbia University Press.

———. 1993. Developing ecological research that is relevant for achieving sustainability. *Ecological Applications* 3:579–81.

———. 2000. Visions of alternative (unpredictable) futures and their use in policy analysis. *Conservation Ecology* 4 (1): 5. http://www.consecol.org/vol4/iss1/art5.

Costanza, R., F. Andrade, P. Antunes, M. van den Belt, D. Boersma, D. F. Boesch, F. Catarino, S. Hanna, K. Limburg, B. Low, M. Molitor, G. Pereira, S. Rayner, R. Santos, J. Wilson, and M. Young. 1998a. Principles for sustainable governance of the oceans, *Science* 281:198–99.

Constanza, R. and M. Ruth. 1998. Dynamic systems modeling for scoping and consensus building. *Ecological Management.*

Costanza, R., J. Cumberland, H. E. Daly, R. Goodland, and R. Norgaard. 1997. *Introduction to ecological economics.* Boca Raton, FL: St. Lucie Press.

Constanza, R. and S. Tognetti, eds. 1996. Integrated adaptive ecological and economic modeling and assessment—a basis for the design and evaluation of sustainable development programs. Synthesis paper. Scientific Committee on Problems of the Environment, 51 Bld de Montmorecy, Paris, France.

Costanza, R., and H. E. Daly. 1987. Toward an ecological economics. *Ecological Modeling* 38:1–7.

Costanza, R., and H. E. Daly. 1992. Natural capital and sustainable development. *Conservation Biology* 6:37–47.

Costanza, R., R. d'Arge, R. de Groot, S. Farber, M. Grasso, B. Hannon, S. Naeem, K. Limburg, J. Paruelo, R. V. O'Neill, R. Raskin, P. Sutton, and M. J. van den Belt. 1997. The value of the world's ecosystem services and natural capital. *Nature* 387:253–60.

Costanza, R., and S. E. Jørgensen, eds. 2002. *Understanding and solving environmental problems in the 21st century: Toward a new, integrated hard problem science.* Amsterdam: Elsevier.

Costanza, R., B. Low, E. Ostrom, and J. Wilson, eds. 2001. *Institutions, ecosystems, and sustainability.* Boca Raton, FL.: Lewis Publishers/CRC Press.

Costanza, R., and M. Ruth. 1998. Using dynamic modeling to scope environmental problems and build consensus. *Environmental Management* 22:185–95.

Costanza, R., O. Segura, and J. Martinez-Alier, eds. 1996. *Getting down to earth: Practical applications of ecological economics.* Washington, DC: Island Press/ISEE.

Costanza, R., F. H. Sklar, and M. L. White. 1990. Modeling coastal landscape dynamics. *BioSci.* 40:91–107.

Costanza, R., A. Voinov, R. Boumans, T. Maxwell, F. Villa, L. Wainger, and H. Voinov. 2002. Integrated ecological economic modeling of the Patuxent River watershed, Maryland. *Ecolog. Monogr.* 72:203–31.

Crawford, J. A., and R. S. Lutz. 1985. Sage grouse populations in Oregon 1941–1983. *Murrelet* 66:69–74.

Cupps, R. A. 1977. Emerging problems of citizen participation. *Pub. Admin. Rev.* 37:478–87.

Daily, G. C., ed. 1997. *Nature's services: Societal dependence on natural ecosystems.* Washington, DC: Island Press.

Dalke, P. D., D. B. Pyrah, D. C. Stanton, J. E. Crawford, and E. F. Schlatterer, 1963. Ecology, productivity, and management of sage grouse in Idaho. *J. Wildl. Manage.* 27:811–41.

Daly, H. E., and J. Cobb. 1989. *For the common good: Redirecting the economy towards community, the environment, and a sustainable future.* Boston: Beacon Press.

Daniels, S. E., and G. B. Walker. 1996. Collaborative learning: Improving public deliberation in ecosystem-based management. *Envir. Impact Assess. Rev.* 16:71–102.

———. 2001. *Working through environmental conflict: The collaborative learning approach.* Westport, CT: Praeger.

Deaton, M., and J. Winebrake. 1999. *Dynamic modeling of environmental Systems.* New York: Springer-Verlag.

DeLong Jr., D. C. 1995. Relationships between vegetational structure and predation of artificial sage grouse nests. *J. Wildl. Manage.* 59, 88–92.

Dovers, S. R., and C. D. Mobbs. 1997. An alluring prospect? Ecology, and the requirements of adaptive management. Chapter 4 in *Frontiers in ecology: Building the links.* Proceedings, Conference of the Ecological Society of Australia, October 1–3, 1997, Charles Sturt University. Oxford, UK: Elsevier Science. http://life.csu.edu.au/esa/esa97/papers/dovers/dovers.htm (accessed November 24, 2002).

Ehrlich, P. R. 2000. *Human natures: Genes, cultures, and the human prospect.* Washington, DC.: Island Press.

Electronic Arts, Inc. SIMEARTH and SIMCITY, 209 Redwood Shores Parkway, Redwood City, CA 94065, Maxis.

Emery, M., and R. E. Purser. 1996. *The search conference: A powerful method for planning organizational change and community action.* San Francisco: Jossey-Bass.

Endenburg, G. 1998. Sociocracy: The organization of decision-making. Sociocratic Engineering Corp.

Eng, R. L., and P. Schladweiler. 1972. Sage grouse winter movements and habitat use in central Montana. *J. Wildlife Management* 36:141–46.

European Commission. 2001. White Paper on Governance. COM (2001) 428. Brussels.

Fish Banks, Ltd. University of New Hampshire, Laboratory for Interactive Learning, Institute for Policy and Social Science Research, Thompson Hall G-01, 105 Main Street, Durham, NH 03824-3547. Phone: (603) 862–2244.

Fisher, R. A., K. P. Reese, and J. W. Connelly. 1996. An investigation on fire effects within xeric sage grouse brood habitat. *J. Range Management* 49:194–98.

Fisher, R. A., A. Sharp, and J. Richardson. 1998. *Getting it done: How to lead when you're not in charge.* New York: HarperBusiness.

Fisher, R. A., W. Ury, and B. Patton. 1991. *Getting to yes.* 2nd ed. New York: Penguin Books.

Fisher, R. A., W. L. Wakkinen, K. P. Reese, and J. W. Connelly. 1997. Effects of prescribed fire on movements of female sage grouse from breeding to summer ranges. *Wilson Bull.* 109:82–91.

Flood, R. L., and M. C. Jackson. 1991. *Creative problem solving: Total systems intervention.* New York: Wiley.

Folke, C., S. Carpenter, T. Elmqvist, L. Gunderson, C. S. Holling, and B. Walker. 2002. Resilience and sustainable development: Building adaptive capacity in a world of transformations. *Ambio* 31:437–40.

Folke, C., J. Colding, and F. Berkes. 2003. Synthesis: Building resilience and adaptive capacity in social-ecological systems. In *Navigating social-ecological systems: Building resilience for complexity and change,* ed. F. Berkes, J. Colding, and C. Folke, 352–87. Cambridge, UK: Cambridge University Press.

Ford, A. 1999. *Modeling the environment.* Washington, DC: Island Press.

Ford, D. N., and J. D. Sterman. 1998. Expert knowledge elicitation to improve formal and mental models, *System Dynamics Review* 14(4):309–40.

Forrester, J. 1961. *Industrial dynamics.* Walthan, MA: Pegasus Communications.

―――. 1969. *Urban Dynamics.* Walthan, MA: Pegasus Communications.

Geernaert, G., C. Humborg, L. Jordão, J. Kohn, H. Langenberg, P. Meier, H. S. Otter, L. Rahm, W. Solomons, M. Vidal, V. Wallbaum. 1998. System Dynamics of the Continuum River Catchment to the Coastal Region, *Workshop Report of the Transdisciplinary Euroconference on Coastal Management Research,* 6–10 December 1997, San Feliu de Guixols, Spain, European Science Foundation pp. 51–61.

Gibeau, M. L., S. Herrero, J. L. Kansas, and B. Benn. 1996. Grizzly bear population and habitat status in Banff National Park. Chapter 6 in *Ecological Outlooks Project: A cumulative effects assessment and futures outlook of the Banff Bow Valley,* ed. J. Green, C. Pacas, L. Cornwell, and S. Bayley. Prepared for the Banff Bow Valley Study. Ottawa: Department of Canadian Heritage.

Gibeau, M. Pers. Communication. Bear expert for the Banff-Bow Valley Study, Parks Canada, Banff, Alberta.

Grant, W. E., E. K. Pedersen, and S. L. Marin. 1997. *Ecology and natural resource management: System analysis and simulation.* New York: John Wiley and Sons. 373pp.

Gray, B. 1989. *Collaborating: Finding common ground for multiparty problems.* San Francisco: Jossey-Bass.

Green, J., C. Pacas, L. Cornwell, and S. Bayley, eds. 1996. *Ecological Outlooks Project: A cumulative effects assessment and futures outlook of the Banff Bow Valley.* Prepared for the Banff Bow Valley Study. Ottawa: Department of Canadian Heritage.

Greenberger, M., M. Crenson, and B. Crissey. 1976. *Models in the policy process.* New York: Russell Sage Foundation.

Gregg, M. A., J. A. Crawford, M. S. Drut, and A. K. DeLong. 1994. Vegetational cover and predation of sage grouse nests in Oregon. *J. Wildlife Management* 58:162–66.

Gunderson, L., C. S. Holling, and S. Light, eds. 1995. *Barriers and bridges to the renewal of ecosystems and institutions.* New York: Columbia University Press.

Haan, C. T., B. J. Barfield, J. C. Hayes. 1994. *Design hydrology and sedimentology for small catchments.* San Diego: Academic Press.

Habermas, J. 1992. *Autonomy and solidarity.* Rev. ed. London: Verso.

Hannon, B., and M. Ruth. 1994. *Dynamic modeling.* New York: Springer-Verlag.

Hare, A. P., H. H. Blumberg, and M. F. Davies. 1994. *Small group research: A handbook.* Norwood, NJ: Ablex.

Harris, H. J., R. B. Wenger, V. A. Harris, and D. S. DeVault. 1994. A method for assessing environmental risk: A case study of Green Bay, Lake Michigan, USA. *Environmental Management* 18:295–306.

Herrero, S. Pers. Communication. Bear Expert for the Banff-Bow Valley Study, University of Calgary, Calgary, Alberta.

Hogarth, R. 1987. *Judgment and choice.* Chichester, UK: Wiley.

Holland, W. D., and G. M. Coen, eds. 1982. *Ecological (biophysical) land classification of*

Banff and Jasper National Parks. Vol. 2, *Soil and vegetation resources.* Alberta Institute of Pedology, Publication SS-82-44.

Holling, C. S., ed. 1978. *Adaptive environmental assessment and management.* London: Wiley.

_____. 1993. Investing in research for sustainability. *International Series on Applied Ecosystem Analysis* Vol. 3. New York: Wiley.

Holroyd, G., and K. Van Tighem. 1983. Ecological (biophysical) Land Classification of Banff and Jasper National Parks. Volume III: The Wildlife Inventory. Canadian Wildlife Services report to Parks Canada, Calgary.

Houston, D. B. 1982. *The northern Yellowstone elk: Ecology and management.* New York: Macmillan.

Huggard, D. J. 1991. Prey selectivity of wolves in Banff National Park. Master's thesis, Department of Zoology, University of British Columbia, Vancouver.

Hurd, T. Pers. Communication. Ungulate expert for the Banff-Bow Valley Study, Parks Canada, Banff, Alberta.

Imperial, M. T. 1999a. Analyzing institutional arrangements for ecosystem-based management: lessons from the Rhode Island Salt Ponds SAM Plan. *Coastal Management* 27:31–56.

_____. 1999b. Institutional analysis and ecosystem-based management: the institutional analysis and development framework. *Environmental Management* 24:449–65.

Jiggins, J. 1993. From technology transfer to resource management. In *Grasslands for our world,* ed. M. J. Baker, 184–189. Wellington, NZ: SIR Publishing.

Johnson, B. L. 1995. Applying computer simulation models as learning tools in fishery management. *N. Am. J. Fish. Manage.* 15:736–47.

Kahane, A. 2000. How to change the world: Lessons for entrepreneurs from activists. Generon speech delivered to Fast Company's Real Time Conference, Orlando. Also in *Reflections: The SOL Journal.* MIT Press, 2001.

Kahnemann, D., P. Slovic, and A. Tversky. 1982. *Judgment under uncertainty: Heuristics and biases.* Cambridge, UK: Cambridge University Press.

Kahnemann, D., and A. Tversky. 1974. Judgment under uncertainty, *Science* 185:1124–31.

Katic, E. 1996. *Overnight facility carrying capacity and use: Banff National Park.* Prepared for the Banff Bow Valley Study. Ottawa: Department of Canadian Heritage.

Kay, C., B. Patton, and C. White. 1994. Assessment of long-term terrestrial ecosystems in the Central Canadian Rockies: a new perspective on ecological integrity and ecosystem management. In R. Linn (ed.), Sustainable Society and Protected Areas. Contributed Papers on the 8th Conference on Research and Resources Management in Parks and on Public Lands. George Wright Society.

Keirsey, D., and M. Bates. 1984. *Please, understand me: Character and temperament types.* Del Mar, CA: Gnosology Books.

Klebenow, D. A. 1969. Sage grouse nesting and brood habitat in *Idaho. J. Wildl. Manage.* 33:649–62.

Kleinmuntz, D. 1985. Cognitive heuristics in a dynamic decision environment. *Management Science* 31:680–702.

Kolb, D. A. 1986. *Experiential learning: Experience as the source of learning and development.* Englewood Cliffs, NJ: Prentice Hall.

Krueger, R. A. 1994. *Focus groups: A practical guide for applied research.* Thousand Oaks, CA: Sage Publications.

Lane, D. C. 1992. Modeling as learning: A consultancy methodology for enhancing learning in management teams. In *Modeling for learning,* by J. D. W. Morecroft and J. D. Sterman. Special issue, *European Journal of Operational Research* 59(1): 64–84.

Langer, E. J. 1997. *The power of mindful learning.* Addison-Wesley Publishing Company.

Lax, D. A., J. and K. Sebenius. 1986. *The manager as negotiator: Bargaining for cooperation and competitive gain.* New York: Free Press.

Lee, K. 1993. *Compass and gyroscope: Integrating science and politics for the environment.* Washington DC: Island Press.

Leighton, D. Pers. Communication. Town of Banff Official, Banff, Alberta.

Levi, A. M., and A. Benjamin. 1977. Focus and flexibility in a model of conflict resolution, *Journal of Conflict Resolution* 21 (3): 405–26.

Levins, R. 1966. The strategy of model building in population biology. *American Scientist* 54:421–31.

Lundin, W., and K. Lundin. 1995. *Working with difficult people.* New York: American Management Association.

Lyons, J., L. Wang, and T. D. Simonson. 1996. Development of an index of biotic integrity for coldwater stream in WI, *N. Am. J. Fish. Manage.* 16:241–56.

Lynam, D. R. 2002. Fledgling psychopathy: A view from personality theory. *Law and Human Behavior* 26(2): 255–59.

Markham, U. 1993. *How to deal with difficult people.* New Delhi, India: HarperCollins.

Martin, N. S. 1970. Sagebrush control related to habitat and sage grouse occurrence. *J. Wildl. Manage.* 34: 313–20.

Mazmanian, D. 1976. Participatory democracy in a federal agency. In *Water politics and public involvement,* ed. J. Piece and H. Doerksen. Ann Arbor, MI: Science Publishers.

Meadows, D. H., and J. M. Robinson. 1985. *The Electronic Oracle: Computer Models and Social Decision.* New York: John Wiley & Sons.

Moore, C. 1986. *The mediation process.* San Francisco: Jossey-Bass.

Morecroft, J. D. W., and J. D. Sterman. 1994. *Modeling for learning organizations.* System Dynamics Series. Portland, OR.: Productivity Press.

Morris, L. E. 1995. Development strategies for the knowledge era. In *Learning organizations: Developing cultures for tomorrow's workplace,* ed. S. Chawla and J. Renesch. 1995. Portland, OR: Productivity Press.

Muchagata, M., and K. Brown. 2000. Colonist farmers' perceptions on fertility and the frontier environment in eastern Amazonia. *Agric. and Human Values* 17:371–84.

Nabhan, G. P. 1997. *Cultures of habitat: On nature, culture, and story.* Washington, DC: Counterpoint.

Nelle, P. J., K. P. Reese, and J. W. Connelly. 2000. Long-term effects of fire on sage grouse habitat. *J. Range Management* 53:586–91.

Nothdurft, W. 1995. Environmental mediation. In *Fairness and competence in citizen participation: Evaluating models for environmental discourse,* ed. O. Renn, T. Webler, and P. Wiedemann. Boston: Kluwer Academic.

Olsson, P., C. Folke, and F. Berkes. 2003. Adaptive co-management for building social-ecological resilience. Manuscript submitted to *Envir. Manage.*

Oreskes, N., K. Shrader-Frechette, K. Berlitz. 1994. Verification, Validation and Confirmation of Numerical Models in Earth Sciences, *Science* 263, 641–46.

Ozawa, C. P. 1991. *Recasting science: Consensual procedures in public policy making.* Boulder: Westview Press.

Pacas, C. 1996. Human use in the Banff Bow Valley: past, present and future. Chapter 3 in *Ecological Outlooks Project: A cumulative effects assessment and futures outlook of the Banff Bow Valley,* ed. J. Green, C. Pacas, L. Cornwell, and S. Bayley. Prepared for the Banff Bow Valley Study. Ottawa: Department of Canadian Heritage.

Pacas, C., D. Bernard, N. Marshall, and J. Green. 1996. *State of the Banff Bow Valley: A compendium of information.* Prepared for the Banff Bow Valley Study. Ottawa: Department of Canadian Heritage.

Paquet, P., Pers. Communication. Wolf expert for the Banff-Bow Valley Study, University of Calgary, Calgary, Alberta.

Paquet, P. C., J. Wierchowski, and C. Callaghan. 1996. Effects of human activity on grey wolves in the Bow River Valley, Banff National Park, Alberta. Chapter 7 in *Ecological Outlooks Project: A cumulative effects assessment and futures outlook of the Banff Bow Valley,* ed. J. Green, C. Pacas, L. Cornwell, and S. Bayley. Prepared for the Banff Bow Valley Study. Ottawa: Department of Canadian Heritage.

Paquet, P., and A. Hackman. 1995. *Large carnivore conservation in the Rocky Mountains.* World Wildlife Fund. Toronto, Ontario.

Parks Canada. 1994. Guiding Principles and Operational Policies. Department of Canadian Heritage, Ottawa, Ontario.

———. 1995. Initial assessment of proposed improvements to the Trans-Canada Highway in Banff National Park. Phase IIIA, Sunshine Interchange to Castle Mountain Interchange. March 1995. Ottawa, Ontario.

———. 1997. Banff National Park Management Plan. Department of Canadian Heritage, Ottawa, Ontario.

———. 1998. National Parks Act. Department of Canadian Heritage, Ottawa, Ontario.

Patterson, R. L. 1952. *The sage grouse in Wyoming.* Denver: Sage Books.

Pedersen, E. K. 2001. Effect of sheep grazing and fire on sage grouse populations in south-eastern Idaho. PhD diss. Texas A&M University, College Station, Texas.

Pedersen, E. K., J. W. Connelly, J. R. Hendrickson, and W. E. Grant. 2003. Effect of sheep grazing and fire on sage grouse populations in Southeastern Idaho. *Ecological Modelling,* 165, 24–37.

Pike, B., and D. Arch. 1997. *Dealing with difficult participants: 127 practical strategies for minimizing resistance and maximizing results in your presentations* San Francisco: Jossey-Bass.

Price Waterhouse. 1995. Canadian Lodging Outlook Hotel Market Trend year-to-date, Edmonton, Alberta.

Prugh, T., R. Costanza, and H. E. Daly. 2000. *The local politics of global sustainability.* Washington, DC: Island Press.

Pyle, W. H., and J. A. Crawford. 1996. Availability of foods of sage grouse chicks following prescribed fire in sagebrush-bitterbrush. *J. Range Manage.* 49, 320–24.

Pyrah, D. B., 1970. Effects of chemical and mechanical sagebrush control on sage grouse. In *Ecological effects of chemical and mechanical sagebrush control,* ed. E. F. Schlatterer and D. B. Pyrah, 8–35. Missoula: Montana Department of Fish and Game.

Raiffa, H. 1982. *The art and science of negotiation.* Cambridge, MA: Harvard University Press.

Richardson, G. P. and D. F. Anderson. 1995. Teamwork in group model building. *System Dynamics Review* 11(2):113–37.

Richmond, B. 1987. *The strategic forum; from vision to strategy to operating policies and back again.* Lyme (NH), Netherlands: High Performance Systems.

––––––. 1997. The strategic forum: Aligning objectives, strategy and process. *Systems Dynamics Review* 13(2):131–48.

Richmond, B., and S. Peterson. 1994. STELLA documentation. High Performance Systems, Inc., Hanover, NH.

Ritchie, M. E., M. L. Wolfe, and R. Danvir. 1994. Predation of artificial sage grouse nests in treated and untreated sagebrush. *Great Basin Nat.* 54:122–29.

Roberts, E. B. 1978. *Managerial applications of system dynamics.* Portland, OR: Productivity Press.

Rogeau, M.-P., and D. Gilbride. 1994. *Forest stand age origin mapping of Banff National Park.* Parks Canada, Banff National Park.

Rosener, J. 1982. Making bureaucracy responsive; a study of impacts of citizen participation and staff recommendation on regulatory decision making, *Public Administration Review* 42:339–45.

Rouwette, E. A. J. A., J. A. M. Vennix, and T. van Mullekom. 2002. Group model building effectiveness: A review of assessment studies. *Sys. Dynam. Rev.* 18(1):5–45.

Schindler, D., and C. Pacas. 1996. Cumulative effects of human activity on aquatic ecosystems in the Bow Valley of Banff National Park. In Green, J., C. Pacas, L. Cornwell, and S. Bayley (eds.). *Ecological Outlooks Project: A Cumulative Effects Assessment and Futures Outlook of the Banff-Bow Valley.* Department of Canadian Heritage, Ottawa, Canada.

Schroeder, M. H., J. R. Young, and C. E. Braun. 1999. Sage grouse (*Centrocercus urophasianus*). In *The birds of North America,* ed. A. Poole and F. Gill, 1–28. Philadelphia.

Senge, P. M. 1990. *The fifth discipline.* New York: Doubleday.

Shoham, Y. 1990. Nonmonotonic reasoning and causation, *Cognitive Science* 14:213–52.

Simon, H. A. 1948. *Administrative behavior: A study of decision-making processes in administrative organizations.* New York: Macmillan.

––––––. 1979. Rational decision-making in business organizations. *Am. Econ. Rev.* 69: 493–513.

––––––. 1985. Human nature in politics: The dialogue of psychology with political science. *Am. Polit. Sci. Rev.* 79:293–304.

Soloman, M. 1990. *Working with difficult people.* Englewood Cliffs, NJ: Prentice Hall.

Statistics Canada. 1991. *Dominion census.* Ottawa: Statistics Canada.

––––––. 1995. *Travelscope international travel.* Ottawa: Statistics Canada.

Stave, K. A. 2002. Using system dynamics to improve public participation in environmental decisions. *System Dynamic Review* 18(2):139–67.

Sterman, J. D. 1989. Modeling managerial behavior: Misperceptions of feedback in a dynamic decision environment, *Manage. Sci.* 35:321–39.

Stern, A .J., and T. Hicks. 2000. *The process of business/environmental collaborations: Partnering for sustainability.* Westport, CT: Quorum Books.

Susskind, L., and J. Cruikshank. 1987. *Breaking the impasse: Consensual approaches to resolving public disputes.* New York: Basic Books.

Susskind, L., P. F. Levy, and J. Thomas-Larmer. 2000. *Negotiating environmental agreements: How to avoid escalating confrontation, needless costs, and unnecessary litigation.* Washington, DC: Island Press.

Susskind, L., S. McKearnan, and J. Thomas-Larmer. 1999. *The consensus building handbook: A comprehensive guide to reaching agreement.* Thousand Oaks, CA: Sage Publications.

Toropov, B. 1997. *The complete idiot's guide to getting along with difficult people.* New York: Alpha Books.

Town of Banff. 1995. The Town of Banff Residential/Commercial Inventory, council file 7622, Banff, Alberta.

Thomas, J. C. 1990. Public involvement in public management; adapting and testing a borrowed theory. *Pub. Admin. Rev.* 50:435–45.

University of Wisconsin. 1997. The Upper Fox River Basin: An Analysis of Demographic Composition, Public Goods and Natural Resources.

van Asselt, M. B. A. 2000. *Perspectives on Uncertainty and Risk: The PRIMA Approach to Decision Support.* Boston: Kluwer Academic.

van den Belt, M., L. Deutsch, and A. Jansson. 1998. A consensus-based simulation model for management in the Patagonian coastal zone. *Ecological Modeling.*

van den Belt, M. J. 1998. *Mediated modeling project: An integrated scoping model of the Upper Fox River Basin.* Green Bay: University of Wisconsin.

———. 2000. Mediated modeling: A collaborative approach for the development of shared understanding and evaluation of environmental policy scenarios, with case studies in the Fox River, Wisconsin and the Ria Formosa, Portugal. PhD diss., University of Maryland.

———. In preparation. 2004. Mediated modeling as a tool for stakeholder involvement concerning socioeconomic impacts of UV-b radiation.

van den Belt, M. J., L. Deutsch, and Å. Jansson. 1998. A consensus-based simulation model for management in the Patagonia coastal zone. *Ecological Modeling* 110:79–103.

van den Belt, M. J., N. Videira, P. Antunes, R. Santos, and S. Gamito. 2000. *Mediated modeling in Ria Formosa, Sea Foundation and Luso.* Lisbon: American Foundation for Development.

Vennix, J. 1996. *Group model building: Facilitating team learning using system dynamics.* London: Wiley.

Vennix, J., D. Andersen, and G. Richardson. 1997. Group model building, art, and science. *Sys. Dynam. Rev.* 13(2).

Vennix, J., and J. W. Gubbels. 1994. Knowledge elicitation in conceptual model building: A case study in modeling a regional Dutch health care system. In *Modeling for learning organizations,* ed. J. D. W. Morecroft and J. D. Sterman, 121–46. Portland, OR: Productivity Press.

Wallestad, R. O. 1971. Summer movements and habitat use by sage grouse broods in central Montana. *J. Wildl. Manage.* 35:129–36.

Wallestad, R. O., and D. B. Pyrah. 1974. Movement and nesting of sage grouse hens in central Montana. *J. Wildl. Manage.* 38:630–33.

Wang, L., J. Lyon, P. Kanehl, and R. Gatli. 1997. Influences of Watershed Land Use on Habitat Quality and Biotic Integrity in Wisconsin Streams. *Fisheries* 22:6–12.

Weiner, B. 1985. "Spontaneous" causal thinking. *Psych. Bull.* 97(1): 74–84.

Weisbord, M. R. 1992. *Discovering common ground: How future search conferences bring people together to achieve breakthrough innovation, empowerment, shared vision and collaborative action.* San Francisco: Berrett-Koehler.

Weisbord, M. R., and S. Janoff. 1995. *Future search: An action guide to finding common ground in organizations and communities.* San Francisco: Berrett-Koehler.

Weisinger, H., 1998. *Emotional intelligence at work: the untapped edge for success.* San Francisco: Jossey-Bass.

Weiss, D. H. 1987. *How to deal with difficult people.* New York: American Management Association.

Wenger, R. G., H. J. Harris, R. Sivanpillai, and D. S. DeVault. 1999. A graph-theoretic analysis of relationships among ecosystem stressors. *J. Envir. Manage.* 57:109–22.

Wilson, K., and G. E. B. Morren. 1990. *Systems approaches for improvements in agriculture and resource management.* New York: Macmillan.

Wolstenholme, E. F. 1982. System dynamics in perspective. *J. Op. Res. Soc.* 33:547–56.

———. 1990. *System enquiry: A system dynamics approach.* Chichester, UK: Wiley.

Wolstenholme, E. F., and R. G. Coyle. 1983. The development of system dynamics as a methodology for system description and analysis, *J. Op. Res. Soc.* 34:569–81.

Wondolleck, J. M., and S. L. Yaffee. 2000. *Making collaboration work: Lessons from innovation in natural resource management.* Washington DC: Island Press.

Woods, J. Pers. Communication. Ungulate expert for the Banff-Bow Valley Study, Parks Canada, Revelstoke, British Columbia.

Woods, J. G. 1987. *Bow Valley elk population characteristics 1985–1987: A discussion paper and example computer simulation of the impacts of the Banff Highway Project.* Natural History Research Division, Ottawa, Environment Canada.

———. 1990. *Effectiveness of fences and underpasses on the Trans-Canada Highway and their impact on ungulate populations in Banff National Park, Alberta.* Calgary: Canadian Parks Service.

———. 1991. Ecology of a partially migratory elk population. PhD. diss., University of British Columbia, Vancouver.

Woods, J. G., L. Cornwell, T. Hurd, R. Kunelius, P. Paquet, and J. Wierchowski. 1996. Elk and other ungulates. Chapter 8 in *Ecological Outlooks Project: A cumulative effects assessment and futures outlook of the Banff Bow Valley,* ed. J. Green, C. Pacas, L. Cornwell, and S. Bayley. 1996. Prepared for the Banff Bow Valley Study. Ottawa: Department of Canadian Heritage.

Yaffee, S. L., A. F. Phillips, I. C. Frentz, and B. E. Thorpe. 1996. *Ecosystem management in the United States: An assessment of current experience.* Washington DC: Island Press.

Zuber-Skerritt, O. 1992. *Action research in higher education: Examples and reflections.* London: Kogan Page.

About the Author

Marjan van den Belt, Ph.D. is an ecological economist and environmental management professional. She is the founder and President of Mediated Modeling Partners, LLC in Burlington, Vermont and a fellow in the Gund Institute of Ecological Economics at the University of Vermont. Her areas of expertise include participatory processes and computer modeling in environmental management and policy making.

Contributors

Marjan van den Belt, Ph.D
Mediated Modeling Partners, LLC
c/o Gund Institute for Ecological Economics
590 Main Street
Burlington, VT 05605
Phone: (802) 658-6689
Email: m.vandenbelt@verizon.net

Ann L. Kenimer, Ph.D., P.E.
Biological and Agricultural Engineering
Texas A&M University
201 Scoates Hall
College Station, TX 77843-2117
Phone: (979) 845-3677
Fax: (979) 847-8828
Email: a-kenimer@tamu.edu

Robert Wenger, Ph.D.
Natural and Applied Sciences
University of Wisconsin Green Bay
2420 Nicolet Drive
Green Bay, WI 54311
Phone: (920) 465-2770
Fax: 920-465-2376
Email: wengerr@uwgb.edu

H. J. (Bud) Harris, Ph.D.
Natural and Applied Sciences
University of Wisconsin Green Bay
2420 Nicolet Drive
Green Bay, WI 54311
Phone: (920) 465-2796
Fax: (920) 465-2376
Email: harrish@uwgb.edu

Tarla Rai Peterson
Communication
University of Utah
LNCO 2400
Salt Lake City, UT 84112-0491
Phone: (801) 581-6527
Fax: (801) 585-6255
Email: trp3@utah.edu

William E. Grant
Department of Wildlife and
Fisheries Sciences
Texas A&M University
College Station, TX 77843-2258
Phone:(979) 845-5702
Fax: (979) 845-3786
Email: wegrant@tamu.edu

Laura Cornwell
1977 Biltmore Street NE
Washington DC, 20009
Email: l-cornwell@hotmail.com

Paula Antunes, Ph.D.
ECOMAN—Ecological Economics and
Environmental Management Centre
College of Sciences and Technology,
New University of Lisbon
Quinta da Torre
2829-516 Caparica
Portugal
Phone: +351 212 948300
Fax: +351 212 948554
Email: mpa@fct.unl.pt

Rui Santos, Ph.D.
ECOMAN—Ecological Economics and
Environmental Management Centre
College of Sciences and Technology,
New University of Lisbon
Quinta da Torre
2829-516 Caparica
Portugal
Phone: +351 212 948300
Fax: +351 212 948554
Email: rfs@fct.unl.pt

Nuno Videira, M.Phil.
Faculty of Marine and Environmental
Sciences
University of Algarve
Campus de Gambelas
8005-139 Faro
Portugal
Phone: +351 289 800900
Fax: + 351 289 818353
Email: nvideira@ualg.pt

Sofia Gamito, Ph.D
Faculty of Marine and Environmental
Sciences
University of Algarve.
Campus de Gambelas, 8005-139 Faro,
Portugal
Phone: +351 289 800900
Fax: +351 289 818353
Email: sgamito@ualg.pt

Ellen Pedersen
1223 Arthur Street
Davis, CA 95616
Phone: (530) 753-4996
Email: ellenkp@frontier. net

Index